The Discursive March of Thought
An Interdisciplinary Roadmap

Ruth Katz

A well-established reference is endowed with power.
Whatever has power also has roots.

– Nelson Goodman

The Discursive March of Thought
An Intedisciplinary Roadmap

Ruth Katz

Published by **ISRAEL ACADEMIC PRESS, New York**
(A subsidiary of MultiEducator, Inc.)
180 E. Prospect Avenue • Mamaroneck, NY 10543
Email: nhkobrin@Israelacademicpress.com

ISBN # 978-1-885881-14–58

© 2015 Israel Academic Press

Cover Image: Marble panel, entitled: "Logic and Dialectic." by Luca della Robbia (15th Century)

Table of Contents

PART III
Conception and Perception Intertwined

PART IV
Mind and Brain Relationship

Acknowledgements

In addition to my obvious debt to the authors, alive and dead, whose works are interpolated in this volume, I wish to thank the following publishers and rights holders for permission to reprint:

Yale University Press for excerpts from Ernst Cassirer's *Philosophy of Symbolic Forms*, 1965;

Dover Publications for the excerpt from Ernst Cassirer's *Language and Myth*, 1946;

The American Psychological Association for excerpts from Amos Tversky's "Features of Similarity," 1977;

Perseus Books for excerpts from Ervin Panofsky's *Idea: A Concept in Art Theory*, 1968;

Phaidon Press for excerpts from E.H. Gombrich's *Art and Illusion: A Study in the Art of Pictorial Representation*, 1972;

The University of Chicago Press for W.J.T. Mitchell's "Representation" from Frank Lentricchia et al, *Critical Turns for Literary Studies*, 1965;

The Aristotelian Society for Max Black's "Metaphor." 1962;

Columbia University Press for excerpts from Patricia Tunstall's "Structuralism and Musicology: An Overview." In *Current Musicology*, Vol. 27;

Cengage Learning for Ruth Katz's "Spocietal Codes for Responding to Dissent," from W. Bennis et al, eds., *The Planning of Change*, 4th edition, 1985;

MIT Press Journals for Semir Zeki's "Art and the Brain," in *Daedalus* Vol.127, 1998;

The Journal of Consciousness Studies for Erich Harth's "The Emergence of Art and Language in the Human Brain," Vol. 6, 1999.

Preface

Allow me to begin by stating unabashedly that had I stumbled during my student days, and even much later, on a book that tried to convey what I attempt to put across in the present volume, I might have been considerably "wiser" much earlier. Wisdom, apparently, does not only require knowledge, but the power to apply it critically. Critical judgment is invariably constrained; it is constrained by the factors that are deemed relevant to the assessment of its value. In a world that undergoes rapid changes, impacted by a variety of old and new factors (social, scientific, technological, etc.), overwhelmed by a deluge of information, it is extremely difficult to determine what impinges on what and how. However, if we accept the notion that all of our preoccupations and actions are man-made, including what we know and think about the *given* world, it becomes somewhat easier to wise-up. Moreover, if we also accept the notion that "no-thing emerges from nothing,"[1] it becomes easier to clear a path, i.e. to distinguish among factors that *might* be relevant to the issue at hand. Although it defies haphazard claims concerning "relatedness," it fails to tell us how far to go and where to stop. Before I proceed, I would like to illustrate what I have in mind via short summaries of two case studies.

While collecting data for my doctoral dissertation on the beginnings of opera, pursuing, as it were, a specific subject matter, I realized that it could not be treated in isolation. I knew, of course, from the start where the emergence of opera took place. I was likewise acquainted with the seminal figures associated with the beginning of opera and familiar with the various artistic genres that contributed their share to the rise of that new musical institution. Historians of music have placed their emphasis on the major constituent elements comprising the opera, and in particular on the stages of their development immediately preceding its rise. Yet the factors underlying these stages of development were

---

[1] Claiming that interactions between things would be impossible unless all were forms of one basic substance, Diogenes of Apollonia (5th century BC) coined the following phrase: "Nothing comes to be from that which is not, nor is anything destroyed into that which is not." See Kirk, G.S. and Raven, J.E. *The Pre-Socratic Philosophers,* (Cambridge University Press, 1957) p. 432.

rarely brought to bear. Emphasis was primarily placed on historical facts concerning theatre and music, as well as on the unveiling and examination of examples of early operas and the variety of other theatrical presentations containing music. Since the boundaries of these investigations were determined by the components of the medium itself, they largely prescribed the trends to be discovered. This did not seem adequate as explanation. To "explain" by pointing out that prior to opera one encounters musical and dramatic forms that have elements similar to opera, is begging the question anew. It is for this reason that a theory concerning the rise of opera that also takes cognizance of factors extrinsic to the medium itself was justified.

Explaining the rise of opera, I attempted to view opera as emerging primarily from the concurrent preoccupation with defining the powers of music, a problem that required the weaving together of an aesthetic strand with roots in philosophy, and an experimental one with roots in magic. It took me years to realize that the rise of opera is integrally connected with, of all things, the scientific revolution of the late sixteenth and early seventeenth century, a revolution that redefined 'knowledge' and the processes that govern its advance. This was not a sudden insight, but the product of a prolonged interdisciplinary quest. Opera, as it turned out, partook in the shift that emphasized the discovery of *hidden* constituents that yield diverse overt manifestations, rather than the other way round. In fact, many of the musical forms of the same period–accompanied monody, the cantata and the opera–may be characterized as partaking in a search for the answer to questions such as: What is music? Wherein resides its "power"? Lacking a semantic of its own, how can music be possessed by "meaning"? Indeed, the aesthetic questions put to the arts by the intellectuals of the period are actually counterparts of scientific concerns. To ask "what is music" is not different than to ask "what is matter." (Parenthetically, it might be noted that the study of music as sound did eventually move to the scientific field of acoustics.) This parallelism relates of course to the fact that the renaissance of aesthetic theory in the arts coincided in time.

It has been argued that the scientific revolution of the seventeenth century addressed itself anew to fundamental questions concerning the makeup– properties and order–of the world, questions which until that time had been officially relegated to the domain of religion. Yet regardless of emphasis and area under discussion, it became abundantly clear that historic events, scientific innovations, aesthetic desiderata, technological changes–and more–are jointly shaped by the social practices that fashion the "world view" they share and reflect. Given that history does not stand still and that change is inevitable, documents of all kinds and a diversity of artifacts, often become the only remnants of bygone times. With luck, effort and ingenuity, they allow us not only to establish "where and when" a major change took place, but to trace the transformations and the interactions of the *ideas* that propelled the change.

Unlike my study of the opera as a turning point in the conception of music and its uniqueness, my study of the waltz-craze that besieged Vienna in the early decades of the nineteenth century was closer to home and led me on a different path. Familiarity with the Straus waltzes was a virtual prerequisite to membership in my family. Trying to explain the "epidemic," my first thought was to examine the demographics of the Viennese dancers and the loci where they assembled. And indeed I discovered that provision had been made for publicly-accessible dance halls in which different strata of society mixed together. This led me to ask how this change came about and what it displaced. I began, accordingly, to examine the attributes of the waltz compared to the major dance that preceded it, i.e. the minuet. My broadened study comprised, however, some unanticipated "steps."

The overt difference between the two dances was easily established. The waltz, I learned, is one of the whirling dances; it is particularly the Landler from which it derived. The couples in close embrace made a turn to each two measures while at the same time following a circular course. The three-four rhythm with the strongly accentuated first beat, characteristic of most Landlers was adopted by the waltz. The waltz attained its true character, however, by being danced like a Schleifer, having given up the skips and turning under the arm of the Landler in favor of dragging the feet along the floor. The skips which represented a certain freedom were replaced by ecstatic gliding motion that really made it possible to "let go." The minuet, by comparison, is a courtly dance whose unrestrained folk origins had been transformed into the classical ideas of clarity, balance and regularity. While outwardly simple, the minuet had to be studied, a fact to which a great number of dance manuals devoted to its rules and regulations attest.

Having examined a goodly number of these manuals, I realized that "onlookers" were an important part of the spectacle; they were saluted with ceremonial bows which preceded the actual dance. Moreover, I also learned that it took a great deal of research to determine who would open the ball, and in what succession each guest should enter the dance. The minuet, it may be said, reflected and incorporated the worldly ranks which its participants brought with them when entering the ballroom. Paradoxically, this was made possible by the very uniformity of the minuet. In the waltz, which has no rules to be studied, save for a few basic steps, the individual is encouraged to introduce his own variations and interpretations. Here, the dancers surrender their worldly identities upon entering the "society of the dance" where individuals take on new roles and where recognition is accorded not by virtue of one's status in the larger society, but by virtue of one's performance in the dance. Sociologists characterize this difference as 'ascription' versus 'achievement', the latter implying 'mobility'. At any rate, the waltz seemed to echo the slogan of the French Revolution.

A close examination of the origins of these dances revealed that the upper classes of Western society borrowed their dances from "the people." Although the dances underwent transformations in the course of their adaptation, two forms of the same dance frequently existed side by side, the upper classes preferring the restrained and calmer version, while the country folk preferred the freer and wilder form. The tie between the two forms was particularly close until the fifteen century. The dances tended to be quite simple until then and their unwritten rules could be learned through observation and participation. From that time forward, however, the focus on simplicity and the "whole" began to be replaced by a liking for multiple elements and attention to small detail. This new "realism of particulars" also found expression in the other arts. In the dance, at any rate, it gave rise to an elaborate vocabulary of steps which had to be learned and memorized. This led eventually to the establishment of a new profession, the dance teacher, and to the crystallization of a 'theory' of the dance, to which the proliferation of dance manuals attest. Consequently, courtly dance and folk dance spread further apart.

I shall not go into all that transpired in the extended period that increased the differences between the two types of dances, but report that the homogeneity of cultural expression declined the more heterogeneous the class structure became. This was accompanied by an abundance of verbal and pictorial documents that severely criticized the spontaneity and licentious character of folk dances, largely emphasizing their moral hazard. It was the waltz, nonetheless, that propelled the legs of the diplomats and delegates that attended the Vienna Congress, held in the years 1814-5. The congress, as is well known, constitutes an important moment in modern European history. The diplomats and delegates consisted of aristocrats of the old regime as well as representatives of other classes who were imbued with post-revolutionary political ideas. The decades that bridge between the French Revolution and The Vienna Congress harbor the transformation of socio-political ideas that found expression in the arts as well. The move from the minuet to the waltz thus constituted an integral part of a significant process of change. That which began with an inquiry into a particular "craze" turned into an extended interdisciplinary study. Incidentally, it also helped to identify some of the "whys and when" high culture and popular culture diverge.

These two case studies–the one that led me from the opera to the Scientific Revolution and the other from the waltz to the French Revolution–exemplify the interrelations among ideas. They highlight four major points: (1) Manifestations and expressions of a given period are jointly shaped by the social practices that fashion the "world view" they share. (2) Knowledge entails the power to apply it critically. (3) "What impinges on what" is neither obvious, nor easily established. (4) Knowledge, applied critically, begets knowledge!

Knowledge, evidently, advances through a continuous process involving problems in search of solutions which sensitize us to relationships we hardly anticipated. Though unable to predict where it will lead, we can retrace how we arrived to where we are. In what follows, I shall identify some of the steps that led to the current "sanctioning" of interdisciplinary activities. Such a review, I believe, helps to explain why and wherefore the issues discussed in this book deserve utmost attention.

From the dawn of civilization humans have been engaged in a relentless attempt to comprehend themselves and their world in intelligible ways.

Motivation, intuition and thought attended these efforts, alongside social and environmental changes. Ideas, beliefs, norms etc., i.e. *Culture*, is the product of Man. Man's own "configurations" thus continue to guide his quest for *Knowledge*, steering also the changes which knowledge undergoes. Human beings clearly use ideas to *think with* about ideas, whether they do or do not know where they come from. At any rate, in light of the history of ideas, knowledge evokes the image of "Connected Vessels." Unlike the interconnectivity that the internet has put at our disposal, 'knowledge'– however defined–is invariably subject to constraints, circumscribed by the very ideas that Man produced in order to understand the world he inhabits, his place within it, and the vast universe which surrounds him.

As the horizon of knowledge grew ever more extensive sifting processes of all kinds accompanied its development. These processes gave rise to divisions and alignments of sorts, increasingly sensitive to what belongs where and is relevant to what and in what way. Areas of concern, the subjects they encompass, the issues they raise, and countless problems that require immediate solutions, continuously challenged accepted notions as to what impinges on what and in what way. The divisions among disciplines kept likewise fluctuating in the course of history, as did the alignments among them. These fluctuations, however, invariably resulted in an assumedly better or "higher" level of understanding. Established disciplines also gave rise, at times, to new ones or were subsumed by others.

Complicated undertakings generally engender a division of labor, which unfortunately is too often accompanied by obliviousness to the enterprise as a whole. The pursuit of knowledge is one of those ongoing enterprises in which the division of labor ideally includes steady awareness of the undertaking as a whole, however complex. Yet since nobody is in the position of knowing all there is to know, or is currently taking place in the various "sub units" of this grand enterprise, interactions among the subdivisions may at times alleviate or aggravate the uncertainties that hover over the "findings"–conclusions, implications and ramifications–of various separate investigations.

The more there is to know the greater the branching off, yet questions concerning "what relates to what and in what way" become nonetheless increasingly clarified. The accelerated pace in the advancement of knowledge in the last century, and of the means that enable its diffusion, contributed no doubt to the celebration of "specialists" in various fields of endeavor. Specialization seemed like a trustworthy road to excellence as far as scientific investigation is concerned. The broader picture, it was thought, could be obtained from the summation of specialized inquiries and their findings. This development also gained impetus by the division of the natural sciences and the human sciences into allegedly "two worlds," as expounded by C.P. Snow.[2]

The natural sciences, accordingly, were designed to investigate the "given" world, in search of its permanent laws of construction, while the "socially constructed" world, with its diversity and ever changing manifestations, was relegated to the human sciences. Interdisciplinary studies–even *within* these separate worlds, let alone between them–encountered marked reservations, as belonging neither here nor there. Yet much of the investigation that researchers conducted in their various areas of specialization took place in institutions of higher learning–equipped with laboratories and libraries–that contributed, in one way or another, to the advancement of knowledge.

The above situation, however, gradually changed, so that by the end of the 20th century the whole approach to scientific achievements, including to those who produce and enjoy them, had undergone drastic transformations. Many of the theories that guided our understanding, including that of marked cultural achievements, have clearly been challenged in recent years. It is abundantly clear that changes occurring in the technological, political and social spheres–embraced by processes such as globalization, multicultural trends, and the diffusion of post-modern ideologies–have exerted pressure on our mental attitudes and frames of mind, not to mention the new issues and dilemmas to which they gave rise.

---

[2] What began with a lecture delivered by Snow at Cambridge was subsequently published as *The Two Cultures and the Scientific Revolution* in 1956. The book exerted great influence on Western public discourse since World War II. The book distinguished between the scientific method embedded within language and culture, and the scientific viewpoint which believes that it is possible to arrive at objective non-culturally imbedded observation about nature.

Interestingly, though the realization that we, as humans, create that which guides our understanding–including that of Nature–is widely accepted by now, the natural sciences are still somehow treated as a pursuit of knowledge divorced from those turns of mind to which social and intellectual life give rise. While the focus on "innovation" is one of the central features of the sciences, we also know that the supposed "timelessness" of scientific innovations often undergoes "new looks" in light of further innovations. Nor is science immune from competing points of view, despite the fact that it generally enjoys a high degree of consensus. Whether in search of embracing principles or of the smallest significant difference, serious investigations, it must be remembered, derive their impetus from the communities of discourse to which they belong. These refer, in one way or another, to the theoretical traditions that stipulate the kind of rigor involved and the sort of speculations licensed. In Man's quest to understand Nature and his place within it, it is of course not easy to attain overriding principles. The human sciences, being an overt and undeniable part of the variety of social life and its changes, are more readily characterized by syntheses of a temporary nature.

The natural sciences, on the other hand, dealing with Nature as an *a priori* given, are clearly after *permanent* principles of regulation. Their investigations thus rest on circumscribed variables in search of causal relationships that can be verified empirically and assure a high degree of predictability. There is a difference, however, between enduring truth and "truth of fact." Overriding principles, we have learned, do not rest solely on causal relationships, but employ theoretical frameworks that lend *meaning* to these relationships. These frameworks are neither natural nor free. They are formulated by human beings who use the cultural resources they have created in order to arrive at better understandings of the issues and the new questions to which they give rise. The history of mankind is replete with examples that reveal the processes whereby seemingly diverse concerns relate to each other and, in turn, give rise to new concerns. The concern with specifics, on the other hand, often creates all kinds of interrelated webs of understanding, the interactions of which give rise to yet new specifics that solicit inquiries of their own. When we pose the question of what all this means for a critical theory of knowledge we may readily conclude that knowledge involves both imminent and far-flung relationships that impact each other in ways that continuously sensitize us to issues we may have never entertained or have taken for granted.

Histories of all kinds, and a host of other scholarly endeavors, do not, as a rule, conceive of themselves as being engaged with questions and processes that are explored in other domains as subjects requiring their own modes of investigation. One gets nonetheless the feeling nowadays that nothing seems relevant unless it can be expediently and advantageously applied. Moreover, the staggering pace of technological advances makes every yesterday seem far behind its morrow, creating a daily feeling that one will miss out on what tomorrow has in store. This acceleration has doubtless hastened the transfer of technologies and methodologies from one arena to another, though the pastures in which they sprouted and the research that engendered them are often overlooked and poorly-supported.

That which holds true for the "exact sciences" holds equally true for the human sciences, though their relevance–taken as a whole–is less transparent. To be sure, not all that we know can be immediately applied, or even readily perceived. Yet, nothing in the great orbit of knowledge is divorced from that web of ideas that flow through its channels, however shrouded or overlooked. In modern times, in the centuries that bridge between the Scientific Revolution and the Cybernetic Revolution, giant steps have been taken that enhance our understanding of the relationship between theoretical and analytical investigations and the ways in which they impact each other in the advancement of knowledge.

Engulfed by a deluge of information (and more in the offing), we are aware nowadays that encyclopedic knowledge is neither possible nor desirable, however much we may once have appreciated Erasmus and his likes. This awareness may in part explain the current shift from discipline to "problem solving," so called. There is nothing new, of course, about problem solving, it occupied center stage in the advancement of knowledge. It has gained saliency, however, because problems define and demarcate the boundaries of investigation more clearly than the disciplines whence they emerge. This development contributed, in turn, to the growth of interdisciplinary studies and to the recognition they presently enjoy. Whether correctly applied or misunderstood, interdisciplinarity has, in fact, become a buzz word. That which was scorned not so long ago has turned into something one takes pride in nowadays.

By now, inter-disciplinary studies have even produced a fair amount of literature that traces their development in "top-down" and "down-up" fashion, as well as the agencies and institutions that initiate such studies. These studies also point to the climate that hovers over academia, whose members are increasingly ready to "change gears." As valuable and informative as these studies are, the "whys" and "wherefores" still await serious explication. Considerable thought is also required regarding the implication of this trend for the organization of teaching and research, and, not least, for the criteria whereby they ought to be judged and evaluated.

Long before interdisciplinary studies became fashionable, educators in charge of curriculum development promoted theories about the desirability of a more "integrated" kind of learning. "Integrated learning" was supposed to mirror the "real world" better than the traditional disciplines. It primarily aimed to empower students to see "connections," to be able to "generalize" and, possibly, to transfer what they have learned to problems they may face in their lives. The educational literature is replete with suggestions that rest on the notion that academic skills are transferable from one area to another. It was also suggested that collective learning experiences may achieve the highest level of concept reinforcement. The most common method of implementing integrated instruction centered on the "thematic unit," in which a common theme is studied in more than one discipline.

With the advancement of cognitive studies, the purpose of the "integrated theme" was to enhance the "pattern-seeking" operations of the brain. Though theories of this kind try to create a better fit between learning schemes and the working of the brain, we are still far from knowing how the brain learns. Nonetheless, instead of imparting bits of knowledge in diverse fields, it clearly seemed preferable to show students how what they learn is somehow "connected" and carries significance to their lives and to the world they encounter. The notion of 'relevance'–spelled out or implied–apparently loomed large in these theories.

Interestingly, that which preoccupied educators for quite some time has by now also reached those in charge of higher education. The latter, however, are also required to *advance* our understanding, i.e. to produce *new* knowledge, not only to transmit what is known in meaningful ways.

The traditional tri-part division—the natural sciences, the social sciences and the humanities—clearly rests on the idea that each of these faculties already consists of disciplines related to each other through some shared epistemological assumptions. Economics, accordingly, can be related to sociology and the latter to anthropology; psychology can be related to social-psychology and the latter to political science. Each faculty can display similar internal relationships. Indeed, "proximities" of this kind were never overlooked in the advancement of knowledge. In the age of information however—unlike earlier times—it became salient that new insights are more likely to be gained by relating *remote* disciplines to each other in sophisticated ways. The "reliability" of such an undertaking, moreover, does not depend on the scholar's expertise in the fields he chooses to relate to each other in a novel and meaningful way. Although the proof of the pudding is in the pudding, one has to have a fair idea, nonetheless, of its *particular* ingredients. In fact, interdisciplinary studies nowadays may be defined by processes that *take apart* entrenched disciplines in order to answer *specific* questions or solve *specific* problems that are, paradoxically, "too complex" to be dealt with by a single discipline or by traditionally related ones.

Yet despite the growing endorsement of interdisciplinary interactions, there is no denying that central disciplines under the umbrella of the so-called humanities have suffered major setbacks, as though they carried no relevance to present day scientific and social developments. I must therefore emphasize that interdisciplinary studies—however applied or understood—do *not* emerge from a simple lumping together of related fields, but from the *theoretical* interrelationships among factors, some of which may have been addressed elsewhere, that seem relevant to the problem under investigation. Although interdisciplinary studies are also related to our inability to cope even with all that a single discipline embraces, they do require a closer look and a better understanding of the issues that impinge on a particular problem, and how and in what way they affect each other. Whereas the "integrated" educational program encouraged the gathering of information–as diverse as possible–about a *given* theme, interdisciplinary studies nowadays try to advance knowledge by detecting unforeseen relationships among *diverse* themes.

In the age of information, information itself has ironically lost much of the standing it previously enjoyed. It engendered, however, an *ars-combinationis* which directly appeals, for better or worse, to our cognitive faculty, expecting increased participation on our part. Although we are expected to exercise our own minds and judgment, it has become exceedingly difficult to do so in a world that has practically blurred the dividing lines between facts and fiction and what was previously meant thereby. In this flood of information and disinformation, invented facts and invented images threaten to overwhelm us. Interdisciplinarity, as it turned out, is also a "combinatorial art" that addresses our understanding rather than imparting sheer information, and it, too, tries to persuade. Thus, in order to assure trustworthy studies, creative and responsible scientific investigations, it behooves us to better understand the "power of reference"–the working of ideas and the "tools" that allow us to *differentiate* between them, to *categorize* them and to *construct* new relationships among them.

The subdivisions of this volume, and their suggested readings, do by no means provide answers to all of the issues that need to be clarified concerning interdisciplinary studies. Rather than contribute to the crystallization of criteria whereby such studies may be judged and evaluated, or the kind of educational changes that it requires, they intend to upgrade, as it were, a mode of "awareness"–attentiveness to one's own reasoning and to the reasoning of others. We all use ideas to *think with* about ideas, yet we rarely stop in daily life to ask ourselves where they come from and in what particular way they serve us. Scientific investigations, unlike ordinary life, require at all times alertness to the ideas one employs–where they come from, the purposes they serve, and the degree of their relevance to the issue under investigation, a fortiori concerning interdisciplinary studies. To be sure, alertness of this kind leaves much room for intellectual creativity, yet it stipulates that scientific innovations do not start from scratch. The advancement of knowledge, it must be remembered, is an interactive process and, similar to the development of natural languages, a collective attainment and realization.

Knowledge, in fact, rests on the capacity of humans to create language, since it is in language that cultures are formed. The first section of this volume thus deals–in broad terms–with the capacity of humans to create features of similarity and difference, signs and symbols, points of reference, etc., i.e. with the bare bones of language. As a creative collective achievement, languages clearly evolve and rest on shared understandings of sorts as to what represents what and refers to what and whereby. The section hence deals with the essentials that set human *communication* in motion. Man's capacity "to refer" apparently established the a-priori status of the non-sensual, i.e. ideas.

Like language, the advancement of knowledge is an interactive enterprise. As such it is also inextricably intertwined with processes of learning, based on past experiences and accomplishments. We continuously reexamine the latter in light of social changes and novel ideas that stand to improve our understanding of the world we inhabit and the universe we are part of. Given the enormity of the enterprise, this ongoing process of "checks and balances" also introduces, willy-nilly, shifts in our points of reference, thereby highlighting *context* as an important factor to reckon with. Context notwithstanding, the advancement of knowledge nonetheless rests on some kind of *order*–referential sequences regarding what refers to what and in what way. These various chains of references create, as it were, a "multi-dimensional matrix," the interrelations of which are neither evident nor readily discernible. In fact, their various cross relationships and intersections invite *discovery*, like the unveiling of the "secrets" of the given world. The second section of this volume thus deals with Delimiting Modes of Organization, i.e. with demarcations–organizational boundaries of investigatory areas and noteworthy theoretical configurations that may unveil analogies or correspondences among diverse issues or subject matters.

The realization that we, as humans, create that which guides our understanding (including our understanding of Nature), raises many questions about the "tools" we employ in order to achieve intelligibility. In order to suggest a coherent picture we often use familiar examples to illustrate certain aspects we wish to convey or emphasize. However unconscious we may be of the function of metaphors, of the nature of representations, of the import of expressions, of the influence of framing, and of analogies of all kinds, they clearly loom large in our use of language. They loom equally large in our attempt to better understand the relationships among diverse bodies of knowledge. These relations are more likely to become apparent on various levels of abstraction that highlight shared features at the expense of individual particularities. Yet comprehension is not based on isolated bits of information, but on relationships that impart significations of sorts. The latter clearly rest on theoretical frameworks formulated by human beings who use the cultural resources they have created in order to arrive at better understandings of the issues involved and the new questions to which they give rise.

Though we as humans create that which guides our understanding, such knowledge involves both pre-conceived notions and inferred understanding. To be sure, the pursuit of knowledge, and the accumulation thereof, rests at all times on insights and discernments, imagination and judgment. The integrative aspect of knowledge, however, results from the interrelationships among the successions of those "referential sequences" that propel its advance. We must thus be able to differentiate between already formed ideas and new ones concerning issues that have never been entertained or have been taken for granted. The third section of this volume–Conception and Perception Intertwined–presents routes and procedures that engender distinctions between pre-conceived notions and inferred understandings.

Although we are still far removed from the full understanding of the workings of our brain, great progress has been made in the last decades towards a better understanding of the mind-brain conundrum. Philosophy has of course been preoccupied with questions concerning the "innate" versus the "learned" for a long time. Yet the advancements of several offshoots of scientific investigations brought questions pertaining to "nature versus nurture" to the forefront. From biology to psychology, from the behavioral sciences to education, and more, the dividing lines between the "bequeathed" and the "acquired" have become central issues in dire need of clarification and guidance.

In the second half of the eighteenth century, the cognitive turn in epistemology constituted a crucial turning point that markedly precipitated the investigation of the brain. It commenced with 'perception' as a subject worthy of study and continued with 'cognition' and with ongoing attempts to better grasp the impact of the former on the latter. Generally speaking, cognitive studies are concerned with the manner in which the mind processes information and structures coherence. However, to move from process to coherence requires some form of construction or representation, based on relationships among the particular particles which are processed. Process, accordingly, is influenced by that which is being processed and coherence, structured as it may be, does not in itself carry meaning. To turn such cohesive patterns into cohesive meanings requires symbolizations. This interlock suggests some kind of mind/brain relationship. The book's fourth section–Mind Brain Relationship–tries to provide some insight to this, as of yet, unsettled conundrum. It is by no means surprising that the brain–the center of all of our abilities and sensitivities–should be addressed by some of its investigators in interdisciplinary terms.

The four sections of this book, I must point out, neither represent the history of ideas, nor do they deal with 'reference' in philosophical terms, though aware of both and of the concerted deliberations that attended, and attend, many of the concepts employed. By listing some of the "tools" that scholars employ in order to arrive at a better understanding of the issues which their investigations involve, this volume only aims to deepen the awareness of readers in looking more critically at the ideas they may employ in their own research and those employed by others. The focus on "modes of reasoning," i.e. the "practical apparatus" that humans devised in order to understand themselves and the world they inhabit, highlights five basic tenets: (1) Knowledge is a collective enterprise. (2) Humans use ideas to *think with* about ideas. (3) Ideas interrelate via referential sequences. (4) Mankind advances knowledge in humanly intelligible ways. (5) As a creative collective enterprise, knowledge advances in "connected vessels."

Given the intent of this volume, it must be evident that the readings I have chosen are not limited to the most recent writings. Rather, the readings aim to present some of the writings whose thoughts carried significance for subsequent deliberations of the issues they addressed. To be sure, the history of ideas is replete with thoughts that benefited from more rigorous formulations at a later time. I tried, however, to avoid the debates that various concepts and schemes engendered in order to highlight some of the *tools* that man devised that enabled him, to begin with, to differentiate and categorize, to characterize and systematize his perceptions and thoughts *en route* to a better understanding of the world which surrounds him and his place within it. These tools continue to serve us, provided one knows how to employ them. Considering the predicament of the Humanities nowadays, it is also hoped that the arguments raised in the various readings will dispel the simplistic approach to the division between the "natural" sciences and the "human" sciences. Since 'Art' is mostly viewed as occupying the opposite pole of 'Science', it is by no means inadvertent that art should loom large in this volume. Were I to be asked "who are the readers you have in mind?" my answer would be: anybody in search of "explanations," i.e. everybody from freshman to post-doc, in whatever discipline. Were I asked "how should one read this book?" my advice would be: in sequence, since it is organized as a "road-map" to still uncharted territories.

Introduction

Introduction

One need not be an astute observer to be aware of the current shift in academia from discipline to "problem solving." Nor can the current appeal of interdisciplinary studies be overlooked. Long the unsung hero of the advancement of knowledge, problem solving seems to have gained saliency nowadays because problems better define and demarcate more clearly the boundaries of investigations than the disciplines from which they emerge. These boundaries invite of course trespassing beyond the bounds set by the disciplines. Even if this has always been the case, it was not formally recognized.

Ironically moreover, although we are engulfed in a deluge of information, information itself has lost much of the standing it previously enjoyed, having given way to the notion of *relevance*. To be sure, factors that had a "bearing on," or were "pertinent to" the issues and matters at hand, always carried significance in the advancement of knowledge, but they, too, gained new saliency in the age of information.

Knowledge apparently grows exponentially. Even in former days, when there was less to know, knowledge was impossible to corral, however much appreciated and desired. In the age of information it has become undesirable even to try, because *and* despite of the increased access to information which the internet provides. No amount of information can displace the "thinking" that lends validation to the various associations that establish what belongs where and relates to what and in what way. The advancement of knowledge is an interactive activity, and however "revolutionary" certain findings turn out to be, they do not start from scratch. By now it is widely accepted that we as humans create that which guides our understanding. Although this, too, has always been the case, it was only gradually formulated in this way. The current wide spread acceptance of the idea that humans are the creators of "truths"–cast in human intelligible ways–imposes greater responsibility on those engaged in the advancement of knowledge. In fact, the more widespread this awareness, the more it constrains scholars to appeal to our cognitive faculty, expecting increased participation on our part.

To be sure, unassisted pronouncements were never accepted in the world of learning. New assertions were invariably accompanied by persuasive arguments that rested on views already held by the group one wished to persuade. Expecting a group to entertain a "new look" on issues or questions that preoccupied its members, required familiarity with prior arguments, even dismissed ones. By now, scholarly communities that propose innovations are no longer as removed from the public eye as they were in former days. In the world we live in, people have not only become more literate and more conscious of factors that impact their daily lives, but also of factors that affect "turns of mind" and public decisions. All of these factors–including the processes whereby they become persuasive–have been extensively studied by social scientists, many of whom have also pointed to the manipulations involved. Agencies and entrepreneurs of all kinds–who are steadily trying to improve their strategies of persuasion–are more disposed to pay attention to such studies than are the people whom they are trying to influence. And although we are expected to exercise our minds and judgment more than ever before, it has become exceedingly difficult to do so in a world that has practically blurred the dividing lines between facts and fiction and what was meant thereby. In this flood of information and disinformation, invented facts and invented images threaten to overwhelm us. This situation raises both ethical and epistemological problems.

Problems of this kind were never overlooked in the course of advancing knowledge. Given the interactive aspect of the pursuit of knowledge, a "language"–a mode of transmission–was developed to empower only facts that have earned consensual agreement. Since facts depend on–or relate to–questions asked, the processes whereby they are established require, likewise, consensual approval. It is by no means a coincidence that the acquisition of knowledge highlighted intellectual honesty. Yet even when this dictum was violated, the built-in checks and balances of the system enabled the discovery of fraud. This does not mean, however, that consensual agreements stay put, or that they do not change. For example, despite their different trajectories and concerns, Copernicus and Darwin both challenged the shared belief in the centrality of Man, namely, his prominence in the universe and among creatures. Nobody still believes that the earth is flat or that the sun orbits around the earth, though ideas of this kind were agreed upon in some earlier times.

Nonetheless, given the ever increasing ease in which information can be defused and manipulated requires alertness even as far as the production of knowledge is concerned. The age of information engendered an *ars-combinationis*, the unconstraint nature of which requires some surveillance even as far as academia is concerned. Interdisciplinarity itself is a "combinatorial art" that addresses our understanding rather than imparting sheer information, and it, too, tries to persuade. It tries to do so, however, in its own particular ways. Thus, in order to assure trust-worthiness, it behooves us to clarify, as best we can, the ways whereby worthy studies may be produced and contribute to the advancement of knowledge.

How we think and what makes sense is evidently of crucial importance at all times. Natural languages in fact contain special words–nouns and verbs–that pertain to essential *mental acts*. Oxford's concise dictionary of English renders some instructive definitions of the following words:

Think	"consider, be of opinion;" "form conception of;" "exercise the mind."
Thought	"process or power of thinking; way of thinking characteristic of a person or class; faculty of reason."
Reflection	"mental faculty dealing with products of sensation and perception;" "idea arising in the mind, mental or verbal."
Refer	"trace or ascribe to person or thing as cause or source, consider as belonging to certain date or place or class."
Reference	"refer of matter for decision or settlement or consideration to some authority, or scope given to such authority;" "relation, respect, correspondence to (x)."
Reason	"facts adduced or serving as argument, motive, cause, or justification; "intellectual faculty characteristic especially of human beings by which conclusions are drawn from premises."

The mental act of *reasoning* obviously rests on the use of arguments that serve to uphold claims, whatever their nature. Persuasion apparently employs all kinds of thinking procedures, but regardless of their diversity, these processes rest on *mental capacities* which are attributed primarily to mankind. In fact, it is these very capacities that enable humans to develop the languages they evolve. A brief survey of several key factors that characterize natural languages may help to grasp the significance of the "tools" highlighted in this book, emphasizing their relevance to scientific investigations and the advancement of knowledge.

The syntax of a language generally *refers* to the grammatical arrangement of words that show their connection and relations to one another within a given sentence and among sentences related to each other. Although the display may be, and frequently is, incorrect, it invariably presupposes the existence of certain customary use of words in combination. In fact, the grammar of a language denotes the mode in which words are connected in order to express a complete *thought*, or a "proposition" (as it is termed by logicians). Thus the grammatical correctness or incorrectness of an expression depends upon its *intelligibility*, that is, upon the ordinary use and custom of a particular language. Whatever is so unfamiliar as not to be generally understood is also ungrammatical, for it is contrary to the habit of a language as determined by common usage and consent.

Since grammatical propriety is but the established usage of a particular body of speakers at a particular time in history, it follows that the grammar of a people undergoes changes concerning all those contrivances whereby the relations of words and sentences are pointed out in the language they hold in common. To establish the "historical grammar," or primary infrastructure, of a single language involves tracing language patterns as far back as documentary evidence allows so as to disclose–through their development and transformations–the morphological uniqueness of the language, that is, the sorts of *distinctions* and degree of *distinctness* its users found necessary to introduce. There is apparently no language that has completely forsaken the relations of elements with which it started. It is thought that this is due to the fact that the essential unit, that of the sentence, resides in the very relations of its several parts. Like the thoughts that they express, sentences are conceived as wholes; their parts are related to each other like the *ideas* they intend to convey. Such relations do not readily change once they succeed in facilitating the utterances and the understanding of the bearers of a given language. Solidifying what has been achieved, they are transformed only gradually, making room for *novel ideas* that seek expression. Thus, indices of grammatical relations may be placed differently in different languages, and some languages may allow for greater subtleties than others, yet fundamental structural relations, once established, do not drastically change their functions, though they may gain in refinement and coherence. It is obvious, therefore, why grammar constitutes the surest and most important basis for the classification of languages.

This brief discussion seeks only to stress that the object of language is to *convey thought*. So long as this object is attained, the machinery for attaining it is of comparatively slight importance. Yet it is the contrivances whereby the relation of words and sentences are pointed out that allow us to follow the thoughts *thus* expressed. Obviously, elaborate machinery is not necessary for simple designations, whereas abstract thought that rests on interrelated ideas, subordinated to one another in a variety of ways, requires machinery crafted to handle complicated mental processes. Although what refers to what and in what way may vary, complicated thought patters invariably necessitate a multilayered referential system that is able to effect hierarchical structures in which the ideas that make up intricate and composite thought may find their proper places. The set of rules governing the grammatical arrangements of sentence structures and the relationships within and among them are cardinal factors for the act of conveying thoughts via language.

Although semantic factors are not essential to the identification of grammatical formulations or parts of speech, we would have difficulty in formulating the rules that make one correct expression acceptable and another not if the morphology of languages did not also include concepts of a higher order to mediate these phenomena of grammar, so as to correspond to the regularities that prevail concerning the behavior involved. Since natural languages relate *to* and function *in* culture, they are used not only for purposes of communication, but also to *code* or *categorize* the environment, thereby constituting an important intellectual feature in the control of behavior. It has thus been suggested that linguistic systems follow an ordinary sequence of increasing differentiation of significant features, relating language development to *perceptual* development. It has likewise been suggested that in addition to phrase structure, languages must also contain a set of transformational rules that, when used, serve to modify a statement from one type to another. Transformations, accordingly, rest on simple sentence models–basic forms of adult utterances–that are transformed, as needed, by the use of transformational rules such as the interrogative, the passive, the negative, and so on.

Even the rudimentary considerations raised here are enough to convey the idea that natural languages obviously stand apart from other communication systems used by humans. This is largely due to the magnitude of their resources. While we are still far from understanding all of the characteristics of language, and even farther from understanding the human nervous system that makes it possible, two things are clear, namely, that humans are capable of inventing both *symbols* and a *duality of patterning* in linguistic structure. Unlike signs, from which the existence of something else is inferred, a symbol is a special kind of sign, one with arbitrary, conventionally assigned meaning. It is apparently uniquely human to be able to assign arbitrary meanings to signs, that is, to invent symbols. Yet the symbols of language, unlike other symbolic systems, are divisible, that is, words divide into morphemes, which, in turn, divide into phonemes–the sound units of spoken language. These diverse sound units, which are meaningless in themselves, are used for the construction of a huge number of meaningful units. It is this duality of patterning–the two level structuring–that bestows on language a quantitative and qualitative superiority over other symbolic systems.

The fact that individual languages are transmitted culturally does not rule out the possibility that mankind has certain unique inborn capacities for linguistic behavior, which culture "naturally" exploits. To be sure, the preoccupation with the innate capacities of the mind did not commence with linguistic studies; it has a time-honored, distinguished history. Nonetheless, because language is a *communal* achievement, an inseparable part of culture, which enables the development, elaboration, transmission, and accumulation of a culture as a whole, it is no wonder that the study of language should have focused on matters concerning *structure* and *meaning*, as related to manifest experiences and behavior. Yet when a particular word, in common usage, designates the object it refers to, the meaning of the word resides in the individual minds of the users of the language; it is not, however, a "thing" they have in mind but, rather, a *relationship* that associates words and objects. In other words, even the minimum units that participate in the arbitrary relationships of meaning, that is, the lexical part of language, already rest on a mind capable of entertaining relationships of this sort. However, since the links between such structural units and meaning are arbitrary, it is their *regularity* that reflects the integration between language and the rest of culture. Again, it is not surprising that regularities of this kind should have attracted the attention of linguists and anthropologists. It is the regularities displayed in the use of language that discloses, after all, not only its syntactic structure but also its semantic meaning and the culture that contributed to their formation.

Human beings clearly communicate in a variety of ways, yet compared to all other systems, 'language' displays the kind of resources most apt to convey thought. Via my brief survey of natural languages, I wished to convey above all the notion that abstract thought that rests on *interrelated* ideas–subordinated to one another in a variety of ways–is inconceivable without language. Language is apparently able to handle *complicated mental processes*. I also wanted to call attention to the fact that language is not only used for purposes of communication, but that it is also used to *code* and *characterize* the environment–of whatever kind–and that various linguistic systems follow an ordinary sequence of *increasing differentiation* of significant features, relating language development to *perceptual* development. Albeit that some languages have a more developed grammar and a richer vocabulary than others, 'language' is one of those collective enterprises that invariably weds *thought* and *meaning*. The increased differentiation of *significant features* may be devised, as well, by a group of people that wishes to register a certain *circumscribed* environment in greater detail, comprising aspects that not all of the speakers of a language are familiar with or care to know about. New words–names and concepts–may thus come into being that meet the needs of a particular group and facilitate the communication among its members.

I also called attention to the ability of humans to invent symbols. Unlike signs, from which the existence of something else is inferred, a symbol, I pointed out, is a special kind of sign, one with arbitrary, conventionally assigned meaning. The modes of symbolization, themselves, dictate what is being symbolized; their meaning, hence, resides in their making. "Images"– of whatever kind–have to be turned into symbols by the very intellect they address, using the content of perception and experience. Symbols, accordingly, are not only made, but disclose themselves through their own making; they are in fact the cultural forms of human activities. In other words, symbolic representations cannot be abstracted from their various manifestations as self-contained isolated existences.

The manner in which the mind processes information and structures coherence preoccupies scholars in diverse fields. It is currently thought that to move from process to coherence requires some form of construction or representation based on the relationships among the particles which are being processed. Process, it is thought, is influenced by that which is being processed. Yet coherence, structured as it may be, does not in itself carry meaning. In other words, coherence "makes sense," but has no meaning. To turn coherence into meaning requires symbolization. This relationship between *coherence* and *meaning* may have given rise to the relationship that pertains between the "syntax" and the "semantics" of languages. Moreover, it may have determined the mind/brain relationship altogether. In fact, the mind/brain relationship preoccupies many scholars nowadays. Yet despite the enormous advances that have been made in the diverse investigations of the brain, the unknown still outweighs the known. One thing is however abundantly clear: the brain is the *locus* that enables and controls all that we are capable of as humans. The brain may be hailed by aestheticians as the ultimate *"Gesamtkunstwerk"*–the "artwork" that enlists all of our senses and abilities.

Given the special power of language to convey thought, language was naturally enlisted to enable the tracing *and* establishment of relations and interrelations among ideas that advance knowledge. Like language itself, the pursuit of knowledge is a collective enterprise, it advances, as it were, in "connected-vessels." By employing the metaphor of connected-vessels, I wish to stress the interconnectedness among ideas (of whatever kind) and the constraints they exert on each other. Considering the vastness of the enterprise, no wonder that humans devised additional "tools" that would allow them to stir through the multitude of issues, the understanding of which may be guided by diverse ideas. The variety of issues and the diversity of ideas often give rise to contradictions and "incommensurables" that require attention. The "tools" discussed in this book do not suffice to prevent all of the mishaps and contradictions that may occur among diverse ideas. They do, however, exemplify–through their applications–how diverse fields of knowledge may be bridged. Such bridging, of course, carries special significance for interdisciplinary studies.

Relating diverse fields to each other invariably requires some common denominator. The latter may vary in kind, depending on the issue addressed and on the level of abstraction employed. For example, a horse-drawn cart, a bicycle and a car—though they differ in speed—are vehicles employing *wheels*. Wheels, however, can no longer serve as a common denominator once an airplane is added to the list. Although they vary in speed, what these vehicles have now in common is *movement*, i.e. the getting from one place to another. The time it takes for getting there is then calculated via the relationship between speed and the distance covered. The idea of relating time to movement—rather than measuring time through additive units—was originally proposed by Aristotle. Thereby, he also opened up the possibility of treating the "character" of its passage. "Experienced time," Bergson suggested, is related to the character of its unfolding. Music, for example, tries hard to convey diverse "qualities" through its unfolding. Since music unfolds in time to begin with, it represents, hence, a kind of "quantification of qualities." Indeed, the decisions and assessments concerning durational relationships within a time span constituted a major problem in the development of musical notation in the west. Yet once the mathematical approach to time was replaced (in the 13th century) by the Aristotelian approach, which defines time qualitatively as an attribute of motion, some of the major problems of notating music's unfolding in time were solved.

The reader may have noticed that the last paragraph created a *chain* of thoughts, commencing with a search for a "common denominator" and terminating with the "quantification of qualities" that are bridged by the gauging of time via movement. However strange these associations may seem, they are by no means arbitrary. They are constrained by a certain chain of interrelationships among ideas. Were I to focus on inventions—from wheels to engines—I might wish to argue that despite the "progress" in speed, the wheel is the more impressive invention as far as movement is concerned, since its inventor had no "shoulders" to stand on. But this may be an exception to the general rule, i.e. that employing chains of interrelated ideas allows one to see "further." Such chains in fact represent *sequences* of ideas that *refer* to each other progressively via common denominators.

Allow me to indulge in a few anecdotes. Some years ago my husband and I visited the impressive Inca ruins on the peak of the Machu Picchu Mountain, looming above the clouds more than two miles overhead. The steep slopes of the mountain and the dense jungle covered for centuries the lost sanctuary of this bygone culture. The gigantic blocks cling to each other creating walls without using cement. These blocks, one is told, were brought from far away quarries where they were fashioned by people using stone tools. They were moved over an inclined plane by levers, since they had neither pulleys nor wheels, but had thousands of patient workers, whose perseverance, determination and achievement are owe inspiring. Since all of this took place only five or six centuries ago, i.e. relatively recently, by what criteria and from what perspective are we supposed to judge their colossal achievement?... On one of our visits to the Chartres cathedral, we joined a group that listened to the explanations of a renowned English tour-guide. Surrounded by people upholding binoculars, he told his audience that the stain-glass windows imparted the familiar biblical stories *visually* to the illiterate believers. "They must have had better eyesight," exclaimed one of the tourists, "since the lens was invented considerably later!" Obviously, the repeated explanation used by the guide–however attractive–cannot be the sole reason for the magnificent windows that adorn the cathedral... Interested in the reliability of oral transmission, I investigated, some years ago, Samaritan music–a three tone music consisting of a central note adorned by an upper and lower vibrated note. What guided my study was, however, the statement of one of my informants who claimed that Samaritan music, unlike Beethoven's music, was very rich and interesting. Beethoven's music, he thought was dull since "nothing happens in that music, it is all the same!"

What refers to what and in what way is of utmost importance. One must remember, however, that what appears to be different on one level may seem alike on another level, depending on what it is one wants to emphasize. Syntheses–of whatever kind–are generally in search of common denominators that would embrace a variety of subjects, related to each other via diverse ideas. The process mostly involves a move from "specifics" in the direction of "abstractions." Yet things which seem alike to begin with, may also differ significantly upon closer scrutiny, once their detailed features are analyzed. Again, it all depends on what it is one wants to know with reference to the issue at hand. What *resembles* what and what *differs* from what and *whereby*, clearly depends on what it is that one is trying to *understand*.

As already stated, 'Knowledge'–however defined–is invariably subject to constraints, circumscribed by the very ideas that humans produced in order to *understand* the world they inhabit, their place within it, and the vast universe which surrounds them. Whether in search of embracing principles or in search of the smallest significant difference, serious investigations derive their impetus from the communities of discourse to which they belong. These refer, in one way or another, to the theoretical traditions that stipulate the kind of rigor that is involved and the sort of speculations that are licensed. The concern with specifics, we must remember, creates all kinds of interrelated webs of understanding, the intersections of which give rise to yet new specifics that solicit inquiries of their own. Knowledge apparently involves both imminent and far-flung relationships that impact each other in ways that continuously sensitize us to issues we may have never entertained or have taken for granted. Knowledge clearly intensifies the *pursuit* of knowledge, which is continually challenged by new discoveries that may throw new light on old assessments. Discoveries, thus, turn into *creative acts* that ignite the "engine" that lends knowledge its forward thrust.

Indeed, although it is human-beings who create the means whereby they further their understanding, the "Acquisition of Knowledge" is an ongoing process that is *constrained* by the very means that enable its progression. The means–which may be characterized by the various processes of "differentiations" and "likenesses" that they create–apparently rest on our mental capacity "to refer," i.e. to *create* distinctions and similarities. 'Sameness' & 'Difference'–in whatever guise–are clearly related to each other in our thought processes. In fact, the advancement of knowledge is inconceivable without this fundamental "binary" that enables and propels the multiple chains of reference that enlarge the scope of our understanding. The study of diverse issues, however, may employ different "referential schemes"–arrangements, outlines, classifications–that provide diverse *points of reference* which, in turn, make it possible to determine how different issues relate to each other.

It may be recalled that in my brief discussion of language I stressed that the study of language focuses on matters concerning *structure* and *meaning,* as related to manifest experiences and behavior. I called attention to the fact that the meaning of words–that designate objects they refer to–resides in the minds of their users, minds capable of entertaining relationships. In other words, it is not "things" they have in mind but, rather, *relationships* that associate words to objects. I also emphasized that it is apparently uniquely human to be able to attribute arbitrary meaning to signs, that is, to invent symbols. Since the modes of symbolization themselves dictate what is symbolized, their meaning resides, hence, in their making. The "power" of language apparently rests on a mind capable of evolving *differentiations*, of entertaining *relationships*, and of fabricating *new relationships* that impart signification. No wonder that the "referential schemes" (to which I alluded in the previous paragraph) should also be imbedded in language; they constitute significant "tools" that help us to establish what relates to what and in what way.

The predisposition for language acquisition also involves, as is well known, vocal abilities (the ability to produce and perceive sound) and the ability to communicate via visual and audible gestures. However, since *ideas*—primarily the way they relate to each other—occupy center stage in this book, the aspects I highlighted above are those that enable 'reference', 'thought', *and* 'reasoning' as a *collective enterprise*. Human beings obviously use ideas to *think with* about ideas, irrespective of issue or concern. The pursuit of knowledge thus rests, willy-nilly, on the interrelationships among ideas. While it is impossible to deal with the multiplicity of relationships at one and the same time, they partake nonetheless in the *thinking processes* that underlie the "multi-dimensional-matrix" that embraces knowledge in its entirety.

Our discussion, so far, has focused primarily on the capacity to "differentiate" as inherent in *thought*, and on the capacity "to refer" as inherent in *language*. The interrelationships among ideas, as we have seen, create *chains* of thoughts, brought about via "common denominators." Each of these chains follows some kind of *order*—a sequence of references that discloses the *thinking processes* implicit in particular investigations. Though investigations—regardless of kind—never start from scratch, their initial point of reference may vary, depending on the issue examined and the perspective employed. The interactions of these various chains create the afore-mentioned "multi-dimensional-matrix" of knowledge, yet the ways in which these chains *relate* to each other require investigations of their own. Investigations of this kind cannot be achieved, however, without taking into account the *contexts* that circumscribed the points of reference relevant to the issues already investigated, and the perspectives which they entertained. This situation of the "chicken and the egg" is due to the fact that the pursuit of Knowledge continually gives rise to new knowledge that sensitizes us to issues we have not entertained.

Nonetheless, by specifying the points of reference relevant to the investigation of diverse issues, contexts seem to provide *frames* of reference that justify different criteria of judgment. Identifiable separations of sorts are obviously necessary in order to be able to create referential chains, i.e. sequences of ideas that impart signification. In fact, it is *demarcations*–organizational boundaries–that make possible the search for meaningful commonalities among different fields of inquiry. The search rests, however, on "schemes" that allow for diverse kinds of comparisons to take place. Given that language depends on a mind capable of (1) developing differentiations, (2) entertaining relationships, and (3) fabricating new relationships that impart signification, no wonder that the schemes that may unveil *new* relationships should also be embedded in language, employing commonly used concepts.

Let us have a look at the definitions supplied by the dictionary for the following terms:

Representation	"Representing or being represented;" "seeking to portray reality;" "what is representative, serving as portrayal or symbol of"
Structure	"Manner in which a building or organism or other complete whole is constructed;" "the essential parts of something"
Form	"Shape, arrangements of parts, visible aspects, or tangible"
Model	"Representation on a small scale;" "simplified description of system etc. to assist calculations and predications, design, style of structure"
Archetype	"Original model, prototype, recurrent symbol or motif, primordial mental image"
Metaphor	"Application of name or descriptive term of phrase to an object or action to which it is not literally applicable"
Expression	"Expressing, wording;" "collection of symbols expressing a quality; aspect of indication, emotion"

Experience	"Actual observation of or practical acquaintance with factsnor events; event that affects one; fact or process of being so affected"
Interpretation	"Make out the meaning of, bring out the meaning of, render, by artistic representation or performance; explain, understand in specified manner"
Frame	"Shape, direct thoughts, acts to a purpose;" "adapt, fit to or into;" "construct by combination of parts"
Name	"Give name to; call by right name; nominate; mention"

All of the above definitions involve–in one way or another–differentiations, relationships, and some bearing on diverse issues. They all establish modes of reference. Despite their diversity, a close examination of these definitions reveals considerable overlap. For example, 'structure' 'form' and 'frame' involve some kind of organization of parts; 'representation' 'model' 'metaphor' and 'archetype' involve portrayals of sorts; 'expression' 'experience' and 'interpretation' relate directly, or indirectly, to "qualities" of kinds. Portrayals, moreover, may be achieved through an emphasis on *essential* parts or via their *organizations*. Mental *images* need not be anchored in reality in order to function symbolically, and *qualities* may reside in the objects observed or in the *experience* of the observer. Although much more can be inferred from the above definitions, it is abundantly clear that the terms, themselves, are ambiguous. They require a great deal of elucidation when employed or applied in scientific investigations, *a fortiori* regarding interdisciplinary studies.

Given that the meaning of symbols resides in their very making, the strategies employed, so as to impart signification, concerns all scientists regardless of their field of inquiry. Indeed, since knowledge advances via diverse chains of reference, the "logic" that governs specific sequences of ideas, i.e. the *reasoning* which it involves, must be spelled out. Only theoretical elucidations of this kind enable us to locate the common denominators that make the bridging among diverse chains of ideas possible. "Separations" and "Combinations" are thus processes of equal importance in the advancement of knowledge. The pursuit of knowledge as a *collective* human enterprise is inconceivable, as we have seen, without the inter-dependence of the "specific" and the "general" that jointly enlarge the scope of our understanding.

The reader may recall that I repeatedly stressed that what *relates* to what and *whereby* requires utmost scrutiny. I deliberately used the words 'relate' and 'whereby' in order not to foreclose the variety of possible answers. This said, it is nonetheless clear that establishing relevance involves delimiting factors–"territorial boundaries," as it were, that lend credence to the ideas employed. Although the borderlines among disciplines have fluctuated in the course of history, and continue to do so, they invariably maintain some differentiation among diverse "areas" of investigation. A particular "subject" may thus be viewed as constituting a part of a given area. A specific "problem" may be considered to be part of a particular subject. A certain "objective" (purpose, intent) may be related to a specific problem, and a given "solution" to a pre-determined objective. Though hierarchies of this kind both circumscribe and contextualize scientific investigations, the *processes of thought* that accompany diverse investigations are disclosed thereby. It is these processes that enable the kind of "cross-fertilization" of ideas that enhances and widens our understanding of self, *and* of the world that surrounds us, in *intelligible* ways. In fact, the history of ideas substantiates the claim that Knowledge (with a capital K) advances in "*connected* vessels," as it were.

Indeed, scientific investigations require continual alertness to the ideas employed–where they come from, the purposes they serve, and the degree of their relevance to the issue under investigation. Critical thinking applies *a fortiori* to interdisciplinary studies. By focusing on some of the "tools" that scholars employ in their investigations, this book aims to alert its readers to look more deeply at the ideas they may employ in their own research. With this in mind, the readings included in this volume consist of: (1) writings whose propositions carry significance for the book as a whole, (2) writings that directly deal with some of the "tools" that enable the advance of knowledge, and (3) writings that *exemplify* the use of basic propositions and seminal tools in their investigations of specific topics.

As already stated, the book neither represents the *history* of ideas, nor does it deal with 'reference' in purely *philosophical* terms. The choice of readings is nonetheless guided by an awareness of: (a) the historical development of seminal ideas, (b) the kind of deliberations which 'reference' enlists, (c) the inherent importance of each of the writings, and (d) their significance for scientific investigations, regardless of the discipline whence they emerged. Consequently, although each of the readings deserves to be read on its own, the book as a whole tries to convey the *interconnectedness* of ideas and the *integrations* which they create, imparting thereby a comprehensive picture of the various settings and routes through which knowledge advances and shapes our understanding and consciousness. As explained in the preface, the book is divided into four major sections, each of which is prefaced by an introduction. The readings in each of the sections are also individually introduced.

In conclusion, I see fit to emphasize that seemingly intricate explanations, once understood, strike us as "common sense." In fact, this book attempts to highlight the truism that Knowledge advances through mechanisms and explications that are both guided by and create the *common* sense, i.e. the *shared* understanding that affects scientific investigations. The natural-sciences and the human-sciences are mutually propelled by the ideas–and the interrelationships thereof–that humans devise to better understand their own "makeup" and that of the world that surrounds them.

PART I

The Fundamentals of Reference

I

The Fundamentals of Reference

INTRODUCTION

By now it is widely accepted that humans alone create and build in a *cumulative* way, guided by webs of understandings that they themselves devise and continue to spin. One of the definitions of the word 'knowledge' refers to the *sum* of these understandings, whether theoretical or practical. Knowledge, in fact, rests on the capacity of humans to create language, since it is in language that cultures are formed. The first section of this book thus deals with the capacity of humans to create features of similarity and difference, symbols and references, i.e. with the bare bones of language and the essentials that set human communication in motion.

Communication apparently requires an ability to differentiate among things–of whatever kind–and an ability to refer to them in some way. Human beings are endowed with the mental capacities that enable both of these activities. However, since differentiations rest on some notion concerning *whereby* one thing differs from another, they are employed in a variety of ways. Objects, for example, that look alike may differ from each other by the functions they serve. The reverse is likewise possible, dissimilar objects may serve the same function. Differentiations, it seems, involve comparisons of sorts that rest on assessments of similarities and differences of diverse kinds. Similarity naturally increases with the addition of common features and decreases with the deletion of features that are distinctive to each of the objects compared. One may wish, nonetheless, to highlight *distinctive* features due to their saliency, their significance, and their relative "weight" in the characterization of the objects unto themselves.

The trajectories one has in mind are clearly impacted by what it is one tries to convey or understand. They are, however, also impacted by their intended audience. Scientific investigations invariably involve communities of discourse that share some agreed upon knowledge that rests on theoretical propositions and prior investigations relevant to the investigation at hand. In fact, the accumulation of knowledge is inconceivable without such communities. They serve a double function, that of judges and custodians, guarantying thereby their contribution to Knowledge as an enduring *collective* enterprise. Yet it is primarily the "reasoning" processes that accompany diverse scientific discourses that enable the detection of the interrelationships among ideas, and of the *thinking patterns* that humans employ that propel both the acquisition of knowledge as well as its advancement.

Aware or not, human beings evidently employ ideas to *think with* about ideas. What enables them to do so, i.e. to refer *via* ideas *to* ideas clearly rests on the capacity of humans to create *distinctions,* as well as, *directives*, or *indications* that point in the direction of–or refer to–those distinctions. The "thinking patterns," to which I alluded above, while resting on the capacities of our species, involve primarily Man's own *creations* in order to better understand the self and the world that surrounds him. Though continuously affected by environmental and social changes–involving diverse objectives and aspirations–this ongoing quest enables nonetheless the advancement of knowledge due to the "devices" that humans create. These devices help further our understanding in a *humanly* intelligible way. The pursuit of knowledge must thus take into account past experiences–acquired insights and understandings–with regard to diverse issues that seem to have solicited satisfactory investigations and persuasive findings. Knowledge clearly advances through what has been "learned." The latter, however, may give rise to new queries the investigations of which may cast new light on former understandings. Indeed, while scientific inquiries may center on diverse issues, the need for common standardized systems of reference–that would both store and manage scientific data efficiently–accompanied the advancement of knowledge all along. Though reasoning is an inherent feature of all human activities, we cannot comprehend the rich and varied symbolic forms of man's cultural life by relying solely on reason, since man's own creations construed a complex web that envelopes *all* of human life, a mesh he cannot escape.

The various branches of philosophy, for example, clearly deal with different issues. It can be argued, moreover, that each of these branches occupied center stage, or was most prominent in different periods in Western history. They all abided, however, by standardized systems of reference that enabled the "spinning" nature of knowledge, thereby contributing their share to its accumulation. Metaphysics, it is thought, loomed large in antiquity since the period was primarily concerned with the *ultimate nature* of reality and the problem of virtue in political context. Logic, interestingly, which deals with laws of *valid reasoning*, loomed large in medieval thought that was inseparable from Christian thought. Beginning with the Renaissance, philosophical inquiries moved in the direction of Epistemology, i.e. towards a concern with the *nature of knowledge* and the *processes* of knowing. Ethics, which deals with problems pertaining to *right conduct,* has always been somehow applied to real life, evolving various conceptions of the good life for man. Aesthetics, however, only became a bona fide branch of philosophy in the eighteenth century, although deliberations concerning 'beauty' already had an extended and venerable history. Despite their different concerns and trajectories, there is a great deal of overlap among these branches of philosophy since the premises of each were, and could be employed in order to substantiate the main arguments of the other. This is largely due to those standardized systems of reference whereby ideas relate to each other in an orderly way that imparts signification in a humanly intelligible way.

At any rate, the history of mankind teaches us how humans progressively developed material and mental "tools" that enabled them to survive in communities facing diverse circumstances. Developments of this kind depended, however, on shared understandings concerning the efficacy of the tools that came into being. The gauging of their efficacy required as well agreed points of reference–former states of development or knowledge in relationship to which judgment could be cast. Thus, for example, the predictable conduct of the Sun, the Moon, and other planets gave rise to the notion that the universe represents some kind of *order*–a preplanned universal *design*. In fact, this belief constituted the point of reference for the ancient concept of "The Harmony of the Spheres" according to which the celestial bodies were thought to revolve around the earth, each in its proper sphere. The spheres, however, were thought to be related to each other by the whole-number ratios of "musical intervals," creating a kind of unheard "harmony" that substantiated the assumption about the uniqueness of the "designer" and of the nature of his "creation."

It may be recalled that by recognizing the ratios of intervals from a keynote, Pythagoras had discovered the mathematical basis that was applied to the spheres. Yet even after the earth was no longer considered the center of the universe, and the movements of the celestial bodies were differently conceived, Pythagoras' discovery remained intact. In fact, the association of the length of a chord with musical tones has been acclaimed as the first known *reduction* of a 'quality' (sound) into a 'quantity' (length and ratios), thereby constituting the starting point of the understanding of Nature through mathematics. The understanding of Nature through mathematics remained to this very day one of the main objectives of science. Pythagoras, in fact, discovered a new "language," the language of numbers. Yet the importance of Pythagoras' discovery does not only rest on the fact, it is the *interpretation* of the fact which became decisive for the future orientation of philosophical and mathematical thought. The Pythagorean thinkers, unlike their descendants, did not conceive of the world of number as a *symbolic* world; they made no distinction between symbol and object, the former replaced the latter. The "substantial reality" of numbers was nonetheless replaced, in due time, by an understanding that 'number' is one of the steps in the process of objectification.

Everyday language also reveals efforts of classification, it cannot lead to an *exact* systematization however, since the symbols of language have no systematic order; every single linguistic term has its special "area" of meaning. If number is superior to the symbolism of speech it is precisely due to the fact that the essence of number is always and invariably *relative*, not absolute. It has no self-contained reality, its meaning is defined by the position it occupies in the whole numerical system. In fact, the transition from the apprehensible to the understandable invariably calls for a new "instrument" of thought. Indeed, observations must be referred to a system of well ordered symbols in order to make them coherent and interpretable in terms of scientific concepts, whether in the, so called, *exact* sciences or *human* sciences.

Many different schemes existed concerning the "Harmony of the Spheres," yet the *design* of the Heaven–of that apparent vault over the Earth, in which sun, moon, and stars are seen–invariably entailed some calculation of proportions, i.e. an organization of the "parts" that were supposed to impart the *unity* of the "whole." The Heavenly design, at any rate, was believed to represent the consummate *order,* the secrets of which could be unveiled through intelligible calculations advanced by humans. Calculations of this sort and their implications were transmitted to medieval Europe via the doctrine of the "Harmony of the Spheres," a doctrine that became manifest not only in philosophy and science, but in the arts and religion as well. We need only think of medieval scholasticism, and of the architecture of those awe inspiring cathedrals, to become fully aware of the impact that proportions of musical and geometrical "harmony" had on medieval thought.

The notion of a divinely ordered universe that emanated from the school of Pythagoras was assimilated by Plato and later on by the Church Fathers. It became a basic premise in religion and science until the seventeenth century when the Pythagorean cosmology was discredited by the Scientific Revolution. This revolution, as is well known, undermined the Aristotelian understanding of Nature that was primarily based on the factual, *visible* world. The revolution of the late sixteenth and early seventeenth centuries reversed this understanding, hoping to extrapolate from the factual world the *invisible* laws of nature–its hypothetical fundamental laws. The Scientific Revolution thus ushered in a new kind of search, a search that aimed to unveil the "secrets" of nature via theories that gained credence through novel processes of verification.

As already stated, the transition from the "graspable" to the "understandable" invariably calls for a new "instrument" of thought, or for the reformulation of previous understandings. In fact, these transitions highlight the processes whereby humans advance knowledge, the ways in which they employ their own creations in order to further their understanding. It practically goes without saying that all of the issues which I barely touch upon received concerted attention and have been carefully studied by scholars in diverse fields, comprising the human and natural sciences. It naturally occupied a venerable place in philosophy and the history of ideas. However, since this book is primarily concerned with Culture as a *man-made* product, it only tries to impart some insights into the ways in which humans employ the "figurations" they themselves devise, figurations that guide their quest for knowledge and the changes which knowledge undergoes.

If language loomed large in what was said so far it is due to the unique capacity of language to convey *thought*. I repeatedly stressed the notion that humans use ideas to *think with* about ideas, but I refrained from discussing the ontological nature of ideas in relationship to all else. It will have been noticed, nonetheless, that with regard to scientific investigations–regardless of kind– the introduction emphasized three major aspects that require special attention and scrutiny: *ideas*, *distinctions* and *symbolic forms*. These three aspects seem to interact with each other in significant ways. 'Reasoning,' accordingly, enables the detection of the *relationship* among ideas; 'differentiation' allows us to *refer* to them; and 'symbolic forms' seem to *constitute* man's cultural life. The readings contained in this section address these fundamental subjects and draw the attention of the reader to their significance and relevance to knowledge and its advance.

Much has been written on the subjects I see fit to emphasize in this book, a situation that makes the choice of readings not easy. However, the choice of readings for this section of the book was relatively easy. The authors chosen are considered by experts to have contributed formative thoughts to our conception of 'knowledge'. This by no means implies a "standstill" concerning further thoughts and clarifications. This book, however, only attempts to promote the awareness of the reader to the kind of *reasoning* that accompanies the pursuit of knowledge, rather than create expertise on certain philosophical debates. With this in mind, it is hard to overlook the thoughts advanced by Plato concerning "ideas," those by Cassirer with regard to "symbolic forms", and the ones by Tversky about "features of similarity."

Plato, as is well known, called our attention to the fact that certain qualities are always the same though they may appear in changing objects, and that many different words and thoughts contain "truth." There are certain qualities or essences, argued Plato, which our minds recognize as permanent realities (such as blueness, beauty, goodness, etc.), Plato called them *Ideas*. In a series of dialogues that began as a monument to Socrates, Plato went on to add thoughts of his own to the legacy he attributed to his beloved master. Plato eventually emerged as a decisive "initiator" of much that is still fruitful in thought to this very day. His approach to the question of how humans advance knowledge involves processes of "reasoning" through which one may arrive at "true" knowledge and understanding.

Ernest Cassirer is generally identified with his profound work concerning symbolic forms. Much has transpired in the centuries that elapsed since Plato, and much has been learned ever since. Cassirer is one of those philosophers who also endeavored to trace this development in order to better understand Man and the Culture he creates. With great insight and vast learning Cassirer investigated the creation of myth, religion, art, language, history and science in order to unveil the unity of a "general function" by which these creations are held together. As the great exponent of the philosophy of symbolic forms, Cassirer emphasized the symbolic nature of man's cultural achievement.

Unlike the above, Amos Tversky was a cognitive and mathematical psychologist, a key figure in the discovery of systematic human cognitive bias and handling of risk. The idea that people make irrational decisions caused Tversky and Kahneman to develop a model that simulates the considerations of decision making. (Their joint work merited in 2002 the Nobel Prize in economics.) Interested in cognitive processes, they were also eager to reveal how different kinds of "framing" may influence our decisions and perceptions of given situations. Among his many studies, Tversky's seminal article, entitled "Features of Similarity" (1984), received much attention upon its appearance and ever since. More than many other studies that deal with similarities and differences, Tversky sensitized us to the *variety* whereby they may be established and accessed.

Plato
(427–347 B.C.)

Introduction

As is well known, Socrates is the presiding speaker in Plato's dialogues, although the ideas he is expressing are often those of his disciple. According to Socrates, men are bad because they are "thoughtless." What the Athenians needed most after their war experience,[1] he argued, is not a return to prosperity and unfounded beliefs, but to a self-examination that might lead to a better life for the individual and for the society at large. Socrates, says Cassirer, introduced "a new activity and function of thought," namely, that "we cannot discover the nature of man in the same way that we can detect the nature of physical things. Physical things may be described in terms of their objective properties, but man may be described and defined only in terms of his consciousness."[2] The method used by Socrates to persuade people became a model for imitation ever since, largely due to Plato's dialogues.

True knowledge, according to Plato, cannot be established by relying solely on our sense impressions since these often deceive us. Neither can opinions based on sensations alone be trusted as a guide to truth. Only reason and learning produce knowledge and understanding. Plato, you may recall, also sensitized us to the fact that different words and thoughts contain truth. There are certain qualities or essences, according to Plato, which our minds learn to recognize as *permanent realities* since their form and character never change (like 'roundness', for example). Plato called them *Ideas*. Moreover, the more we examine *with reason* that which we perceive through our senses, the more likely we are to detect the *essential* connection between diverse objects or thoughts that previously seemed unconnected. Having highlighted *reason* and the

---

[1] The Peloponnesian War that began in 431 B.C. and lasted twenty-seven years.
[2] Cassirer, Ernst, *An Essay on Man: An Introduction to Human Culture,* Anchor Books, New York, 1954, p. 20.

unifying function of *ideas*, Plato also addressed the fundamental issues, that preoccupied the society to which he belonged. Like Socrates, he, too, believed that humans need to know how to make the best of living. Aware of the rifts among the Athenians of his time, he produced a detailed plan for a new social order that required no less than a total reorganization of the society.

The new order was not only expected to promote wisdom through education, but to enact it in everyday life. Above all, the governing institutions of the new social order must be administered by those who have acquired the wisdom needed to fulfill so responsible a tusk. Plato, accordingly, conjured-up a "blueprint" for an ideal state. He outlined the institutions that such a state is in need of and the kinds of people in whose hands they may be entrusted in order to assure a just, well ordered state–a state that may benefit both the individual citizen as well as the collective. Since the running of such a state requires a great deal of wisdom, it is hardly surprising that Plato should privilege those who have already acquired wisdom to be in charge.

Many theories were advanced since those ancient times concerning what may constitute an *ideal* state and how it might be achieved. Plato's *Republic* received, nonetheless, much attention although it was written over two millennia ago. The many issues which Plato addressed in this magnum opus required, after all, a great deal of *wisdom*. It has often been remarked that ever since Plato, and his luminous student Aristotle, philosophy consisted largely of "footnotes." Indeed, between them they set the foundation for the thought that accompanied scientific development in the West, regardless of the field of endeavor and despite the changes that took place ever since. Their philosophical horizon was apparently vast enough so as to carry significance even for inquiries which they themselves could hardly have anticipated. Interestingly, it is largely the division between Plato's and Aristotle's philosophical orientation that continued to run throughout the whole history of Western philosophy. Plato became identified with all that pertains to 'idealism' and 'realism,' whereas Aristotle became identified with 'rationalism' and 'empiricism.'

Here, however, I only wish to direct the reader's attention to Plato's so-called "Theory of Forms"–a metaphysical and epistemological theory that grants

Ideas a seminal function in the search for truth. Correct answers, according to the theory, do not rest on what we think, but on an accurate description of an independent "entity"–a Form. Forms are *mind-independent entities* and their existence and nature is independent of our beliefs and judgments about them. Plato called these forms *ideas*. The nature of these "mind-independent entities" are however only graspable *by* the mind. The forms, according to Plato, help us to distinguish knowledge from opinion or belief. Moreover, they help us to determine whether there are certain permanent "real things" behind the changing phenomena that can be perceived.

Though central to Plato's thought, the "Theory of Forms" is nowhere systematically argued for; it is dispersed among his several writings. It appears, however, more markedly in his *Phaedo* and the *Republic*. In the dialogue that carries Phaedo's name, Phaedo–one of Socrates' disciples–reports to a group of friends about the discussion that took place among Socrates and the friends who spent the last hours with Socrates, before he was executed. The dialogue vividly imparts Socrates' astuteness and, no less, his inspiring composure in the face of death. He does not fear death since *ideas* are the immortal and unchangeable causes of the world. The dialogue, according to Plato scholars, is made up partly of genuine memories of Socrates' last words and partly of Plato's own mature reasoning. Although the dialogue also elaborates at length on the "immortality of the soul," the sections represented here are those that best convey Plato's thoughts concerning *Ideas*their role and function.

PLATO
from ***Phaedo****

Cebes added: "Your favorite doctrine, Socrates, that knowledge is simply recollection, if true, also necessarily implies a previous time in which we have learned that which we now recollect. But this would be impossible unless our soul had been in some place before existing in the form of man; here then is another proof of the soul's immortality."

"But tell me, Cebes," said Simmias, interposing, "what arguments are urged in favor of this doctrine of recollection. I am not very sure at the moment that I remember them."

"One excellent proof," said Cebes, "is afforded by questions. If you put a question to a person in a right way, he will give a true answer of himself, but how could he do this unless there were knowledge and right reason already in him? And this is most clearly shown when he is taken to a   diagram[1] or to anything of that sort."

"But if," said Socrates, "you are still incredulous, Simmias, I would ask you whether you may not agree with me when you look at the matter in another way—I mean, if you are still incredulous as to whether knowledge is recollection?"

"Incredulous I am not," said Simmias; "but I want to have this doctrine of recollection brought to my own recollection, and, from what Cebes has said, I am beginning to recollect and be convinced: but I should still like to hear what you were going to say."

"This is what I would say," he replied. "We should agree, if I am not mistaken, that what a man recollects he must have known at some previous time."

"Very true."

"And what is the nature of this knowledge or recollection? I mean to ask whether a person who, having seen, or heard, or in any way perceived anything,

---

* From *Phaedo,* trans by B. Jowett (Walter J. Black, New York, 1942), pp. 104-110 and pp. 133-143.

[1] In the *Meno,* an earlier dialogue, Plato had represented Socrates as drawing from an untaught slave boy the right answer to a geometrical problem, thus proving, he said, that knowledge is often recollection of things known in a past existence.

knows not only that, but has a conception of something else which is the subject, not of the same but of some other kind of knowledge, may not be fairly said to recollect that of which he has the conception?"

"What do you mean?"

"I mean what I may illustrate by the following instance: The knowledge of a lyre is not the same as the knowledge of a man?"

"True."

"And yet what is the feeling of lovers when they recognize a lyre, or a garment, or anything else which the beloved has been in the habit of using? Do not they, from knowing the lyre, form in the mind's eye an image of the youth to whom the lyre belongs? And this is recollection. In like manner anyone who sees Simmias may remember Cebes; and there are endless examples of the same thing."

"Endless, indeed," replied Simmias.

"And recollection is most commonly a process of recovering that which has been already forgotten through time and inattention."

"Very true," he said.

"Well; and may you not also from seeing the picture of a horse or a lyre remember a man? and from the picture of Simmias, you may be led to remember Cebes?"

"True."

"Or you may also be led to the recollection of Simmias himself?"

"Quite so."

"And in all these cases, the recollection may be derived from things either like or unlike?"

"It may be."

"And when the recollection is derived from like things, then another consideration is sure to arise, which is whether the likeness in any degree falls short or not of that which is recollected?"

"Very true," he said.

"And shall we proceed a step further, and affirm that there is such a thing as equality, not of one piece of wood or stone with another, but that, over and above this, there is absolute equality? Shall we say so?"

"Say so, yes," replied Simmias, "and swear to it, with all the confidence in life."

"And do we know the nature of this absolute essence?"

"To be sure," he said.

"And whence did we obtain our knowledge? Did we not see equalities of material things, such as pieces of wood and stones, and gather from them the idea of an equality which is different from them? For you will acknowledge that there is a difference. Or look at the matter in another way: Do not the same pieces of wood or stone appear at one time equal, and at another time unequal?"

"That is certain."

"But are real equals ever unequal? Or is the idea of equality the same as of inequality?"

"Impossible, Socrates."

"Then these (so-called) equals are not the same with the idea of equality?"

"I should say, clearly not, Socrates."

"And yet from these equals, although differing from the idea of equality, you conceived and attained that idea?"

"Very true," he said.

"Which might be like, or might be unlike them?"

"Yes."

"But that makes no difference: whenever from seeing one thing you conceived another, whether like or unlike, there must surely have been an act of recollection?"

"Very true."

"But what would you say of equal portions of wood and stone or other material equals? And what is the impression produced by them? Are they equals in the same sense in which absolute equality is equal? Or do they fall short of this perfect equality in a measure?"

"Yes," he said, "in a very great measure too."

"And must we not allow, that when I or anyone, looking at any object, observes that the thing which he sees aims at being some other thing, but falls short of, and cannot be, that other thing, but is inferior, he who makes this observation must have had a previous knowledge of that to which the other, although similar, was inferior?"

"Certainly."

"And has not this been our own case in the matter of equals and of absolute equality?"

"Precisely."

"Then we must have known equality previously to the time when we first saw the material equals, and reflected that all these apparent equals strive to attain absolute equality, but fall short of it?"

"Very true."

"And we recognize also that this absolute equality has only been known, and can only be known, through the medium of sight or touch, or of some other of the senses, which are all alike in this respect?"

"Yes, Socrates, as far as the argument is concerned, one of them is the same as the other."

"From the senses then is derived the knowledge that all sensible things aim at an absolute equality of which they fall short?"

"Yes."

"Then before we began to see or hear or perceive in any way, we must have had a knowledge of absolute equality, or we could not have referred to that standard the equals which are derived from the senses?–for to that they all aspire, and of that they fall short."

"No other inference can be drawn from the previous statements."

"And did we not see and hear and have the use of our other senses as soon as we were born?"

"Certainly."

"Then we must have acquired the knowledge of equality at some previous time?"

"Yes."

"That is to say, before we were born, I suppose?"

"True."

"And if we acquired this knowledge before we were born, and were born having the use of it, then we also knew before we were born and at the instant of birth not only the equal or the greater or the less, but all other ideas; for we are not speaking only of equality, but of beauty, goodness, justice, holiness, and of all which we stamp with the name of essence in the dialectical process, both when we ask and when we answer questions. Of all this we may certainly affirm that we acquired the knowledge before birth?"

"We may."

"But if, after having acquired, we have not forgotten what in each case we acquired, then we must always have come into life having knowledge, and shall always continue to know as long as life lasts–for knowing is the acquiring and retaining knowledge and not forgetting. Is not forgetting, Simmias, just the losing of knowledge?"

"Quite true, Socrates."

"But if the knowledge which we acquired before birth was lost by us at birth, and if afterwards by the use of the senses we recovered what we previously knew, will not the process which we call learning be a recovering of the knowledge which is natural to us, and may not this be rightly termed recollection?"

"Very true."

"So much is clear–that when we perceive something, either by the help of sight, or hearing, or some other sense, from that perception we are able to obtain a notion of some other thing like or unlike which is associated with it but has been forgotten. Whence, as I was saying, one of two alternatives follows: either we had this knowledge at birth, and continued to know through life; or, after birth, those who are said to learn only remember, and learning is simply recollection."

"Yes, that is quite true, Socrates."

"And which alternative, Simmias, do you prefer? Had we the knowledge at our birth, or did we recollect the things which we knew previously to our birth?"

"I cannot decide at the moment."

"At any rate, you can decide whether he who has knowledge will or will not be able to render an account of his knowledge? What do you say?"

"Certainly, he will."

"But do you think that every man is able to give an account of these very matters about which we are speaking?"

"Would that they could, Socrates, but I rather fear that tomorrow, at this time, there will no longer be anyone alive who is able to give an account of them such as ought to be given."

"Then you are not of opinion, Simmias, that all men know these things?"

"Certainly not."

"They are in process of recollecting that which they learned before?"

"Certainly."

"But when did our souls acquire this knowledge? Not since we were born as men?"

"Certainly not."

"And therefore, previously?"

"Yes."

"Then, Simmias, our souls must also have existed without bodies before they were in the form of man, and must have had intelligence."

"Unless indeed you suppose, Socrates, that these notions are given us at the very moment of birth; for this is the only time which remains."

"Yes, my friend, but if so when do we lose them? for they are not in us when we are born, that is admitted. Do we lose them at the moment of receiving them, or if not at what other time?"

"No, Socrates, I perceive that I was unconsciously talking nonsense."

"Then may we not say, Simmias, that if, as we are always repeating, there is an absolute beauty, and goodness, and an absolute essence of all things; and if to this, which is now discovered to have existed in our former state, we refer all our sensations, and with this compare them, finding these ideas to be pre-existent and our inborn possession—then our souls must have had a prior existence, but if not, there would be no force in the argument? There is the same proof that these ideas must have existed before we were born, as that our souls existed before we were born; and if not the ideas, then not the souls."

"Yes, Socrates; I am convinced that there is precisely the same necessity for the one as for the other; and the argument retreats successfully to the position that the existence of the soul before birth cannot be separated from the existence of the essence of which you speak. For there is nothing which to my mind is so patent as that beauty, goodness, and the other notions of which you were just now speaking have a most real and absolute existence; and I am satisfied with the proof."

... Socrates paused awhile, and seemed to be absorbed in reflection. At length he said: "You are raising a tremendous question, Cebes, involving the whole nature of generation and corruption, about which, if you like, I will give you my own experience; and if anything which I say is likely to avail towards the solution of your difficulty you may make use of it."

"I should very much like," said Cebes, "to hear what you have to say."

"Then I will tell you," said Socrates. "When I was young, Cebes, I had a prodigious desire to know that department of philosophy which is called the investigation of nature; to know the causes of things, and why a thing is and is created or destroyed appeared to me to be a lofty profession; and I was always agitating myself with the consideration of questions such as these: Is the growth of animals the result of some decay which the hot and cold principle contracts, as some have said?[2] Is the blood the element with which we think, or the air, or the fire? or perhaps nothing of the kind—but the brain may be the originating power of the perceptions of hearing and sight and smell, and memory and opinion may come from them, and science may be based on memory and opinion when they have attained fixity. And then I went on to examine the corruption of them, and then to the things of heaven and earth, and at last I concluded myself to be utterly and absolutely incapable of these inquiries, as I will satisfactorily prove to you. For I was fascinated by them to such a degree that my eyes grew blind to things which I had seemed to myself, and also to others, to know quite well; I forgot what I had before thought self-evident truths; e.g. such a fact as that the growth of man is the result of eating and drinking; for when by the digestion of food flesh is added to flesh and bone to bone, and whenever there is an aggregation of congenial elements, the lesser bulk becomes larger and the small man great. Was not that a reasonable notion?"

"Yes," said Cebes, "I think so."

"Well; but let me tell you something more. There was a time when I thought that I understood the meaning of greater and less pretty well; and when I saw a great man standing by a little one, I fancied that one was taller than the other by a head; or one horse would appear to be greater than another horse: and still more clearly did I seem to perceive that ten is two more than eight, and that two cubits are more than one, because two is the double of one."

"And what is now your notion of such matters?" said Cebes.

---

[2] This sentence might be better translated: "Do heat and cold by a sort of fermentation bring about the growth of living things, as some people say?"

"I should be far enough from imagining," he replied, "that I knew the cause of any of them, by heaven I should; for I cannot satisfy myself that, when one is added to one, the one to which the addition is made becomes two, or that the two units added together make two by reason of the addition. I cannot understand how, when separated from the other, each of them was one and not two, and now, when they are brought together, the mere juxtaposition or meeting of them should be the cause of their becoming two: neither can I understand how the division of one is the way to make two; for then a different cause would produce the same effect—as in the former instance the addition and juxtaposition of one to one was the cause of two, in this the separation and subtraction of one from the other would be the cause. Nor am I any longer satisfied that I understand the reason why one or anything else is either generated or destroyed or is at all, but I have in my mind some confused notion of a new method, and can never admit the other.

"Then I heard someone reading, as he said, from a book of Anaxagoras,[3] that mind was the disposer and cause of all, and I was delighted at this notion, which appeared quite admirable, and I said to myself: If mind is the disposer, mind will dispose all for the best, and put each particular in the best place; and I argued that if anyone desired to find out the cause of the generation or destruction or existence of anything, he must find out what state of being or doing or suffering was best for that thing, and therefore a man had only to consider the best for himself and others, and then he would also know the worse, since the same science comprehended both. And I rejoiced to think that I had found in Anaxagoras a teacher of the causes of existence such as I desired, and I imagined that he would tell me first whether the earth is flat or round; and whichever was true, he would

---

[3] The philosopher Anaxagoras had taught that in the beginning Mind or Intelligence, by separating substances, had brought form and order into the chaotic universe, thereby laying down the general principle that Mind was the cause of the universe. However, he never went on to show either how Mind acted on matter to produce its results or why it saw fit to produce these results and no others. In specific instances he spoke of physical substances as if they, taken alone, were sufficient explanation.

proceed to explain the cause and the necessity of this being so, and then he would teach me the nature of the best and show that this was best; and if he said that the earth was in the center, he would further explain that this position was the best, and I should be satisfied with the explanation given, and not want any other sort of cause.

"And I thought that I would then go on and ask him about the sun and moon and stars, and that he would explain to me their comparative swiftness, and their returnings and various states, active and passive, and how all of them were for the best. For I could not imagine that when he spoke of mind as the disposer of them, he would give any other account of their being as they are, except that this was best; and I thought that when he had explained to me in detail the cause of each and the cause of all, he would go on to explain to me what was best for each and what was good for all. These hopes I would not have sold for a large sum of money, and I seized the books and read them as fast as I could in my eagerness to know the better and the worse.

"What expectations I had formed, and how grievously was I disappointed! As I proceeded, I found my philosopher altogether forsaking mind or any other principle of order, but having recourse to air, and ether, and water, and other eccentricities. I might compare him to a person who began by maintaining generally that mind is the cause of the actions of Socrates, but who, when he endeavored to explain the causes of my several actions in detail, went on to show that I sit here because my body is made up of bones and muscles; and the bones, as he would say, are hard and have joints which divide them, and the muscles are elastic, and they cover the bones, which have also a covering or environment of flesh and skin which contains them; and as the bones are lifted at their joints by the contraction or relaxation of the muscles, I am able to bend my limbs, and this is why I am sitting here in a curved posture—that is what he would say; and he would have a similar explanation of my talking to you, which he would attribute to sound, and air, and hearing, and he would assign ten thousand other causes of the same sort, forgetting to mention the true cause, which is, that the Athenians have thought fit to condemn me, and accordingly

I have thought it better and more right to remain here and undergo my sentence; for I am inclined to think that these muscles and bones of mine would have gone off long ago to Megara or Boeotia—by the dog they would, if they had been moved only by their own idea of what was best, and if I had not chosen the better and nobler part, instead of playing truant and running away, of enduring any punishment which the state inflicts.

"There is surely a strange confusion of causes and conditions in all this. It may be said, indeed, that without bones and muscles and the other parts of the body I cannot execute my purposes. But to say that I do as I do because of them, and that this is the way in which mind acts, and not from the choice of the best, is a very careless and idle mode of speaking. I wonder that they cannot distinguish the cause from the condition, which the many, feeling about in the dark, are always mistaking and misnaming. And thus one man makes a vortex all round and steadies the earth by the heaven; another gives the air as a support to the earth, which is a sort of broad trough. Any power which in arranging them as they are arranges them for the best never enters into their minds; and instead of finding any superior strength in it, they rather expect to discover another Atlas[4] of the world who is stronger and more everlasting and more containing than the good; of the obligatory and containing power of the good they think nothing; and yet this is the principle which I would fain learn if anyone would teach me. But as I have failed either to discover myself, or to learn of anyone else, the nature of the best, I will exhibit to you, if you like, what I have found to be the second best mode of inquiring into the cause."

"I should very much like to hear," he replied.

Socrates proceeded: "I thought that as I had failed in the contemplation of true existence, I ought to be careful that I did not lose the eye of my soul; as people may injure their bodily eye by observing and gazing on the sun during an eclipse, unless they take the precaution of only looking at the image reflected in the water, or in some similar medium. So in my own case, I was afraid that my soul might be blinded altogether if I looked at things

---

[4] The mountain in Libya that was popularly supposed to support heaven on its crest.

with my eyes or tried to apprehend them by the help of the senses. And I thought that I had better have recourse to the world of mind and seek there the truth of existence. I daresay that the simile is not perfect—for I am very far from admitting that he who contemplates existences through the medium of thought, sees them only 'through a glass darkly,' any more than he who considers them in action and operation. However, this was the method which I adopted: I first assumed some principle which I judged to be the strongest, and then I affirmed as true whatever seemed to agree with this, whether relating to the cause or to anything else; and that which disagreed I regarded as untrue. But I should like to explain my meaning more clearly, as I do not think that you as yet understand me."

"No, indeed," replied Cebes, "not very well."

"There is nothing new," he said, "in what I am about to tell you; but only what I have been always and everywhere repeating in the previous discussion and on other occasions: I want to show you the nature of that cause which has occupied my thoughts. I shall have to go back to those familiar words which are in the mouth of everyone, and first of all assume that there is an absolute beauty and goodness and greatness, and the like; grant me this, and I hope to be able to show you the nature of the cause, and to prove the immortality of the soul."

Cebes said: "You may proceed at once with the proof, for I grant you this."

"Well," he said, "then I should like to know whether you agree with me in the next step; for I cannot help thinking, if there be anything beautiful other than absolute beauty, should there be such, that it can be beautiful only in so far as it partakes of absolute beauty—and I should say the same of everything. Do you agree in this notion of the cause?"

"Yes," he said, "I agree."

He proceeded: "I know nothing and can understand nothing of any other of those wise causes which are alleged; and if a person says to me that the bloom of color, or form, or any such thing is a source of beauty, I leave all that, which is only confusing to me, and simply and singly, and perhaps foolishly, hold and am assured in my own mind that nothing makes a thing beautiful but the presence and participation of beauty in whatever way or manner obtained; for as to the manner I am uncertain, but I stoutly contend that by beauty all beautiful things become beautiful. This appears to me to be the safest answer which I can give, either to myself or to another, and to this I cling, in the persuasion that this principle will never be overthrown, and that to myself or to anyone who asks the question, I may safely reply, that by beauty beautiful things become beautiful. Do you not agree with me?"

"I do."

"And that by greatness only great things become great and greater, and by smallness the less become less?"

"True."

"Then if a person were to remark that A is taller by a head than B, and B less by a head than A, you would refuse to admit his statement, and would stoutly contend that what you mean is only that the greater is greater by, and by reason of, greatness, and the less is less only by, and by reason of, smallness; and thus you would avoid the danger of saying that the greater is greater and the less less by the measure of the head, which is the same in both, and would also avoid the monstrous absurdity of supposing that the greater man is greater by reason of a head, which is small. You would be afraid to draw such an inference, would you not?"

"Indeed, I should," said Cebes, laughing.

"In like manner you would be afraid to say that ten exceeded eight by, and by reason of, two; but would say by, and by reason of, number; or you would say that two cubits exceed one cubit not by a half, but by magnitude?—for there is the same liability to error in all these cases."

"Very true," he said.

"Again, would you not be cautious of affirming that the addition of one to one, or the division of one, is the cause of two? And you would loudly asseverate that you know of no way in which anything comes into existence except by participation in its own proper essence, and consequently, as far as you know, the only cause of two is the participation in duality—this is the way to make two, and the participation in one is the way to make one. You would say: I will let alone puzzles of division and addition, wiser heads than mine may answer them; inexperienced as I am, and ready to start, as the proverb says, at my own shadow, I cannot afford to give up the sure ground of a principle. And if anyone assails you there, you would not mind him, or answer him, until you had seen whether the consequences which follow agree with one another or not, and when you are further required to give an explanation of this principle, you would go on to assume a higher principle, and a higher, until you found a resting place in the best of the higher; but you would not confuse the principle and the consequences in your reasoning, like the Eristics[5] —at least if you wanted to discover real existence. Not that this confusion signifies to them, who never care or think about the matter at all, for they have the wit to be well pleased with themselves however great may be the turmoil of their ideas. But you, if you are a philosopher, will certainly do as I say."

"What you say is most true," said Simmias and Cebes, both speaking at once.

ECHECRATES: Yes, Phaedo; and I do not wonder at their assenting. Anyone who has the least sense will acknowledge the wonderful clearness of Socrates' reasoning.

PHAEDO: Certainly, Echecrates; and such was the feeling of the whole company at the time.

ECHECRATES: Yes, and equally of ourselves, who were not of the company, and are now listening to your recital. But what followed?

PHAEDO: After all this had been admitted, and they had agreed that ideas exist, and that other things participate in them and derive their names from them, Socrates, if I remember rightly, said:

"This is your way of speaking; and yet when you say that Simmias is greater than Socrates and less than Phaedo, do you not predicate of Simmias both greatness and smallness?"

[5] The name given to a philosophic school in Megara, where much attention was paid to the art of disputation.

"Yes, I do."

"But still you allow that Simmias does not really exceed Socrates, as the words may seem to imply, because he is Simmias, but by reason of the size which he has; just as Simmias does not exceed Socrates because he is Simmias, any more than because Socrates is Socrates, but because he has smallness when compared with the greatness of Simmias?"

"True."

"And if Phaedo exceeds him in size, this is not because Phaedo is Phaedo, but because Phaedo has greatness relatively to Simmias, who is comparatively smaller?"

"That is true."

"And therefore Simmias is said to be great, and is also said to be small, because he is in a mean between them, exceeding the smallness of the one by his greatness, and allowing the greatness of the other to exceed his smallness." He added, laughing, "I am speaking like a book, but I believe that what I am saying is true."

Simmias assented.

"I speak as I do because I want you to agree with me in thinking, not only that absolute greatness will never be great and also small, but that greatness in us or in the concrete will never admit the small or admit of being exceeded: instead of this, one of two things will happen, either the greater will fly or retire before the opposite, which is the less, or at the approach of the less has already ceased to exist; but will not, if allowing or admitting of smallness, be changed by that; even as I, having received and admitted smallness when compared with Simmias, remain just as I was, and am the same small person. And as the idea of greatness cannot condescend ever to be or become small, in like manner the smallness in us cannot be or become great; nor can any other opposite which remains the same ever be or become its own opposite, but either passes away or perishes in the change."

"That," replied Cebes, "is quite my notion."

Hereupon one of the company, though I do not exactly remember which of them, said: "In heaven's name, is not this the direct contrary of what was admitted before—that out of the greater came the less and out of the less the greater, and that opposites were simply generated from opposites; but now this principle seems to be utterly denied."

Socrates inclined his head to the speaker and listened. "I like your courage," he said, "in reminding us of this. But you do not observe that there is a difference in the two cases. For then we were speaking of opposites in the concrete, and now of the essential opposite which, as is affirmed, neither in us nor in nature can ever be at variance with itself: then, my friend, we were speaking of things in which opposites are inherent and which are called after them, but now about the opposites which are inherent in them and which give their name to them; and these essential opposites will never, as we maintain, admit of generation into or out of one another." At the same time, turning to Cebes, he said: "Are you at all disconcerted, Cebes, at our friend's objection?"

"No, I do not feel so," said Cebes; "and yet I cannot deny that I am often disturbed by objections."

"Then we are agreed, after all," said Socrates, "that the opposite will never in any case be opposed to itself?"

"To that we are quite agreed," he replied.

"Yet once more let me ask you to consider the question from another point of view, and see whether you agree with me: There is a thing which you term heat, and another thing which you term cold?"

"Certainly."

"But are they the same as fire and snow?"

"Most assuredly not."

"Heat is a thing different from fire, and cold is not the same with snow?"

"Yes."

"And yet you will surely admit, that when snow, as was before said, is under the influence of heat, they will not remain snow and heat; but at the advance of the heat, the snow will either retire or perish?"

"Very true," he replied.

"And the fire too at the advance of the cold will either retire or perish; and when the fire is under the influence of the cold, they will not remain as before, fire and cold."

"That is true," he said.

"And in some cases the name of the idea is not only attached to the idea in an eternal connection, but anything else which, not being the idea, exists only in the form of the idea, may also lay claim to it. I will try to make this clearer by an example: The odd number is always called by the name of odd?"

"Very true."

"But is this the only thing which is called odd? Are there not other things which have their own name, and yet are called odd, because, although not the same as oddness, they are never without oddness?—that is what I mean to ask—whether numbers such as the number three are not of the class of odd. And there are many other examples: would you not say, for example, that three may be called by its proper name, and also be called odd, which is not the same with three? and this may be said not only of three but also of five, and of every alternate number—each of them without being oddness is odd; and in the same way two and four, and the other series of alternate numbers, have every number even, without being evenness. Do you agree?"

"Of course."

"Then now mark the point at which I am aiming: not only do essential opposites exclude one another, but also concrete things, which, although not in themselves opposed, contain opposites; these, I say, likewise reject the idea which is opposed to that which is contained in them, and when it approaches them they either perish or withdraw. For example: Will not the number three endure annihilation or anything sooner than be converted into an even number, while remaining three?"

"Very true," said Cebes.

"And yet," he said, "the number two is certainly not opposed to the number three?"

"It is not."

"Then not only do opposite ideas repel the advance of one another, but also there are other natures which repel the approach of opposites."

"Very true," he said.

Ernst Cassirer
(1874-1945)

Introduction

In a lecture delivered by Nelson Goodman at the University of Hamburg on the one-hundredth anniversary of the birth of Ernst Cassirer he opened with the following statement:

> "Countless worlds made from nothing by use of symbols—so might a satirist summarize some major themes in the work of Ernst Cassirer. These themes—the multiplicity of worlds, the speciousness of 'the given', the creative power of the understanding, the variety and formative function of symbols— are also integral to my own thinking. Sometimes, though, I forget how eloquently they have been set forth by Cassirer, partly perhaps because his emphasis on myth, his concern with the comparative study of cultures, and his talk of the human spirit have been mistakenly associated with current trends toward mystical obscurantism, anti-intellectual intuitionism, or anti-scientific humanism. Actually these attitudes are as alien to Cassirer as to my own skeptical, analytic, constructionist orientation."[1]

Goodman's aim was less to defend certain theses that he and Cassirer shared than to take a hard look at some crucial questions they raise such as: In just what sense are there many worlds? What distinguishes genuine from spurious worlds? What are worlds made of? How are they made? What role do symbols play in the making? And how is world-making related to knowing?[2] These questions must be faced, claimed Goodman, even if full and final answers are far off. Goodman nonetheless assured his audience that Cassirer and like-minded

[1] Goodman, Nelson. *Ways of World-making* (Indianapolis, 1978) p. 1.
[2] Ibid.

pluralists accept the sciences at full value and that a reduction from one system to another can make "a genuine contribution to understanding the interrelationships among world-versions." However, since reductions in any reasonably strict sense are rare, the pluralists' acceptance of "versions other than physics," according to Goodman, does not imply a relaxation of rigor, but a realization that "standards different from, yet no less exacting than those applied in science, are appropriate for appraising what is conveyed in perceptual or pictorial or literary versions." So long as contrasting right versions are not reducible in a strict sense, "unity is to be sought," says Goodman, "in an overall organization embracing them."[3] Cassirer, accordingly, undertook the "search" through a cross-cultural study of the development of myth, religion, language, art, and sciences. Goodman's approach, unlike Cassirer's, was through an analytic study of types and functions of symbols and symbolic systems.

Cassirer developed his philosophy of culture as a theory of symbols founded on a phenomenology of knowledge. The systematic reflection and analysis of human *consciousness* provided Cassirer with a firm basis for all of human knowledge, including scientific knowledge. Cassirer's approach to symbolic forms rests on the notion that humans create their own universe of symbolic meaning that structures and shapes their perception of reality. Moreover, humans are able to conceive of progress in the form of culture only via this kind of structuring. The world, in other words, is not directly perceived via sensory perception, but via the means that humans create whereby it is perceived. According to Cassirer the human world is created through a variety of symbolic forms of thought–linguistic, scientific and artistic. He treated the various branches of culture as symbolic constructions, each with its own criteria of validity and capability to assert its distinct truth.

Born into a well-educated assimilated Jewish family, Cassirer imbibed the liberal ideal of German culture. He completed his doctoral dissertation in Marburg under the direction of Hermann Cohen, one of the leading figures of the German neo-Kantian movement known for its emphasis on epistemology and science. In fact, much of Cassirer's early work was in epistemology, philosophy of

---

[3] Ibid., p. 5.

science, and logic. Given the decline of German speculative idealism and the rise of philosophical interests in the empirically oriented natural and human sciences in the mid-nineteenth-century, the revival of Kant's speculative attitude appealed to Cassirer. As a representative of the Marburg school of neo-Kantianism, he wrote a series of important works on the history and theory of physics, mathematic, and logic. Cassirer actually began his career as an intellectual historian, contributing profound original works to both the history of philosophy and the history of science. Although he already belonged to a later generation when neo-Kantianism came increasingly under attack, his aim was to uphold, against the onslaughts of positivism, a broadly Kantian conception of science as an expression of the creativity of human reason.

Cassirer's mature thought moved, however, from science in the direction of culture in general. As professor of philosophy at the University of Hamburg (1919-1933), he came into contact with circles whose interests centered on domains of culture other than the exact sciences.[4] Widely educated and steeped in culture, as Cassirer was, he took genuine interest in the thinking of these circles and was impressed by the rigor that their members brought to their subject matters–a factor that, no doubt, influenced his mature thinking. In fact, the "creativity of reason" gradually lost its centrality in Cassirer's thought; it appeared more and more as but one aspect of a deeper and more general creativity, a creativity that seemed to affect all of the forms of human culture. Cassirer came to realize that the variety of the cultural life of humans cannot be adequately comprehended via reason. The entire gamut of human experience with its diversities may be subsumed, however, by the fact that all of these forms of human culture are symbolic.

Unlike the traditional understanding of symbol as pointing to something other than what it represents, Cassirer's symbolic forms contain, unto themselves, the significations of human experience in its variety. Cassirer's symbolic forms do

---

[4] Cassirer took special interest in the circle that surrounded the art historian and cultural theorist Aby Warburg whose private library for cultural studies eventually became the foundation of the famous Warburg Institute in London. Warburg's interest in image-based thinking engendered at the Institute profound studies of the Hermetic Tradition and of the mnemonic practices that animated the human mind.

not create a distinction between the symbolizing activity of consciousness and its schematizing function. Cassirer's symbolic forms represent a fusion, as it were, between the activity and its function. Jointly they embody the ways in which human beings construct their reality through the "worlds" which they create such as language, myth, religion, science and art. The structuring of reality is however an ongoing process since the human spirit progressively deepens its grasp of the meaning it confers upon experience. This historical unfolding rather than provide a foundation for truth withstanding historical contingencies, it furthers man's understanding of the part he plays in the creation of the world he lives in. The idea that man is the custodian of his own destiny precludes forever final truth, but it imposes on humans a continuous search for an ethical universalism that would both benefit the individual and mankind at large. Evidently, emancipation–in whatever guise–is not wholly a blessing because the "emancipated" need to rely on their own resourcefulness and to surmount unforeseeable difficulties on their own.

History, according to Cassirer, does not simply rest on "facts," since factual truth implies a theoretical truth. When we speak of facts, says Cassirer "we do not simply refer to our immediate sense data," we are thinking of "objective facts." This objectivity, however, is not given, for it always implies "a complicated process of judgment." Thus, "if we wish to know the difference between scientific facts– between the facts of physics, of biology, of history–we must always begin with an analysis of judgment. We must study the modes of knowledge by which these facts are accessible." The historian like the physicist lives in a material world, yet his search is not that of physical objects but that of "a symbolic universe–a world of symbols."[5] The methods of the natural sciences while essential for the construction of history, historical knowledge is a theoretical knowledge that can only be reflective. In short, history studies "facts," i.e. the particular, but its efforts consist in finding universals. The universality of logic and the differentiated unity of knowledge preclude the distinction between the humanities and the natural sciences.

From my all too brief explication of some of Cassirer's thoughts, it must have become apparent that his philosophy of "symbolic forms" and his conception of "history" must have engendered considerable debates both in his lifetime

---

[5] Cassirer, *An Essay on Man,* p. 174.

and ever since. Indeed, Cassirer's overall embracement of the world of culture as *the* arena in which the "self realization of man" and the goal of life are taking place, was seriously challenged by positivists and by philosophers who claimed that the secular idols of "humanity" and "progress" were dead.[6] Though Cassirer seemed "outmoded" by positivists and existentialists alike, nobody could accuse him for lacking a thorough understanding of the exact sciences on the one hand, and of the arts and the humanities on the other. Given his vast and profound learning in both the natural and the human sciences, he confronted his adversaries with sound arguments. In fact, Cassirer considered the schism that came to the fore between these "worlds" of knowledge as a misunderstanding of the integrative makeup of Knowledge and of the processes whereby it advances.

The schism which Cassirer refused to indorse was nonetheless more and more echoed in the course of the twentieth century, leaving considerable imprints on academic life. The natural sciences, accordingly, were steadily promoted while the human sciences were increasingly demoted. The former became unreservedly identified with knowledge that can be verified and substantiated, while the latter seemed to retain forever a "speculative" garb. The cleavage between these two worlds became, consequently, "unbridgeable," as C. P. Snow exclaimed in mid century. The speedy advances in the technological sphere no doubt precipitated this development. Equipped with all kinds of instrumentation, the natural sciences were better able to obtain more precise and specified results. It must be remembered that the language of "number and measurement" became the hallmark of science ever since Pythagoras.

---

[6] In 1929, a famous debate took place at Davos (a Swiss resort) between Cassirer–the leading representative of the idealist tradition–and Martin Heidegger who had shaken this tradition to its foundation in his recently published work *Being and Time*. Rudolf Carnap (a leader of the Vienna Circle of logical empiricists), who is best known for his explicit attempt to create a radical break with the metaphysical tradition, attended the meeting. Much has been written about the debate and about each of these figures, yet the reason I see fit to mention the three is Michael Friedman's illuminating book– *A Parting of the Ways: Carnap, Cassirer, and Heidegger* (Illinois: Carus Publishing Company, 2000). Friedman has shown how the Davos debate constituted a seminal philosophical watershed, that of the divide between the "analytic" philosophical tradition of the English speaking world and the continental tradition that dominated the European scene.

Cassirer, to be sure, is not the only philosopher to have conceived of knowledge as a man-made world. Almost three hundred years ago Vico's vision of the "wholeness" of man's activities led him to propose in his *Scienza Nuova* (1732) that mathematics is nearer to history than physics, for in both, man is the maker of that which he eventually recognizes as "true." Nor is Vico the first thinker to have tried to understand the processes whereby man achieves "true" knowledge. Plato, as we have seen, suggested an elaborate process whereby man achieves such knowledge. Indeed, the world as "perceived" or "contemplated" engendered many theories in the course of history, theories that grappled with questions concerning the "truly real" in nature. Is the truly real known by inferences or directly, objectively or subjectively? Questions like these–and many other related ones–were, in fact, asked and subjected to refined scrutiny, yielding interesting insights and enlightening arguments. Nonetheless, if I chose to mention Vico it is because his "anthropological historicism" enabled Isaiah Berlin to summarize his contribution in the following way:

> Vico's boldest contribution is that there can be a science of mind that is the history of its development, the realization that ideas evolve, that knowledge is not a static network of eternal, universal, clear truth, either Platonic or Cartesian, but social process, that this process is traceable through (indeed is in a sense identical with) the evolution of symbols–words, gestures, and their altering patterns, functions, structures, and uses.[7]

Cassirer was of course aware of Vico's contribution; like Vico, he called attention to the variety of "schemes" that man created–linguistic, scientific and artistic that structure his reality. Unlike Vico, however, he wished to drive home the idea that from the dawn of civilization man has been manufacturing symbols that *embrace* the logic in which they are embedded in order to make "sense" of his life and of the world which he inhabits. The investigations of the variety of the symbolic forms that man created thus allow us to trace the development of man, including the processes, whereby he developed a world of knowledge

---

[7] Berlin, Isaiah, *Against the Current: Essays in the History of Ideas* (Oxford, 1981), p. 113.

that is intelligible to mankind. In short, Cassirer's approach to symbolic forms rests on the notion that humans create their own universe of symbolic *meaning* that structures and shapes their perception of reality and only thus can they conceive of progress in the form of human culture. The world, in other words, is not directly perceived via sensory perception, but via the means humans create whereby it is perceived. Though Vico's type of historicism and social theory already exerted considerable influence in nineteenth century historical and social thought, it is only in the twentieth century that it became possible to appreciate the full scope of his "new science." It is during this century that it has become clear that understanding science, in fact any science, requires historical awareness which takes into account man's consciousness.

Born into a Jewish family, Cassirer was forced to leave Germany when the Nazis came to power. He first moved to England, where he lectured at Oxford University for two years (1933-1935). Subsequently he moved to Sweden, to the Gothenburg University where he stayed for six years (1935-1941). Feeling unsafe in Sweden, he moved to the United States, where he served as a visiting professor at Yale University for two years (1941-1943) and later at Columbia University where he lectured until his death (1943-1945). I mention these trying years since they forced Cassirer, who was not essentially concerned with problems of politics, to have a new look at the autonomy of science and culture which he so ardently defended. Given that in Nazi Germany–like in primitive societies–every aspect of life became "ritualized," totalitarian societies could be construed as a sort of "regression" to a mythic state. Yet unlike myth, which is unconscious to its own acts, totalitarianism constitutes a resolute, purposeful mode of acting. Cassirer grappled with these issues in his later writings.

There is much that can be said, and has been said, about Cassirer's contribution to the "theory of knowledge" that this introduction hardly touched upon. Cassirer was clearly dissatisfied with the "theory of knowledge" that concerned itself solely with the appreciation of "facts" and the philosophical deliberations about facts as they evolved since the Middle Ages. Cassirer, says Susanne Langer, realized that man's prime instrument of reason, i.e. *language*, "reflects his mythmaking tendency more than his rationalizing tendency," and that language–as the symbolization of thought–"exhibits two entirely different modes of thought." In both modes, the mind is powerful and creative, "it expresses itself in different forms, one of which is discursive logic, the other creative imagination."[8] According to Cassirer, reason is not man's primitive endowment, but his achievement, the seeds of which lie in language. Language gives rise to logic "when that greatest of symbolic modes is mature."

I mentioned the "wandering years" of Cassirer because they presented a greater challenge to Cassirer's liberal outlook than did his former adversaries. In a way, my portrayal of Cassirer does an injustice to the breadth and profoundness of his thinking. Although he seemed "outmoded" by some of his contemporaries and irrelevant by the following generation, he was never overlooked. The scope of his knowledge–his dazzling erudition and arresting intelligence–enlisted continuous interest in his work, primarily among those who looked for a reliable source concerning the history of ideas. If Cassirer enjoys a "resurrection" nowadays, it is not least because of what has been learned in the meantime in the various fields of knowledge which Cassirer so diligently addressed. I chose to include Cassirer in the present book because of the following reasons: 1) Cassirer highlighted–more than anybody else–the notion that knowledge is man-made. 2) He has shown how the diverse symbolic forms create their own criteria of validity and capability to assert their distinct truths. 3) He has persuasively shown how the universality of logic and the differentiated unity of knowledge *prevent* the distinction between the humanities and the natural sciences.

[8] See Susanne K. Langer's preface to her translation of Cassirer's *Language and Myth,* Harper and Brothers, 1946, pp. viii-ix.

CASSIRER
from **Symbolic Forms**[*]

1. The Concept of Symbolic Form and the System of Symbolic Forms

Philosophical speculation began with the concept of *being*. In the very moment when this concept appeared, when man's consciousness awakened to the unity of being as opposed to the multiplicity and diversity of existing things, the specific philosophical approach to the world was born. But even then man's thinking about the world remained for a long while imprisoned within the sphere of existing things, which it was seeking to relinquish and surpass. The philosophers attempted to determine the beginning and origin, the ultimate "foundation" of all being: the question was stated clearly, but the concrete, determinate answers given were not adequate to this supreme, universal formulation. What these thinkers called "the essence", the substance of the world was not something which in principle went beyond it; it was a fragment taken from this very same world. A particular, specific and limited existing thing was picked out, and everything else was genetically derived from it and "explained by it." Much as these explanations might change in content, their general form remained within the same methodological limits. At first a particular material substance, a concrete *prima materia*, was set up as the ultimate foundation of all phenomena; then the explanations became more ideal and the substance was replaced by a purely rational "principle," from which everything was derived. But on closer inspection this "principle" hung in midair between the "physical" and "spiritual." Despite its ideal coloration, it was closely connected with the world of existing things. The number of the Pythagoreans, the atom of Democritus, though removed from the original substance of the Ionians, remained a methodological hybrid, which had not found its true nature and had not, as it were, chosen its true spiritual home. This inner uncertainty was not definitely overcome until Plato developed his

[*] From: Ernst Cassirer: *The Philosophy of Symbolic Forms,* vol. I, translated by Ralph Mannheim, New Haven, Yale, 1955 , pp.73-77; 84-89 ("Introduction and Presentation of the Problem").

theory of ideas. The great systematic and historical achievement of this theory is that here, for the first time, the essential intellectual premise for any philosophical understanding and explanation of the world took on explicit form. What Plato sought for, what he called "idea," had been effective as an immanent principle in the earliest attempts to explain the world, in the Eleatic philosophers, in the Pythagoreans, in Democritus; but Plato was the first to be conscious of this principle and its significance. Plato himself took this to be his philosophical achievement. In his late works, where he sees the logical implications of his doctrine most clearly, he characterizes the crucial difference between his speculation and that of the Pre-Socratics: the Pre-Socratics identified being with a particular existing thing and took it as a fixed point of departure, while he for the first time recognized it as a *problem*. He no longer simply inquired into the order, condition and structure of being, but inquired into the concept of being and the meaning of that concept. Compared with the sharpness of Plato's question and the rigor of his approach, all earlier speculations paled to tales or myths about being.[1] It was time to abandon these mythical, cosmological explanations for the true, dialectical explanation of being, which no longer clings to its mere facticity but discloses its intelligible *meaning*, its systematic, teleological order. And with this, thought, which in Greek philosophy since Parmenides had appeared as a concept interchangeable with that of being, gained a new and profounder meaning. Only where being has the sharply defined meaning of a *problem*, does thought attain to the sharply defined meaning and value of a *principle*. It no longer runs parallel to being, a mere reflection "about" being, but by its own inner form, it now determines the inner form of being.

The same typical process was repeated at different stages in the historical development of idealism. Where a materialist view of the world contented itself with some ultimate attribute of things as the basis of all cognition–idealism turned this very same attribute into a question for thought. And this process is discernible not only in the history of philosophy but in the specialized sciences as well. The road does not lead solely from "data" to "laws" and from laws back to "axioms" and "principles": the axioms and principles themselves, which at a certain stage of knowledge represent the ultimate and most complete solution,

---

[1] Cf. especially *The Sophists* 243 C ff.

must at a later stage become once more a problem. Accordingly, what science designates as its "being" and its "object," ceases to appear as a simple and indivisible set of facts; every new type or trend of thought discloses some new phase in this complex. The rigid concept of being seems to be thrown into flux, into general movement, and the unity of being becomes conceivable only as the aim, and no longer as the beginning of this movement. As this insight develops and gains acceptance in science itself, the naïve *copy theory* of knowledge is discredited. The fundamental concepts of each science, the instruments with which it propounds its questions and formulates its solutions, are regarded no longer as passive images of something given, but as *symbols* created by the intellect itself.

Mathematicians and physicists were first to gain a clear awareness of this symbolic character of their basic implements.[2] The new ideal of knowledge, to which this whole development points, was brilliantly formulated by Heinrich Hertz in the introduction to his *Principles of Mechanics*. He declares that the most pressing and important function of our natural science is to enable us to foresee future experience–and he goes on to describe the method by which science derives the future from the past: We make "inner fictions or symbols" of outward objects, and these symbols are so constituted that the necessary logical consequences of the images are always images of the necessary natural consequences of the imaged objects.

> Once we have succeeded in deriving images of the required nature from our past experience, we can with them as models soon develop the consequences which will be manifested in the outward world much later or as consequences of our own intervention. . . . The images of which we are speaking are our ideas of things; they have with things the one essential agreement which lies in the fulfillment of the stated requirement, but further agreement with things is not necessary to their purpose. Actually we do not know

[2] This is discussed in greater detail in my book *Zur Einstein'schen Relativitätstheorie* (Berlin, B. Cassirer, 1921); cf. especially the first section on "Massbegriffe und Denkbegriffe."

and have no means of finding out whether our ideas of things accord with them in any other respect than in this one fundamental relation.[3]

The epistemology of the physical sciences, on which the work of Heinrich Hertz is based and the theory of "signs" as first fully developed by Helmholtz, was still couched in the *language* of the copy theory of knowledge - but the concept of the "image" had undergone an inner change. In place of the vague demand for a similarity of content between image and thing, we now find expressed a highly complex logical relation, a general intellectual *condition*, which the basic concepts of physical knowledge must satisfy. Its value lies not in the reflection of a given existence, but in what it accomplishes as an instrument of knowledge, in a unity of phenomena which the phenomena must produce out of themselves. A system of physical concepts must reflect the relations between objective things as well as the nature of their mutual dependency, but this is only possible in so far as these concepts pertain from the very outset to a definite, homogeneous intellectual orientation. The object cannot be regarded as a naked thing in itself, independent of the essential categories of natural science: for only within these categories which are required to constitute its form can it be described at all.

In this sense, Hertz came to look upon the fundamental concepts of mechanics, particularly the concepts of mass and force, as "fictions" which, since they are created by the logic of natural science, are subordinate to the universal requirements of this logic, among which the *a priori* requirement of clarity, freedom from contradiction, and unambiguousness of reference takes first place.

With this critical insight, it is true, science renounces its aspiration and its claim to an "immediate" grasp and communication of reality. It realizes that the only objectivization of which it is capable is, and must remain, mediation. And in this insight, another highly significant idealistic consequence is implicit. If the object of knowledge can be defined only through the medium of a particular logical and conceptual structure, we are forced to conclude that a variety of

---

[3] H. Hertz, *Die Prinzipien der Mechanik* (Leipzig, F. A. Barth, 1894), cf. p. 1 ff.

media will correspond to various structures of the object, to various meanings for "objective" relations. Even in "nature," the physical object will not coincide absolutely with the chemical object, nor the chemical with the biological–because physical, chemical, biological knowledge *frame their questions* each from its own particular standpoint and, in accordance with this standpoint, subject the phenomena to a special interpretation and formation. It might also seem that this consequence in the development of idealistic thought had conclusively frustrated the expectation in which it began. The end of this development seems to negate its beginning–the unity of being, for which it strove, threatens once more to disintegrate into a mere diversity of existing things. The One Being, to which thought holds fast and which it seems unable to relinquish without destroying its own form, eludes *cognition*. The more its metaphysical unity as a "thing in itself" is asserted, the more it evades all possibility of knowledge, until at last it is relegated entirely to the sphere of the unknowable and becomes a mere "X." And to this rigid metaphysical absolute is juxtaposed the realm of phenomena, the true sphere of the knowable, with its enduring multiplicity, finiteness and relativity. But upon closer scrutiny the fundamental postulate of unity is not discredited by this irreducible diversity of the methods and objects of knowledge; it merely assumes a new form. True, the unity of knowledge can no longer be made certain and secure by referring knowledge in all its forms to a "simple" common object which is related to all these forms as the transcendent prototype to the empirical copies. But instead, a new task arises: to gather the various branches of science with their diverse methodologies–with all their recognized specificity and independence–into one system, whose separate parts precisely through their necessary diversity will complement and further one another. This postulate of a purely functional unity replaces the postulate of a unity of substance and origin, which lay at the core of the ancient concept of being.

And this creates a new task for the philosophical critique of knowledge. It must follow the special sciences and survey them as a whole. It must ask whether the intellectual symbols by means of which the specialized disciplines reflect on and describe reality exist merely side by side or whether they are not diverse manifestations of the same basic human function. And if the latter hypothesis should be confirmed, a philosophical critique must formulate the universal conditions of this function and define the principle underlying it. Instead of dogmatic metaphysics, which seeks absolute unity in a substance to which all the particulars of existence are reducible, such a philosophical critique seeks after a rule governing the concrete diversity of the functions of cognition, a rule which, without negating and destroying them, will gather them into a unity of deed, the unity of a self-contained human endeavor.

..... If we can find a medium through which all the configurations effected in the separate branches of cultural life must pass, but which nevertheless retains its particular nature, its specific character–we shall have found the necessary intermediary link for an inquiry which will accomplish for the *totality* of cultural forms what the transcendental critique has done for pure *cognition*. Our next question must therefore be: do the diverse branches of cultural life actually present such an intermediate field and mediating function, and if so, does this function disclose typical traits, by means of which it can be recognized and described?

2. Universal Function of the Sign. The Problem of Meaning

In seeking an answer to this question we shall first go back to the concept of the "symbol," as Heinrich Hertz characterized it from the standpoint of natural science. What the physicist seeks in phenomena is a statement of their necessary connection. But in order to arrive at this statement, he must not only leave behind him the immediate world of sensory impressions, but must seemingly turn away from them entirely. The concepts with which he operates, the concepts of space and time, of mass and force, of material point and energy, of the atom or the ether, are free "fictions." Cognition devises them in order to dominate the world of sensory experience and survey it as a world ordered by law, but nothing in the sensory data themselves immediately corresponds to them, yet although there is no such correspondence–and perhaps precisely *because* there is none–the conceptual world of physics is entirely self-contained. Each particular concept, each special fiction and sign is like the articulated *word* of a *language* meaningful in itself and ordered according to fixed rules. In the very beginnings of modern physics, in Galileo, we find the metaphor that the "book of nature" is written in mathematical language and can be read only through mathematical ciphers. And since then, the entire development of exact natural science shows that every step forward in the formulation of its problems and concepts has gone hand-in-hand with the increasing refinement of its *system of signs*. A clear understanding of the fundamental concepts of Galileo's mechanics became possible only when the universal logical locus of these concepts was, as it were, determined and a universally valid mathematical-logical sign for them was created in the algorism of the differential calculus. And then, taking as his point of departure the problems connected with the discovery of the analysis of infinity, Leibniz was soon able to formulate the universal problem inherent in the function of symbolism, and to raise his universal "characteristic" to a truly philosophical plane. In his view, the logic of things, i.e., of the material concepts and relations on which the structure of a science rests, cannot be separated from the logic of signs. For the sign is no mere accidental cloak of the idea, but its necessary and essential organ. It serves not merely to communicate a complete and given thought-content, but is an instrument, by means of which this content develops and fully defines itself. The conceptual definition of a content goes hand-in-hand with its stabilization in some characteristic sign. Consequently, all truly strict and exact thought is sustained by the *symbolics* and *semiotics* on which it is based. Every "law" of nature assumes for our thinking the form of a universal "formula"–and a formula can be expressed only by a combination of universal and specific signs. Without the universal signs provided by arithmetic and algebra, no special relation in physics, no special law of nature would be expressible. It is, as it were, the fundamental principle of cognition that the universal can be perceived only in the particular, while the particular can be thought only in reference to the universal.

This mutual relation is not limited to science but runs through all the other fundamental forms of cultural activity. None of them can develop its appropriate and peculiar type of comprehension and configuration without, as it were, creating a definite sensuous substratum for itself. This substratum is so essential that it sometimes seems to constitute the entire content, the true "meaning" of these forms. Language seems fully definable as a system of phonetic symbols–the worlds of art and myth seem to consist entirely in the particular, sensuously tangible forms that they set before us. Here we have in fact an all-embracing medium in which the most diverse cultural forms meet. The content of the spirit is disclosed only in its manifestations; the ideal form is known only by and in the aggregate of the sensible signs which it uses for its expression. If it were possible to achieve a systematic survey of the various directions which this kind of expression has taken; if it were possible to show their typical and consistent features as well as their special gradations and inner differences, the ideal of a "universal characteristic," formulated by Leibniz for cognition, would be fulfilled for the whole of cultural activity. We should then possess a kind of grammar of the symbolic function as such, which would encompass and generally help to define its special terms and idioms as we encounter them in language and art, in myth and religion.

The idea of such a grammar implies a broadening of the traditional and historical concept of idealism. Idealism has always aimed at juxtaposing to the *mundus sensibilis* another cosmos, the *mundus intelligibilis*, and at defining the boundary between these two worlds. But the usual means of drawing this boundary was to say that the intelligible world is governed by the principle of pure action, while the sensible world is dominated by the principle of receptivity. The free spontaneity of the mind prevails in the former, the confinement, the passivity of the senses in the latter. But for the "universal characteristic" which now stands before us in the broadest outlines as problem and project, *this* opposition is no longer irreconcilable and exclusive. For the senses and the spirit are now joined in a new form of reciprocity and correlation. Their metaphysical dualism seems bridged, since it can be shown that precisely the pure *function* of the spirit itself must seek its concrete fulfillment in the sensory world. Within the sensory sphere, a sharp distinction must be made between mere "reaction" and pure "action," between "impression" and "expression." Dogmatic sensationalism underestimates the importance of the purely intellectual factors and moreover, though it insists on sensibility as the basic factor in the life of the spirit, it by no means encompasses either the whole concept of sensibility or its whole effect. Dogmatic sensationalism presents an inadequate and distorted picture of sensibility, which it limits to "impressions," to the immediate givenness of simple sensations. In so doing, it fails to recognize that there is also an activity of the sensibility itself, that, as Goethe said, there is also an "exact sensory imagination," which operates in the most diverse spheres of cultural endeavor. We find indeed that, beside and above the world of perception, all these spheres produce freely their own *world of symbols* which is the true vehicle of their immanent development–a world whose inner quality is still wholly sensory, but which already discloses a formed sensibility, that is to say, a sensibility governed by the spirit. Here we no longer have to do with a sensible world that is simply given and present, but with a system of diverse sensory factors which are produced by some form of free creation.

The process of language formation shows for example how the chaos of immediate impressions takes on order and clarity for us only when we "name" it and so permeate it with the function of linguistic thought and expression. In this new world of linguistic signs the world of impressions itself acquires an entirely new "permanence," because it acquires a new intellectual articulation. This differentiation and fixation of certain contents by words, not only designates a definite intellectual quality through them, but actually endows them with such a quality, by virtue of which they are now raised above the mere immediacy of so-called sensory qualities. Thus language becomes one of the human spirit's basic implements, by which we progress from the world of mere sensation to the world of intuition and ideas. It contains in germ that intellectual effort which is afterwards manifested in the formation of scientific concepts and in the logical unity of their form. Here lies the first beginning of that universal function of separation and association, which finds its highest conscious expression in the analyses and syntheses of scientific thought. And beside the world of linguistic and conceptual signs stands the world of myth and art, incommensurate with it and yet related in spiritual origin. For deeply rooted as it is in sensibility, mythical fantasy also goes far beyond the mere passivity of sensation. If we judge it by the ordinary empirical standards provided by our sensory experience, its creations cannot but seem "unreal," but precisely in this unreality lies the spontaneity and inner freedom of the mythical function. And this freedom is by no means arbitrary and lawless. The world of myth is no mere product of whim or chance, it has its own fundamental laws of form, which are at work in all its particular manifestations. And when we consider art, it is immediately clear that the conception of an aesthetic form in the sensible world is possible only because we ourselves create the fundamental elements of form. All understanding of spatial forms, for example, is ultimately bound up with this activity of their inner production and with the law governing this production. And so we see that the very highest and purest spiritual activity known to consciousness is conditioned and mediated by certain modes of sensory activity. Here again the authentic and essential life of the pure idea comes to us only when phenomena "stain the white radiance of eternity." We can arrive at a system of the manifold manifestations of the mind only by pursuing the different directions taken by its original imaginative power. In them we see reflected the essential nature of the human spirit—for it can only disclose itself to us by shaping sensible matter.

Another indication that the creation of the various systems of sensuous symbols is indeed a pure activity of the mind is that from the outset all these symbols lay claim to objective value. They go beyond the mere phenomena of the individual consciousness, claiming to confront them with something that is universally valid. This claim may possibly prove unwarranted in the light of subsequent critical inquiry with its more highly developed concept of truth; but the mere fact that it is made belongs to the essence and character of the particular cultural forms themselves. They themselves regard their symbols not only as objectively valid, but for the most part as the very core of the objective and "real." It is characteristic, for example, of the first seemingly naïve and unreflecting manifestations of linguistic thinking and mythical thinking, that they do not clearly distinguish between the content of the "thing" and the content of the "sign," but indifferently merge the two. The name of a thing and the thing itself are inseparably fused; the mere word or image contains a magic force through which the essence of the thing gives itself to us. And we need only transfer this notion from the real to the ideal, from the material to the functional, to find that it contains a kernel of justification. In the immanent development of the mind the acquisition of the *sign* really constitutes a first and necessary step towards knowledge of the objective nature of the thing. For consciousness the sign is, as it were, the first stage and the first demonstration of objectivity, because through it the constant flux of the contents of consciousness is for the first time halted, because in it something enduring is determined and emphasized. No mere *content* of consciousness as such recurs in strictly identical form once it has passed and been replaced by others. Once it has vanished from consciousness, it is gone forever as that which it was. But to this incessant flux of contents, consciousness now juxtaposes its own unity and the unity of its form. Its identity is truly demonstrated not in what it is or has, but in what it does. Through the sign that is associated with the content, the content itself acquires a new permanence. For the sign, in contrast to the actual flow of the particular contents of consciousness, has a definite ideal *meaning*, which endures as such. It is not, like the simple given sensation, an isolated particular, occurring but once, but persists as the representative of a totality, as an aggregate of potential contents, beside which it stands as a first "universal." In the symbolic function of consciousness—as it operates in language, in art, in myth—certain unchanging fundamental forms, some of a conceptual and some of a purely sensory nature, disengage themselves from the stream of consciousness; the flux of contents is replaced by a self-contained and enduring unity of form.

CASSIRER
*Language and Conception**

To know and understand the peculiar nature of mythico-religious conception not only through its results, but through the very principle of its formation, and to see, furthermore, how the growth of linguistic concepts is related to that of religious ideas and in what essential traits they coincide–this requires us, indeed, to reach far back into the past. We must not hesitate to take a roundabout way through general logic and epistemology, for it is only upon this basis that we may hope to determine precisely the *function* of this sort of ideation and to distinguish it clearly from the conceptual forms which serve theoretical thinking. According to the traditional teachings of logic, the mind forms concepts by taking a certain number of objects which have common properties, i.e., coincide in certain respects, together in thought and abstracting from their differences, so that only the similarities are retained and reflected upon, and in this way a general idea of such-and-such a class of objects is formed in consciousness. Thus the concept *(notio, conceptus)* is that idea which represents the totality of *essential* properties, i.e., the essence of the objects in question. In this apparently simple and obvious explanation, everything depends on what one means by a "property," and how such properties are supposed to be originally determined. The formulation of a general concept presupposes *definite* properties; only if there are fixed characteristics by virtue of which things may be recognized as similar or dissimilar, coinciding or not coinciding, is it possible to collect objects which resemble each other into a class. But–we cannot help asking at this point–how can such differentiae exist prior to language? Do we not, rather, *realize* them only by means of language, through the very act of naming them? And if the latter be the case, then by what rules and what criteria is this act carried out? What is it that leads or constrains language to collect just *these* ideas into a single whole and denote them by a word? What causes it to select, from the ever-flowing,

* From: Ernest Cassirer, *Language and Myth,* trans. by Susanne K. Langer (Dover, N.Y. 1942), pp. 23-43.

ever-uniform stream of impressions which strike our senses or arise from the autonomous processes of the mind, certain pre-eminent forms, to dwell on them and endow them with a particular "significance"? As soon as we cast the problem in this mold, traditional logic offers no support to the student and philosopher of language; for its explanation of the origin of generic concepts presupposes the very thing we are seeking to understand and derive–the formulation of linguistic notions.[7] The problem becomes even more difficult, as well as more urgent, if one considers that the form of that ideational synthesis which leads to the primary verbal concepts and denotations is not simply and unequivocally determined by the object itself, but allows scope for the free operation of language and for its specific mental stamp. Of course, even this freedom must have its rules, and this original, creative power has a law of its own. Can this law be set forth, and can it be brought into relation with the principles that govern other spheres of spiritual expression, especially the rules of mythical, religious, and purely theoretical, i.e., scientific, conception?

Beginning with the last of these branches, we can show that all the intellectual labor whereby the mind forms general concepts out of specific impressions is directed toward breaking the isolation of the datum, wresting it from the "here and now" of its actual occurrence, relating it to other things and gathering it and them into some inclusive order, into the unity of a "system." The logical form of conception, from the standpoint of theoretical knowledge, is nothing but a preparation for the logical form of judgment; all judgment, however, aims at overcoming the illusion of singularity which adheres to every particular content of consciousness. The apparently singular fact becomes known, understood and conceptually grasped only in so far as it is "subsumed" under a general idea, recognized as a "case" of a law or as a member of a manifold or a series. In this sense every genuine judgment is synthetic; for what it intends and strives for is just this synthesis of parts into a whole, this weaving of particulars into a system. This synthesis cannot be achieved immediately and at a single stroke; it has to be worked out step-by-step, by a progressive activity of relating separate notions or sense impressions with each other, and then gathering up the resultant wholes into the resultant wholes into greater complexes, until finally the union of all these

---

[7] For more detailed discussion of this point see my *Philosophie der symbolischen Formen*, I, 244ff.

separate complexes yields the coherent picture of the totality of things. The will to this totality is the vivifying principle of our theoretical and empirical conception. This principle, therefore, is necessarily "discursive"; that is to say, it starts with a particular case, but instead of dwelling upon it, and resting content in sheer contemplation of the particular, it lets the mind merely start from this instance to run the whole gamut of Being in the special directions determined by the empirical concept. By this process of running through a realm of experience, i.e., of discursive thinking, the particular receives its fixed intellectual "meaning" and definite character. It has different appearances according to the ever-broadening contexts in which it is taken; the place it holds in the totality of Being, or rather the place which the progressive march of thought assigns to it, determines its content and its theoretical significance.

How this ideal of knowledge controls the rise of science, especially the construction of mathematical physics, requires no further elucidation. All the concepts of physics have no other aim than to transform the "rhapsody of perceptions," by which the world of sense is actually presented to us, into a system, a coherent epitome of laws. Each individual datum becomes a phenomenon and object of "nature" only as it meets this requirement–for "nature" in the theoretical sense, according to the Kantian definition, is nothing but the existence of things as determined by general laws.

A distinction has often been drawn between the "individualizing" mode of historical thought and the "generalizing" mode of science. While in the latter any concrete case is merely regarded as an instance of a general law, and while the "here" and "now" has no significance save in so far as it reveals a universal rule, it is said that history deliberately seeks out this here and now, in order to grasp it ever more precisely in just this character. But even in historical thinking the particular fact is significant only by virtue of the relationships into which it enters. Although it cannot be regarded as an instance of a general law, yet in order to be historically conceived, to appear *sub specie* the mode of history, it must take its place as a *member* of a course of events or belong to some teleological nexus. Its determination in time is the exact opposite of its temporal separateness; for historically it has meaning only if and as it refers back to a past and forward to a future. Thus all genuine historical reflection, instead of losing itself in contemplation of the *merely* singular and non-recurrent, must strive, like the morphological thought of Goethe, to find those "pregnant" moments in the course of events where, as in focal points, whole series of occurrences are epitomized. In such points, phases of reality that are temporally widely separated become connected and linked for historical conception and understanding. As certain high moments are culled from the uniform stream of time, and are related to each other, and concatenated in series, the origin and end of all happenings, their whence and whither, is gradually illumined. So historical conception, too, is characterized by the fact that through it a thousand connections are forged by one stroke; and it is not so much the contemplation of particulars as an awareness of such relationships that constitutes the peculiar historicity, or what we call the historical significance of facts.

But let us not dwell longer on such general observations, because our concern is not primarily with the structure of scientific concepts; we are considering this structure only in order to clarify another, namely, the form and character of the primordial linguistic concepts. While this remains to be done, the purely logical theory of conception cannot be completely developed. For all the concepts of theoretical knowledge constitute merely an upper stratum of logic which is founded upon a lower stratum, that of the logic of language. Before the intellectual work of conceiving and understanding of phenomena can set in, the work of *naming* must have preceded it, and have reached a certain point of elaboration. For it is this process which transforms the world of sense impression, which animals also possess, into a mental world, a world of ideas and meanings. All theoretical cognition takes its departure from a world already pre-formed by language; the scientist, the historian, even the philosopher, lives with his objects only as language presents them to him. This immediate dependence is harder to realize than anything that the mind creates mediately, by conscious thought processes. It is easy to see that logical theory, which traces concepts back to an act of generalizing "abstraction," is of little use here; for this "abstraction" consists of selecting from the wealth of *given* properties certain ones which are common to several sensory or intuitive experiences; but our problem is not the choice of properties already given, but the *positing* of the properties themselves. It is to comprehend and illuminate the nature and direction of *noticing*, which must precede mentally the function of "denoting." Even those thinkers who have concerned themselves most actively with the problem of the "origin of language" have thought it necessary to stop at this point, and have simply assumed a "faculty" of the soul for the process of "noticing."

"When man attained that condition of reflection which is peculiar to him," says Herder in his essay on the origins of language, "and when this reflection first achieved free play, he invented speech." Suppose a certain animal, say a lamb, to pass before the eyes of a human being: what image, what view of it will present itself to him? Not the same that would arise for wolves or lions; they would smell and taste it mentally, be overcome by sensuality, and instinct would throw them upon it. Nor would man's image be like that of another animal to whom the lamb was of no direct interest; for such an animal would let it glide vaguely past, because its own instinct was turned in another direction. "But with man, not so! As soon as he is in a position to become acquainted with the lamb, there is no instinct to interfere with him; there is no sensuality to draw him into too close contact with it, or to repel him from it; it stands before him just as it meets his senses. White, gentle, woolly–his mind in its conscious exercise seeks a characteristic for it–the lamb bleats! He has found the differentia. His inner sense is activated. This bleating, which has made the liveliest impression on his mind, that freed itself from all other properties of sight and touch, stood forth, and entered most deeply into his experience–'Ah! You are the bleating one!'–remains with him; he feels that he has recognized it *humanly,* has interpreted it, in that he knows it by a property ... By a property, then? And is that anything but by an inward *denoting word*? The sound of bleating, thus apprehended by a human being as the character of the sheep, became, through the medium of reflection, the *name* of the sheep, even though his tongue had never attempted to utter it."[8]

In these statements of Herder's one can still hear quite dearly the echoes of those theories which he was combating–the traces of the language theories of the Enlightenment, which derived language from conscious reflection and considered it as something "invented." Man looks for a differentia because he needs it; because his reason, his specific faculty of "reflection" demands it. This demand itself remains something un-derived–a "basic power of the soul." Thus the explanation has really progressed in a circle: for the end and goal of language formation, the act of denotation by specific properties, must be regarded as also the principle of its beginning.

---

[8] "Ueber den Ursprung der Sprache," Werke (ed. Supham), V, 3 f.

Humboldt's notion of the "inward form of language" seems to lead in another direction. For he no longer considers the "whence" of linguistic concepts, but is concerned purely with their "what"; not their origin, but the demonstration of their character constitutes his problem. The form of observation, which underlies all speech and language development, always expresses a peculiar spiritual character, a special way of conceiving and apprehending. The difference between the several languages, therefore, is not a matter of different sounds and marks, but of different world conceptions. If the moon is denoted in Greek as the Measuring One (μήν), in Latin as the Shining One (luna), or if even in one and the same language, as in Sanskrit, the elephant is called now the Twice Drinker, now the Two-Tusked One, now the Handed One–that goes to show that language never denotes simply objects, things as such, but always conceptions arising from the autonomous activity of the mind. The nature of concepts, therefore, depends on the way this active viewing is directed.

But even this notion of the inward form of language really has to presuppose that which it professes to prove and reveal. For, on the one hand, speech is here the vehicle of any world perspective, the medium through which thought must pass before it can find itself and assume a definite theoretical form; but, on the other hand, just this sort of form, this definite perspective has to be presupposed, in order to explain the particular character of any given language, its special way of seeing and denoting. So the question of the origin of language tends always to become–even for the thinkers who have taken it most profoundly and struggled hardest with it–a veritable monkey puzzle. All the energy devoted to it seems only to lead us about in a circle and finally leave us at the point from which we started.

And yet the very nature of such fundamental problems entails that the mind, though it despairs of ever finally solving them, can never quite let them alone. And we receive something like a new hope of a solution if, instead of comparing the primary linguistic forms with the forms of logical conception, we try to compare them with those of mythical ideation. What holds these two kinds of conception, the linguistic and the mythical, together in one category, and opposes both of them to the form of logical thought, is the fact that they both seem to reveal the same sort of intellectual apprehension, which runs counter to that of our theoretical thought processes. The aim of theoretical thinking, as we have seen, is primarily to deliver the contents of sensory or intuitive experience from the isolation in which they originally occur. It causes these contents to transcend their narrow limits, combines them with others, compares them, and concatenates them in a definite order, in an all-inclusive context. It proceeds "discursively," in that it treats the immediate content only as a point of departure, from which it can run the whole gamut of impressions in various directions, until these impressions are fitted together into one unified conception, one closed system. In this system there are no more isolated points; all its members are reciprocally related, refer to one another, illumine and explain each other. Thus every separate event is ensnared, as it were, by invisible threads of thought, that bind it to the whole. The theoretical significance which it receives lies in the fact that it is stamped with the character of this totality.

Mythical thinking, when viewed in its most elementary forms, bears no such stamp; in fact, the character of intellectual unity is directly hostile to its spirit. For in this mode, thought does not dispose freely over the data of intuition, in order to relate and compare them to each other, but is captivated and enthralled by the intuition which suddenly confronts it. It comes to rest in the immediate experience; the sensible present is so great that everything else dwindles before it. For a person whose apprehension is under the spell of this mythico-religious attitude, it is as though the whole world were simply annihilated; the immediate content, whatever it be, that commands his religious interest so completely fills his consciousness that nothing else can exist beside and apart from it. The ego is spending all its energy on this single object, lives in it, loses itself in it. Instead of a widening of intuitive experience, we find here its extreme limitation; instead of expansion that would lead through greater and greater spheres of being, we have here an impulse toward concentration; instead of extensive distribution, intensive compression. This focusing of all forces on a single point is the prerequisite for all mythical thinking and mythical formulation. When, on the one hand, the entire self is given up to a single impression, is "possessed" by it and, on the other hand, there is the utmost tension between the subject and its object, the outer world; when external reality is not merely viewed and contemplated, but overcomes a man in sheer immediacy, with emotions of fear or hope, terror or wish fulfillment: then the spark jumps somehow across, the tension finds release, as the subjective excitement becomes objectified, and confronts the mind as a god or a daemon.

Here we have the mythico-religious proto-phenomenon which Usener has sought to fix with the term "momentary god." "In absolute immediacy," he says, "the individual phenomenon is deified, without the intervention of even the most rudimentary class concept; that *one* thing which you see before you, that and nothing else is the god" (p. 280). To this day, the life of primitive races shows us certain features in which this process is almost tangibly clear. We may recall the examples of it which Spieth adduces: water found by a thirsty person, a termite mound that hides and saves someone, any new object that inspires a man with sudden terror–all these are transformed directly into gods. Spieth summarizes his observations with the words: "To the mind of the Evé, the moment in which an object or any striking attributes of it enter into any noticeable relation, pleasant or unpleasant, with the life and spirit of man, that moment a Trõ is born in his consciousness." It is as though the isolated occurrence of an impression, its separation from the totality of ordinary, commonplace experience produced not only a tremendous intensification, but also the highest degree of *condensation,* and as though by virtue of this condensation the objective form of the god were created so that it veritably burst forth from the experience.

Now it is here, in this intuitive creative form of myth, and not in the formation of our discursive theoretical concepts, that we must look for the key which may unlock for us the secrets of the original conceptions of language. The formulation of language, too, should not be traced back to any sort of reflective contemplation, to the calm and clearheaded comparison of given sense impressions and the abstraction of definite attributes; but here again we must abandon this static point of view for the comprehension of the dynamic process which produces the verbal sound out of its own inner drive. To be sure, this retrospect in itself is not enough; for through it we are merely brought to the further, more difficult question, how it is possible for anything permanent to result from such a dynamism, and why the vague billowing and surging of sensory impressions and feelings should give rise to an objective, verbal "structure." The modern science of language, in its efforts to elucidate the "origin" of language, has indeed gone back frequently to Hamann's dictum, that poetry is "the mother-tongue of humanity"; its scholars have emphasized the fact that speech is rooted not in the prosaic, but in the poetic aspect of life, so that its ultimate basis must be sought not in preoccupation with the objective view of things and their classification according to certain attributes, but in the primitive power of subjective feeling.[9] But although this doctrine may seem, at first sight, to evade the vicious circle into which the theory of logical expression is ever lapsing, in the end it also cannot bridge the gulf between the purely denotative and the expressive function of speech. In this theory, too, there always remains a sort of hiatus between the lyrical aspect of verbal expression and its logical character; what remains obscure is exactly that *emancipation* whereby a sound is transformed from an emotional utterance into a denotative one.

Here we may be guided once more by consideration of how the "momentary gods" were generated. If such a god is, in his origin, the creation of a moment, if he owes his existence to some entirely concrete and individual, never-recurring situation, he yet achieves a certain substantiality which lifts him far above this accidental condition of his origin. Once he has been divorced from the immediate exigency, the fear or hope of the moment, he becomes an independent being, which henceforth lives on by a law of its own, and has gained form and continuity. He appears to men not as a creature of the hour, but as an objective and superior power, which they adore and which their cult endows with more and more definite form. The image of the momentary god, instead of merely preserving the memory of what he originally meant and was–a deliverance from fear, the fulfillment of a wish and a hope–persists and remains long after that memory has faded and finally disappeared altogether.

The same function which the image of the god performs, the same tendency to permanent existence, may be ascribed to the uttered sounds of language. The word, like a god or a daemon, confronts man not as a creation of his own, but as something existent and significant in its own right, as an objective reality. As soon as the spark has jumped across, as soon as the tension and emotion of the

[9] See Otto Jespersen, *Progress in Language* (London, 1894), esp. pp. 35 f.

moment has found its discharge in the word or the mythical image, a sort of turning point has occurred in human mentality: the inner excitement which was a mere subjective state has vanished, and has been resolved into the objective form of myth or of speech. And now an ever-progressive objectification can begin. In the same measure in which the autonomous activity of man extends over a widening sphere, and becomes adjusted and organized within that sphere, his mythical and verbal *world* undergoes a progressive organization and ever more definite articulation. The "momentary gods" are succeeded by gods of activity, as Usener has shown us through the examples of the Roman "functional gods" and the corresponding Lithuanian deities. Wissowa summarizes the basic character of Roman religion with the words: "All their deities are entirely practically conceived, so to speak–conceived as being effective in those things with which the Roman dealt in his ordinary life: the local environment in which he moved, the various occupations in which he engaged, the occasions that determine and shape the life of the individual as well as the community–all these things are in the keeping of clearly conceived gods with definitely recognized powers. For the Roman, even Jupiter and Tellus were gods of the Roman community, gods of the hearth and the heath, of wood and wold, seedtime and harvest, of growth and flower and fruit."[10] Here one can trace directly how humanity really attains its insight into objective reality only through the medium of its own activity and the progressive differentiation of that activity; before man thinks in terms of logical concepts, he holds his experiences by means of clear, separate, mythical images. And here, too, the development of language appears to be the counterpart of the development which mythical intuition and thought undergo; for one cannot grasp the true nature and function of linguistic concepts if one regards them as copies, as representations of a definite world of facts, whose components are given to the human mind *ab initio* in stark and separate outlines. Again, the limits of things must first be posited, the outlines drawn, by the agency of language; and this is accomplished as man's activity becomes internally organized, and his conception of Being acquires a correspondingly clear and definite pattern.

[10] G. Wissowa, *Religion und Kultus der Römer* (Munich, 1912), Vol. 2, pp. 24f.

We have already demonstrated that the primary function of linguistic concepts does not consist in the comparison of experiences and the selection of certain common attributes, but in the concentration of such experiences, so to speak, in distilling them down to one point. But the manner of this concentration always depends upon the direction of the subject's interest, and is determined not so much by the content of the experience as by the teleological perspective from which it is viewed. Whatever appears important for our wishing and willing, our hope and anxiety, for acting and doing: that and only that receives the stamp of verbal "meaning." Distinctions in meaning are the prerequisite for that solidification of impressions which, as we said above, is a necessary condition for their denotation by words. For only what is related somehow to the focus point of willing and doing, only what proves to be essential to the whole scheme of life and activity, is selected from the uniform flux of sense impressions, and is "noticed" in the midst of them–that is to say, receives a special linguistic accent, a name. The beginnings of this process of "noticing" must undoubtedly be attributed even to animal mentality; for in their world of experience, too, those elements upon which their impulses and instincts center are singled out by their conscious apprehension. Only something that arouses a single impulse, such as the nutritional or the sexual impulse, or anything that relates to it, "is there" for an animal as an objective content of its feeling and apperception. But such a presence always fills just the actual moment in which the impulse is evoked, is directly stimulated. As soon as the excitation abates, and the desire is fulfilled, the world of Being, the order of perceptions collapses again. When a new stimulus reaches the animal's consciousness, this world may be resurrected; but it is always held in the narrow confines of actual drives and excitations. Its successive beginnings always fill just the present moment, without ranging themselves in any progression; the past is but dimly retained, the future does not become an image, a *prospect*. Only symbolic expression can yield the possibility of prospect and retrospect, because it is only by symbols that distinctions are not merely *made*, but *fixed* in consciousness. What the mind has once created, what has been culled from the total sphere of consciousness, does not fade away again when the spoken word has set its seal upon it and given it definite form.

Here, too, the recognition of function precedes that of Being. The aspects of Being are distinguished and coordinated according to a measure supplied by action–hence they are guided, not by any "objective" similarity among things, but by their appearance through the medium of practice, which relates them within a purposive nexus. This teleological character of verbal concepts may be readily supported and clarified by means of examples from the history of language.[11] A great many of the phenomena which philologists commonly treat under the general heading of "changes of meaning" can really be understood in principle only from this angle. If altered conditions of life, the changes that attend the advance of culture, have brought men into a new practical relation with their environment, the concepts inherent in language do not retain their original "sense." They begin to shift, to move about, in the same measure as the bounds of human activity tend to vary and efface each other. Wherever, for any reason, the distinction between two activities loses its importance and meaning, there is wont to be a corresponding shift of verbal meanings, namely, of the words which marked that distinction. A very characteristic instance of this sort of thing may be found in an article which Meinhof has published under the title, "On the Influence of Occupation on the Language of the Bantu Tribes in Africa." According to Meinhof, "The Herero have a word, *rima*, to denote sowing, which is phonetically identical with *lima*, the word for hoeing, cultivating, in other Bantu languages. The reason for this peculiar change of meaning is that the Herero neither sow nor cultivate the ground. They are cowherds, and their whole vocabulary smells of cows. Sowing and cultivating they deem unworthy occupations for a man; so they do not find it worth while to draw nice distinctions among such inferior tasks."[12]

Primitive languages especially furnish many further examples in support of the principle that the order of nomenclature does not rest on the external similarities among things or events, but that different items bear the same name, and are subsumed under the same concept, whenever their *functional* significance is the same, i.e., whenever they hold the same place or at least analogous places in the order of human activities and purposes. Certain Indian tribes, for instance, are said to use the same word for "dancing" and for "working"[13]–obviously

---

[11] In regard to the "teleological" structure of language, cf. the more detailed study in my *Philosophie d. symbolischen Formen,* I, 245ff.

[12] "Ueber die Einwirkung der Beschaftigung auf die Sprache bei den Bantustämmen Afrikas," *Globus,* Vol. 75 (1899), p. 361.

[13] "Die Tarahumara tanzen überhaupt nur zu Zauberzwecken bzw. als 'Gebet.' Tanzen ist ihnen daher . . . gleich arbeiten, was aus der Bedeutung des Wortes tanzen nolávoa hervorgeht." Preuss, "Der Ursprung der Religion und Kunst," *Globus,* Vol. 87 (1905), p. 336.

because the distinction between these two activities is not immediately apparent to them, since in their scheme of things dance analogous places in the order of human activities and purposes. Certain Indian tribes, for instance, are said to use the same word for "dancing" and for and agriculture serve essentially the same purpose of providing the means of livelihood. The growth and prosperity of their crops seems to them to depend as much or more on the correct performance of their dances, their magical and religious ceremonies, than on prompt and proper attention to the soil.[14] Such a fusion of activities gives rise to the identification of their respective names, the "concepts" of language. When the natives along the Swan River in Africa were first introduced to the sacrament of Communion, they called it a dance;[15] which goes further to show how a unity may be posited by language in spite of all distinctions and even complete disparity of appearances, as long as the contents contents of experience agree in their functional import - in this case, their religious significance.[16]

Here is one of the basic motives by virtue of which mythical thinking transcends the original vagueness of "complex" intuitions and proceeds to concretely defined, distinctly sundered, and individualized mental constructions. This process, too, is determined primarily by the lines which activity takes; so much so that the forms of mythical invention reflect, not the objective character of *things,* but the forms of human practices. The primitive god, like primitive action, is limited to a very restricted sphere. Not only does every occupation have its particular god, but each phase of the total action becomes the domain of an independent god or daemon who governs this precise sphere of action.

[14] E. Reclus, *Le primitif d'Australie,* p. 28.

[15] Cf. Preuss, *Religion und Mythologie der Uitoto* (Göttingen and Leipzig, 1923), I, 123ff.; II, 637f.

[16] Here we may adduce a further striking example of this "teleological" construction of language, which I owe to a verbal communication from my colleague Professor Otto Dempwolff. In the Kate language, which is current in New Guinea, there is a word *bilin,* which denotes a certain kind of grass with tough stems and roots that are wedged firmly in the soil; the latter are said to hold the earth together during earthquakes, so that it does not break apart. When nails were first introduced by Europeans, and when their use became popularly known, the natives applied this word to them - as also to wire and to iron rods, in short, to everything that served the purpose of holding things together. Similarly, one may often observe in nursery language the creation of such teleological identities, which do not meet our class concepts at all, and seem even to defy them. Cf. Clara and William Stern, Die Kindersprache (Leipzig, 1906), pp. 26, 172, et al.

The Roman *Fratres Arvales,* when making atonement for the removal of trees from the sacred grove of the goddess Dia, divided the deed into a number of separate acts, for each of which a special deity was invoked: *Deferenda* for fetching down the wood, *Commolenda* for chopping it up, *Coinquenda* for splitting it, and *Adolenda* for burning up the brushwood.[17] The same phenomenon may be seen in primitive languages, which often divide an action into several sub-actions, and instead of comprehending it all under one term, denote each part by a separate verb, as though they had to break up the idea into little pieces in order to handle it. Perhaps it is not mere chance that in the language of the Evé, who have such a wealth of "momentary gods" and "special gods," this peculiarity should be very pronounced.[18] And even where both language and myth have risen considerably above such momentary, sense-bound intuition, where they have broken through their original fetters, they long remain quite inseparably involved with each other. Their connection is, in fact, so close that it is impossible to determine on a basis of empirical data which of them takes the lead in their progress toward universal formulation and conception, and which one merely follows suit. Usener, in a section of his work that is philosophically one of the most significant parts, has sought to prove that all general terms in language have had to go through a certain mythical phase. The fact that in the Indo-Germanic languages abstract concepts are usually denoted by feminine nouns, with the feminine ending -a (-η), proves, according to Usener, that the idea this feminine form expresses was originally not conceived as an abstractum, but apprehended and felt as a female *deity.*

"Can there be any doubt," he asks further, "whether $Φόβος$ came first, or $φόβος$, the divine image or the condition? Why should the condition be denoted as something of masculine gender, not as neuter, like τὸ δέος? The first creation of the word must have been inspired by some idea of a living, personal Being, the "Startler," the "Flight Producer"; in countless applications of the supposed abstract word, this Being still appears: εἰσῆλθεν or ἐνέπεδε Φόβος, the Startler stalks, or attacks, me! The same process must be assumed for the making of all feminized abstractions. The feminine adjective only became an abstraction after

---

[17] Wissowa, *Religion und Kultus der Römer,* Vol. 2, p. 25.

[18] Westermann, *Grammatik der Ewe-Sprache* (Berlin, 1907), p. 95.

it had denoted a female personage, and in primitive times, this could not have been conceived as anything but a goddess" (p. 375).

But does not the science of language as well as that of religion show signs of a converse process as well? Should we not suppose, for instance, that the way which inflected languages have of endowing every noun with a particular gender may have influenced the conceptions of mythico-religious imagination and bent them after its own fashion? Or may we deem it mere chance that among peoples whose language does not differentiate genders, but employs other and more complex principles of classification, the realm of myth and religion also exhibits an entirely different structure–that it represents all phases of existence not under the auspices of personal, divine powers, but orders it according to totemic groups and classes? We shall content ourselves with merely proposing this question, which would have to be answered by detailed scientific research. But whatever the verdict might be, it is evident that myth and language play similar roles in the evolution of thought from momentary experience to enduring conceptions, from sense impression to formulation, and that their respective functions are mutually conditioned. Together and in combination they prepare the soil for the great syntheses from which our mental creation, our unified vision of the cosmos springs.

Amos Tversky
(1937-1996)

Ð

Introduction

The ass that bears the name of Buridan–a 14th century cleric philosopher–is often identified with the notion that humans faced by alternative courses of action are likely to choose the greater good. Buridan's ass, according to the fable, remains indeterminate since he is faced by equidistant and equally tempting piles of hay. By eliminating all reasons for a preferable course of action, the ass eventually dies of starvation. Humans are rarely caught between two equivalent solutions or by options that readily disclose the greater good. What it is that humans consider "advantageous" may vary and consequently yield different courses of action. Decisions, like some dilemmas, may also reveal conflict between logic and will, raising queries as to where to invest one's energy. Moreover, whereby one thing differs from the other, or resembles the other, largely depends on what it is that we wish to emphasize. Nonetheless, recognition, judgment and learning presuppose an ability to categorize stimuli and classify situations by kinds of similarity. In fact, our human sense of similarity is considered basic to thought and language.

According to Leibniz two things sharing every attribute are not only similar, but are the same thing. The concept of "sameness" has given rise to the general concept of "identity," including personal and social identities. Any difference, thus, may give rise to a separate identity since identity relates to whatever makes an entity definable and recognizable in terms of possessing a set of qualities or characteristics that distinguish it from other entities. It has been argued that analogy-making and the perception of sameness, rather than representing two different cognitive processes, are two sides of the same coin. The theory is based on the notion that the building-up and the manipulation of representations are inseparable aspects of mental functioning, and that analogy making is an extension of our constant background process of perceiving.

Tversky's "Features of Similarity" is an attempt to represent various entities in terms of many qualitative features, rather than in terms of a few quantitative dimensions. Similarity relations, he argues, are better represented by the comparison of features than by the comparison of metric distance between points. He also argues against viewing similarity via symmetric relations, emphasizing that the choice of subject and referent depends on the relative salience of the objects. Humans apparently tend to select the prototype as a referent and the variant as subject, e.g. "Sara resembles her mother," rather than "Sara's mother resembles Sara." Tversky claims that this asymmetry in choice of similarity statements is associated with asymmetry in judgment of similarity in which the variant is more similar to the prototype than vice versa. The directionality and asymmetry of similarity relations are also most noticeable in similes and metaphors.

Tversky argues that the representation of stimuli in terms of their many qualitative *features* is more intuitive than a few qualitative dimensions, given that the perceived similarity between items depends on features they may have in common. Similarity between items clearly increases the more features they have in common and decreases the more features on which they differ. Yet common and distinctive features are *weighted* differently, depending on context and the particular task at hand.

In some of his investigations of how best to represent similarity relations, Tversky also considered the representation of similarity data in the form of additive trees, disregarding the afore-mentioned asymmetries. In the additive tree model dissimilarity between objects is the length of the path joining them. Certain common features can be better captured by a tree structure than by spatial representation, and in many semantic fields a focal element is the nearest relation of most of the instances of the category. Though hierarchical classification involving various *qualitative attributes* may be better captured by tree representations, emotions, for example, may be characterized by few dimensions that differ in *intensity* and thus fit a dimensional representation. In their joint study, Tversky and Gati[1] found that common features loom larger than distinctive features in verbal stimuli, whereas in pictorial stimuli distinctive features loom larger than common features.

---

[1] Amos Tversky and Itamar Gati, "Studies of Similarity," in *Preference, Belief, and Similarity*, edited by Eldar Shafir, A Bradford Book (M.I.T. Press, 2004).

Similarity or dissimilarity data apparently appear in different forms. Judging two identical stimuli as same rather than different is not constant for all stimuli. Moreover, similarity rarely evokes symmetrical relations. Similarity assessments extract from our data base a limited list of *relevant* features on the basis of which the required task is performed. The representation of an object as a collection of features is thus viewed as a product of prior processes of contemplation and extraction. Like other judgments, similarity depends on context and frame of reference. At times the relevant frame of reference is explicitly specified. In general, however, the relevant feature-space is not specified but must be inferred from the general context. Wittgenstein, one may recall, also sensitized us to the fact that natural categories may not have any attribute that is shared by all their members, and by them alone—like 'games', for example. Natural categories and concepts he proposed are commonly characterized and understood in terms of "family resemblance," that is, a network of similarity relations that link the various members of the class.

I repeatedly stated that *what refers to what and whereby* is of utmost importance for communication and understanding. This dictum carries *a fortiori* significance with regard to interdisciplinary studies. Indeed, the identification of "contingencies" among seemingly unrelated fields of investigation requires great awareness to the "features" one enlists that enable the establishment of "sameness" on some structural level or from a specified perspective. Though the term "feature" generally denotes the value of a binary variable—same/different—the establishment of "which is what" is far from simple.

I am fully aware of the difficulties that the following article presents to readers not familiar with the kind of experiments and analyses exemplified by Tversky's profound work. I shortened the article considerably by skipping the descriptions of the experiments and their enlightening analyses, retaining only some of the conclusions which highlight the complexity that assessments of "sameness" involve. I suggest that the reader make an effort to follow at least some of his arguments and seminal findings. Tversky, I repeat, was a key figure in the discovery of systematic human cognitive bias. He contributed a major share to the development of models that simulate the considerations of decision making. His systematic studies also revealed how different kinds of "framing" influences perceptions and decisions of given situations. All of these factors– no less than *ideas* and *symbolic forms*–must be entertained when approaching interdisciplinary work.

Born in Palestine (later Israel), Tversky received his undergraduate education at the Hebrew University of Jerusalem and his doctorate from the University of Michigan. He first taught at the Hebrew University and subsequently at Stanford University. In his all too short life, Tversky had an illustrious academic career. He was widely recognized as a breaker of new grounds in cognitive psychology. He was both a fellow of the American Academy of Arts and Science and of the National Academy of Sciences. He was the recipient of the MacArthur Fellowship and of the Grawemeyer Award for Psychology. Although the Nobel Prize is not awarded posthumously, it is widely accepted that the prize awarded to Kahneman (Tversky's close collaborator) in 2002 was a joint prize.

TVERSKY
from *Features of Similarity**

Similarity plays a fundamental role in theories of knowledge and behavior. It serves as an organizing principle by which individuals classify objects, form concepts, and make generalizations. Indeed, the concept of similarity is ubiquitous in psychological theory. It underlies the accounts of stimulus and response generalization in learning, it is employed to explain errors in memory and pattern recognition, and it is central to the analysis of connotative meaning.

Similarity or dissimilarity data appear in different forms: ratings of pairs, sorting of objects, communality between associations, errors of substitution, and correlation between occurrences. Analyses of these data attempt to explain the observed similarity relations and to capture the underlying structure of the objects under study.

The theoretical analysis of similarity relations has been dominated by geometric models. These models represent objects as points in some coordinate space such that the observed dissimilarities between objects correspond to the metric distances between the respective points. Practically all analyses of proximity data have been metric in nature, although some (e.g., hierarchical clustering) yield tree-like structures rather than dimensionally organized spaces. However, most theoretical and empirical analyses of similarity assume that objects can be adequately represented as points in some coordinate space and that dissimilarity behaves like a metric distance function. Both dimensional and metric assumptions are open to question.

It has been argued by many authors that dimensional representations are appropriate for certain stimuli (e.g., colors, tones) but not for others. It seems more appropriate to represent faces, countries, or personalities in terms of many qualitative features than in terms of a few quantitative dimensions. The assessment

---

* From: Amos Tversky: "Features of Similarity," in *Preference, Belief, and Similarity,* edited by Edgar Shafir (M.I.T., 2004), pp. 7; 8-12; 14-15; 23-24; 26; 28-29; 33-34; 40-41.

of similarity between such stimuli, therefore, may be better described as a comparison of features rather than as the computation of metric distance between points.

A metric distance function, δ, is a scale that assigns to every pair of points a non-negative number, called their distance, in accord with the following three axioms:

> Minimality: $\delta(a, b) \geq \delta(a, a) = 0$.
>
> Symmetry: $\delta(a, b) = \delta(b, a)$.
>
> The triangle inequality: $\delta(a, b) + \delta(b, c) \geq \delta(a, c)$.

To evaluate the adequacy of the geometric approach, let us examine the validity of the metric axioms when δ is regarded as a measure of dissimilarity. The minimality axiom implies that the similarity between an object and itself is the same for all objects. This assumption, however, does not hold for some similarity measures. For example, the probability of judging two identical stimuli as "same" rather than "different" is not constant for all stimuli. Moreover, in recognition experiments the off-diagonal entries often exceed the diagonal entries; that is, an object is identified as another object more frequently than it is identified as itself. If identification probability is interpreted as a measure of similarity, then these observations violate minimality and are, therefore, incompatible with the distance model.

Similarity has been viewed by both philosophers and psychologists as a prime example of a symmetric relation. Indeed, the assumption of symmetry underlies essentially all theoretical treatments of similarity. Contrary to this tradition, the present paper provides empirical evidence for asymmetric similarities and argues that similarity should not be treated as a symmetric relation.

Similarity judgments can be regarded as extensions of similarity statements, that is, statements of the form "a is like b." Such a statement is directional; it has a subject, a, and a referent, b, and it is not equivalent in general to the converse similarity statement "b is like a." In fact, the choice of subject and referent depends, at least in part, on the relative salience of the objects. We tend to select the more salient stimulus, or the prototype, as a referent, and the less salient stimulus, or the variant, as a subject. We say "the portrait resembles the person" rather than "the person resembles the portrait." We say "the son resembles the father", rather than "the father resembles the son." We say "an ellipse is like a circle," not "a circle is like an ellipse," and we say "North Korea is like Red China", rather than "Red China is like North Korea."

As will be demonstrated later, this asymmetry in the *choice* of similarity statements is associated with asymmetry in *judgments* of similarity. Thus, the judged similarity of North Korea to Red China exceeds the judged similarity of Red China to North Korea. Likewise, an ellipse is more similar to a circle than a circle is to an ellipse. Apparently, the direction of asymmetry is determined by the relative salience of the stimuli; the variant is more similar to the prototype than vice versa.

The directionality and asymmetry of similarity relations are particularly noticeable in similes and metaphors. We say "Turks fight like tigers" and not "tigers fight like Turks." Since the tiger is renowned for its fighting spirit, it is used as the referent rather than the subject of the simile. The poet writes "my love is as deep as the ocean," not "the ocean is as deep as my love," because the ocean epitomizes depth. Sometimes both directions are used but they carry different meanings. "A man is like a tree" implies that man has roots; "a tree is like a man" implies that the tree has a life history. "Life is like a play" says that people play roles. "A play is like life" says that a play can capture the essential elements of human life. The relations between the interpretation of metaphors and the assessment of similarity are briefly discussed in the final section.

The triangle inequality differs from minimality and symmetry in that it cannot be formulated in ordinal terms. It asserts that one distance must be smaller than the sum of two others, and hence it cannot be readily refuted with ordinal or even interval data. However, the triangle inequality implies that if a is quite similar to b, and b is quite similar to c, then a and c cannot be very dissimilar from each other. Thus, it sets a lower limit to the similarity between a and c in terms of the similarities between a and b and between b and c. The following example (based on William James) casts some doubts on the psychological validity of this assumption. Consider the similarity between countries: Jamaica is similar to Cuba (because of geographical proximity); Cuba is similar to Russia (because of their political affinity); but Jamaica and Russia are not similar at all.

This example shows that similarity, as one might expect, is not transitive. In addition, it suggests that the perceived distance of Jamaica to Russia exceeds the perceived distance of Jamaica to Cuba, plus that of Cuba to Russia–contrary to the triangle inequality. Although such examples do not necessarily refute the triangle inequality, they indicate that it should not be accepted as a cornerstone of similarity models.

It should be noted that the metric axioms, by themselves, are very weak. They are satisfied, for example, by letting $\delta(a, b) = 0$ if $a = b$, and $\delta(a, b) = 1$ if $a \neq b$. To specify the distance function, additional assumptions are made (e.g., intra-dimensional subtractivity and inter-dimensional additivity) relating the dimensional structure of the objects to their metric distances. For an axiomatic analysis and a critical discussion of these assumptions, see Beals, Krantz, and Tversky (1968), Krantz and Tversky (1975), and Tversky and Krantz (1970).

In conclusion, it appears that despite many fruitful applications (see e.g., Carroll & Wish, 1974; Shepard, 1974), the geometric approach to the analysis of similarity faces several difficulties. The applicability of the dimensional assumption is limited, and the metric axioms are questionable. Specifically, minimality is somewhat problematic, symmetry is apparently false, and the triangle inequality is hardly compelling.

The next section develops an alternative theoretical approach to similarity, based on feature matching, which is neither dimensional nor metric in nature. In subsequent sections this approach is used to uncover, analyze, and explain several empirical phenomena, such as the role of common and distinctive features, the relations between judgments of similarity and difference, the presence of asymmetric similarities, and the effects of context on similarity. Extensions and implications of the present development are discussed in the final section.

Feature Matching

Let $\Delta = \{a, b, c,...\}$ be the domain of objects (or stimuli) under study. Assume that each object in Δ is represented by a set of features or attributes, and let A,

B, C denote the sets of features associated with the objects a, b, c, respectively. The features may correspond to components such as eyes or mouth; they may represent concrete properties such as size or color; and they may reflect abstract attributes such as quality or complexity. The characterization of stimuli as feature sets has been employed in the analysis of many cognitive processes such as speech perception (Jakobson, Fant, & Halle, 1961), pattern recognition (Neisser, 1967), perceptual learning (Gibson, 1969), preferential choice (Tversky, 1972); and semantic judgment (Smith, Shoben, & Rips, 1974).

Two preliminary comments regarding feature representations are in order. First, it is important to note that our total database concerning a particular object (e.g., a person, a country, or a piece of furniture) is generally rich in content and complex in form. It includes appearance, function, relation to other objects, and any other property of the object that can be deduced from our general knowledge of the world. When faced with a particular task (e.g., identification or similarity assessment) we extract and compile from our database a limited list of relevant features on the basis of which we perform the required task. Thus, the representation of an object as a collection of features is viewed as a product of a prior process of extraction and compilation.

Second, the term *feature* usually denotes the value of a binary variable (e.g., voiced vs. voiceless consonants) or the value of a nominal variable (e.g., eye color). Feature representations, however, are not restricted to binary or nominal variables; they are also applicable to ordinal or cardinal variables (i.e., dimensions). A series of tones that differ only in loudness, for example, could be represented as a sequence of nested sets where the feature set associated with each tone is included in the feature sets associated with louder tones. Such a representation is isomorphic to a directional unidimensional structure. A non-directional unidimensional structure (e.g., a series of tones that differ only in pitch) could be represented by a chain of overlapping sets. The set-theoretical representation of qualitative and quantitative dimensions has been investigated by Restle (1959).

Let s(a, b) be a measure of the similarity of a to b defined for all distinct a, b in Δ. The scale s is treated as an ordinal measure of similarity. That is, s(a, b) > s(c, d) means that a is more similar to b than c is to d. The present theory is based on the following assumptions.

1. MATCHING:

$$s(a, b) = F(A \cap B, A - B, B - A).$$

The similarity of a to b is expressed as a function F of three arguments: $A \cap B$, the features that are common to both a and b; $A - B$, the features that belong to a but not to b; $B - A$, the features that belong to b but not to a. A schematic illustration of these components is presented in figure 1.1.

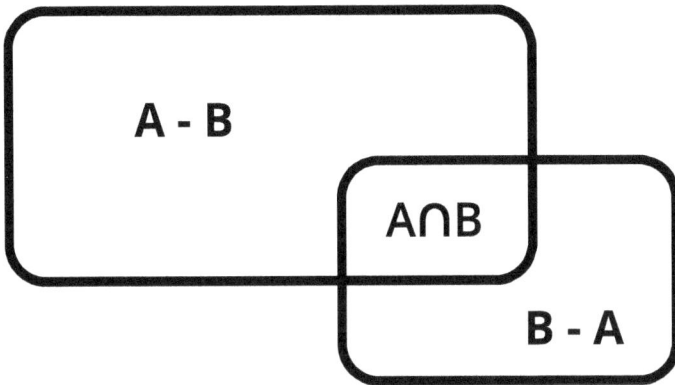

Figure 1.1
A graphical illustration of the relation between two feature sets.

2. MONOTONICITY:

$$s(a, b) \geq s(a, c)$$

whenever

$$A \cap B \supset A \cap C, A - B \subset A - C,$$

and

$$B - A \subset C - A.$$

Moreover, the inequality is strict whenever either inclusion is proper.

That is, similarity increases with addition of common features and/or deletion of distinctive features (i.e., features that belong to one object but not to the other). The monotonicity axiom can be readily illustrated with block letters if we identify their features with the component (straight) lines. Under this assumption, E should be more similar to F than to I because E and F have more common features than E and I. Furthermore, I should be more similar to F than to E because I and F have fewer distinctive features than I and E.

Any function F, satisfying assumptions 1 and 2, is called a *matching function*. It measures the degree to which two objects–viewed as sets of features–match each other. In the present theory, the assessment of similarity is described as a feature-matching process. It is formulated, therefore, in terms of the set-theoretical notion of a matching function rather than in terms of the geometric concept of distance.

In order to determine the functional form of the matching function, additional assumptions about the similarity ordering are introduced. The major assumption of the theory (independence) is presented next; the remaining assumptions and the proof of the representation theorem are presented in the appendix. Readers who are less interested in formal theory can skim or skip the following paragraphs up to the discussion of the representation theorem. . . .

3. INDEPENDENCE:
Suppose the pairs (a, b) and (c, d), as well as the pairs (a', b') and (c', d'), agree on the same two components, while the pairs (a, b) and (a', b'), as well as the pairs (c, d) and (c', d'), agree on the remaining (third) component. Then $s(a,b) \geq s(a',b')$ if $(c,d) \geq s(c',d')$.

To illustrate the force of the independence axiom consider the stimuli presented in figure 1.2, where

$A \cap B = C \cap D$ = round profile = X,
$A' \cap B' = C' \cap D'$ = sharp profile = X',
$A - B = C - D$ = smiling mouth = Y,
$A' - B' = C' - D'$ = frowning mouth = Y',
$B - A = B' - A'$ = straight eyebrow = Z,
$D - C = D' - C'$ = curved eyebrow = Z'.

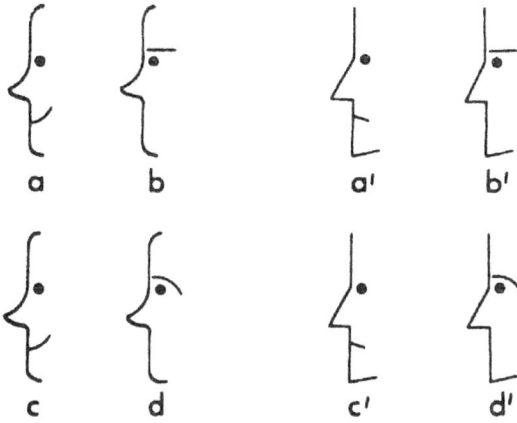

Figure 1.2 An illustration of independence.

By independence, therefore,

$s(a, b) = F(A \cap B, A - B, B - A)$
$\qquad = F(X,Y,Z) \geq F(X',Y',Z)$
$\qquad = F(A' \cap B', A' - B', B' - A')$
$\qquad = s(a', b')$

if and only if

$s(c, d) = F(C \cap D, C - D, D - C)$
$\qquad = F(X,Y,Z') \geq F(X',Y',Z')$
$\qquad = F(C \cap D', C' - D', D' - C')$
$\qquad = s(c', d')$

Thus, the ordering of the joint effect of any two components (e.g., X, Y vs. X', Y') is independent of the fixed level of the third factor (e.g., Z or Z') . . .

. . . In addition to matching (1), monotonicity (2), and independence (3), we also assume solvability (4), and invariance (5), Solvability requires that the feature space under study be sufficiently rich that certain (similarity) equations can be solved. Invariance ensures that the equivalence of intervals is preserved across factors. A rigorous formulation of these assumptions is given in the Appendix, along with a proof of the following result.

Representation Theorem

Suppose assumptions 1, 2, 3, 4, and 5 hold. Then there exist a similarity scale S and a nonnegative scale f such that for all a, b, c, d in Δ,

  (i) $S(a, b) \geq S(c,d)$ if $s(a, b) \geq s(c,d)$;

  (ii) $S(a, b) = \theta f(A \cap B) - \alpha f(A - B) - \beta f(B - A)$, for some $\theta, \alpha, \beta \geq 0$;

  (iii) f and S are interval scales.

The theorem shows that under assumptions 1-5, there exists an interval similarity scale S that preserves the observed similarity order and expresses similarity as a linear combination, or a contrast, of the measures of the common and the distinctive features. Hence, the representation is called the *contrast model*. In parts of the following development we also assume that f satisfies feature additivity. That is, $f(X \cup Y) = f(X) + f(Y)$ whenever X and Y are disjoint, and all three terms are defined.[1]

Note that the contrast model does not define a single similarity scale, but rather a family of scales characterized by different values of the parameters θ, α, and β. For example, if $\theta = 1$ and α and β vanish, then $S(a, b) = f(A \cap B)$; that is, the similarity between objects is the measure of their common features. If, on the other hand, $\alpha = \beta = 1$ and θ vanishes then $S(a, b) = f(A - B) + f(B - A)$; that is, the dissimilarity between objects is the measure of the symmetric difference between the respective feature sets. Restle (1961) has proposed these forms as models of similarity and psychological distance, respectively. Note that in the former model ($\theta = 1$, $\alpha = \beta = 0$), similarity between objects is determined only by their common features, whereas in the latter model ($\theta = 0$, $\alpha = \beta = 1$), it is determined by their distinctive features only. The contrast model expresses similarity between objects as a weighted difference of the measures of their common and distinctive features, thereby allowing for a variety of similarity relations over the same domain.

---

[1] To derive feature additivity from qualitative assumptions, we must assume the axioms of an extensive structure and the compatibility of the extensive and the conjoint scales; see Krantz et al. (1971, section 10.7).

The major constructs of the present theory are the contrast rule for the assessment of similarity, and the scale f, which reflects the salience or prominence of the various features. Thus, f measures the contribution of any particular (common or distinctive) feature to the similarity between objects. The scale value f(A) associated with stimulus a is regarded, therefore, as a measure of the overall salience of that stimulus. The factors that contribute to the salience of a stimulus include intensity, frequency, familiarity, good form, and informational content. The manner in which the scale f and the parameters (θ, α, β) depend on the context and the task are discussed in the following sections.

Let us recapitulate what is assumed and what is proven in the representation theorem. We begin with a set of objects, described as collections of features, and a similarity ordering which is assumed to satisfy the axioms of the present theory. From these assumptions, we derive a measure f on the feature space and prove that the similarity ordering of object pairs coincides with the ordering of their contrasts, defined as linear combinations of the respective common and distinctive features. Thus, the measure f and the contrast model are derived from qualitative axioms regarding the similarity of objects.

The nature of this result may be illuminated by an analogy to the classical theory of decision under risk (von Neumann & Morgenstern, 1947). In that theory, one starts with a set of prospects, characterized as probability distributions over some consequence space, and a preference order that is assumed to satisfy the axioms of the theory. From these assumptions one derives a utility scale on the consequence space and proves that the preference order between prospects coincides with the order of their expected utilities. Thus, the utility scale and the expectation principle are derived from qualitative assumptions about preferences. The present theory of similarity differs from the expected-utility model in that the characterization of objects as feature sets is perhaps more problematic than the characterization of uncertain options as probability distributions. Furthermore, the axioms of utility theory are proposed as (normative) principles of rational behavior, whereas the axioms of the present theory are intended to be descriptive rather than prescriptive. . . . .

Discussion

The conjunction of the contrast model and the focusing hypothesis implies the presence of asymmetric similarities. This prediction was confirmed in several experiments of perceptual and conceptual similarity using both judgmental methods (e.g., rating) and behavioral methods (e.g., choice).

The asymmetries discussed in the previous section were observed in *comparative* tasks in which the subject compares two given stimuli to determine their similarity. Asymmetries were also observed in *production* tasks in which the subject is given a single stimulus and asked to produce the most similar response. Studies of pattern recognition, stimulus identification, and word association are all examples of production tasks. A common pattern observed in such studies is that the more salient object occurs more often as a response to the less salient object than vice versa. For example, "tiger" is a more likely associate to "leopard" than "leopard" is to "tiger." Similarly, Garner (1974) instructed subjects to select from a given set of dot patterns one that is similar- -but not identical--to a given pattern. His results show that "good" patterns are usually chosen as responses to "bad" patterns and not conversely.

This asymmetry in production tasks has commonly been attributed to the differential availability of responses. Thus, "tiger" is a more likely associate to "leopard" than vice versa, because "tiger" is more common and hence a more available response than "leopard." This account is probably more applicable to situations where the subject must actually produce the response (as in word association or pattern recognition) than to situations where the subject merely selects a response from some specified set (as in Garner's task).

Without questioning the importance of response availability, the present theory suggests another reason for the asymmetry observed in production tasks. Consider the following translation of a production task to a question-and-answer scheme. Question: What is a like? Answer: a is like b. If this interpretation is valid and the given object a serves as a subject rather than as a referent, then the observed asymmetry of production follows from the present theoretical analysis, since $s(a, b) > s(b, a)$ whenever $f(B) > f(A)$.

In summary, it appears that proximity data from both comparative and production tasks reveal significant and systematic asymmetries whose direction is determined by the relative salience of the stimuli. Nevertheless, the symmetry assumption should not be rejected altogether. It seems to hold in many contexts, and it serves as a useful approximation in many others. It cannot be accepted, however, as a universal principle of psychological similarity. ...

Similarity versus Difference

It has been generally assumed that judgments of similarity and difference are complementary; that is, judged difference is a linear function of judged similarity with a slope of -1. This hypothesis has been confirmed in several studies. For example, Hosman and Kuennapas (1972) obtained independent judgments of similarity and difference for all pairs of lowercase letters on a scale from 0 to 100. The product-moment correlation between the judgments was -.98, and the slope of the regression line was -.91. We also collected judgments of similarity and difference for 21 pairs of countries using a 20-point rating scale. The sum of the two judgments for each pair was quite close to 20 in all cases. The product-moment correlation between the ratings was again -.98. This inverse relation between similarity and difference, however, does not always hold.

Naturally, an increase in the measure of the common features increases similarity and decreases difference, whereas an increase in the measure of the distinctive features decreases similarity and increases difference. However, the relative weight assigned to the common and the distinctive features may differ in the two tasks. In the assessment of similarity between objects the subject may attend more to their common features, whereas in the assessment of difference between objects the subject may attend more to their distinctive features. Thus, the relative weight of the common features will be greater in the former task than in the latter task. ...

Similarity in Context

Like other judgments, similarity depends on context and frame of reference. Sometimes the relevant frame of reference is specified explicitly, as in the questions, "How similar are English and French with respect to sound?"

"What is the similarity of a pear and an apple with respect to taste?" In general, however, the relevant feature space is not specified explicitly but rather inferred from the general context.

When subjects are asked to assess the similarity between the USA and the USSR, for instance, they usually assume that the relevant context is the set of countries and that the relevant frame of reference includes all political, geographical, and cultural features. The relative weights assigned to these features, of course, may differ for different people. With natural, integral stimuli such as countries, people, colors, and sounds, there is relatively little ambiguity regarding the relevant feature space. However, with artificial, separable stimuli, such as figures varying in color and shape, or lines varying in length and orientation, subjects sometimes experience difficulty in evaluating overall similarity and occasionally tend to evaluate similarity with respect to one factor or the other (Shepard, 1964) or change the relative weights of attributes with a change in context (Torgerson, 1965).

In the present theory, changes in context or frame of reference correspond to changes in the measure of the feature space. When asked to assess the political similarity between countries, for example, the subject presumably attends to the political aspects of the countries and ignores, or assigns a weight of zero to, all other features. In addition to such restrictions of the feature space induced by explicit or implicit instructions, the salience of features and hence the similarity of objects are also influenced by the effective context (i.e., the set of objects under consideration). To understand this process, let us examine the factors that determine the salience of a feature and its contribution to the similarity of objects.

The Diagnosticity Principle

The salience (or the measure) of a feature is determined by two types of factors: intensive and diagnostic. The former refers to factors that increase intensity or signal-to-noise ratio, such the brightness of a light, the loudness of a tone, the saturation of a color, the size of a letter, the frequency of an item, the clarity of a picture, or the vividness of an image. The diagnostic factors refer to the classificatory significance of features, that is, the importance or prevalence of the classifications that are based on these features. Unlike the intensive factors, the diagnostic factors are highly sensitive to the particular object set under study. For example, the feature "real" has no diagnostic value in the set of actual animals since it is shared by all actual animals and hence cannot be used to classify them. This feature, however, acquires considerable diagnostic value if the object set is extended to include legendary animals, such as a centaur, a mermaid, or a phoenix.

When faced with a set of objects, people often sort them into clusters to reduce information load and facilitate further processing. Clusters are typically selected so as to maximize the similarity of objects within a cluster and the dissimilarity of objects from different clusters. Hence, the addition and/or deletion of objects can alter the clustering of the remaining objects. A change of clusters, in turn, is expected to increase the diagnostic value of features on which the new clusters are based, and therefore, the similarity of objects that share these features. This relation between similarity and grouping–called the diagnosticity hypothesis–is best explained in terms of a concrete example. Consider the two sets of four schematic faces (displayed in figure 1.4), which differ in only one of their elements (p and q).

The four faces of each set were displayed in a row and presented to a different group of 25 subjects who were instructed to partition them into two pairs. The most frequent partition of set 1 was c and p (smiling faces) versus a and b (non-smiling faces). The most common partition of set 2 was b and q (frowning faces) versus a and c (non-frowning faces). Thus, the replacement of p by q changed the grouping of a: In set 1 a was paired with b, while in set 2 a was paired with c.

According to the above analysis, smiling has a greater diagnostic value in set 1 than in set 2, whereas frowning has a greater diagnostic value in set 2 than in set 1. By the diagnosticity hypothesis, therefore, similarity should follow the grouping. That is, the similarity of a (which has a neutral expression) to b (which is frowning) should be greater in set 1, where they are grouped together, than in set 2, where they are grouped separately. Likewise, the similarity of a to c (which is smiling) should be greater in set 2, where they are grouped together, than in set 1, where they are not. ...

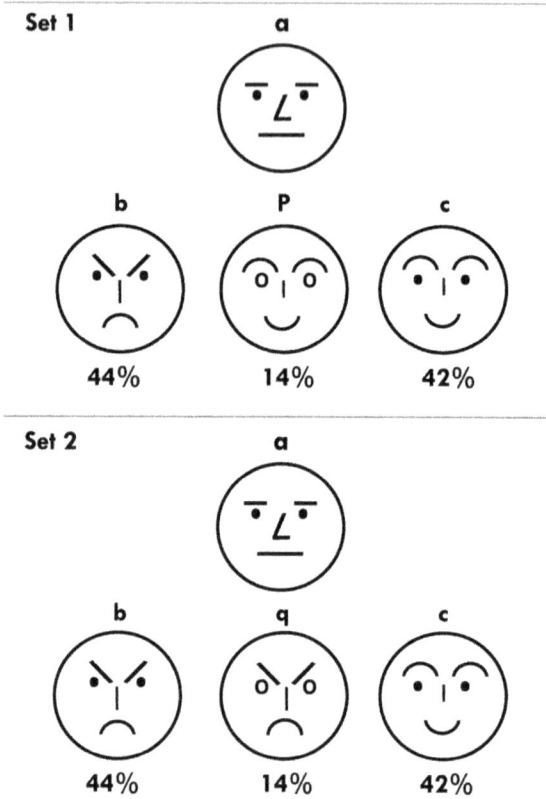

Figure 1.4
Two sets of schematic faces used to test the diagnosticity hypothesis.
The percentage of subjects who selected each face (as most similar to the target)
is presented below the face.

The Two Faces of Similarity

According to the present analysis, the salience of features has two components: intensity and diagnosticity. The intensity of a feature is determined by perceptual and cognitive factors that are relatively stable across contexts. The diagnostic value of a feature is determined by the prevalence of the classifications that are based on it, which change with the context. The effects of context on similarity, therefore, are treated as changes in the diagnostic value of features induced by the respective changes in the grouping of the objects.

This account was supported by the experimental finding that changes in grouping (produced by the replacement or addition of objects) lead to corresponding changes in the similarity of the objects. These results shed light on the dynamic interplay between similarity and classification. It is generally assumed that classifications are determined by similarities among the objects. The preceding discussion supports the converse hypothesis: that the similarity of objects is modified by the manner in which they are classified. Thus, similarity has two faces: causal and derivative. It serves as a basis for the classification of objects, but it is also influenced by the adopted classification. The diagnosticity principle which underlies this process may provide a key to the analysis of the effects of context on similarity. . . .

Similes and Metaphors

Similes and metaphors are essential ingredients of creative verbal expression. Perhaps the most interesting property of metaphoric expressions is that despite their novelty and non-literal nature, they are usually understandable and often informative. For example, the statement that Mr. X resembles a bulldozer is readily understood as saying that Mr. X is a gross, powerful person who overcomes all obstacles in getting a job done. An adequate analysis of connotative meaning should account for man's ability to interpret metaphors without specific prior learning. Since the message conveyed by such expressions is often pointed and specific, they cannot be explained in terms of a few generalized dimensions of connotative meaning, such as evaluation or potency (Osgood, 1962). It appears that people interpret similes by scanning the feature space and selecting the features of the referent that are applicable to the subject (e.g., by selecting features of the bulldozer that are applicable to the person). The nature of this process is left to be explained.

There is a close tie between the assessment of similarity and the interpretation of metaphors. In judgments of similarity one assumes a particular feature space, or a frame of reference, and assesses the quality of the match between the subject and the referent. In the interpretation of similes, one assumes a resemblance between the subject and the referent and searches for an interpretation of the space that would maximize the quality of the match. The same pair of objects, therefore, can be viewed as similar or different depending on the choice of a frame of reference.

One characteristic of good metaphors is the contrast between the prior, literal interpretation, and the posterior, metaphoric interpretation. Metaphors that are too transparent are uninteresting; obscure metaphors are un-interpretable. A good metaphor is like a good detective story. The solution should not be apparent in advance to maintain the reader's interest, yet it should seem plausible after the fact to maintain coherence of the story. Consider the simile "An essay is like a fish." At first, the statement is puzzling. An essay is not expected to be fishy, slippery, or wet. The puzzle is resolved when we recall that (like a fish) an essay has a head and a body, and it occasionally ends with a flip of the tail.

References

Beals, R., Krantz, D. H., & Tversky, A. "Foundations of multidimensional scaling," in *Psychological Review*, 1968, *75*, 127-142.

Carroll, J. D., & Wish, M. "Multidimensional perceptual models and measurement methods," in E. C. Carterette & M. P. Friedman (Eds.), *Handbook of Perception*. New York: Academic Press, 1974.

Garner, W. R. *The Processing of Information and Structure*. New York: Halsted Press, 1974.

Gibson, E. *Principles of Perceptual Learning and Development*. New York: Appleton-Century-Crofts, 1969.

Hosman, J., & Kuennapas, T. *On the Relation between Similarity and Dissimilarity Estimates* (Report No. 354). University of Stockholm, Psychological Laboratories, 1972.

Jakobson, R., Fant, G. G. M., & Halle, M. *Preliminaries to Speech Analysis: The Distinctive Features and their Correlates*. Cambridge, Mass.: MIT Press, 1961.

Krantz, D. H., Luce, R. D., Suppes, P., & Tversky, A. *Foundations of Measurement* (Vol. 1). New York: Academic Press, 1971.

Krantz, D. H., & Tversky, A. "Similarity of Rectangles: An analysis of subjective dimensions," in *Journal of Mathematical Psychology*, 1975, *12*, 4-34.

Neisser, U. *Cognitive Psychology*. New York: Appleton-Century-Crofts, 1967.

Osgood, C. E. "Studies on the Generality of Affective Meaning Systems," in *American Psychologist*, 1962, *17*, 10-28.

Restle, F. "A Metric and an Ordering on Sets," in *Psychometrika*, 1959, *24*, 207-220.

Shepard, R. N. "Attention and the Metric Structure of the Stimulus Space," in *Journal of Mathematical Psychology*, 1964, *1*, 54-87.

Shepard, R. N. "Representation of Structure in Similarity Data: Problems and Prospects," in *Psychometrika*, 1974, *39*, 373-421.

Smith, E. E., Shoben, E. J., & Rips, L. J. "Structure and Process in Semantic Memory: A featural model for semantic decisions,' in *Psychological Review*, 1974, *81*, 214-241.

Torgerson, W. S. "Multidimensional Scaling of Similarity," in *Psychometrika*, 1965, *30*, 379-393.

Tversky, A. "Elimination by Aspects: A Theory of Choice," in *Psychological Review*, 1972, *79*, 281-299.

Tversky, A. & Krantz, D. H. "The Dimensional Representation and the Metric Structure of Similarity Data," in *Journal of Mathematical Psychology*, 1970, *7*, 572-597.

von Neumann, J., & Morgenstern, O. *Theory of Games and Economic Behavior*. Princeton, N.J.: Princeton University Press, 1947.

PART II

Delimiting Modes of Organization

II

Delimiting Modes of Organization

Introduction

It deserves repeating that knowledge, like language, is a collective enterprise. Yet unlike language, knowledge advances in "Connected Vessels." By the metaphoric use of connected vessels, I wish to emphasize that the acquisition of knowledge is a highly constrained interrelated process. While it is possible to identify problems that impinge on each other and processes that constrain each other, it is humanly impossible to have a total grasp of the many venues of the entire enterprise and the ways in which they affect each other.

Despite the complexity which this venerable quest of mankind has created, it must be remembered that knowledge represents at all times the attempt of humans to understand the world that surrounds them, and their place within it, in *humanly* intelligible ways. Thus we continuously re-examine former understandings in light of social changes and novel discoveries that stand to improve, or alter our understanding. This ongoing process of "checks and balances" also sensitizes us to shifts in understandings caused by altered "frames of reference," highlighting *context* as an important factor to reckon with. Ambient conditions of various kinds, historical, geographical, sociological, and many others create demarcation lines–*frames*, as it were–that facilitate our understanding of diverse *perspectives* by taking into account the double entendre of the phrase "different points of view."

'Context' generally applies to a set of circumstances–situations or facts–that surround a particular event that influences its meaning. Like parts of a written or spoken statement that precede or follow a specific utterance, context circumscribes meaning and directs our attention to what is *implied* rather than expressed, denoted rather than indicated. Quoting an utterance out of context is often viewed as having misconstrued its intent. Political parties in power, for example, often justify their changed rhetoric arguing that "what one sees from *here* one doesn't see from *there*." The biblical story of Balaam, in fact, makes this point. When the prophet-magician fails to curse the people of Israel, as Balak–the King of Moab–expected him to do, the king proposed that they ascend another mountain to see the enemy encampment from a different vantage point, from which he might produce a pronouncement that would lend support to Moab's own encampment.[1] Contextualization, it seems fair to claim, is a procedure that takes into consideration the conditions–environmental, social, economic etc.–of the moment in which given events transpire.

It can also be shown, however, that identical ideas have emerged in a variety of different historical contexts. Historians frequently reveal that what passes for novel already existed in earlier times. Although factors of this kind must be taken into consideration in the general delineation of a specific event, they must be carefully scrutinized in the attempt to establish the uniqueness of the cultural expressions of the period. Perception, we are told is "the action by which the mind refers its sensations to the external objects as cause."[2] Indeed, time and place dictate the *prism* through which ideas and concepts are perceived; old ideas may be subsumed by new "looks." Thus a shift of "vision"–a new perspective–does not apply solely to our understanding of past events, but may equally affect contemporary cultural activities. Yet what generally passes under the rubric of "reception studies" applies primarily to the *ensuing history* of events, to their influences and subsequent implications.

Interestingly, the search for progress led Ecclesiastes, the biblical skeptic, to say "there is nothing new under the sun." The "new," he observed, "hath been already, in the ages which were before." The reason he gave for "that which hath been is that which shall be" was based on the insight that "there is no remembrance of them of former times; neither shall there be any remembrance of them of later times."[3] There is much truth in his "circular" theory of progress, however depressing. Nonetheless, his implication that "sameness" prevents "newness" seems to overlook the fact that in *human* life–unlike the natural phenomena that occupied Ecclesiastes–the very same things may be differently *perceived*, depending on contexts and points of view.

[1] See *Numbers* 23:13.
[2] See the Oxford Dictionary of Current English.
[3] See *Ecclesiastes* 1:9-11.

Phenomena of all kinds must, of course, also be examined for their own effectiveness, for what they, themselves, profess and display. Yet regardless of kind and perspective, the advancement of knowledge invariably rests on referential sequences concerning what refers to what and in what way.[4] The various chains of references create interrelationships and intersections that are neither evident nor readily discernible. Thus despite the diversity of investigatory boundaries and the diversity of theoretical underpinnings, the advancement of knowledge allows us to reveal certain analogies, correspondences and contingencies that unveil relationships that further our grasp of the *inter*-relationships among different issues and different subject matters. Analogies, for example, may refer to processes of *reasoning,* to modes of *construction,* or the *functions* of essentially different investigatory areas. Correspondences may imply prior *agreements* of sorts, but they must specify whereby. Contingencies involve, *a priori, specified* conditions.

As we all know, complicated explications often supply familiar cases that "exemplify" their arguments. Yet the cases, while familiar, are supposed to draw draw our attention to some aspects we may have overlooked although they may have "guided" our understanding of the case. Indeed, we rarely overlook the literalness of a tale, but the nature of its unfolding—the structure and the dynamics that constitute essential parts of the tale—often eludes us. The latter mostly involve schemes that affect our minds in ways that supersede the literal

---

[4] There is an enormous amount of literature about the notion of reference. In trying to establish how references relate to their referents, the philosophy of language has given rise to debates among prominent philosophers concerning the varieties of reference. Their theories do not only deal with the determination of the reference of proper names and how communication and information are thereby effected, but also with the ways in which thought and belief affect the information. Neither have philosophers overlooked the existence of references without referents. However enlightening and relevant these debates are to the topics raised in this book, we shall overlook them. As repeatedly stated, I only wish to upgrade the awareness of the reader to the "circumscriptions" entailed by those ordinary and habitual "tools"—which we all inevitably use—once they are employed in scientific investigations, *a fortiori* in interdisciplinary studies. The following short list is for those who wish to acquaint themselves with the debates concerning 'reference': Gareth Evans, *The Varieties of Reference* (Oxford, 1982); Catherine Z. Elgin, *With Reference to Reference* (Hackett, 1983); R. M. Sainsbury, *Reference without Referents* (Oxford, 2005) and David Boersema, *Pragmatism and Reference* (MIT, 2009).

wording of the tale. In fact, it is abstract schemes of this kind that enable the bridging between issues and subject matters that, of hand, differ from each other markedly. Interestingly, that which promotes our understanding–and possibly the "interconnectivity" of our brain– rests primarily on "syntheses" of kinds that unveil commonalities among diversities.

The transition from the apprehensible to the understandable invariably calls for *ordered* symbols so as to make them coherent and interpretable in terms of scientific concepts, whether in the, so called, "exact" sciences or "human" sciences. If the language of numbers seems superior to the symbolism of speech, it is largely due–as explained earlier–to the fact that the essence of number is invariably *relative*, not absolute. It has no self-contained reality; its meaning is defined by the position it occupies in the whole numerical system. Indeed, relationships and interrelationships of all kinds can be expressed via abstract formulations. Given that the symbolism of speech invariably addresses a reality of sorts that carries its own meaning, it can rarely be translated into the language of numbers. It must engage other schemes that enable the abstractions of communalities from amidst diversities. Though the reduction of qualities to quantities represents the highest degree of objectification, it must be remembered that the language of numbers is not part of the "given" world, but a manufactured system, no less than the other schemes, that allow humans to advance knowledge in humanly intelligible ways.

Knowingly or not, we all use metaphors. In fact, language is replete with metaphors which go unnoticed, like for example in "I *see* what he was *driving* at, but his theory is *half-baked.*" Language in essence is metaphorical; it contains all kinds of figures of speech that construct analogies between things and ideas that enable the further structuring of reference. Metaphors clearly use words figuratively, not literally–figures of speech in which implicit comparisons are made between things that actually have nothing in common. A conceptual metaphor refers to the understanding of one idea, or conceptual domain, in terms of another. While constituting an inherent aspect in speech and writing, metaphors are pervasive in every-day life, not just in language, but also in thought and action. Indeed, while the understanding and experiencing of one kind of thing in terms of another is characteristic of metaphors,

metaphors may differ from each other in the ways they are brought about and the functions they serve. In short, metaphor may reveal the underlying nature of language, thought and communication. As such, it has elicited a goodly number of theories, all of whom contributed, in one form or another, to our better understanding of their use. Metaphors are by no means simply an ornamental aspect of language.[5]

The study of metaphor has in fact revealed that it is constraint by different communicative forces. It has been shown, for example, that diverse contexts have given rise to specific metaphorical usage. Some studies have even revealed a simultaneous presence of neural, linguistic and psychological forces that challenge the simplistic definitions of metaphor. However defined, metaphors clearly take part in human *meaning-making* practices, involving language, mind, and aspects of culture that invite categorizations of sorts that enable diverse comparison processes. Yet despite their significance and dominance, we are hardly aware of the metaphors we use in our daily lives, not to mention their diversity. In fact, some metaphors have become so entrenched in our use of language that they are often referred to as "dead metaphors." Even the incongruity of "I *see* your point," uttered by a blind man, may pass unnoticed.

Nonetheless, metaphors *are* constrained; the functions they serve and what they imply may vary from one domain to another. Being privy to the presuppositions of the domain in which they are used, enforces the communicative process by preventing misunderstandings of sorts. For example, as a meaningful statement about our perception of the universe, art may be viewed as a representation in accord with mythology, religion, nature, and many other delimited arias. In fact, many different elements have at one time or another been considered as the rudimental components of reality. From history we learn that numbers, energy, primary qualities, and other factors were deemed at different times to represent the "intrinsic ingredients" of the universe, impacting as well our conception of reality.

---

[5] The sheer leafing through *The Cambridge Handbook of Metaphor and Thought* (edited by Raymond W. Gibbs, Jr., Cambridge, 2008) will allow the inquisitive reader to get an idea about the variety of studies which metaphor engendered and about the centrality of metaphor in thought.

I chanced to mention in an earlier section of the book the influence exerted by numbers–as defined by the Pythagoreans–on thought and artistic manifestations in the middle age. The interrelationships between celestial orbits also suggested the notion of a well "tuned" cosmic order, as reflected in the phrase "The Harmony of the Spheres." In his seminal study of Pythagorean Cosmology–*Touches of Sweet Harmony*[6]–Heninger argued that the study of Renaissance Poetics must take into account the cosmological assumptions shared by both artists and their respective percipients. For art forms to be effective, he claimed, there must be some kind of prior "agreement," since art always pertains to the reality which it ventures to interpret. The notion of a divinely ordered universe, we learn, emanated from the school of Pythagoras. It was subsequently assimilated by the Platonists and from there by the Church Fathers. It became an unstated premise for both humanists and scientists until the advent of the scientific revolution. The Scientific Revolution–of the late sixteenth and early seventeenth century–challenged, as is well known, this very premise, hoping to extrapolate from the perceptible world the *invisible* laws of nature.

Whether we accept or reject Heninger's overall thesis concerning Renaissance Poetics, we must admit that Pythagorean cosmology does lend specific meaning to Lorenzo's depiction of heaven in *The Merchant of Venice*. Contemplating the beauty of heaven, Lorenzo calls Jessica's attention to the "*sweet harmony*" and the "*sounds of music*" of the "*stillness*" night. Clearly, when a musician states that he dislikes the harmony because it is too *sweet*, he clearly refers to *audible* music as organized sound, and employs a metaphor the meaning of which is understood by his colleagues. Though I am no expert in the field, and without further deliberating on the thoughts of those who systematically dealt and deal with the subject, I wish nonetheless to convey the idea that metaphor takes part in the creation of meaning. Moreover, if it is true that utterances of all kind display ways in which language is being used, then they must evidently also refer to a "broader" system of meaning in order to

---

[6] S.K. Heninger, Jr. *Touches of Sweet Harmony: Pythagorean Cosmology and Renaissance Poetics*, The Huntington Library, San Marino, California, 1974.

be comprehensible, involving conventions appropriate to a specific context or community of discourse.

In an earlier section of the book I called the reader's attention to the fact that we use ideas to *think with* about ideas, whether we do or do not know where they come from. I stressed the importance of knowing where they come from, once they are employed in scientific research. The same holds true for metaphors. Unlike the "dead metaphors" we use in daily life that are understood without further ado, the transference of metaphors from one scientific domain to another requires inquiry into their particular meaning in the domain whence they come from. However trivial all of this may sound, overlooking such aspects has caused many a misunderstanding among scientists in the past. I am fully aware of the fact that the creation of meaning–and the diverse processes of communication which it involves–embraces many complex issues that received much attention by scholars who delved into the subject. All I am trying to do is to call the reader's attention to some factors he may have never entertained. That these seemingly "elementary" factors deserve special attention concerning interdisciplinary studies goes without saying.

I mentioned above that 'Art'–as a meaningful statement about the universe–may be viewed as a *representation* in accord with a variety of delimited areas, such as nature, religion, politics, etc. The perception of specific symbolic material depends however on effective communication, which rests on prior knowledge and expectation. Expectation clearly partakes in the *illusion* created by art, involving a communality of sorts between the producers of the artifacts and their audience. This holds no less true for abstract art than it does for figurative art, since all representation relies on "guided projection." No matter how realistic a work of art may be, it too rests on chosen signs which the artist considers essential in order to convey the image he creates, while allowing our imagination to forgo, or complete the rest.

Like symbolic forms, *representations* seem to partake in the organization of the world and reality via the _creation_ and _manipulation_ of signs that stand for, or take the place of, something else. Though largely associated with aesthetics and semiotics, representations refer to that which they represent in a variety of ways and carry a large range of meaning. Yet regardless of the differences among them, representations are expected to "bring to mind"–via their characteristics–that which they supposedly represent. Given the importance and scope of their function, it hardly comes as a surprise that 'representation' should have occupied philosophers since ancient times. Nor is it surprising that representation–whether verbal, musical or visual–should have also elicited many attempts to differentiate between their forms and modes. Interestingly, though Aristotle viewed representation as an essential human activity for learning processes and a basic procedure of being in the world, Plato feared the illusions that representations create. Both agreed, however, that humans, unlike animals, are able to *create* and *manipulate* signs. (Plato clearly feared that representations might displace the "real things" he was after. See my introduction to Plato in section I). In retrospect it seems that both of them were right. Indeed, humans need signs whereby they organize the world and reality, while the "manipulations" of the signs deserve utmost attention *and* caution.

Language naturally looms large in the deliberations about representations, not least because they involve questions about the sorts of "agreements" whereby their understanding occurs. It has become clear over time that representations cannot be divorced from the cultures which produce them and the subject matters that restrict the kinds of representational signs they employ. Moreover, the need to express reality via representations also continued to produce throughout history new modes and forms, in line with changes that imposed new ways of "seeing" reality. Consequently, many of those codes and agreements that were informally arrived at were, likewise, subject to change. In short, representational relationships may be differently categorized since "meanings" are invariably fashioned by humans whose "scope" of understanding is impacted by social and cultural circumstances.

Given the diversity of modes of representation, and their altering forms, led to an interesting attempt to supersede these differences by an analysis of their structures. Surface characteristics, it was claimed, do not reveal that which they may hold in common, i.e. something that is more apt to disclose the systematic ordering activity of the mind. Yet, though the organization of the characteristics of different representations may disclose similar overall structures, they do not necessarily suggest a "systematic" mental activity, however interesting and helpful. In fact, the belief that human beings are *inherently* rational (a long held Western theoretical presupposition) and, as such, capable of arriving at some kind of objective reality, was clearly challenged–like much else–by the encounter with unfamiliar modes of thought displayed by nonwestern cultures. Nonetheless, it may be "reasonable" to assume that the number of possible structures is considerably smaller than the number of the features which they are likely to contain. It may be possible, hence, to examine the "placing," i.e. the position of each of the features that different modes of thought display via the structures which they employ.

Structural analyses, as is well known, became a popular research approach in a range of academic fields in the second half of the twentieth century. It had its origin in Ferdinand Saussure's general linguistic theory, which holds that language is a self-contained system of signs. Language, accordingly, may be analyzed as a formal system of differential elements *apart* from real-time production and comprehension. Languages, observed Saussure, seem to function in a similar way in that their "wholes" are greater than the sum of their parts. They have nonetheless *different* relational conceptions about their elements since the connotation of words are defined by comparing and contrasting their meanings to one another, highlighting their function rather than their inherent "qualities." The social nature of language, accordingly, provides a larger context for the analysis of its structures. The cultural theories of Claude Levi-Strauss–a highly influential cultural anthropologist–held that cultures, like languages, can be viewed as systems of signs and can be analyzed in terms of the structural relation among their elements. Central to his structuralism is the notion that binary opposition (for example: raw/cooked, female/male) reveal the unconscious logic or "grammar" of a system.

Structuralism, though applied in diverse sub-fields of language, culture and society, became most prominent in anthropology and literary studies. Indeed, it is easy to show how cultural anthropology and literary theory explored the meanings of social life, i.e. patterns of sociality and the underlying logic of social behavior and thought. In fact, cultural anthropologists are trained in the interpretations of narratives, rituals and a variety of symbolic behavior in relation to the context in which they are embedded. The notion that specific cultures or domains of culture might be better understood by means of their structures, distinct from the organization of ideas, seemed not only attractive and promising, but yielded important and interesting studies.

But how about areas of investigation whose structures are more readily perceived than the features which they contain? Must the "wholes" be grounded in the composition of the parts or, conversely, should the functions of the parts result from the peculiarity of the whole? Can one always eliminate the difference between structure and function, between the arrangement and the coherence of parts? A sound quality, for example, that is separated from the other ones has no real existence in music, since only the note as the embodiment of its features is concrete. Thus the concept of 'parameter' is tangential to accustomed musical categories–melody, rhythm and dynamics. Timbre, for example, is a sound quality not a parameter, since its variability depends on other parameters. In traditional music, a description of "interactions" is a retrospective procedure, an attempt to explain "complexes" that present themselves to our immediate perception as complete and un-dissected. The categories in music apparently constitute forms of contemplation that seem to regulate our perception. They do not merely present perceptual data, but "points of view," as it were, from which notes or groups of notes are to be brought together and related to each other. More can be said, and more has been said about 'structure' concerning music. I only wished to draw attention to the fact that however ingenious a new analytical theory might be, it requires utmost scrutiny once employed. Concerning music, at any rate, 'structure' seems more closely allied with the "genesis" of musical works i.e. their processes of production, whereas 'form' constitutes an aesthetic category which refers to their audible shape.

Aside from structuralism, the confused reader may rightly ask why I bother to sensitize him to "tools" we all use–aware or unaware–with a modicum of success. Indeed, what held true for 'ideas' holds equally true for those tools. We need to know where they come from and the ways in which they are employed in order to prevent misunderstandings. We have to be aware of the hazards entailed by these seeming "self-evident" tools once they are employed in scholarly work, *a fortiori* concerning interdisciplinary studies. This said, it must be clear that I do not expect the reader to become acquainted with the vast literature that deals with the subjects that I barely touch upon. Yet those who intend to partake in the *advancement* of knowledge must be mindful of the fact that what "looks alike" is not necessarily "the same."

The readings in this section make this abundantly clear. ▲ Panofsky's tracing of the "discourse" that provided the context for the rise of a *theory* of art, allows us to gain insight into deliberations that give rise to "viewpoints" and social action. ▲ Gombrich's focus on the problems entailed in the *making* and *perception* of art reveals that *expectations* may create *illusions* that mold what we see, i.e. that representations rely on "guided projection." ▲ Focusing on the "*politics*" of interpretations, Mitchell, unlike Gombrich, treats images as a kind of interaction between the object and the viewer who may transform the *meaning* of the picture. Although it is possible to differentiate between one medium and another, images, insists Mitchell, do not belong exclusively to any discipline. Their study, hence, enlists an interdisciplinary approach. ▲ Steeped in the philosophy of language and mathematics, Black calls our attention to the *imaginative* aspects that accompanies scientific thought. His explication of metaphors highlights the *creativity* involved in their communicative function and contribution to language and thought. ▲ Goodman's theory of knowledge makes no room for a separation between 'Art' and 'Science'–between "concreteness" and "abstraction"–since they are likewise dominated by specific characteristics of symbols. It is the "*denotations*" of the symbols that vary and undergo change. ▲ Tunstall's overview of structuralism presents in a concise and responsible way *the search* for a "formal system" that might unveil how humans "structure reality" apart from cultural diversity.

Erwin Panofsky
(1892-1968)

Introduction

Erwin Panofsky was an important art-historian, known primarily for his definition of modern 'iconography' and 'iconology'. These two concepts are most frequently associated with the matching of the subject matter of works of art to a symbolic syntax of meaning drown from literature and other sources of knowledge.

Born in Germany, Panofsky migrated to the United States following the rise of the Nazi regime. Prior to his arrival in the U.S., he studied philosophy, philology and art-history in various German universities. His interest in art-history became, however, increasingly pronounced over the years. His scientific investigations concerning art concentrated primarily on the circumstance and ideas that impact its diverse manifestations and development. At the University of Hamburg where he chaired the art-history department, he befriended Ernst Cassirer and Aby Warburg with whom he established an intimate intellectual relationship. Cassirer's philosophy of symbolic forms and Warburg's interest in "secret signs" and hermetic "images" have exerted considerable influence on Panofsky, who admired the knowledge and profoundness of his colleagues. The three also became active members of the famous research institute which Warburg helped to establish. The Warburg Institute, as is well known, produced over the years seminal studies that unveiled the important input of the hermetic tradition to the advancement of science and the arts.

Although already well-known in Germany, Panofsky accomplished his major scientific investigations in the decades he spent in America. He became particularly known, however, for his studies of symbols and iconography concerning works of art. The understanding of art, according to Panofsky, entails several levels: The first level is devoid of added cultural knowledge, like, for example, the portrayal of an angel addressing a young woman. The second level adds knowledge of the subject matter, e.g. the Annunciation. The third level attempts to understand the work as a product of its historical moment, i.e. of its immediate social and cultural environment. The last level tries to understand whereby one depiction of the annunciation differs from another. Answers, for example, to questions like "who commissioned the work" and "under what circumstance the work was established" may help to ascertain why certain aspects were "emphasized" and "in what way" in a given depiction of a well known subject. This last stage constitutes a synthesis, as it were, that enables the art-historian to unveil the *meaning* of the work, i.e. the uniqueness of the depiction. Panofsky's search of meaning was intrinsic to his understanding of art. He convincingly argued that ideas play a major role in the "imitations" of the world of perception. This, of course, includes the configurations of art and art theories; or conversely, the ideas that propel the arts are manifested as well in other domains of culture. Jointly, according to Panofsky, they reflect the social and cultural environment in which they are embedded.

Given Panofsky's immense erudition, he was fully aware of the fact that the definition and the conception of the term 'idea' underwent changes in the course of history. His meticulous scholarship, thus, invariantly took note of these changes. In fact, these very "turns of mind" constituted an integral part of his efforts to "contextualize" the subjects –the uniqueness of the depictions he was investigating–so as to grasp what they meant to their producers and respective audiences. Establishing the relation of art to artists, and artists to concurrent thought is well exemplified in his study *Gothic Architecture and Scholasticism*. While relations of this kind characterize all of Panofsky's explorations, I chose to mention the one concerning Gothic Architecture because the title, itself, conveys the affinity between art and thought.

In the introduction to this section of the book I argued that "context" is a factor one needs to reckon with since it invariably applies to a particular set of circumstances that influences its meaning. "Time and place," accordingly, dictate the *prism* through which ideas and concepts are perceived. Indeed, old ideas may be subsumed by new looks, and new looks may engender new ideas. The advancement of knowledge takes of course note of this ongoing process of "continuity and change;" it constitutes a significant part of its overall "checks and balances." With this in mind, it must be obvious that the intent of the following excerpt from *Idea: A concept in Art Theory* is not a round-about way to bring the reader closer to art, but to draw his attention to the notion of 'context' and its significance. Art theories, no less than styles, seem to undergo transformations impacted by "turns of mind" that yield new processes of conceptualization. Rather than include an essay about 'context', I chose to entrust Panofsky to show us how it actually works via a specific example of *"contextualization at work."* Indeed, Panofsky's tracing of the "turn of mind" in the Renaissance that gave birth to a theory of art, allows us to gain insight about other developments that have given rise to new ideas, which, in turn, gave rise to new theories that dictated and defined new beliefs and social activities.

PANOFSKY
Art Theory and Its Concepualization[*]

IN CONTRAST TO MEDIEVAL THOUGHT the theoretical and historical literature about the art of the Italian Renaissance emphasized, with an insistence and indefatigability perhaps understandable only from the attitudes discussed in the preceding chapter, that the task of art is the direct imitation of reality. To the modern reader it may seem somewhat strange that Cennino Cennini–whose treatise is otherwise deeply rooted in medieval workshop traditions–advised the artist who wants to depict a mountain landscape to take some rough rocks and copy them in appropriate size and lighting;[1] yet this prescription signifies the beginning of a new cultural epoch. When the painter was advised to use a natural model (even if so strangely chosen as here), art theory lifted from a thousand years of oblivion the notion–self-evident in classical antiquity, purged away by Neoplatonism, and hardly even considered in medieval thought–that the work of art is a faithful reproduction of reality. And not only did art theory lift this notion from oblivion; it consciously elevated it to the status of an artistic program. All this was something extraordinarily new.

From the very beginning the literature of the Renaissance took it for granted that the innovation and the glory of the great artists of the fourteenth and fifteenth centuries was to have called art, "antiquated and childishly deviating from the truth of nature"[2] and founded merely on a usage handed down by tradition,[3] back to "verisimilitude." When Leonardo da Vinci said that "that painting is most praiseworthy that has the most similarity to the thing reproduced, and I say this to refute such painters as want to improve upon the

[*] From his *Idea: A Concept in Art Theory,* trans. by Joseph J. S. Peake (New York, 1968), pp. 47-68 (Ch.4). Although I numbered Panofsky's footnotes, I decided to omit their texts. The texts include further quotations from the sources he cited and additional ones from other sources. The footnotes, more than they add to his main arguments, reveal his overwhelming erudition and meticulous scholarship. The numbering of the notes is for readers who which to explore certain points Panofsky saw fit to highlight.

things of nature,"[4] he expressed an opinion which for centuries no one would have dared contradict.

Parallel to this idea of "imitation," which included the requirement of formal and objective "correctness,"[5] art literature in the Renaissance placed the thought of "rising above nature," just as art literature had done in antiquity. On the one hand, nature could be overcome by the freely creative "phantasy" capable of altering appearances above and beyond the possibilities of natural variation and even of bringing forth completely novel creatures such as centaurs and chimeras. On the other hand, and more importantly, nature could be overcome by the artistic intellect, which–not so much by "inventing" as by selecting and improving–can, and accordingly should, make visible a beauty never completely realized in actuality. The constantly repeated admonitions to be faithful to nature are matched by the almost as forceful exhortations to choose the most beautiful from the multitude of natural objects,[6] to avoid the misshapen, particularly in regard to proportions,[7] and in general–here the notorious painter Demetrius is again a warning example–to strive for beauty above and beyond mere truth to nature. Let us listen to Leone Battista Alberti:

> And of all the parts [the painter should] not only render a true likeness but also add beauty to them; for in painting, loveliness is not so much pleasing as it is required. Demetrius, the ancient painter, failed to gain the highest praise because he strove to make things similar to nature rather than lovely.

> For this it will help to take from all beautiful bodies each praiseworthy part, and one must always exert himself with study and skill to learn great loveliness; this may well be difficult, for perfect beauty is not in one body alone, but [beautiful parts] are dispersed and rare in rnany bodies, yet one must give all his labor to investigate and learn it. It will happen that one who is accustomed to aim at and undertake great things will be easily capable of lesser things. And nothing is so difficult that it cannot be mastered by study and application.[8]

With the same enthusiasm with which the anecdotes of the sparrows and the horses were circulated and occasionally supplemented by "well-authenticated" examples from recent times[9] there was repeated—and even more often—that other anecdote about Zeuxis's selective rendering of the Crotonian maidens. This anecdote even Ariosto did not spare his readers.[10]

Thus the Renaissance, at first seeing no contradiction therein, demanded of its works of art truth to nature and beauty at the same time, just as antiquity had done (the idea of *imitatio* is, after all, just as much an inheritance from antiquity as is the idea of *electio*). In fact, from the standpoint of the Renaissance both of these demands, incompatible only in later times, seemed like the parts of a single postulate: the demand that the artist confront reality anew in each work of art, be it as corrector or imitator.[11] Warnings against "imitation" of other masters are characteristic of the Renaissance,[12] but they were not as yet voiced because such imitation would reveal the imitator's poverty of ideas; this could not become important until "idea" had become the central concept of art theory.[13] Rather those warnings were given quite simply because nature is infinitely richer than the works of painters, so that he who imitates other painters' works would lower himself to being the grandchild of nature, when he was capable of being her son.[14]

Birth of an Actual "Art Theory"

Now this double demand, to face reality directly—imitating and nevertheless improving upon it—would have been impossible to fulfill during this epoch if the expressly rejected workshop tradition,[15] which, as it were, spared the artist the necessity of finding his own terms for dealing with nature, had not been replaced by something completely different which made this "coming to terms with nature" possible. The artist was rather like someone driven out of a confined, but protected, residential area into a vast and still uncharted countryside, and there arose, and was bound to arise, that discipline that today is customarily called art theory. In many respects it was built upon antique foundations, but on the whole it is specifically modern. It differs from the earlier literature of art by no longer answering the question "how to do it?" but the quite different and thoroughly unmedieval question "what abilities and, above all, what kind of knowledge enable the artist to confront nature with confidence whenever he is required to do so?"

In its attitude toward art the Renaissance thus differed fundamentally from the Middle Ages in that it removed the object from the inner world of the artist's imagination and placed it firmly in the "outer world." This was accomplished by laying a distance between "subject" and "object" much as in artistic practice perspective placed a distance between the eye and the world of things–a distance which at the same time objectifies the "object" and personalizes the "subject." [16]

One would think that this basically novel attitude would immediately raise the problem that until this day has been the focus of scientific thought about art: the problem of the relationships between "I" and the world, spontaneity and receptivity, given material and active forming power–in short, the problem which for the sake of brevity may be called the "subject-object problem." But the opposite is the case. The purpose of art theory as it was developed in the fifteenth century was primarily practical, only secondarily historical and apologetic, and in no way speculative. That is, it aimed at nothing more than, on the one hand, to legitimize contemporary art as the genuine heir of Greco-Roman antiquity and to wrest a place for it among the *artes liberales* by enumerating its dignity and merits; and, on the other hand, to provide artists with firm and scientifically grounded rules for their creative activity. This second and most important goal, however, could be reached only on the presupposition (quite universally recognized) that above the "subject" as well as above the "object" there exists a system of universal and unconditionally valid laws from which the artistic rules are to be derived, and that the understanding of these laws was the specifically "art-theoretical" task.

As naïvely as this new discipline posed the two demands of correctness and beauty as naïvely did it believe in its ability to pave and indicate the way to their fulfillment. Formal and objective correctness seemed to be guaranteed if the artist observed, on the one hand, the laws of perspective and, on the other, the laws of anatomy, of the doctrine of psychological and physiological movements, and of physiognomy. He would achieve beauty if he chose a *bella invenzione,* [17] avoided "indecorousness" and "contradictions," and lent to the appearance that harmony that was considered to be a rationally ascertainable *concinnitas* (concinnity) of colors[18] qualities, and especially proportions. The doctrine of proportion[19] raised the questions of how to ascertain what is harmonious and therefore pleasing, and what constitutes the basis of this pleasingness. The answers, however they might be expressed in an individual case, all agreed that in any event the subjective and individual judgment of the artist does not suffice to legitimize good proportions as "good": if the authors didn't refer to the basic laws of either mathematics or music (which for that time meant almost the same thing), they appealed to the utterances of venerable authorities or to the testimony of antique statues.[20] And even scholars critical or sceptical in this respect, such as Alberti or Leonardo, tried at least to abstract a kind of norm from material sifted by the judgment of public opinion or by the opinion[21] of "experts[22]" and to contrast this norm with judgments based merely on individual taste.

Un-Platonic Orientation of Real Art Theory in the Early Renaissance

Medieval thought saw no problem in artistic creativity, because basically it denied the "subject" as well as the "object": art was nothing more than the materialization of a form that neither depended upon the appearance of a real "object" nor was called into being by the activity of a living "subject"; rather this form pre-existed as a *vorgêndes bilde* (antecedent image) in the mind of the artist.[23] Neither could this problem become apparent to Renaissance thinkers, since they considered the nature and behavior of the "subject" as well as the "object" to be determined by definite rules either valid *a priori* or demonstrable empirically. This explains the peculiar fact that the discipline of art theory, newly arisen in the fifteenth century, was at first almost completely independent of the revival of Neoplatonic philosophy taking place at the same time and within the same Florentine cultural circle. For this metaphysical, even mystical, philosophy that conceived of Plato not as a critical philosopher but as a cosmologist and theologian, that never even sought to distinguish between Platonism and Neoplatonism,[24] that attempted a magnificent combination of the Platonic and the Plotinian, of late Greek cosmology and Christian mysticism, of Homeric myth and Jewish cabala, of Arabic natural science and medieval Scholasticism–such a philosophy could give the most manifold stimulation to a speculative theory *about* art (and, as we will see, later did just that); but it could not be of any essential value for a practical and rationalistically oriented theory *for* art such as the Early Renaissance required and devised.

This kind of art theory was not as yet ready for thoughts such as those that Marsilio Ficino read out of Plotinus and the Pseudo-Dionysius and into Plato. Because of its naturalistic orientation it would have been forced to reject a theory according to which the human soul contains a notion of the perfect man, lion, or horse impressed upon it by the divine mind and according to which it is by this notion that the soul judges the products of nature.[25] The prosaically logical enumeration of the "seven possibilities of motion"[26] in such an art theory had little in common with the mystical doctrine of Neoplatonism, for which straight motion signified the divine initiative, oblique motion the continuity of divine creation, and circular motion the divine identity with itself.[27]

Beauty as Symmetry

At one time Ficino defined beauty, in close accord with Plotinus, as a "clearer similarity of the bodies with the Ideas" or as a "victory of divine reason over matter."[28] At another time he designated it, more nearly approaching Christian Neoplatonism, as a "radiance from the face of God" that first enlightens the angels, then illumines the human soul, and finally the world of corporeal matter.[29] Alberti, fully agreeing with his fellow theorists and predetermining the position of art theory for more than a century, opposed to this metaphysical interpretation of beauty the purely phenomenal definition of the Greek classic age:

> . . . thus we may say that beauty is a certain agreement and
> harmony of parts within that to which they belong, with regard to
> a definite number, proportionality, and order, such as concinnity
> (i.e., the absolute and primary law of nature) demands.[30]

An even clearer formulation: "First one must observe that the single members fit together well, and they will fit together well if in relation to size and measure, character, color, and other similar things they harmonize and form one unified beauty."[31] Harmony of proportions and harmony of colors and qualities–this is what Alberti and other art theorists in the Early Renaissance understood to be the nature of beauty. Precisely that definition of beauty to which Plotinus had vigorously objected, because it seized only the external characteristics of appearance but not the inner essence and meaning of beauty, was helped by Alberti to a long-lasting victory: "(the) proportion of the parts to one another and to the whole, with the addition of a pleasant hue." This definition is important just because it renounces any metaphysical explanation of the beautiful, so that its acceptance loosened for the first time the ancient bond between the *pulchrum* (the beautiful) and the *bonum* (the good), even though this was done, at the beginning, less by expressly denying such a bond as by silently suppressing it. The autonomy of the aesthetic experience, which would not be theoretically proved for more than three centuries but which in the interim, as we will see, was quite often in question again, was recognized *de facto* even if not as yet *de jure*.

Thus one may maintain that Early Renaissance art theory in Italy was hardly affected by the revival of Neoplatonism.[32] Art theorists were able to gain access to Euclid, Vitruvius, and Alhazen, on the one side, and to Quintilian and Cicero, on the other; but they could not gain access to Plotinus or Plato, whom Alberti still referred to only as a painter.[33] In fact, Plato's influence became effective on a larger scale for the first time in the *Divina proporzione* (1509) by Luca Pacioli, who was not so much an art theorist in the strict sense of the term as a mathematician and cosmologist.[34]

In only one respect does the Platonic revival seem to have influenced art theory from the beginning: at first only in isolated cases and in relatively unimportant places, but gradually more often and with greater emphasis, one encounters the concept of the artistic "Idea." But perhaps nothing so clearly illuminates the depth of the essential difference between the original premise of art theory and the original premise of Platonism as the fact that it was possible to connect the theory of Ideas with art theory only by sacrificing certain aspects of either the one or the other, and in most cases of both. The more influence the Idea concept had and the closer it approached its inherent (i.e., metaphysical) meaning (which first happened in the so-called "mannerist" period), the further art theory retreated from its originally practical goals and its originally unproblematical premises. And vice versa, the stronger art theory adhered to these practical goals and unproblematical premises (as was true during the actual Renaissance and then again during the period of "classicism"), the more the Idea concept forfeited its original metaphysical, or at least *a priori*, validity.

Ficino

According to the view of the *Academia Platonica,* as conclusively formulated by Marsilio Ficino, the Ideas are metaphysical realities. They exist as "true substances," while earthly things are only *imagines* of them (i.e., of the essences having real being);[35] and aside from their substantiality Ideas were regarded as "simple, immovable, and without conflicting admixtures."[36] They are immanent in the mind of God (also occasionally in the mind of the angels),[37] and in accordance with Plotinus and the patristic writers they were called *exempla rerum in mente divina.* The human consciousness is capable of cognition only because "impressions" (Latin: *formulae)* of the Ideas are inherent to the human soul from its supraterrestrial pre-existence.[38] Like unto "sparks from the divine primordial light," these impressions "are almost extinguished" as a result of long inactivity, but they can be revived by "instruction" and can be caused to flash up again in the light of the Ideas "as the visual rays are by starlight":

> Finally he [Plato] adds that in the mind thus affected the light of truth is lit not slowly in the manner of human love, but suddenly. But from where? From the fire, i.e. from God which shoots forth and emits sparks. By sparks he designates the Ideas. . . and he also thus designates the impressions *[formulas]* of these Ideas innate in us, which, formerly benumbed by lack of use, are rekindled by the breeze of teaching, and they are brightened by the Ideas just as the rays emitted by the eyes [are] by starlight.[39]

What was true of cognition in general was true (and to an even higher degree) of the cognition of beauty in particular. The Idea of the beautiful is also impressed in our minds as a *formula,* and only by means of this inborn notion are we–that is, what is most spiritual in us–able to perceive visible beauty, since we relate it to an invisible beauty and enjoy the triumph of the *Eidos* over matter thus revealed to our eyes. That earthly object is beautiful that most nearly agrees with the Idea of beauty (and at the same time with its own Idea), and we perceive this agreement by referring the sensory appearance back to its *formula* preserved within us.[40]

Alberti

Leone Battista Alberti assigned a completely different ethos to the Idea concept. In the middle of discussing the postulate of beauty, following the censure of the ancient realist Demetrius and immediately before the unavoidable story of Zeuxis and the Crotonian maidens, there appears, as though a warning against the other extreme, a sharp attack against those who believe that they can produce something beautiful without any study of nature:

> But in order not to lose time and effort, one should avoid the custom of some fools who, boasting their own talent, seek to win a painter's fame by their own resources alone, completely without a natural model which they would follow with eye and mind. These never learn to paint well, but they habituate themselves to their own errors. *That idea of beauty, which even the most experienced mind can hardly perceive, escapes the inexperienced one.*

> Zeuxis, a most excellent . . . painter, when he was going to make a painting to set up in public in the Temple of Lucina among the Crotonians, did not trust foolishly his own native talent, as every painter does today; but because he did not think he could find in a single body all the beauties he sought. . .[41]

"That idea of beauty, which even the most experienced mind can hardly perceive, escapes the inexperienced one." Without doubt this statement proves that Alberti, too, was affected in some way by the Platonic movement, since the notion of an *idea delle bellezze* (idea of the beauties) that appears to the mental eye of the painter or sculptor is utterly unmedieval. Yet it is understandable that those who see Alberti as a real "Neoplatonist" unanimously pass over this statement in silence. For the same Idea concept which Cicero and Plotinus used to demonstrate the unlimited power of artistic genius and its essential independence from any external experience, serves here to warn this artistic genius against overvaluing itself and to call it back to the contemplation of nature. "The idea of beauty, which even the most experienced mind can hardly perceive, escapes the inexperienced one." This means nothing else than that Renaissance theory, neither willing nor able to sacrifice its hard-won realistic creed to the Idea concept, had now altered this concept to such an extent that it could be reconciled with that realistic creed and could even be used to support it. Petrarch, a premature but genuine Neoplatonist, understood the ability to visualize beauty by means of color and line only in terms of a divine vision;[42]Alberti believed that the mental ability to perceive beauty could be attained only by experience and practice. And in fact, even though Cennini[43] and after him Leonardo[44] granted the artist the ability to emancipate himself from reality by varying and inventing, no Renaissance thinker would have dared to consider beauty the child of "phantasy," as Dion and Cicero had done.

Significantly it was a rather long time before Italian art theorists gave greater importance to the concept of Idea–and even longer before they became fully aware of the consequences. Alberti made only that one rather parenthetical statement about it. Leonardo, so far as I know, never used the term "idea" at all. And it is not uncharacteristic of the High Renaissance attitude to art that Castiglione, who in his *Cortigiano* defines and celebrates love in a thoroughly Platonic panegyric, bases the judgment of art on no other criterion than that of adequate imitation.[45]

Raphael

Only Raphael, in his world-famous letter to Castiglione written in 1516, took up the Idea concept; but he spoke his mind even less than Alberti had done about how we are to understand the relationship between "idea" and "experience." Indeed he expressly refused to discuss this question. He says in the letter: "in order to paint a beautiful woman I should have to see many beautiful women, and this under the condition that you were to help me with making a choice; but since there are so few beautiful women and so few sound judges, I make use of a certain idea that comes into my head. Whether it has any artistic value I am unable to say; I try very hard just to have it [the idea]."[46] These wonderful sentences, gracefully hiding artistic conviction behind a compliment to the great connoisseur of women, should not be subjected to the acid test of epistemological criticism. They prove that, on the one hand, Raphael was aware that he could form the image of perfect femininity only from an "inner notion" no longer dependent on the concrete single object, but that, on the other, he ascribed to this inner notion neither a normative validity nor a metaphysical origin. In fact, he could designate its nature only with the expression *certa idea*. Somehow it came into his mind, but whether it was of any value or correctness, he didn't know and did not care to know. If he had been asked whence it came to him, he probably would not have denied that the sum of sensory experiences had in some way been transformed into an inner mental image, in a similar way as Dürer spoke of a *versammlet heimlichen Schatz des Herzen* (secret collected treasure of the heart) which comes into existence only if the artist has *durch viel Abmachens sein Gemüt voll gefasst* (through much sorting-out filled his mind) and out of whose fullness he can create in his heart a *neue Kreatur in der Gestalt eins Dings* (new being- in the shape of a thing).[47] But Raphael's final answer would have been: *Io non so* (I don't know).

Vasari

Vasari, influenced to a certain extent by the new Mannerist theory of art though on the whole rather retrospective in his art-theoretical attitude, expressed himself somewhat more fully in the second edition of his *Lives*. He still did not go beyond stating the situation and refrained from providing a philosophic analysis of this situation as well as from drawing theoretical conclusions therefrom.[48] Alberti–for Raphael, we recall, did not commit himself with regard to this question—had thought that the *idea delle bellezze,* which for him had still preserved something of its metaphysical nimbus, was dependent on "experience"; but he had not as yet said that it originated in "experience." He thought that it abides in a mind familiar with nature in preference to a mind that dispenses with concrete observation; but this does not mean that it is, to use Kant's terminology, "abstracted" from natural objects. Vasari said:

> Design, the father of our three arts[49] ... derives a general judgment from many things: a form or idea of all the things in nature, as it were, which in its proportions is exceedingly regular. So it is that design recognizes, not only in human and animal bodies but also in plants, buildings, sculptures, and paintings, the proportion of the whole in relation to its parts as well as the proportion of the parts to one another and to the whole. And since from this recognition there arises a certain judgment, that forms in the mind the thing which later, formed by the hand, is called a design, one may conclude that this design is nothing but a visual expression and clarification of that concept which one has in the intellect, and that which one imagines in the mind and builds up in the idea....[50]

This says, then, that the Idea not just presupposes but actually originates in experience; not only can the idea be readily combined with observation of reality, it *is* observation of reality, only clarified and made more universally valid by the mental act of choosing the individual from the many and then combining the individual choices into a new whole. This interpretation amounts to a redefinition of "idea" both according to its nature—which presupposes and proves a complete misunderstanding of the Platonic, let alone the Plotinian, theory of Ideas[51]—and also according to its function. Since an idea is no longer present *a priori* in the mind of the artist (i.e., it does not precede experience) but is brought forth by him *a posteriori* (i.e., it is engendered on the basis of experience), its role is no longer that of a competitor with, much less that of an archetype for, the reality perceived by the senses, but rather that of a derivative of reality. For the same reasons an idea functions no longer as the given content or even as the transcendent object of human cognition, but as its product. This change is clearly recognizable even in purely semantic terms. From now on an idea no longer "dwells" or "pre-exists" in the soul of the artist, as Cicero[52] and Thomas Aquinas[53] had put it, and still less is it "innate" to him, as genuine Neoplatonism had expressed it.[54] Rather "it comes into his mind,"[55] "arises,"[56] is "derived" from reality,[57] "acquired,"[58] nay, "formed and sculpted."[59] In the middle of the sixteenth century it even became customary to designate not only the content of artistic imagination but also the capacity for artistic imagination with the expression "idea," so that the term approximated the word *imagizione*.[60] Thus Vasari could say in the passage just quoted: *concetto che si ha fabbricato nell' idea* (concept which one builds up in the idea);[61] and elsewhere we encounter such phrases as: *le cose immaginate nell' Idea* (the things imagined in the idea),[62] *quella forma di corpo, che nell' Idea mi sono stabilita* (that form of body, which has been stabilized for me in the idea)[63] *quella forma di corpo, che nell' Idea della artefice e disegnata* (that form of body which is inscribed in the Idea of the artifact)[64], etc.

Redefinition of Idea in High Renaissance Art Theory

It is clear from what has been said that the "subject-object problem" was now ripe for a basic clarification. For as soon as the "subject" is given the task of obtaining the laws of artistic production from reality by his own effort instead of being allowed to presuppose them above reality (and above himself), there necessarily arises the question of when and for what reasons he is justified in claiming to have these laws correct. Yet–and this is particularly significant–it was only the definitely "Mannerist" school of thought which first achieved a basic clarification of this problem, or at least consciously demanded it.

Renaissance thinkers could consider the "subject-object problem" to have been solved (by their modified theory of Ideas itself) even before it had been expressly stated. Since an "idea" engendered in the artist's mind and revealed in his design did not really originate within the artist himself but was taken from nature by way of a *giudizio universale* (universal judgment), the idea, even if actually recognized and realized by the "subject," seemed potentially prefigured in the "objects." Characteristically, Vasari based the possibility of arriving at an Idea on the reasoning that, because nature itself is so regular and consistent in its formations, one can recognize the whole of a thing in a single part of it *(ex ungue leonem)*, This thought was not formulated in the Renaissance, as it was later,[65] nor was it necessary to do so. It seemed self-evident that the Idea, obtained by the artist from observation, at the same time revealed the actual purposes of nature "creating according to laws"–that "subject" and "object," mind and nature, did not stand in hostile or even opposite relation to each other but that the Idea, itself derived from experience, necessarily corresponded to experience, supplementing or even replacing it. Thus Raphael could say of himself exactly as the classicistically oriented Guido Reni did a century later[66]–that because he lacked sufficiently beautiful models, he made use of a *certa idea.* And thus a later Spaniard, though thoroughly imbued with the spirit of classicism, could formulate the peculiar relationship of mutual supplementation between viewing nature and forming Ideas by stating that the good painter must "adjust" or "correct" his inner notions by observing nature, but that where this observation is lacking, he may make use of the "beautiful Ideas that he has acquired": "For perfection consists in passing from the Ideas to the natural model and from the natural model to the Ideas."[67]

In the High Renaissance, then, the art-theoretical doctrine of Ideas, insofar as it is concerned with the problem of beauty (and in being so concerned it essentially differs from the medieval doctrine of Ideas), seems almost like a more spiritualized form of the old selection theory–spiritualized in the sense that beauty is achieved not by an external combination of separate parts but by an inner vision that combines individual experiences into a new whole.[68] The classical thinkers themselves, even though the selection theory was a commonplace to them, had not identified the "Idea" with the *paradeigma* obtained by choosing from among the most beautiful things. They had conceived of Idea not as a compromise between the mind and nature but as that which guarantees the mind's independence of nature. But Renaissance thinkers understood the Idea concept in the light of a fundamentally novel attitude toward art which identified the world of ideas with a world of heightened realities. Even though this thought was not explicitly formulated before the rise of seventeenth-century classicism,[69] the concept of the "Idea" was already transformed into the concept of the "ideal" *(le beau idéal)* during the Renaissance. This stripped the Idea of its metaphysical nobility but at the same time brought it into a beautiful and almost organic conformity with nature: an Idea which is produced by the human mind but, far from being subjective and arbitrary, at the same time expresses the laws of nature embodied in each object, achieves basically the same thing by intuitive synthesis that Alberti, Leonardo, and Dürer had tried to achieve by discursive synthesis when they summarized and systematized a rich material, gained by observation and approved by expert judgment, into a theory of proportion: the perfection of the "natural" by means of art.

Vasari, in the passage quoted above, answered not so much the question of whether it is possible to realize beauty as the question of whether artistic representation as such is possible: the question of *disegno.* In the philosophy of the High Middle Ages, marked as it was by Aristotelianism, the term "idea"–or, more exactly, "quasi-idea"–was not connected with the concept of *idea della bellezza* (which was first revived in Renaissance Platonism and later developed into the "ideal") but with "artistic conception pure and simple," no matter whether the content of this conception be "beautiful" or "unbeautiful." It is clear that Renaissance thinkers found themselves unable to abandon this wider meaning of "idea"; that is, they subsequently used the expression "idea" in about the same sense as *pensiero* ("thought") or *concetto* ("concept"). But it is also clear that they had to redefine "artistic conception pure and simple" as something no less functional and *a posteriori* than the "idea of beauty" in the narrower sense. What seemed to enable the artist to "devise" or "design" any work of art was the same *giudizio universale* that enabled him to visualize beauty (or, conversely, ugliness).[70] The possibility, guaranteed by the Idea, of *"enhancing* a form that originates in the observation of nature and yet surpasses the actual natural objects," corresponded to the possibility of *conceiving* a form that likewise originates in the observation of nature and yet is independent thereof.

The expression "idea," then, even if we disregard the loose usage according to which it could mean imaginative ability or power of conception (that is, not *forma* or *conceptus* but *mens* or *imaginatio),* had two essentially different art-theoretical meanings in the sixteenth century:

(1) As Alberti and Raphael used the word, "idea" meant the mental image of a beauty that surpasses nature, that is, about the same thing that "the ideal" was to denote at a later time.

(2) As Vasari and others used it, "idea" meant any image conceived in the artist's mind, that is, about the same thing as the expressions *pensiero* and *concetto,* which had been so used as early as the thirteenth and fourteenth centuries.[71] In this sense, which even came to be predominant in the late sixteenth century but tended to disappear in the seventeenth when the concept of "the ideal" was explicitly formulated, the expression "idea" designates every notion that, conceived in the artist's mind, precedes the actual depiction.[72] It can even designate what we customarily call "subject" or "theme."[73]

Often these two meanings were not kept clearly separated. And they could not be, since the second, as the broader of the two, could include the first one under given circumstances; it is for this reason that occasionally an adjective like *bella* or *hermosa* was added to the word "idea" when the word is used in the sense of definition number one.[74] Ultimately, after all, the two definitions agree in that in both spheres–in the realization of beauty as well as in artistic representation as such–the relationship between subject and object is essentially analogous.

Insofar as the formation of ideas was connected in Renaissance art theory with observation of nature, it was placed into a realm that, while not yet that of individual psychology, was nevertheless no longer that of metaphysics. This was the first step toward recognizing that which today is called "genius." Early Renaissance thought had already presupposed an actual artistic "subject" as the counterpart of an actual artistic "object," just as the visible "thing" and the perceiving "eye" had been posited simultaneously by the discovery of central perspective. But as we have seen, laws were also believed to exist that, equally suprasubjective and supraobjective, seemed able to regulate the creative process almost as if handed down by a higher court. The acknowledgement of such suprasubjective and supraobjective rules was in basic contradiction to the notion of a creative artist freely following his own genius, and therefore their validity was gradually limited by the concept of the artistic Idea. It was assumed that the artistic mind was able intuitively to transform reality into an Idea, to effect an autonomous synthesis of the objective data, and such a mind no longer needed such regulations, valid *a priori* or empirically confirmed, as mathematical laws, the concurrence of public opinion, and the testimonials of ancient writers. Rather the artist's privilege and obligation is to acquire by his own efforts the *perfetta cognizione dell' obietto intelligibile* ("the perfect awareness of the intelligibility of the object"), as "idea" was described from this time on in the sixteenth and seventeenth centuries.[75] Giordano Bruno's almost Kantian statement according to which only the artist creates rules and true rules exist only insofar and only in such number as there are true artists,[76] can be wholly understood only in connection with the theory of ideas. But– and this is the important point–the Renaissance proper no more arrived at this explicit, almost polemical emphasis on artistic genius than it did at an express formulation of the concept of "the ideal." It knew no more of a conflict between genius and rule than of a conflict between genius and nature; and the compatibility of these two opposites, not as yet set apart from each other, was clearly expressed by the concept of Idea as reinterpreted in the Renaissance: this concept secured freedom to the artistic mind and at the same time limited this freedom vis-à-vis the claims of reality.

E. H. Gombrich

(1909-2001)

Introduction

Like other acknowledged domains whose development can be traced, Art has produced a goodly number of outstanding historians. Gombrich is undeniably one of them. Like his colleagues, he, too, took special note of the changes that artistic styles undergo. Though fully aware of the social transformations and the collective attitudes that impact art and aesthetic desiderata, Gombrich was primarily interested in what can be learned from the historical development of art that goes beyond art. Art, he believed, may unveil something about our mental makeup that, to begin with, *enables* visual representations and the comprehension of their displayed images. The production and consumption of art clearly involve some kind of interrelationship between visual representations and visual perception. Visual representations, Gombrich tells us, involve fundamental mental processes which art had to grapple with in its various attempts to achieve both perceptibility and comprehension. The history of art, accordingly, tells an interesting story about the ways in which artists went about to solve this fundamental problem—an issue they could hardly ignore. Indeed, if it is true that "artists learned more from artists than from nature," it is largely due to the "problems" they managed to solve.

Born in Vienna into an assimilated Jewish bourgeois family, Gombrich enjoyed a solid classical education and a keen interest in science. His family was part of a social and intellectual milieu whose members included some of the most famous artists, playwrights and thinkers of the time. His father was a lawyer—a former classmate of Hugo von Hofmannsthal—and his pianist mother had been a pupil of Anton Bruckner. The circle included not only famous composers like Brahms and Mahler, but also innovators like Schoenberg and Freud.

Before coming to Britain (1936), where he remained for the rest of his life, Gombrich had studied art history at the University of Vienna where he became familiar with the entire range of Western and ancient art, including the written sources related to the field. In England he started as a research assistant at the Warburg Institute which had migrated from Hamburg to London. During World War II Gombrich was employed by the BBC World Service to monitor German radio broadcasts. As we shall see from the following excerpt from his *Art and Illusion*, the monitoring experience of these radio broadcasts provided Gombrich with some basic insights about the relationship between *anticipation* and *projection*. After the war he returned to the institute, which was to become the center of his activities. From the position of a Research Fellow in 1946, he rose to the position of the director of the institute in 1959. By then, he had already accomplished many research projects that were highly acclaimed. His work was recognized by numerous academies of science, many institutions of higher learning, and he was the recipient of honors, titles and prizes.

An examination of Gombrich's magisterial output readily reveals that he was much less interested in making historical "discoveries" than in the *analyses* of the "problems" which art history involved. Like his friend Karl Popper,[1] Gombrich saw art history as posing problems that required rigorous investigations. He wished to sensitize us to scientific questions that were raised by the very making and perception of art. In fact, his most widely-read book *The Story of Art*–originally meant for teen-agers–does not discuss artistic change in terms of style, but emphasizes the practical problems that artists faced and the means they adopted to solve them. It is due to its novel approach and the insights which this introductory book displayed that art departments, the world over, decided to adopt it as a basic textbook. Though Gombrich invariably deals with complicated issues, it is important to note that his writing is at all times lucid and comprehensible. He always *teaches* while informing; he *explains* while revealing;

[1] Born in Austria, Karl Popper (1902–1994) belongs to a generation of émigré scholars that profoundly influenced thought in the English speaking countries. His greatest contributions are in the philosophy of science and in political and social philosophy. Gombrich's father served his law apprenticeship with Popper's father. The sons reunited in England and Gombrich helped Popper in finding a publisher for his famous book *The Open Society and its Enemies*.

he evokes the curiosity of the reader in "problems" he never entertained and invites him to *witness*, as it were, the solution of intricate "puzzles."

Among Gombrich's influential works, *Art and Illusion* (1960) is considered by art critics and by scientists, who explore various brain processes, as his most far-reaching work. In this book Gombrich grapples with the enigmatic subject of *illusion*, progressively unveiling the psychological factors that partake in visual perception. He examines the history of visual representations, accordingly, as a unique route of "experimentation"–experiments undertaken by artists in their desire to depict the visual world persuasively. While examining the ways in which artists solved the problems they faced, Gombrich provides a host of original ideas by way of explanations. His insightful ideas impacted many subsequent investigations of 'illusion' and related subjects.

In *Art and Illusion* Gombrich gave us a way of looking into the invisible realm of the mind. Gombrich believed that to describe reality artists invariably need a medium and a schema–a "vocabulary" which can be modified. Since the perception of symbolic materials depend on effective communication, artists do not examine the nature of the physical world, but the nature of our reactions to it. This explains why artists have learned throughout history more from artists than from nature, they took note of the "inventions" of their predecessors, rather than making direct observations of the physical world. The history of art, accordingly, is the history of artists whose admirable endeavors not only enhanced our lives, but also revealed that the distinction between perception and illusion is far from rigid. Through seeking a meeting ground between science and the humanities, Gombrich's investigation of the history of art in fact sensitized cognitive scientists to the notion that all representation may rely, in one way or another, on "guided projection" and that expectations may create "illusions," i.e. they may mold what we see.

This said, it must be clear that the issues discussed above do not replace the influences which social changes exert on styles. The interrelationship between visual representation and perception is fundamental, independent of styles of whatever kind. It must also be clear that unveiling the social factors that impact styles does not solve the problem posed by interpretation. Attempts to describe the relationship between the *conceptions* of artistic works and their *interpretations* seem burdened by the difficulty of establishing unequivocally which aspects of the conception are supposed to be comprehended in the first place and who determines which features and facts are aesthetically constitutive. Having abandoned the long-held conviction that the artist's intention is the decisive factor for the understanding of his work, a reception "perspective" ensued that could not escape the demands of resolving the "meaning" of works into innumerable modes of interpretation, without laying down certain forms of conception as adequate and rejecting others as inadequate. Indeed, the naïve concept of reality has by now been displaced by a skepticism that spread from philosophy to infect the public in general. In short, reality is no longer treated as a "given," but as the composite of a relationship between the materials received by the senses and the categorical forms contributed by the perceiving consciousness. We need to remember, however, that "interpretations" are nonetheless constrained, since in the advancement of knowledge persuasive evidence *must* be brought to bear on claims, regardless of their nature.

GOMBRICH

from Conditions of Illusion[*]

The mind, having received of sense a small beginning of remembrance, runneth on infinitely, remembering all what is to be remembered. Our senses therefore, which stand as it were at the entry of the mind, having received the beginning of anything, and having proffered it to the mind; the mind likewise receiveth this beginning and goeth over all what followeth: the lower part of a long and slender pike being but slightly shaken, the motion runneth thorough the whole length of the pike, even to the speares-head . . . so does our mind need but a small beginning to the remembrance of the whole matter.

After MAXIMUS TYRIUS as in FRANCISCUS JUNIUS, *The Painting* of *the Ancients*

I

THE EXAMPLES in the last chapter have confirmed the ideas which Philostratus attributes to his hero Apollonius of Tyana, the idea that "those who look at works of painting and drawing must have the imitative faculty" and that "no one could understand the painted horse or bull unless he knew what such creatures are like." All representation relies to some extent on what we have called "guided projection." When we say that the blots and brushstrokes of the impressionist landscapes "suddenly come to life," we mean we have been led to project a landscape into these dabs of pigment.

Psychologists class the problem of picture reading with what they call "the perception of symbolic material." It is a problem which has engaged the attention

---

[*] From: E.H.Gombrich: *Art and Illusion: A Study in the Psychology of Pictorial Representation* (Princeton, 1972), chap. VII, pp.203-211; 222-231.

of all who investigate effective communication, the reading of texts or displays or the hearing of signals. The basic facts were described by William James with his usual lucidity in his *Talks to Teachers* before the turn of the century:

"When we listen to a person speaking or read a page of print, much of what we think we see or hear is supplied from our memory. We overlook misprints, imagining the right letters, though we see the wrong ones; and how little we actually hear when we listen to speech, we realize when we go to a foreign theatre; for there what troubles us is not so much that we cannot understand what the actors say as that we cannot hear their words. The fact is that we hear quite as little under similar conditions at home, only our mind, being fuller of English verbal associations, supplies the requisite material for comprehension upon a much slighter auditory hint."

It so happens I had an opportunity to study this aspect of perception in a severely practical context during the war. I was employed for six years by the British Broadcasting Corporation in their "Monitoring Service," or listening post, where we kept constant watch on radio transmissions from friend and foe. It was in this context that the importance of guided projection in our understanding of symbolic material was brought home to me. Some of the transmissions which interested us most were often barely audible, and it became quite an art, or even a sport, to interpret the few whiffs of speech sound that were all we really had on the wax cylinders on which these broadcasts had been recorded. It was then we learned to what an extent our knowledge and expectations influence our hearing. You had to know what might be said in order to hear what was said. More exactly, you selected from your knowledge of possibilities certain word combinations and tried projecting them into the noises heard. The problem then was a twofold one–to think of possibilities and to retain one's critical faculty. Anyone whose imagination ran away with him, who could hear any words–as Leonardo could in the sound of bells– could not play that game. You had to keep your projection flexible, to remain willing to tryout fresh alternatives, and to admit the possibility of defeat. For this was the most striking experience of all: once your expectation was firmly set and your conviction settled, you ceased to be aware of your own activity, the noises appeared to fall into place and to be transformed into the expected words. So strong was this effect of suggestion that we made it a practice never to tell a colleague our own interpretation if we wanted him to test it. Expectation created illusion.

While I was struggling with these practical tasks, I did not know that these problems of transmission and reception of communication–terms such as "message" and "noise"–were destined to become a most important, not to say fashionable, field of study under the name of "Information Theory." The technical and mathematical aspects of this science will always remain a closed book to me, but my experience enabled me to appreciate at least one of its basic concepts, the function of the message to select from an "ensemble of possible states." The knowledge of possibilities in the monitor is the knowledge of the language and the contexts in which it is used. If there is only one possibility, his receptor apparatus is likely to jump ahead and anticipate the result at what William James called the slightest "auditory hint." But it also follows from this theory that where there is only one such possibility the hint is in itself redundant and there is, in fact, no special message. The word we must expect in a given context will not add to our "information." We receive no message in the strict sense of the word when a friend enters a room and says "good morning." The word has no function to select from an ensemble of possible states, though situations are conceivable in which it would have.

The most interesting consequence of this way of looking at communication is the general conclusion that the greater the probability of a symbol's occurrence in any given situation, the smaller will be its information content. Where we can anticipate we need not listen. It is in this context that projection will do for perception.

The difficulty in distinguishing between the two in seeing as well as in hearing was well brought out in a fiendish experiment. The subjects were seated in the dark in front of a screen and were told their sensitivity to light was to be tested. At the request of the experimenter, the assistant projected a very faint light onto the screen and slowly increased its intensity, each person being asked to record exactly when he perceived it. But once in a while when the experimenter made the request no light was, in fact, shown. It was found that the subjects still saw it appearing. Their firm expectation of the sequence of events had actually led to a hallucination.

I suspect there is no class of people better able to bring about such phantom perceptions than conjurers. They set up a train of expectations, a semblance of familiar situations, which makes our imagination run ahead and complete it obligingly without knowing where we have been tricked. There are simple parlor tricks which show the problem in its most elementary form. Anyone who can handle a needle convincingly can make us see a thread which is not there. The conjuring trick is turned into art when a magician such as Charlie Chaplin performs a dance with a pair of forks and a couple of rolls that turn into nimble legs in front of our eyes.

II

To the student of the visual image, these experiences are of relevance because they show how the context of action creates conditions of illusion. When the hobbyhorse leans in the corner, it is just a stick; as soon as it is ridden it becomes the focus of the child's imagination and turns into a horse. The images of art, we remember, also once stood in context of action. It must have been an uncanny sight to see the painting of a bison belabored with spears in the darkness of the cave-if our ideas about these origins are right. What we do know is that the fetishes and cult images of early cultures stood in such contexts of action; they were bathed, anointed, clothed, and carried in procession. What wonder that illusion settled on them and that the faithful saw them smiling, frowning, or nodding behind the clouds of incense.

It was when art withdrew from the Pygmalion phase of action that it had to cast around for means to strengthen the illusion and to create the twilight realm of suspended disbelief which the Greeks first explored. But here and ever since, illusion could turn into deception only when the context of action set up an expectation which reinforced the artist's handiwork. The most famous story of illusion in classical antiquity illustrates the point to perfection; it is the anecdote from Pliny, how Parrhasios trumped Zeuxis, who had painted grapes so deceptively that birds came to peck at them. He invited his rival to his studio to show him his own work, and when Zeuxis eagerly tried to lift the curtain from the panel, he found it was not real but painted, after which he had to concede the palm to Parrhasios who had deceived not only irrational birds but an artist. In the cool light of reason, Parrhasios' feat is somewhat less admirable. Within the experience of poor Zeuxis, the probability of a curtain's being painted was surely nil. A few strokes of light and shade may therefore have been sufficient to make him "see" the curtain he expected, all the more so as he was keyed up for the next phase, the picture he wanted to reveal. The trompe l'oeil painters have ever since relied on the mutual reinforcement of illusion and expectation: the painted fly on the panel, the painted letters on the letter rack [168]; indeed, the most successful trompe l'oeil I have ever seen was on the level of Parrhasios' trick-painting simulating a broken glass pane in front of a picture.

168   PETO : *Old Scraps. 1894*

Where these expectations cannot be controlled they have to be created. We read of one such attempt in classical antiquity to transcend the dream-reality of painting. The painter Theon revealed his painting of a soldier to the accompaniment of a blast of trumpets, and we are assured that the illusion was greatly increased. Those of us who still remember the first talking films can imagine something of the effect.

But whatever the eulogists of artists may have said, paintings and statues had no voice, and art had to be satisfied with working its wonders within its own medium and within its own isolated world. Even within this world of conscious make-believe, it was found, genuine illusion held its own: we have seen how the incomplete painting can arouse the beholder's imagination and project what is not there. Some of the history of this development was told in the last chapter; we have now to turn to its psychological interpretation. There are obviously two conditions that must be fulfilled if the mechanism of projection is to be set in motion. One is that the beholder must be left in no doubt about the way to close the gap; secondly, that he must be given a "screen," an empty or ill-defined area onto which he can project the expected image.

169 Monochrome wall painting from the house of *Livia, Rome.* I *century* A.D.

The passage from Philostratus suggests that classical art understood these means of arousing our "imitative faculty," and many of the illusionist paintings from Pompeii and Rome confirm this impression of sovereign mastery. The grisaille from the house of Livia [169], with its emphatic indications of form and its empty areas waiting to be filled in by our imagination, shows that these decorators could play this conjurer's trick with wonderful deftness.

But no tradition of art had a deeper understanding of what I have called the "screen" than the art of the Far East. Chinese art theory discusses the

170 From the "Mustard Seed Garden Manual of Painting." 1679-1701

171 UNKNOWN CHINESE ARTIST:
A Fisherman's Abode after the Rain
XII-XIII *century, ink and tint on silk*

power of expressing through *absence* of brush and ink. "Figures, even though painted without eyes, must seem to look; without ears, must seem to listen. . . . There are things which ten hundred brushstrokes cannot depict but which can be captured by a few simple strokes if they are right. That is truly giving expression to the invisible." [170] The maxim into which these observations were condensed might serve as a motto of this chapter: "i *tao pi pu* tao–idea present, brush may be spared performance."

Perhaps it is precisely the restricted visual language of Chinese art, with its kinship to calligraphy that encouraged these appeals to the beholder to complete and project. The empty surface of the shining silk is as much a part of the image as are the strokes of the brush [171]. "When the highest point of a pagoda reaches the sky," says another Chinese treatise, "it is not necessary to show the main part of its structure. It should seem as if it is there, and yet is not there; as if it exists above and yet also exists below. Hillocks and earth mounds show only the half; the grass huts and thatched arbors should be represented only by their rough outlines."

ILLUSION 172

We do not know precisely how either the inhabitants of Pompeii or the Chinese art lover "saw" these empty spaces. But it is easy to demonstrate that, given both conditions–familiarity and an empty screen–it really becomes as hard as it was for the listener to wartime broadcasts to distinguish the phantom from reality. Take the type of lettering known as Shadow Antiqua ("Granby Shadow"), in which the familiar forms of letters are only indicated by what would be the shaded side if they were formed of ribbons standing up [172]. The distance between the shades indicates there is a slight band along the thickness of the ribbon. There is no such band, but many observers see it running along the whole top of the letter. It is easy to destroy the illusion in two ways: either by isolating individual forms so that the familiar image of the letter disappears, or by destroying the "screen." Place the same shape on a strongly patterned background and the "subjective contour," or phantom ridge, will disappear. We see it only as long as nothing in our field of vision contradicts our most likely hypothesis.

Those whose job it is to interpret images for the purpose of information have a story to tell of the tricks that these phantoms can play on perception. Intelligence officers intent on the reading of aerial reconnaissance photographs, X-ray specialists basing a diagnosis on the faintest of shadows visible in a tissue, learn in a hard school how often "believing is seeing" and how important it therefore is to keep their hypothesis flexible. The art lover adopts the opposite mental set. Unless he is a restorer, he may go through life without ever realizing to what an extent the pictures he loves are crisscrossed by subjective contours of his own making. If he were ever to strip them of these projections, merely a meaningless armature might well be all that would remain.

IV

But at this point the reader will want a question answered that may well have been in his mind for some time. Is it permissible to look at the reading of pictures in the same way we approach the hearing of speech? Are we not putting the cart before the horse when we thus concentrate on the beholder's share and neglect the painter's commerce, not with the public, but with nature herself? Is not the true reason why the painter blurs his image, particularly of distant objects, quite simply that this is how distant objects appear to his eye? Of course they do appear blurred. An early Chinese treatise already reminds the painter of the fact that "distant men have no eyes, distant trees have no branches." But though it is easy to specify what the eye cannot see in the distance, it is less easy to describe exactly what the eye does see. There is an amusing passage in Henry Peacham's book, *The Gentleman's Exercise,* that shows how seventeenth-century thinkers, trained in scholastic thought, still tried to tackle this problem in terms of Aristotelian philosophy:

"Have a regard, the farther your Landtskip goeth to those *universalia,* which, as Aristotle saith ... (in respect of their particulars concealed from our senses) are *notiora:* as in discerning a Building ten or twelve miles off, I cannot tell whether it be Church, Castle, House, or the like: so that in drawing of it, I must expresse no particular sign, as Bell, Portculleis, etc. but shew it as weakly and as faintly as mine eye judgeth of it, because all those particulars are taken away by the greatnesse of the distance. I have seen a man painted coming down a Hill some mile and a half from me, as I judged by the Landtskip, yet might you have told all the buttons of his doublet: whether the Painter had a quick invention, or the Gentleman's buttons were as big as those in fashion, when Monseeur came into England, I will leave to my Reader's judgement."

Peacham's passage may be one of the first to ridicule pictures that are too meticulously painted and to condemn the absurdity of these "conceptual" methods in the name of visual truth. The criticism is undoubtedly justified in the sense that such paintings contradict every possible experience. We do not see buttons at a great distance. But when we ask ourselves exactly what it is that we do see, the question is far less easily answered. Oculists who test our eyesight know very well why they present us with random letters. Where we can guess, we cannot disentangle seeing from knowing, or rather, from expecting. Peacham unwittingly shows this dominance of "conceptual" knowledge over the process of sight in his description of the generalizing tendencies of distance. It is no doubt true that as we travel away from a village we notice the loss of detail which he describes: first we can no longer read the clock-face of the church steeple, then we lose the clock, and finally the distinctive features of the church become so blurred it might be any building. But it is a mistake to think the same process happens in reverse when we approach the village—at least it is by no means sure that the progression will be so orderly, so according to Aristotelian logic. In certain circumstances we may easily take a rock for a building and a building for a rock, and we may hold on to this wrong interpretation till it suddenly gives way to a different reading. Another seventeenth-century author has recaptured this experience more truly than Peacham.

There is an impressive description of these uncertainties and the activity they provoke in the searching mind in one of Calderon's plays, *The Constant Prince.* Relating the appearance of the hostile fleet during a voyage, one of Calderon's characters is reminded of the blurred distances of the subtle painter. The passage is so rich in beauty and insight that it warrants lengthy quotation even in translation.

> *For, as on the coloured canvas*
> *Subtle pencils softly blend*
> *Dark and light in such proportions*
> *That the dim perspectives end—*
> *Now perhaps like famous cities,*
> *Now like caves or misty capes,*
> *For remoteness ever formeth*
> *Monstrous or unreal shapes . . .*
> *So it was, while I alone,*
> *Saw their bulk and vast proportions*
> *But their form remained unknown.*
> *First they seemed to us uplifting*
> *High in heaven their pointed towers,*
> *Clouds that to the sea descended,*
> *To conceive in sapphire showers*
> *What they would bring forth in crystal.*
> *And this fancy seemed more true,*
> *As from their untold abundance*
> *They, methought, could drink the blue*

Drop by drop. Again sea monsters
Seemed to us the wandering droves,
Which, to form the train of Neptune,
Issued from their green alcoves.
For the sails, when lightly shaken,
Fanned by zephyrs as by slaves,
Seemed to us like outspread pinions
Fluttering o'er the darkened waves;
Then the mass, approaching nearer,
Seemed a mighty Babylon,
With its hanging gardens pictured
By the streamers fluttering down.
But at last our certain vision
Undeceived, becoming true,
Showed it was a great armada
For I saw the prows cut through
Foam ....

V

The passage repays study, for the poet succeeds where many psychologists have failed in describing the panorama of illusions that may be evoked by the indeterminate. It is the power of expectation rather than the power of conceptual knowledge that molds what we see in life no less than in art. Were we to voyage in the Mediterranean we would, alas, be unlikely to see the train of Neptune's suite so convincingly conjured up as did the seventeenth-century traveler steeped in the reading of the classics and the experience of mythological paintings. But since we all probe the distant and indeterminate for possible classifications, which we then test and elaborate in a game of projections, Calderon's beautiful text provides us with the desired justification for comparing the reading of indeterminate pictures with the reading of indeterminate scenery. The experience of the radio "monitor" confronted with indistinct speech and that of the sailor confronted with indistinct shapes on the horizon are not incommensurate. We must always rely on guesses, on the assessment of probabilities, and on subsequent tests, and in this there is an even transition from the reading of symbolic material to our reaction in real life. When we wait at the bus stop and hope the Number Two is coming into sight, we probe the indistinct blot that appears in the distance for the possibility of projecting the number "two" into it. When we are successful in this projection, we say we now see the number. This is a case of symbol reading. But is it different with the bus itself? Certainly not on a foggy night, nor even in full daylight, if the distance is sufficiently great. Every time we scan the distance we somehow compare our expectation, our projection, with the incoming message. If we are too keyed up, as is well known, the slightest stimulus will produce an illusion. Here as always it remains our task to keep our guesses flexible, to revise them if reality appears to contradict, and to try again for a hypothesis that might fit the data. But it is always we who send out these tentacles into the world around us, who grope and probe, ready to withdraw our feelers for a new test.

As with the hypothesis of the monitor who listens to speech, so the fitting interpretation will inevitably transform the data beyond recognition. There are countless psychological experiments and observations that confirm this. A characteristic example is quoted from an article by G. K. Adams in M. D. Vernon's book *Visual Perception:*

"I was looking out of the window, watching for the street car, and I saw through the shrubs by the fence the brilliant red slats of the familiar truck; just patches of red, brilliant scarlet. As I looked, it occurred to me that what I was really seeing were dead leaves on a tree; instantly the scarlet changed to a dull chocolate brown. I could actually 'see' the change, as one sees changes in a theatre with a shift of lighting. The scarlet seemed positively to fall off the leaves, and to leave behind it the dead brown. I tried to recover the red by imagining the truck, and found that 1 could redden the leaves somewhat; then 1 made them leaves again, and found that I could brown them somewhat; but I could not get either the original scarlet or the later dead chocolate. I went out to see what the colour 'really' was, and found it to be a distinctly reddish brown. . . ."

Once more the effect experienced by the trained observer can be most conveniently imitated in the perception of images. It has been found in a well-known experiment that a familiar shape will induce the expected color; if we cut out the shape of a leaf and of a donkey from identical material and ask observers to match their exact shade from a color wheel, they will tend to select a greener shade of felt for the leaf and a grayer one for the donkey. We remember that the result of this experiment was anticipated by our ancient author Philostratus: "Even if we drew one of these Indians with white chalk," Apollonius concludes, "he would seem black, for there would be his flat nose and stiff curly locks and prominent jaw ... to make the picture black for all who can use their eyes." He was right. Interpreting, classing a shape affects the way we see its color. We need only analyze our own reactions when we look at black-and-white art to confirm these findings [185]. Objectively, the marble statue in Tiepolo's print is not whiter than the garment of St. Joseph, but it stands out in our minds as a luminous white against the dark foliage, while it is difficult even to remember the garments of the travelers as white. The print serves as a screen for a tentative projection which does not lead to illusion and yet "colors" the way we see it. Perhaps the correct way to describe this experience would be to say we see the garment as potentially dark. The psychologist Hering spoke of "memory color." Here we might speak of "color expectations."

185 G. D. TIEPOLO: *Holy Family Passing near a Statue. 1752, etching*

VI

What we called "mental set" may be precisely that state of readiness to start projecting, to thrust out the tentacles of phantom colors and phantom images which always flicker around our perceptions. And what we call "reading" an image may perhaps be better described as testing it for its potentialities, trying out what fits. The activation of these phantoms has been most frequently tested in the many psychological experiments in which an image is flashed on the screen for a brief moment only. There are many accounts of the wide range of different things which subjects report to have "seen," that is to say, of the images they were induced to project onto the screen by the clues presented to them just long enough to induce a hypothesis but not long enough to check it. A recent experiment has neatly demonstrated the persistence of these visual tentacles and their influence on subsequent fantasies. It appears that negative shapes, i.e., the accidental forms presented by the background, induced such fantasies if the picture was removed sufficiently fast. We may assume that such misreadings constantly flit through our minds but are usually discarded before we become aware of them because they are overlaid by the more consistent and more tenable hypothesis.

Once a projection, a reading, finds anchorage in the image in front of us, it becomes much more difficult to detach it. This is an experience familiar in the reading of puzzle pictures. Once they are solved, it is hard, or even impossible, to recover the impression they made on us while we were searching for the solution.

The possibility that all recognition of images is connected with projections and visual anticipations is strengthened by the results of recent experiments. It appears that if you show an observer the image of a pointing hand or arrow, he will tend to shift its location somehow in the direction of the movement. Without this tendency of ours to see potential movement in the form of anticipation, artists would never have been able to create the suggestion of speed in stationary images.

But here as always this projection needs a "screen," an empty field in which nothing contradicts our anticipation. This is the reason why the impression of movement, and thereby of life, is so much more easily obtained with a few energetic strokes than through elaboration of detail. The fact is familiar, but the explanation that is usually given appeals too confidently to the visual experience we "really have" in the presence of movement. The situation is similar to the blurring of perception with distance. In both instances it is easy to say what we cannot distinguish in such situations. The criticism of traditional methods of representation again took its starting point from this undeniable fact. In the same period when Peacham upbraided a painter who had painted the buttons of the doublet of a man miles away, the painter Philip Angel in Holland criticized his fellow artists for painting the spokes of a wheel when the carriage is supposed to be in motion; "Whenever a cart wheel or a spinning wheel is turned with great force, you will notice that because of the rapid turning no spokes can really be seen but only an uncertain glimpse of them *[een twijfelachtige schemeringe derselves]*, but though I have seen many cart wheels represented I have never yet seen this as it should appear because every spoke is always drawn as if the carriage did not appear to move."

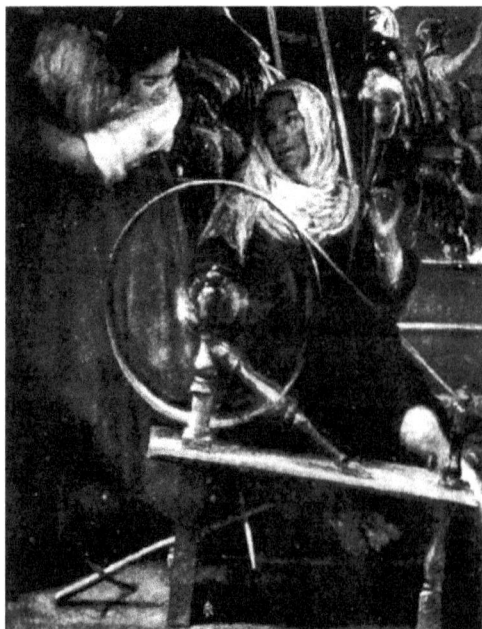

186 VELÁSQUEZ: *Hilanderas, detail.* c. *1660*

Angel was of course right that the sight of these spokes destroys the illusion of movement, but there is no evidence that he found a remedy. It needed the imagination and skill of a Velazquez to invent a means of suggesting that "uncertain glimpse" in the spinning wheel of the *Hilanderas* [186], which appears to catch the so-called "stroboscopic effect," the streaking after-image that trails its path across the field of vision when an object is whizzing past.

187

The suggestion of this effect belongs now to the commonplace language of the cartoonist or comic-strip artist. There is hardly a picture narrative in which speed is not conveniently rendered by a few strokes which act like negative arrows showing where the object has been a moment before [187]. Surely in such a case there can be no question of realism. By no stretch of imagination do figures chasing each other across a precipice look like Al Capp's heroes. But the success of this formula proves that while detail contradicts the illusion of movement, the strokes somehow confirm it. The pre-image, if one may coin this word for our anticipation of where the figure will be next, is confirmed by an anchorage for the after-image.

But the most important effect of these anticipatory probings which accompany the reading of images is that aura of space which appears to surround any naturalistic representation. The mere sign stands out as a figure against a neutral background, but this same ground recedes and assumes potential extension as soon as it forms part of the representation. It is an effect which can be observed with any picture or poster where letterpress is embodied.

We are so trained in assigning to each image its potential living space that we have no difficulty whatever in adjusting our reading to a configuration in which each figure is surrounded by its own particular aura. This happens every time a group of figures is assembled within one frame without being intended to share a common spatial setting. Once more we read such images by applying a rapid test of consistency. We understand without hesitation that the animals on the drawing by Maria Sibylla Merian [188] are to be read as individual specimens. Looking at J. Hoefnagel's plate [189] with its decorative assembly of plants and animals, we always supply the appropriate ground to the figure; the lizard sits on a slope, while some insects, throwing shadows, are imagined against a flat ground, and others are seen as flying. Without knowing it, we have carried out a rapid succession of tests for consistency and settled on those readings which make sense. Without such a test, even the images of traditional art may yield as variegated and fantastic a result as the proverbial shapes of clouds and inkblots.

188   MERIAN: *Snake, lizard and electric eel. c. 1700*

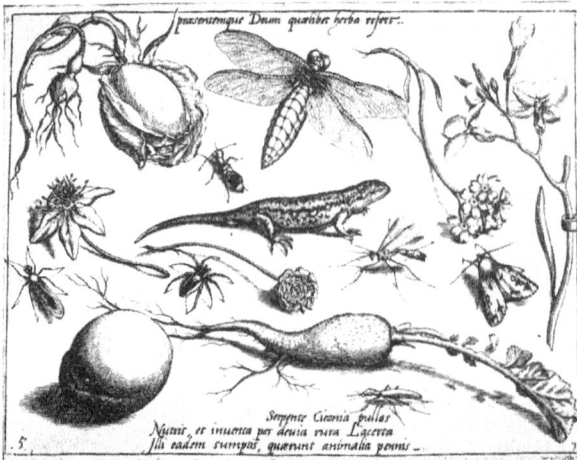

189   HOEFNAGEL: *From "Archetypa studiaque.", 1592*

W. J. T. Mitchell
(b. 1942)

Introduction

Mitchell is a distinguished professor of literature and art history at the University of Chicago. He is also the editor of the interdisciplinary journal *Critical Inquiry* which is devoted to critical theory in the human sciences.

His writings on literary and visual culture center on verbal and visual representations in the context of social, psychological and political issues. As such, they also cover an array of contemporary subjects, like identity, ethnicity, the politics of interpretation, and other topics that loom large in the post-colonial world of globalization and multiculturalism. In the wake of post-modernism, says Mitchell, it seems clear that the last half-century has decisively undermined any notion of "purely visual art." In fact, the "purely visual," he believes, constitutes the exception, whereas the "mixed media" represented all along the basic norm. The realization that images of all kinds do not exclusively belong to any discipline does not mean that it is impossible to differentiate between one medium and another. It does mean, however, that their study forces us to be interdisciplinary.

Mitchell does not believe in any mode of analysis as uniquely privileged for the understanding. Pictures create a critical space in which images can function as "cases" that might deconstruct the method that is brought to them. In other words, pictures might themselves be the sites of theoretical discourse, rather than objects subject to some master-discourse. Mitchell treats images as "living" entities that create a kind of interaction between the viewer and the picture that may transform the meaning of the picture. Pictures, in other words, invite narratives that can appropriate meaning, a change of context, as it were.

Mitchell argues that in contemporary culture and theory, images, pictures and the entire realm of the visual have become as important and worthy of serious study as the realm of language. By emphasizing the non-linguistic symbol systems, this "pictorial turn" invites close observation and informed criticism concerning the role of visual culture in our social lives. Given that texts also create images of sorts, Mitchell endeavors to tell us whereby images differ from signs and elaborates on ideology and its relationship to images. Images, claims Mitchell, is the thing that allows matter to have "memory." Pictorial turns have nonetheless existed before, since pictures have been subjected to different contexts. While we may agree what images are in the literal sense of the word, the mental and verbal images seem to be images only in some metaphoric sense. Although there is no way to check up on mental images objectively, they are clearly different from real, material pictures. Nor are mental images permanent the way real images are, they vary moreover from person to person.

But even proper images are not stable in any metaphysical sense, they, too, may be perceived differently by different viewers and may involve different apprehensions and interpretations. Idols and totems, for example, differ from each other in terms of their "demands" and the functions they serve. Verbal images, unlike mental images, are likewise not simply affairs of "consciousness," but public expressions that are out there like all other kind of material representations we create, whether pictures, maps, statues, etc. They all function as public symbols that project states of affairs about which we can reach provisional agreements. Wittgenstein, Mitchell reminds us, argued that thinking is not a private, occult process, but "the activity of working with signs" both verbal and pictorial.

The "image," according to Mitchell, is to be understood not as a "picture," but as a "likeness," i.e. a matter of spiritual similarity. The distinction between the spiritual and the material, between the inner and the outer image, says Mitchell, was never simply a matter of theological doctrine. It was invariably a question of politics–a struggle between conservative and reform movements. Moreover, knowledge itself is a social product, a matter of dialogue between different versions of the world, comprising different languages, ideologies and modes of representations. There is no scientific method, says Mitchell, that can contain all of those differences, because scientific progress is as much a matter of rhetoric and assumptions which contradict the apparent facts, as it is of methodical observation and information gathering. "Facts are only there as part of some other theory which has come to seem natural."

Mitchell claims that his "pictorial turn" marks in a way the end of postmodernism, although it itself was already part of the postmodern. However defined, it became manifest not only in art history, media studies, philosophy and other disciplines, but also in popular culture. In short, we currently live in a world dominated by images. Images, according to Mitchell, are "life forms." Objects are the bodies they "animate." The various media are the habitats in which they "come alive." By taking all of these factors into account, Mitchell's critical analysis clearly harbors implications concerning the entire realm of intellectual disciplines, in particular the human sciences.

Mitchell naturally elaborates at great length on each of the topics I barely touched upon. His arguments invariably rest on a thorough familiarity with the materials he discusses, and he addresses each issue with rigor. I chose to include Mitchell's short essay on 'representation,' because his overall critical position is echoed in a vast number of intellectual circles nowadays, regardless of discipline.

MITCHELL
*Representation**

PROBABLY the most common and naive intuition about literature is that it is a "representation of life." Unlike many of the terms in this collection, "representation" has always played a central role in the understanding of literature. Indeed, one might say that it has played the definitive role insofar as the founding fathers of literary theory, Plato and Aristotle, regarded literature as simply one form of representation. Aristotle defined all the arts–verbal, visual, and musical–as modes of representation, and went even further to make representation the definitively human activity:

> From childhood men have an instinct for representation and
> in this respect man differs from the other animals that he is far
> more imitative and learns his first lessons by representing things.

Man, for many philosophers both ancient and modem, is the "representational animal," *homo symbolicum*, the creature whose distinctive character is the creation and manipulation of signs–things that "stand for" or "take the place of" something else.

Since antiquity, then, representation has been the foundational concept in aesthetics (the general theory of the arts) and semiotics (the general theory of signs). In the modem era (i.e., in the last three hundred years) it has also become a crucial concept in political theory, forming the cornerstone of representational theories of sovereignty, legislative, authority, and relations of individuals to the state. We now think of "representative government" and the accountability of representatives to their constituents as fundamental postulates of modem government. One obvious question that comes up in contemporary theories of representation, consequently, is the relationship between aesthetic or semiotic

* From: *Critical Terms for Literary Studies* (second edition), edited by Frank Lentricchia and
  Thomas McLaughlin (Chicago, 1995), pp. 11-22.

representation (things that "stand for" other things) and political representation (persons who "act for" other persons). And one obvious place where these two forms of representation come together is the theater, where persons (actors) stand for or "impersonate" other (usually fictional) persons. There are vast differences, of course, between Laurence Olivier playing Hamlet and Ronald Reagan playing the role of the president–the difference, say, between playing and real life; between a rigid script and an open, improvised performance; or between an aesthetic contract and a legal one–but these should not blind us to the structural similarities of the two forms of representation or to the complex interaction between playful fantasy and serious reality in all forms of representation. The fact that Ronald Reagan began his career as an actor and has continually exploited the symbolic, theatrical character of the presidency only makes the links between aesthetic/semiotic and political forms of representation more unavoidable.

What is the "structure" that is common to both the political and semiotic forms of representation? One way to think of it is as a triangular relationship: representation is always *of* something or someone, *by* something or someone, *to* someone. It seems that only the third angle of representation need be a person: we can represent stones with dabs of paint or letters or sounds, but we can represent things only *to* people. The other two angles can be occupied by people but need not be: I can represent a man with a stone, or a stone with a man; but it would seem very odd to speak of representing either a stone or a man *to* a stone. There also may be a fourth dimension to representation not captured by our triangle, and that would be the "intender" or "maker" of the representation, the one who says, "let this dab of paint stand for this stone to someone." This more complete picture of representation might be mapped as a quadrilateral with two diagonal axes, one connecting the representational object to that which it represents, the other connecting the maker of the representation to the beholder:

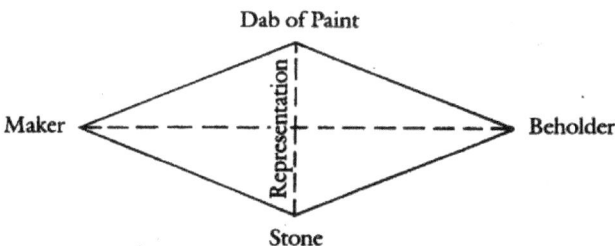

We might call these connecting lines the "axis of representation" (linking the dab of paint to the stone) and the "axis of communication" (linking the persons who understand the relation of paint to stone), respectively. The crossing of these axes suggests, I hope, one of the potential problems that comes-up with representations: they present a barrier that "cuts across," as it were, our lines of communication with others, presenting the possibility of misunderstanding, error, or downright falsehood. As soon as we begin to *use* representations in any social situation–to claim, for instance, that this dab of paint represents *the fact that* this stone is in that place and looks like this–then representation begins to play a double role, as a means of communication which is also a potential obstacle to it.

So far I am speaking of simple, almost "atomistic" cases of representation, in which one thing stands for one other thing. But clearly the business of representation is much more complex than this. Representation is an extremely elastic notion which extends all the way from a stone representing a man to a novel representing a day in the life of several Dubliners. Sometimes one thing can stand for a whole group of things, as when the word "tree" stands for a concept that "covers" a multitude of individual things, or a political representative stands for a people, or a stick figure stands for the general concept of man, or a narrative represents a whole series of events. And the representational sign never seems to occur in isolation from a whole network of other signs: the dab of paint that stands for a stone will probably do so only in the context of a whole field of dabs of paint that represent other things adjacent to the stone–grass, earth, trees, sky, other stones. Take the dab of paint out of that context, and it ceases to represent, becomes merely a dab of paint. In a similar way, the word "tree" represents a certain class of objects only in the context of a language, just as a note or a musical phrase has meaning only in relation to a larger piece and familiar systems of tonality. These "systems" (tonality, language, representational schemes in painting) may be called "codes," by which I simply mean a body of rules for combining and deciphering representational signs. When something stands for something to somebody, it does so by virtue of a kind of social agreement–"let us agree that this will stand for that"–which, once understood, need not be restated on every occasion. In fact, the decision to let

A stand for B may (and usually does) open up a whole new realm of possibilities for representation: B becomes a likely candidate to stand for C, and so on.

Aristotle says that representations differ from one another in three ways: in object, manner, and means. The "object" is that which is represented; the "manner" is the way in which it is represented; the "means" is the material that is used. What I am calling "codes" here are basically the same thing as Aristotle's "means"–that is, language, musical forms, paint. But the "manner" suggests yet another feature of representation, and that is the particular way a representational code is employed. The "means" of literary representation is language, but there are many ways of employing that means (dramatic recitation, narration, description) to achieve all sorts of effects (pity, admiration, laughter, scorn) and represent all sorts of things. Similarly, all paintings may employ shapes, shades, and colors on a two-dimensional surface (and this may be called the painter's "code"), but there are many ways of depicting a tree, many ways of applying paint to a surface. Some of them may become institutionalized as styles or genres, and these, like codes, are social agreements ("let us agree to represent this with that used in *this way*"), only of a more specialized nature. These "mini-codes" associated with styles of representation are usually called "conventions." The difference between a code and a convention may be illustrated by thinking of the difference between a medium and a genre: film is a medium, a material means of representation with a complex set of rules for combining and deciphering its signs; whereas the Hollywood Western is a particular kind of film, a genre that is recognized by the persistence of certain conventional elements (shootouts, wide open spaces, cowboys, Indians) from one example to another. In a similar way, we might think of language as one medium of representation, "literature" as the name of the aesthetic use of that medium, and things like poetry, the novel, and drama as very large genres within that medium.

One crucial consideration that enters into any analysis of representation is the *relationship* between the representational material and that which it represents. A stone may stand for a man, but how? By virtue of *what* "agreement" or understanding does representation occur? Semioticians generally differentiate three types of representational relationships under the names of icon, symbol, and index. An iconic account of the relation "stone-represents-man" would stress *resemblance:* a certain stone might stand for a man because it is upright, or because it is hard, or because its shape resembles that of a man. ("Mimesis" and "imitation" are thus iconic forms of representation that transcend the differences between media: I can imitate–i.e., mimic or produce a resemblance of–a sound, speech act, gesture, or facial expression and, thus, iconically reproduce it; icons are not just pictures.) Symbolic representations, by contrast, are not based on the resemblance of the sign to what it signifies, but on arbitrary stipulation: the stone stands for a man because "we say so," because we have agreed to regard it this way. Representation in language is "symbolic," in that letters, words, and whole texts represent sounds and states of affairs without in the least resembling what they represent. Indexical representation, finally, explains "standing for" in terms of cause and effect or some "existential" relation like physical proximity or connectedness: the stone represents a man because a man set it up as a marker, to indicate (like a trace or footprint) the fact that he was here; a glove, a strand of hair, or a fingerprint are, to the skillful detective, all representations by "indication" of the person who left them behind. There is nothing, of course, to prevent any particular representation from employing more than one of these relationships: a written text may symbolically represent (describe or narrate or dramatize) an action, and it may also indexically represent (indicate the presence of) its author as the "cause" of which it is an "effect." Photographs are commonly thought to combine iconic and indexical representation, standing for visual objects by virtue of both resemblance and cause and effect.

Now it is important to realize that the long tradition of explaining literature and the other arts in terms of representation is matched by an equally long tradition of discomfort with this notion. Plato accepted the common view that literature is a representation of life, but for that very reason he thought it should be banished from the ideal state. Representations, Plato reasoned, are mere substitutes for the things themselves; even worse, they may be false or illusory substitutes that stir up anti-social emotions (violence or weakness), and they may represent bad persons and actions, encouraging imitation of evil. Only certain kinds of representations, carefully controlled by the state, were to be permitted into Plato's republic of rational virtue.

Although Plato's hostility to representation may seem extreme, we should recognize that some prohibitions or restrictions on representations have been practiced by every society that has produced them. Taboos against graven images, against writing or uttering the name of God, against the representation of the human form, against the representation of evil or ugly objects, against sex or violence, are an equally important part of the "social agreements" that constitute representation. The formula "let this stand for that to them" is regularly subjected to restrictions on subject matter ("let this stand for *anything but* that") or on the audience/spectator ("let this stand for that, but *not* to them"). Sometimes the prohibition may be directed at particular types of representational relationships: iconic representations, especially pictures and statues, are generally subjected to more stringent restrictions than symbolic or verbal representations. Greek dramatic conventions allowed the narrative, descriptive representation of violence but not its direct, visual portrayal on the stage. Pornography provides the most interesting examples of all these attempts to limit the triangle of representation, either by specifying the kind of persons who may witness the representation ("adults"; "18 and over"; "men only") or by restricting the kind of things that may be represented (no frontal nudity; no genitals; no actual sex acts), or by restricting the kind of representational signs that may be employed (dirty pictures and movies are usually subjected to more stringent prohibitions than dirty books).

It should be clear that representation, even purely "aesthetic" representation of fictional persons and events, can never be completely divorced from political and ideological questions; one might argue, in fact, that representation is precisely the point where these questions are most likely to enter the literary work. If literature is a "representation of life," then representation is exactly the place where "life," in all its social and subjective complexity, gets into the literary work.

There have been many other challenges to the notion of literary representation. Most of them, like prohibitions against idolatry or pornography, accept the basic model of the representational triangle, but try to restrict or modify it in the service of some set of values. Thus, "idealist" theories of the arts will often posit some "higher nature" as the preferred object of representation and consign the representation of ordinary life to "lower" genres, such as caricature or satire, or some non-aesthetic genre, like "documentary" or "history." Realist theories of the arts tend to consign the idealist genres to the realm of "romance" and to see them as merely imaginary, fanciful representations. Both theories adopt the representational model of art: they simply disagree about what is to be represented (what Aristotle called the "object").

More strenuous challenges to representation come from the traditions of expressionism and formalism. Expressionism generally posits an unrepresentable essence (God, the soul, the author's intention) that is somehow manifested in a work. The "somehow" is the key: the unrepresentable is often construed as the invisible, the unpicturable, even the unspeakable–but not, generally, as the unwritable. Writing, arbitrary marks, hieroglyphics, and allegory are the signs that "encrypt" representation in a secret code. Thus, the cult of the artistic genius and the aura-laden artifact often accompany the expressive aesthetic. The aesthetic object does not "represent" something, except incidentally; it "is" something, an object with an indwelling spirit, a trace in matter of the activity of the immaterial. The anthropological model for the expressive aesthetic is fetishism, which does not treat its sacred objects as icons (i.e., representations by resemblance; pictures) or, in a sense, as representations at all (though they are frequently describable as indexes). The mimetic aesthetic, by contrast, finds its anthropological counterpart in the notion of idolatry, the worship of graven images that represent by resemblance.

Formalist or "abstract" theories of art have provided the most fundamental challenges to representational models in the modern era. Many of these theories take music (which, for obvious reasons, is hard to describe in representational terms) as the paradigm for all the arts. Formalism emphasizes the representational means and manner–the materiality and organization of the "signifier" or representational object–and de-emphasizes the other two angles of the representational triangle. The represented object may even disappear when the medium turns itself back on its own codes, engaging in self-reflexive play. The potential witnesses to the representational act are reduced finally to an elite of technical experts and connoisseurs who appreciate the ostensibly nonrepresentational object. Modernism frequently presents itself as having "grown out of" representational models of art, language, and mind, and it has, in the modern era, been very unfashionable to talk about literature or the other arts as representations of life. To the formalist, literature is about itself: novels are made out of other novels; all poems are about language. If representation sneaks back in, it is likely to be turned backward: life imitates art, reality (nature, society, the unconscious) is a text, and there is nothing outside the text.

Once this turn is made, then the opposition between "life" and "literature" which animates the traditional notion of literary representation begins to fall apart. But the structure of representation itself, as a relation of standing for seems to come back with a vengeance. Postmodern culture is often characterized as an era of "hyper-representation," in which abstract, formalist painting has been replaced by experiments like photorealism, and reality itself begins to be experienced as an endless network of representations. The paradigm for the arts shifts from the pure nonrepresentational formalism of abstract painting and music to mass media and advertising, in which everything is indefinitely reproducible and representable as a commodity. Categories such as "the thing itself," the "authentic," and "the real" which were formerly considered the objects of representation (or as the presence achieved by formal purity) now become themselves representations, endlessly reduplicated and distributed.

A survey of postmodern experiments in literary representation would be outside the scope of this essay, which in any case is intended to raise the issue of representation as a problem that runs throughout the history of literary production. Suffice it to say that concepts such as the identity of the text, the determinacy of meaning, the integrity of the author, and the validity of interpretation all play a role in the representational (or anti-representational) character of literary texts. The highly self-conscious fictive "labyrinths" of Jorge Luis Borges, with their pastiches of scholarly and historical documentation, deadpan realism, and bizarre fantasy, are often cited as paradigms of postmodern literary representation.

But it may be more useful to take as an example of literary representation a more traditional text, one that initiates a historic shift in conventions of literary representation and that takes the activity of representation itself as a theme. Robert Browning's "My Last Duchess" provides an especially interesting case study because it draws together so many different conventions of literary representation (lyric, dramatic, and narrative), and because it reflects as well on other modes of representation, including the pictorial and the political. Browning's text, to begin with, is a representation of a speech act, and thus of a speaker, a listener, and a specific setting. The Duke of Ferrara is "presented" to us (represented, that is, as if he were immediately present to us), describing a painting of his late wife ("My Last Duchess") to the agent of a certain count whose daughter is engaged to be married to the duke.

My Last Duchess
FERRARA

That's my last duchess painted on the wall,
Looking as if she were alive. I call
That piece a wonder, now: Frà Pandolf's hands
Worked busily a day, and there she stands.
Will't please you sit and look at her? I said
"Frà Pandolf" by design, for never read
Strangers like you that pictured countenance,
The depth and passion of its earnest glance,
But to myself they turned (since none puts by
The curtain I have drawn for you, but I)
And seemed as they would ask me, if they durst,
How such a glance came there; so, not the first
Are you to turn and ask thus. Sir, 'twas not
Her husband's presence only, called that spot
Of joy into the Duchess' cheek: perhaps
Frà Pandolf chanced to say "Her mantle laps
Over my lady's wrist too much," or "Paint
"Must never hope to reproduce the faint
"Half-flush that dies along her throat": such stuff
Was courtesy, she thought, and cause enough
For calling up that spot of joy. She had
A heart—how shall I say?—too soon made glad,
Too easily impressed; she liked whate'er
She looked on, and her looks went everywhere.
Sir, 'twas all one! My favor at her breast,
The dropping of the daylight in the West,
The bough of cherries some officious fool
Broke in the orchard for her, the white mule

She rode with round the terrace–all and each Would
draw from her alike the approving speech,
Or blush, at least. She thanked men–good! but thanked
Somehow–I know not how–as if she ranked
My gift of a nine-hundred-years-old name
With anybody's gift. Who'd stoop to blame
This sort of trifling? Even had you skill
In speech–which I have not–to make your will
Quite clear to such an one, and say, "Just this
Or that in you disgusts me; here you miss,
Or there exceed the mark"–and if she let
Herself be lessoned so, nor plainly set
Her wits to yours, forsooth, and made excuse,
–E'en then would be some stooping; and I choose
Never to stoop. Oh sir, she smiled, no doubt,
Whene'er I passed her; but who passed without
Much the same smile? This grew; I gave commands;
Then all smiles stopped together. There she stands
As if alive. Will't please you rise? We'll meet
The company below, then. I repeat,
The Count your master's known munificence
Is ample warrant that no just pretense
Of mine for dowry will be disallowed;
Though his fair daughter's self, as I avowed
At starting, is my object. Nay, we'll go
Together down, sir. Notice Neptune, though,
Taming a sea-horse, thought a rarity,
Which Claus of Innsbruck cast in bronze for me!

The first thing that may strike us about this poem is the way that Browning renounces any direct representation of his own views. the poet does not lyrically describe the painting, or narrate any events in his own voice; he lets his invented character, the duke, do all the talking, as if he were a character in a play. The second thing that may strike us is that this is not a play but something like a fragment or extract–a single speech or "monologue"–presented, however, as a whole poem. Browning has, in other words, deliberately collapsed the distinction between two kinds of literary representation–the brief, self-sufficient lyric utterance of the poet, and the dramatic speech that would conventionally belong in a more extended representation–in order to create a new hybrid genre, the dramatic monologue. This "collapse" of lyric and dramatic conventions is itself an act of representation in which what would have been a part or fragment (a dramatic speech) is allowed to "stand for" or take the place of the whole. And, indeed, one of the pleasures of reading this brief monologue is the unfolding of the whole drama that it represents in miniature. We quickly surmise that the duke is an obsessively jealous husband who had his last duchess killed because she was too free with her affections and approval–"she liked whate'er / She looked on, and her looks went everywhere."

The truly tantalizing mystery, however, is the meaning of the drama that this speech represents in little. Why is the duke telling this story to the agent of his bride-to-be's father? Is he trying to impress the emissary with his power and ruthlessness? Is he indirectly doing what he was unable to do with his last duchess, "stooping" to warn his next duchess that she had better be more discreet in her behavior? Is his speech better understood as a calculated threat in which signs of spontaneity are disguises for a deep plot or as an unwitting confession of the duke's inability to control the affections of women? What state of affairs (including "state of mind") does the duke's speech really represent? And (a rather different, but related problem) what authorial intention or meaning is conveyed by Browning's presentation of the duke in just this way? What judgment are we being invited to make about the speaker and his words? It would seem clear enough that we are meant to disapprove, but what specific form does this disapproval take?

One way of getting at these questions is to reflect on the role of yet another character in the poem, that of the auditor, whose reactions are represented to us by the duke. The auditor is, of course, a representative of his "master" the count, a go-between who presumably is working out details about the dowry (the duke is evidently confident that the count's "known munificence" guarantees that he will make money on the marriage: "no just pretense / Of mine for dowry will be disallowed"), though the duke protests that he is really marrying for love ("his fair daughter's self, as I avowed / At starting, is my object"). But if the emissary represents the count to the duke in the implied drama of Browning's poem, he also represents the *reader* in its implied lyric address: like us, he is the auditor of the speech. What does this mean? What role are we, as readers, being coerced into by having ourselves represented within the poem?

One possibility is that Browning wants to place his reader in a position of weakness and servitude, forced to hear a repugnant, menacing speech but deprived of any voice or power to counteract it. The count's representative, presumably, has the responsibility for seeing that negotiations go smoothly in a marriage that will raise the count's daughter in the sociopolitical order (the difference between a duke and a count, exemplary representatives of feudal hierarchy, is crucial here). Should he warn the count that he's marrying his daughter to a Bluebeard? Should he warn the daughter to watch her step? Neither of these actions really opposes the duke's will; on the contrary, they are ways of carrying out his will, of "stooping" on the duke's behalf to convey warnings the duke would never "stoop" to make in person. If the duke represents the aristocratic, feudal social order, understood here principally as a system giving some men absolute power over others, and particularly over women in a system of exchange, the emissary represents a servant class or (as a representative of the reader) the new bourgeois class of nineteenth-century readers who may hear this speech as the echo of a bygone era, the "bad old days" of absolute power–a power which may be deplored, but which still has a power to fascinate, and which lies beyond our intervention.

The only representation in this poem that seems to have some power to intervene is the portrait of the duchess, which seems still to mock the duke with its free looks from the wall. He may control who can see her by drawing aside or closing the curtain that veils the painting, but he cannot control the way the painting looks. He could, of course, destroy it, just as he destroyed its original, the duchess herself; but he chooses not to. Is that because he wants it as a reminder that now he has her under his power? Or because he is, in some sense, no more capable of destroying the duchess's smiling image than he is of destroying those galling, disgusting memories of her behavior that he pours out on the envoy? If the painting functions as a representation of the duke's power, it also seems to be a continual reminder of his weakness, his inability to "make [his] will / Quite clear" to his wife. In a similar way, the duke's whole performance, his boasting speech to the envoy, is an expression of a wish for absolute power that has just the opposite effect, revealing the duke as someone who is so lacking in confidence about his power that he needs constant reassurance. His final appeal to the envoy to "notice" his statue of Neptune "taming a sea horse" is a transparent invitation to see the duke as a god "taming" nature, much as he "tamed" his duchess by having her painted on his wall. The duke thinks of his power as something that is certified by his control of representations–by his painting of the duchess hidden behind a curtain that only he can draw, by the statue of Neptune "cast in bronze for me," by his control over the envoy's attention (and those whom the envoy represents) with a strategic display of his gallery of representations. What Browning shows us, however, is the uncontrollability of representations, the way they take on a life of their own that escapes and defies the will to determine their meaning. If the duke truly has his last duchess (or himself) under control, why does he need to veil her image with a curtain? If he is so sure of his choosing "never to stoop" to make his will clear, why is he so conspicuously "stooping" to an underling, seducing a mere representative with this odd mixture of boasting and self-betrayal?

These, at any rate, are some of the questions that arise with respect to the duke's manipulation of representations within the mini-drama that makes up the poem. But what if we raised similar sorts of questions about the poem *as itself* a representation? Suppose, for instance, we think of this poem as itself a kind of dramatic portrait, a "speaking picture" in the gallery of Robert Browning's poetry? To what extent is Browning himself-or the commentator who claims to speak for Browning's intentions–playing a role like that of the duke, showing off his own power by displaying his mastery over representation? Should we think of Browning's poem, and the readings it evokes, as something we might call "My Last Duke"? Most readers of this poem have registered some version of Robert Langbaum's insight that "condemnation" is "the least interesting response" to the duke's outrageous display of evil. Just as the duke seems to hypnotize the envoy, Browning seems to paralyze the reader's normal moral judgment by his virtuosic representation of villainy. His poem holds us in its grip, condemning in advance all our attempts to control it by interpretation as mere repetitions of the duke's attempt to control his gallery of representations.

Browning's poem should make it clear why there would be a strong impulse in literature, and in literary criticism, to escape from representation and why such an escape can never succeed. Representation is that by which we make our will known and, simultaneously, that which alienates our will from ourselves in both the aesthetic and political spheres. The problem with representation might be summarized by reversing the traditional slogan of the American Revolution: instead of "No taxation without representation," no representation without taxation. Every representation exacts some cost, in the form of lost immediacy, presence, or truth, in the form of a gap between intention and realization, original and copy ("Paint / Must never hope to reproduce the faint / Half-flush that dies along her throat"). Sometimes the tax imposed by representation is so slight that we scarcely notice, as in the perfect copy provided by a laser disk recording ("Is it real or is it Memorex?"). Sometimes it is as ample as the gap between life and death: "That's my last Duchess painted on the wall, / Looking as if she were alive." But representation does give us something in return for the tax it demands, the gap it opens. One of the things it gives us is literature.

FURTHER READING:

Aristotle. *Poetics.*

Auerbach, Erich. [1946]. 1953. *Mimesis: The Representation of Reality in Western Literature.*

Baudrillard, Jean. 1981. *For a Critique of the Political Economy of the Sign.*

Cavell, Stanley. 1979. *The World Viewed: Reflections on the Ontology of Film.*

Derrida, Jacques. 1978. "The Theater of Cruelty and the Closure of Representation." In *Writing and Difference.*

Eco, Umberto. *1976. A Theory of Semiotics.*

Goodman, Nelson. 1976. *The Languages of Art.*

Langbaum, Robert. 1957. *The Poetry of Experience.*

Meltzer, Françoise. 1987. *Salome and the Dance of Writing.*

Mitchell, W.J.T. 1986. *Iconology: Image, Text, Ideology.*

Peirce, Charles Sanders. 1931-58. "The Icon, Index, and Symbol." In *Collected Works.*

Pitkin, Hanna. 1967. *The Concept of Representation.*

Plato. *Republic,* Book 10.

Max Black
(1909-1988)

Introduction

Black was an analytical philosopher who was concerned with the nature of clarity and meaning in language. He is famed for his contribution to the philosophy of language, and to the philosophy of mathematics and science. He is also famous for his studies of the work of seminal philosophers like Wittgenstein and Frege.

The phases in Black's intellectual development exemplify the working of an "open mind," and convincingly display how different disciplines maybe related to each other via "abstractions." Indeed, Black's particular "shifts" were far from arbitrary. His interest in the *nature* of clarity may be said to underlie his development. Accordingly, Black had a keen interest in mathematics and in the study of the various historical conceptions of the field. Yet before he decided on a career in mathematics, he was immersed in music and in its abstract nature. His early involvement in these "languages" seems to have evoked an interest in language in general. Thus, while at Cambridge (where he completed his undergraduate studies), he came under the influence of Wittgenstein and Russell and eventually produced a comprehensive study of Wittgenstein's work. Having befriended students who were interested in the *philosophy* of mathematics (not least because of their teachersRussell, Wittgenstein, Ramsey and other famous thinkers), Black became more interested in philosophy, though he never completely relinquished mathematics. In fact, the year he spent at Göttingen (a fellowship he was awarded) he devoted to mathematics, and later lectured in mathematics at the Institute of Education in London. While continuing to roam among disciplines, he accepted an appointment as professor of philosophy at the University of Illinois, and, subsequently, he transferred to Cornell.

In my introduction to this part of the book, I claimed that metaphors may reveal the underlying nature of language, thought and communication. I also mentioned the fact that, as such, it has elicited a goodly number of theories that have greatly contributed to our understanding of their use. Keenly interested in the nature of *clarity* and *meaning* in language, Black naturally wished, like all those who followed, to better understand metaphors–their diversity, use and function. I chose to include Black's early essay on metaphor, in preference to more recent works on the subject, because it served as an eye-opener for me many decades ago, when I still believed that language aspires to "mirror reality" rather than strive to convey the regularities of experience. In fact, all of the essays that appeared in his *Models and Metaphors* (1962) constituted a revelatory moment in my scholarly development. Unlike some analytical philosophers, Black never "mystifies" the reader. His explications of complicated mater are invariably clear and can be readily understood, even without the examples which he provides.

Aware of our limitations as humans to understand all that requires understanding, Black chose to focus on the various ways in which mankind "copes" with this situation. "Clearing intellectual jungles," says Black, "is a respectable occupation." And despite his keen interest in mathematics, Black was ready to proclaim: "Perhaps every science must start with metaphor and end with algebra; and perhaps without the metaphor there would never have been any algebra."[1] He confessed, moreover, that he emphasized the importance of scientific models, "because of a conviction that the imaginative aspects of scientific thought have in the past been too much neglected. For science, like the humanities, like literature, is an affair of the imagination."[2]

[1] Max Black, *Models and Metaphors: Studies in Language and Philosophy*, (Cornell University, 1962), p. 242.
[2] Ibid. p. 243.

BLACK

Metaphor[*]

Metaphors are no arguments, my pretty maiden.
The Fortunes of Nigel, Book 2, Chapter 2

TO DRAW attention to a philosopher's metaphors is to belittle him–like praising a logician for his beautiful handwriting. Addiction to metaphor is held to be illicit, on the principle that whereof one can speak only metaphorically, thereof one ought not to speak at all. Yet the nature of the offence is unclear. I should like to do something to dispel the mystery that invests the topic; but since philosophers (for all their notorious interest in language) have so neglected the subject, I must get what help I can from the literary critics. They, at least, do not accept the commandment, "Thou shalt not commit metaphor," or assume that metaphor is incompatible with serious thought.

1

The questions I should like to see answered concern the "logical grammar" of "metaphor" and words having related meanings. It would be satisfactory to have convincing answers to the questions: "How do we recognize a case of metaphor?" "Are there any criteria for the detection of metaphors?" "Can metaphors be translated into literal expressions?" "Is metaphor properly regarded as a decoration upon 'plain sense'?" "What are the relations between metaphor and simile?" "In what sense, if any, is a metaphor 'creative'?" "What is the point of using a metaphor?" (Or, more briefly, "What do we *mean* by 'metaphor'?" The questions express attempts to become clearer about some uses of the word "metaphor"–or, if one prefers the material mode, to analyze the notion of metaphor.)

---

[*] From: *Models and Metaphors: Studies in Language and Philosophy* (Ithaca, 1962), pp.25-47 (chap.3).

The list is not a tidy one, and several of the questions overlap in fairly obvious ways. But I hope they will sufficiently illustrate the type of inquiry that is intended.

It would be helpful to be able to start from some agreed list of "clear cases" of metaphor. Since the word "metaphor" has some intelligible uses, however vague or vacillating, it must be possible to construct such a list. Presumably, it should be easier to agree whether any given item should be included than to agree about any proposed analysis of the notion of metaphor.

Perhaps the following list of examples, chosen not altogether at random, might serve:

(i)   "The chairman plowed through the discussion."
         "A smoke screen of witnesses."

(ii)   "An argumentative melody."

(iii)   "Blotting-paper voices" (Henry James).

(iv)   "The poor are the negroes of Europe" (Chamfort).

(v)   "Light is but the shadow of God" (Sir Thomas Browne).

(vi)   "Oh dear white children, casual as birds,
         Playing amid the ruined languages" (Auden).

I hope all these will be accepted as unmistakeable *instances* of metaphor, whatever judgments may ultimately be made about the meaning of "metaphor." The examples are offered as clear cases of metaphor, but, with the possible exception of the first, they would be unsuitable as "paradigms." If we wanted to teach the meaning of "metaphor" to a child, we should need simpler examples, like "The clouds are crying" or "The branches are fighting with one another." (Is it significant that one hits upon examples of personification?) But I have tried to include some reminders of the possible complexities that even relatively straight-forward metaphors may generate.

Consider the first example—"The chairman plowed through the discussion." An obvious point to begin with is the contrast between the word "plowed" and the remaining words by which it is accompanied. This would be commonly expressed by saying that "plowed" has here a metaphorical sense, while the other words have literal senses. Although we point to the whole sentence as an instance (a "clear case") of metaphor, our attention quickly narrows to a single word, whose presence is the proximate reason for the attribution. And similar remarks can be made about the next four examples in the list, the crucial words being, respectively, "smoke screen," "argumentative," "blotting-paper," and "negroes."

(But the situation is more complicated in the last two examples of the list. In the quotation from Sir Thomas Browne, "Light" must be supposed to have a symbolic sense, and certainly to mean far more than it would in the context of a textbook on optics. Here, the metaphorical sense of the expression "the shadow of God" imposes a meaning richer than usual upon the subject of the sentence. Similar effects can be noticed in the passage from Auden–consider for instance the meaning of "white" in the first line. I shall have to neglect such complexities in this paper.)

In general, when we speak of a relatively simple metaphor, we are referring to a sentence or another expression in which *some* words are used metaphorically while the remainder are used non-metaphorically. (An attempt to construct an entire sentence of words that are used metaphorically results in a proverb, an allegory, or a riddle. No preliminary analysis of metaphor will satisfactorily cover even so trite an example as "In the night all cows are black." And cases of symbolism (in the sense in which Kafka's castle is a "symbol") also need separate treatment.

2

"The chairman plowed through the discussion." In calling this sentence a case of metaphor, we are implying that at least one word (here, the word "plowed") is being used metaphorically in the sentence, and that at least one of the remaining words is being used literally. Let us call the word "plowed" the *focus* of the metaphor, and the remainder of the sentence in which that word occurs the *frame*. (Are *we* now using metaphors–and mixed ones at that? Does it matter?) One notion that needs to be clarified is that of the "metaphorical use" of the focus of a metaphor. Among other things, it would be good to understand how the presence of one frame can result in metaphorical use of the complementary word, while the presence of a different frame for the same word fails to result in metaphor.

If the sentence about the chairman's behavior is translated word for word into any foreign language for which this is possible, we shall of course want to say that the translated sentence is a case of the *very same* metaphor. So, to call a sentence an instance of metaphor is to say something about its *meaning,* not about its orthography, its phonetic pattern, or its grammatical form.[1] (To use a well-known distinction, "metaphor" must be classified as a term belonging to "semantics" and not to "syntax"–or to any *physical* inquiry about language.)

Suppose somebody says, "I like to plow my memories regularly." Shall we say he is using the same metaphor as in the case already discussed, or not? Our answer will depend upon the degree of similarity we are prepared to affirm on comparing the two "frames" (for we have the same "focus" each time). Differences in the two frames will produce *some* differences in the interplay[2] between focus and frame in the two cases. Whether we regard the differences as sufficiently striking to warrant calling the sentences *two* metaphors is a matter for arbitrary decision. "Metaphor" is a loose word, at best, and we must beware of attributing to it stricter rules of usage than are actually found in practice.

So far, I have been treating "metaphor" as a predicate properly applicable to certain expressions, without attention to any occasions on which the expressions are used, or to the thoughts, acts, feelings, and intentions of speakers upon such occasions. And this is surely correct for *some* expressions. We recognize that to call a man a "cesspool" is to use a metaphor, without needing to know who uses the expression, or on what occasions, or with what intention. The rules of our language determine that some expressions must count as metaphors; and a speaker can no more change this than he can legislate that "cow" shall mean the same as "sheep." But we must also recognize that the established rules of

---

[1] Any part of speech can be used metaphorically (though the results are meager and uninteresting in the case of conjunctions); any form of verbal expression may contain a metaphorical focus.

[2] Here I am using language appropriate to the "interaction view" of metaphor that is discussed later in this paper.

language leave wide latitude for individual variation, initiative, and creation. There are indefinitely many contexts (including nearly all the interesting ones) where the meaning of a metaphorical expression has to be reconstructed from the speaker's intentions (and other clues) because the broad rules of standard usage are too general to supply the information needed. When Churchill, in a famous phrase, called Mussolini "that *utensil*," the tone of voice, the verbal setting, the historical background, helped to make clear *what* metaphor was being used. (Yet, even here, it is hard to see how the phrase "that utensil" could ever be applied to a man except as an insult. Here, as elsewhere, the general rules of usage function as limitations upon the speaker's freedom to mean whatever he pleases.) This is an example, though still a simple one, of how recognition and interpretation of a metaphor may require attention to the *particular circumstances of its* utterance.

It is especially noteworthy that there are, in general, no standard rules for the degree of *weight* or *emphasis* to be attached to a particular use of an expression. To know what the user of a metaphor means, we need to know how "seriously" he treats the metaphorical focus. (Would he be just as content to have some rough synonym, or would only *that* word serve? Are we to take the word lightly, attending only to its most obvious implications–or should we dwell upon its less immediate associations?) In speech we can use emphasis and phrasing as clues. But in written or printed discourse, even these rudimentary aids are absent. Yet this somewhat elusive "weight" of a (suspected or detected)[3] metaphor is of great practical importance in exegesis.

To take a philosophical example: Whether the expression "logical form" should be treated in a particular frame as having a metaphorical sense will depend upon the extent to which its user is taken to be conscious of some supposed analogy between arguments and other things (vases, clouds, battles, jokes) that are also said to have "form." Still more will it depend upon whether the writer wishes the analogy to be active in the minds of his readers; and how much his own thought depends upon and is nourished by the supposed analogy.

---

[3] Here, I wish these words to be read with as little "weight" as possible.

We must not expect the "rules of language" to be of much help in such inquiries. (There is accordingly a sense of "metaphor" that belongs to "pragmatics" rather than to "semantics"–and this sense may be the one most deserving of attention.)

3

Let us try the simplest possible account that can be given of the meaning of "The chairman plowed through the discussion," to see how far it will take us. A plausible commentary (for those presumably too literal-minded to understand the original) might run somewhat as follows: "A speaker who uses the sentence in question is taken to want to say *something* about a chairman and his behavior in some meeting. Instead of saying, plainly or *directly,* that the chairman dealt summarily with objections, or ruthlessly suppressed irrelevance, or something of the sort, the speaker chose to use a word ('plowed') which, strictly speaking, means something else. But an intelligent hearer can easily guess what the speaker had in mind."[4] This account treats the metaphorical expression (let us call it *"M"*) as a substitute for some other literal expression (*"L,"* say) which would have expressed the same meaning, had it been used instead. On this view, the meaning of *M,* in its metaphorical occurrence, is just the *literal* meaning of *L.* The metaphorical use of an expression consists, on this view, of the use of that expression in other than its proper or normal sense, in some context that allows the improper or abnormal sense to be detected and appropriately transformed. (The reasons adduced for so remarkable a performance will be discussed later.)

Any view which holds that a metaphorical expression is used in place of some equivalent *literal* expression, I shall call *substitution view* of *metaphor.* (I should like this label to cover also any analysis which views the entire sentence that is the locus of the metaphor as replacing some set of literal sentences.) Until recently, one or another form of a substitution view has been accepted by most writers (usually literary critics or writers of books on rhetoric) who have had anything

[4] Notice how this type of paraphrase naturally conveys some implication of *fault* on the part of the metaphor's author. There is a strong suggestion that he ought to have made up his mind as to what he really wanted to say–the metaphor is depicted as a way of glossing over un-clarity and vagueness.

to say about metaphor. To take a few examples: Whately defines a metaphor as "a word substituted for another on account of the Resemblance or Analogy between their significations."[5] Nor is the entry in the Oxford Dictionary (to jump to modern times) much different from this: "Metaphor: The figure of speech in which a name or descriptive term is transferred to some object different from, but analogous to, that to which it is properly applicable; an instance of this, a metaphorical expression."[6] So strongly entrenched is the view expressed by these definitions that a recent writer who is explicitly arguing for a different and more sophisticated view of metaphor, nevertheless slips into the old fashion by defining metaphor as "saying one thing and meaning another."[7]

According to a substitution view, the focus of a metaphor, the word or expression having a distinctively metaphorical use within a literal frame, is used to communicate a meaning that might have been expressed literally. The author substitutes *M* for *L;* it is the reader's task to invert the substitution, by using the literal meaning of *M* as a clue to the intended literal meaning of *L*. Understanding a metaphor is like deciphering a code or unraveling a riddle.

If we now ask why, on this view, the writer should set his reader the task of solving a puzzle, we shall be offered two types of answer. The first is that there may, in fact, be no literal equivalent, *L,* available in the language in question. Mathematicians spoke of the "leg" of an angle because there was no brief literal expression for a bounding line; we say "cherry lips," because there is no form of

---

[5] Richard Whately, *Elements of Rhetoric* (7th rev. ed., London, 1846), p. 80.

[6] Under "Figure" we find: "Any of the various 'forms' of expression, deviating from the normal arrangement or use of words, which are adopted in order to give beauty, variety, or force to a composition; e.g., Aposiopesis, Hyperbole, Metaphor, etc." If we took this strictly we might be led to say that a transfer of a word not adopted for the sake of introducing "beauty, variety, or force" must necessarily fail to be a case of metaphor. Or will "variety" automatically cover every transfer? It will be noticed that the O.E.D.'s definition is no improvement upon Whately's. Where he speaks of a "word" being substituted, the O.E.D. prefers "name or descriptive term." If this is meant to restrict metaphors to nouns (and adjectives?) it is demonstrably mistaken. But, if not, what is "descriptive term" supposed to mean? And why has Whately's reference to "Resemblance or Analogy" been trimmed into a reference to analogy alone?

[7] Owen Barfield, "Poetic Diction and Legal Fiction," in *Essays Presented to Charles Williams* (Oxford, 1947), pp. 106-117. The definition of metaphor occurs on p. 111, where metaphor is treated as a special case of what Barfield calls "tarning." The whole essay deserves to be read.

words half as convenient for saying quickly what the lips are like. Metaphor plugs the gaps in the literal vocabulary (or, at least, supplies the want of convenient abbreviations). So viewed, metaphor is a species of *catachresis,* which I shall define as the use of a word in some new sense in order to remedy a gap in the vocabulary; catachresis is the putting of new senses into old words.[8] But if a catachresis serves a genuine need, the new sense introduced will quickly become part of the *literal* sense. "Orange" may originally have been applied to the color by catachresis; but the word is now applied to the color just as "properly" (and un-metaphorically) as to the fruit. "Osculating" curves do not kiss for long, and quickly revert to a more prosaic mathematical contact, and similarly for other cases. It is the fate of catachresis to disappear when it is successful.

There are, however, many metaphors where the virtues ascribed to catachresis cannot apply, because there is, or there is supposed to be, some readily available and equally compendious literal equivalent. Thus in the somewhat unfortunate example,[9] "Richard is a lion," which modern writers have discussed with boring insistence, the literal meaning is taken to be the same as that of the sentence, "Richard is brave."[10] Here, the metaphor is not supposed to enrich the vocabulary.

When catachresis cannot be invoked, the reasons for substituting an indirect, metaphorical, expression are taken to be stylistic. We are told that the metaphorical expression may (in its literal use) refer to a more concrete object than would its literal equivalent; and this is supposed to give pleasure to the reader (the pleasure of having one's thoughts diverted from Richard to the irrelevant lion). Again,

---

[8] The O.E.D. defines catachresis as: "Improper use of words; application of a term to a thing which it does not properly denote; abuse or perversion of a trope or metaphor." I wish to exclude the pejorative suggestions. There is nothing perverse or abusive in stretching old words to fit new situations. Catachresis is merely a striking case of the transformation of meaning that is constantly occurring in any living language.

[9] Can we imagine anybody saying this nowadays and seriously meaning anything? I find it hard to do so. But in default of an authentic context of use, any analysis is liable to be thin, obvious, and unprofitable.

[10] A full discussion of this example, complete with diagrams, will be found in Gustaf Stern's *Meaning and Change of Meaning* (Göteborgs Högskolas Årsskrift, vol. 38, 1932, part 1), pp. 300 ff. Stern's account tries to show how the reader is led by the context to *select* from the connotation of "lion" the attribute (bravery) that will fit Richard the man. I take him to be defending a form of the substitution view.

the reader is taken to enjoy problem-solving–or to delight in the author's skill at half-concealing, half-revealing his meaning. Or metaphors provide a shock of "agreeable surprise" and so on. The principle behind these "explanations" seems to be: When in doubt about some peculiarity of language, attribute its existence to the pleasure it gives a reader. A principle that has the merit of working well in default of any evidence.[11]

Whatever the merits of such speculations about the reader's response, they agree in making metaphor a *decoration*. Except in cases where a metaphor is a catachresis that remedies some temporary imperfection of literal language, the purpose of metaphor is to entertain and divert. Its use, on this view, always constitutes a deviation from the "plain and strictly appropriate style" (Whately).[12] So, if philosophers have something more important to do than give pleasure to their readers, metaphor can have no serious place in philosophical discussion.

4

The view that a metaphorical expression has a meaning that is some transform of its normal literal meaning is a special case of a more general view about "figurative" language. This holds that any figure of speech involving semantic change (and not merely syntactic change, like inversion of normal word order) consists in some transformation of a *literal* meaning. The author provides, not his intended meaning, m, but some function thereof, $f(m)$; the reader's task is to apply the inverse function, f^{I}, and so to obtain $f^{I}(f(m))$, i.e., m, the original

---

[11] Aristotle ascribes the use of metaphor to delight in learning; Cicero traces delight in metaphor to the enjoyment of the author's ingenuity in over-passing the immediate, or in the vivid presentation of the principal subject. For references to these and other traditional views, see E. M. Cope, *An Introduction to Aristotle's Rhetoric* (London, 1867), Book III, Appendix B, Ch. 2, "On Metaphor."

[12] Thus Stern *(op. cit.)* says of all figures of speech that "they are intended to serve the expressive and purposive functions of speech better than the 'plain statement'" (p. 296). A metaphor produces an "enhancement" *(Steigerung)* of the subject, but the factors leading to its use "involve the expressive and effective (purposive) functions of speech, not the symbolic and communicative functions" (p. 290). That is to say, metaphors may evince feelings or predispose others to act and feel in various ways - but they do not typically *say* anything.

meaning. When different functions are used, different tropes result. Thus, in irony, the author says the *opposite* of what he means; in hyperbole, he *exaggerates* his meaning; and so on.

What, then, is the characteristic transforming function involved in metaphor? To this the answer has been made: either, *analogy* or *similarity*. M is either similar or analogous in meaning to its literal equivalent L. Once the reader has detected the ground of the intended analogy or simile (with the help of the frame, or clues drawn from the wider context) he can retrace the author's path and so reach the original literal meaning (the meaning of L).

If a writer holds that a metaphor consists in the *presentation* of the underlying analogy or similarity, he will be taking what I shall call a *comparison view* of metaphor. When Schopenhauer called a geometrical proof a mousetrap, he was, according to such a view, *saying* (though not explicitly): "A geometrical proof is *like* a mousetrap, since both offer a delusive reward, entice their victims by degrees, lead to disagreeable surprise, etc." This is a view of metaphor as a condensed or elliptical *simile.* It will be noticed that a "comparison view" is a special case of a "substitution view." For it holds that, the metaphorical statement might be replaced by an equivalent literal *comparison.*

Whately says: "The Simile or Comparison may be considered as differing in form only from a Metaphor; the resemblance being in that case *stated,* which in the Metaphor is implied."[13] Bain says that "the metaphor is a comparison implied in the mere use of a term" and adds, "It is in the circumstance of being confined to a word, or at most to a phrase, that we are to look for the peculiarities of the metaphor–its advantages on the one hand, and its dangers and abuses on the other."[14] This view of the metaphor, as condensed simile or comparison, has been very popular.

---

[13] Whately, *loc. cit.* He proceeds to draw a distinction between "Resemblance, strictly so called, i.e., *direct* resemblance between the objects themselves in question, (as when we speak of '*table-land*', or compare great waves to *mountains*)" and "Analogy, which is the resemblance of Ratios–a similarity of the relations they bear to certain other objects; as when we speak of the 'light of reason', or of 'revelation'; or compare a wounded and captive warrior to a stranded ship."

[14] Alexander Bain, *English Composition and Rhetoric* (enl. ed., London, 1887), p. 159.

The chief difference between a substitution view (of the sort previously considered) and the special form of it that I have called a comparison view may be illustrated by the stock example of "Richard is a lion." On the first view, the sentence means approximately the same as "Richard is brave"; on the second, approximately the same as "Richard is *like* a lion (in being brave)," the added words in brackets being understood but not explicitly stated. In the second translation, as in the first, the metaphorical statement is taken to be standing in place of some literal equivalent. But the comparison view provides a more elaborate paraphrase, inasmuch as the original statement is interpreted as being about lions as well as about Richard.[15]

The main objection against a comparison view is that it suffers from a vagueness that borders upon vacuity. We are supposed to be puzzled as to how some expression (M), used metaphorically, can function in place of some literal expression (L) that is held to be an approximate synonym; and the answer offered is that what M stands for (in its literal use) is *similar* to what L stands for. But how informative is this? There is some temptation to think of similarities as "objectively given," so that a question of the form, "Is A like B in respect of P?" has a definite and predetermined answer. If this were so, similes might be governed by rules as strict as those controlling the statements of physics. But likeness always admits of degrees, so that a truly "objective" question would need to take some such form as "Is A more like B than C on such and such a scale of degrees of P?" Yet, in proportion as we approach such forms, metaphorical statements lose their effectiveness and their point. We need the metaphors in just the cases when there can be no question as yet of the precision of scientific statement. Metaphorical statement is not a substitute for a formal comparison or any other kind of literal statement, but has its own distinctive capacities

---

[15] Comparison views probably derive from Aristotle's brief statement in the *Poetics*: "Metaphor consists in giving the thing a name that belongs to something else; the transference being either from genus to species, or from species to genus, or from species to species, or on grounds of analogy" (1457b). I have no space to give Aristotle's discussion the detailed examination it deserves. An able defense of a view based on Aristotle will be found in S. J. Brown's *The World of Imagery* (London, 1927, esp. pp. 67 ff.).

and achievements. Often we say, "*X* is *M*," evoking some imputed connection between *M* and an imputed *L* (or, rather, to an indefinite system, *L₁, L₂, L₃,* ...) in cases where, prior to the construction of the metaphor, we would have been hard put to it to find any literal resemblance between M and *L*. It would be more illuminating in some of these cases to say that the metaphor creates the similarity than to say that it formulates some similarity antecedently existing.[16]

5

I turn now to consider a type of analysis which I shall call an *interaction view* of metaphor. This seems to me to be free from the main defects of substitution and comparison views and to offer some important insight into the uses and limitations of metaphor.[17]

Let us begin with the following statement: "In the simplest formulation, when we use a metaphor we have two thoughts of different things active together and supported by a single word, or phrase, whose meaning is a resultant of their interaction."[18] We may discover what is here intended by applying Richard's remark to our earlier example, "The poor are the negroes of Europe." The substitution view, at its crudest, tells us that something is being

---

[16] Much more would need to be said in a thorough examination of the comparison view. It would be revealing, for instance, to consider the contrasting types of case in which a formal comparison is preferred to a metaphor. A comparison is often a prelude to an explicit statement of the grounds of resemblance whereas we do not expect a metaphor to explain itself. (Cf. the difference between *comparing* a man's face with a wolf mask by looking for points of resemblance–and seeing the human face as vulpine.) But no doubt the line between some metaphors and *some* similes is not a sharp one.

[17] The best sources are the writings of I. A. Richards, especially Chapter 5 ("Metaphor") and Chapter 6 ("Command of Metaphor") of his *The Philosophy of Rhetoric* (Oxford, 1936). Chapters 7 and 8 of his *Interpretation in Teaching* (London, 1938) cover much the same ground. W. Bedell Stanford's *Greek Metaphor* (Oxford, 1936) defends what he calls an "integration theory" (see esp. pp. 101 ff.) with much learning and skill. Unfortunately, both writers have great trouble in making clear the nature of the positions they are defending. Chapter 18 of W. Empson's *The Structure of Complex Words* (London, 1951) is a useful discussion of Richards' views on metaphor.

[18] *The Philosophy of Rhetoric*, p. 93. Richards also says that metaphor is "fundamentally a borrowing between and intercourse of *thoughts,* a transaction between contexts" (p. 94). Metaphor, he says, requires two ideas "which co-operate in an inclusive meaning" (p. 119).

indirectly said about the poor of Europe. (But what? That they are an oppressed class, a standing reproach to the community's official ideals, that poverty is inherited and indelible?) The comparison view claims that the epigram presents some comparison between the poor and the negroes. In opposition to both, Richards says that our "thoughts" about European poor and American negroes are "active together" and "interact" to produce a meaning that is a resultant of that interaction.

I think this must mean that in the given context the focal word "negroes" obtains a new meaning, which is not quite its meaning in literal uses, nor quite the meaning which any literal substitute would have. The new context (the "frame" of the metaphor, in my terminology) imposes extension of meaning upon the focal word. And I take Richards to be saying that for the metaphor to work the reader must remain aware of the extension of meaning–must attend to both the old and the new meanings together.[19]

But how is this extension or change of meaning brought about? At one point, Richards speaks of the "common characteristics" of the two terms (the poor and negroes) as "the ground of the metaphor" (*The Philosophy of Rhetoric,* p. 117), so that in its metaphorical use a word or expression must connote only a *selection* from the characteristics connoted in its literal uses. This, however, seems a rare lapse into the older and less sophisticated analyses he is trying to supersede.[20] He is on firmer ground when he says that the reader is forced to "connect" the two ideas (p. 125). In this "connection" resides the secret and the mystery of metaphor. To speak of the "interaction" of two thoughts "active together" (or, again, of their "inter-illumination" or "co-operation") is to *use* a metaphor emphasizing the dynamic aspects of a good reader's response to a nontrivial metaphor. I have no quarrel with the use of metaphors (if they are good ones) in talking about metaphor. But it may be as well to use several, lest we are misled by the adventitious charms of our favorites.

---

[19] It is this, perhaps, that leads Richards to say that "talk about the identification or fusion that a metaphor effects is nearly always misleading and pernicious" (*ibid.,* p. 127).

[20] Usually, Richards tries to show that similarity between the two terms is at best *part* of the basis for the interaction of meanings in a metaphor.

Let us try, for instance, to think of a metaphor as a filter. Consider the statement, "Man is a wolf." Here, we may say, are *two* subjects–the principal subject, Man (or: men) and the subsidiary subject, Wolf (or: wolves). Now the metaphorical sentence in question will not convey its intended meaning to a reader sufficiently ignorant about wolves. What is needed is not so much that the reader shall know the standard dictionary meaning of "wolf"–or be able to use that word in literal senses–as that he shall know what I will call the *system of associated commonplaces*. Imagine some layman required to say, without taking special thought, those things he held to be true about wolves; the set of statements resulting would approximate to what I am here calling the system of commonplaces associated with the word "wolf." I am assuming that in any given culture the responses made by different persons to the test suggested would agree rather closely and that even the occasional expert, who might have unusual knowledge of the subject, would still know "what the man in the street thinks about the matter." From the expert's standpoint, the system of commonplaces may include half-truths or downright mistakes (as when a whale is classified as a fish); but the important thing for the metaphor's effectiveness is not that the commonplaces shall be true, but that they should be readily and freely evoked. (Because this is so, a metaphor that works in one society may seem preposterous in another. Men who take wolves to be reincarnations of dead humans will give the statement "Man is a wolf" an interpretation different from the one I have been assuming.)

To put the matter in another way: Literal uses of the word "wolf" are governed by syntactical and semantical rules, violation of which produces nonsense or self-contradiction. In addition, I am suggesting, literal uses of the word normally commit the speaker to acceptance of a set of standard beliefs about wolves (current platitudes) that are the common possession of the members of some speech community. To deny any such piece of accepted commonplace (e.g., by saying that wolves are vegetarians–or easily domesticated) is to produce an effect of paradox and provoke a demand for justification. A speaker who says "wolf" is normally taken to be implying in some sense of that word that he is referring to something fierce, carnivorous, treacherous, and so on. The idea of a wolf is part of a system of ideas, not sharply delineated, yet sufficiently definite to admit of detailed enumeration.

The effect, then, of (metaphorically) calling a man a "wolf" is to evoke the wolf-system of related commonplaces. If the man is a wolf, he preys upon other animals, is fierce, hungry, engaged in constant struggle, a scavenger, and so on. Each of these implied assertions has now to be made to fit the principal subject (the man) either in normal or in abnormal senses. If the metaphor is at all appropriate, this can be done–up to a point at least. A suitable hearer will be led by the wolf-system of implications to construct a corresponding system of implications about the principal subject. But these implications will *not* be those comprised in the commonplaces *normally* implied by literal uses of "man." The new implications must be determined by the pattern of implications associated with literal uses of the word "wolf." Any human traits that can without undue strain be talked about in "wolf-language" will be rendered prominent, and any that cannot, will be pushed into the background. The wolf-metaphor suppresses some details, emphasizes others–in short, *organizes* our view of man.

Suppose I look at the night sky through a piece of heavily smoked glass on which certain lines have been left clear. Then I shall see only the stars that can be made to lie on the lines previously prepared upon the screen, and the stars I do see will be seen as organized by the screen's structure. We can think of a metaphor as such a screen and the system of "associated commonplaces" of the focal word as the network of lines upon the screen. We can say that the principal subject is "seen through" the metaphorical expression–or, if we prefer, that the principal subject is "projected upon" the field *or* the subsidiary subject. (In the latter analogy, the implication-system of the focal expression must be taken to determine the "law of projection.")

Or take another example. Suppose I am set the task of describing a battle in words drawn as largely as possible from the vocabulary of chess. These latter terms determine a system of implications which will proceed to control my description of the battle. The enforced choice of the chess vocabulary will lead some aspects of the battle to be emphasized, others to be neglected, and all to be organized in a way that would cause much more strain in other modes of description. The chess vocabulary filters and transforms: it not only selects, it brings forward aspects of the battle that might not be seen at all through another medium. (Stars that cannot be seen at all, except through telescopes.)

Nor must we neglect the shifts in attitude that regularly result from the use of metaphorical language. A wolf is (conventionally) a hateful and alarming object; so, to call a man a wolf is to imply that he too is hateful and alarming (and thus to support and reinforce dyslogistic attitudes). Again, the vocabulary of chess has its primary uses in a highly artificial setting, where all expression of feeling is formally excluded: to describe a battle as if it were a game of chess is accordingly to exclude, by the choice of language, all the more emotionally disturbing aspects of warfare. (Similar by-products are not rare in philosophical uses of metaphor.)

A fairly obvious objection to the foregoing sketch of the "interaction view" is that it has to hold that some of the "associated commonplaces" themselves suffer metaphorical change of meaning in the process of transfer from the subsidiary to the principal subject. And these changes, if they occur, can hardly be explained by the account given. The primary metaphor, it might be said, has been analyzed into a set of subordinate metaphors, so the account given is either circular or leads to an infinite regress.

This might be met by denying that *all* changes of meaning in the "associated commonplaces" must be counted as metaphorical shifts. Many of them are best described as extensions of meaning, because they do not involve apprehended connections between two systems of concepts. I have not undertaken to explain how such extensions or shifts occur in general, and I do not think any simple account will fit all cases. (It is easy enough to mutter "analogy," but closer examination soon shows all kinds of "grounds" for shifts of meaning with context—and even no ground at all, sometimes.)

Secondly, I would not deny that a metaphor may involve a number of subordinate metaphors among its implications. But these subordinate metaphors are, I think, usually intended to be taken less "emphatically," i.e., with less stress upon their implications. (The implications of a metaphor are like the overtones of a musical chord; to attach too much "weight" to them is like trying to make the overtones sound as loud as the main notes—and just as pointless.) In any case, primary and subordinate metaphors will normally belong to the same field of discourse, so that they mutually reinforce one and the same system of implications. Conversely, where substantially new metaphors appear as the primary metaphor is un-raveled, there is serious risk of confusion of thought (compare the customary prohibition against "mixed metaphors").

But the preceding account of metaphor needs correction, if it is to be reasonably adequate. Reference to "associated commonplaces" will fit the commonest cases where the author simply plays upon the stock of common knowledge and common misinformation) presumably shared by the reader and himself. But in a poem, or a piece of sustained prose, the writer can establish a novel pattern of implications for the literal uses of the key expressions, prior to using them as vehicles for his metaphors. (An author can do much to suppress unwanted implications of the word "contract," by explicit discussion of its intended meaning, before he proceeds to develop a contract theory of sovereignty. Or a naturalist who really knows wolves may tell us so much about them that *his* description of man as a wolf diverges quite markedly from the stock uses of that figure.) Metaphors can be supported by specially constructed systems of implications, as well as by accepted commonplaces; they can be made to measure and need not be reach-me-downs.

It was a simplification, again, to speak as if the implication system of the metaphorical expression remains unaltered by the metaphorical statement. The nature of the intended application helps to determine the character of the system to be applied (as though the stars could partly determine the character of the observation-screen by which we looked at them). If to call a man a wolf is to put him in a special light, we must not forget that the metaphor makes the wolf seem more human than he otherwise would.

I hope such complications as these can be accommodated within the outline of an "interaction view" that I have tried to present.

6

Since I have been making so much use of example and illustration, it may be as well to state explicitly (and by way of summary) some of the chief respects in which the "interaction" view recommended differs from a "substitution" or a "comparison" view.

In the form in which I have been expounding it, the "interaction view" is committed to the following seven claims:

(1) A metaphorical statement has two distinct subjects—a "principal" subject and a "subsidiary" one.[21]

(2) These subjects are often best regarded as "systems of things," rather than "things."

(3) The metaphor works by applying to the principal subject a system of "associated implications" characteristic of the subsidiary subject.

(4) These implications usually consist of "commonplaces" about the subsidiary subject, but may, in suitable cases, consist of deviant implications established *ad hoc* by the writer.

(5) The metaphor selects, emphasizes, suppresses, and organizes features of the principal subject by implying statements about it that normally apply to the subsidiary subject.

(6) This involves shifts in meaning of words belonging to the same family or system as the metaphorical expression; and some of these shifts, though not all, may be metaphorical transfers. (The subordinate metaphors are, however, to be read less "emphatically.")

(7) There is, in general, no simple "ground" for the necessary shifts of meaning—no blanket reason why some metaphors work and others fail.

It will be found, upon consideration, that point (1) is incompatible with the simplest forms of a "substitution view," point (7) is formally incompatible with a "comparison view"; while the remaining points elaborate reasons for regarding "comparison views" as inadequate.

But it is easy to overstate the conflicts between these three views. If we were to insist that only examples satisfying all seven of the claims listed above should be allowed to count as "genuine" metaphors, we should restrict the correct uses of the word "metaphor" to a very small number of cases. This would be to advocate a persuasive definition of "metaphor" that would tend to make all metaphors

---

[21] This point has often been made. E.g.: "As to metaphorical expression, that is a great excellence in style, when it is used with propriety, for it gives you two ideas for one" (Samuel Johnson, quoted by Richards, *ibid.* p. 93). The choice of labels for the "subjects" is troublesome. See the "note on terminology" (n. 23, below).

interestingly complex.[22] And such a deviation from current uses of the word "metaphor" would leave us without a convenient label for the more trivial cases. Now it is in just such trivial cases that "substitution" and "comparison" views sometimes seem nearer the mark than "interaction" views. The point might be met by classifying metaphors as instances of substitution, comparison, or interaction. Only the last kind are of importance in philosophy.

Substitution-metaphors and comparison-metaphors can be replaced by literal translations (with possible exception for the case of catachresis) by sacrificing some of the charm, vivacity, or wit of the original, with no loss of *cognitive* content. But "interaction metaphors" are not expendable. Their mode of operation requires the reader to use a system of implications (a system of "commonplaces"–or a special system established for the purpose in hand) as a means for selecting, emphasizing, and organizing relations in a different field. This use of a "subsidiary subject" to foster insight into a "principal subject" is a distinctive intellectual operation (though one familiar enough through our experiences of learning anything whatever), demanding simultaneous awareness of both subjects but not reducible to any comparison between the two.

Suppose we try to state the cognitive content of an interaction-metaphor in "plain language." Up to a point, we may succeed in stating a number of the relevant relations between the two subjects (though in view of the extension of meaning accompanying the shift in the subsidiary subject's implication system, too much must not be expected of the literal paraphrase). But the set of literal statements so obtained will not have the same power to inform and enlighten as the original. For one thing, the implications, previously left for a suitable reader to educe for himself, with a nice feeling for their relative priorities and degrees of importance, are now presented explicitly as though having equal weight. The literal paraphrase inevitably says too much–and with the wrong emphasis. One of the points I most wish to stress is that the loss in such cases is a loss in cognitive content; the relevant weakness of the literal paraphrase is not that it

---

[22] I can sympathize with Empson's contention that "The term ['metaphor'] had better correspond to what the speakers themselves feel to be a rich or suggestive or persuasive use of a word, rather than include uses like the *leg* of a table" (*The Structure of Complex Words,* p. 333). But there is the opposite danger, also, of making metaphors too important by definition, and so narrowing our view of the subject excessively.

may be tiresomely prolix or boringly explicit (or deficient in qualities of style); it fails to be a translation because it fails to give the insight that the metaphor did.

But "explication," or elaboration of the metaphor's grounds, if not regarded as an adequate cognitive substitute for the original, may be extremely valuable. A powerful metaphor, will no more be harmed by such probing than a musical masterpiece by analysis of its harmonic and melodic structure. No doubt metaphors are dangerous - and perhaps especially so in philosophy. But a prohibition against their use would be a willful and harmful restriction upon our powers of inquiry.[23]

[23] *(A note on terminology):* For metaphors that fit a substitution or comparison view, the factors needing to be distinguished are: (i) some word or expression E, (ii) occurring in some verbal "frame" F, so that (iii) F(E) is the metaphorical statement in question; (iv) the meaning m'(E) which E has in F(E), (v) which is the same as the literal meaning, m(X), of some literal synonym, X. A sufficient technical vocabulary would be: "metaphorical expression" (for E), "metaphorical statement" (for F(E)), "metaphorical meaning" (for m') and "literal meaning" (for m).

Where the interaction view is appropriate, the situation is more complicated. We may also need to refer to (vi) the principal subject of F(E), say P (roughly, what the statement is "really" about); (vii) the subsidiary subject, S (what F(E) would be about if read literally); (viii) the relevant system of implications, *I,* connected with S; and (ix) the resulting system of attributions, A, asserted of P. We must accept at least so much complexity if we agree that the meaning of E in its setting F depends upon the transformation of I into A by using language, normally applied to S, to apply to P instead.

Richards has suggested using the words "tenor" and "vehicle" for the two *"thoughts"* which, in his view, are "active together" (for "the *two* ideas that metaphor, at its simplest, gives *us*" – *The Philosophy of Rhetoric,* p. 96, my italics) and urges that we reserve "the word 'metaphor' for the whole double unit" *(ibid.).* But this picture of *two* ideas working upon each other is an inconvenient fiction. And it is significant that Richards himself soon lapses into speaking of "tenor" and "vehicle" as "things" (e.g. on p. 118). Richards' "vehicle" vacillates in reference between the metaphorical expression (E), the subsidiary subject (S) and the connected implication system *(I).* It is less clear what his "tenor" means: sometimes it stands for the principal subject (P), sometimes for the implications connected with that subject (which I have not symbolized above), sometimes, in spite of Richards' own intentions, for the *resultant* meaning (or as we might say the "full import") of E in its context, F(E).

There is probably no hope of getting an accepted terminology so long as writers upon the subject are still so much at variance with one another.

Nelson Goodman
(1906-1998)

Introduction

Goodman was an analytical philosopher interested in areas of applied logic, epistemology, and the philosophy of science. He was a rigorous philosopher whose unorthodox approach to art constituted a general approach to knowledge and reality. Goodman's interest in aesthetics is closely related to cognitive and constructive factors that make it possible to view the arts as "ways" that contribute to our understanding. According to Goodman art is not markedly different from science since all of the branches of knowledge rest on symbols that classify "reality" as we know and experience it.

Goodman's interest in art came to the fore long before he completed his studies in philosophy. Prior to having produced a dissertation on "qualities" (*A Study of Qualities*, 1941), he directed an art gallery for eleven years. The gallery brought him in close touch with artists and the ways in which they create their "visual worlds." His first book, *The Structure of Appearance* (1951), and his later book, *Ways of World Making* (1978), are no doubt related to his experience as director of an art gallery and as a passionate collector of art. Most of Goodman's aesthetics is, however, contained in his *Languages of Art* (1968), which preceded *Ways of World Making* as part of his inquiry into the theory of knowledge.

In *Languages of Art* Goodman claims that works of art are sets of symbols belonging to particular symbolic systems, and that the manifold means of symbolization attest to the diversity of human understanding. However, given that everything that can be referred to by symbols falls within our understanding, and since creating and using symbols holds also true for science, the difference between art and science, says Goodman, is not that of "induction and inferences, synthesis and analysis, concreteness and abstraction," but rather "a difference in domination of certain specific characteristics of symbols." Art, in other words, must be taken no less seriously than the sciences as modes of discovery and enlargement of knowledge, in the broad sense of advancement of the understanding. This being the case since scientific theories, according to Goodman, are no less the "makers" of worlds and "fabricators" of facts than art, mythology, literature and all the other social and humanistic subjects.

Goodman also makes room for art-forms that do not use language. As a musicologist, I have been intrigued for many years by the development of Western musical notation. The notation, familiar to most of us who ever played a Western musical instrument, only came into being after several centuries of development. Having taught notation and aware of its development, I naturally had some ideas as to what had taken place concerning the various attempts to commit sound to script. Goodman's uncanny rigor and mastery of symbolic logic put, however, order into my diffused thoughts, and not only those concerning notation. I was lucky to be able to test my understanding of Goodman with Goodman himself and pleased that he expressed genuine interest in my presentation of the *historical* development of notation as "compliance" to his theory. I borrowed the term 'compliance' from Goodman, whose theory regarding notation stipulates that a mark is ambiguous if it has different complaints at different times. If scores are to be correlated with performances, says Goodman, whatever is denoted by a symbol must comply with it. The development of Western musical notation, in fact, reveals recurrent attempts to rid itself of ambiguities so as to assure "identities." In short, musical notation, as it evolved in the centuries bridging the early Middle-Ages and the Renaissance, incorporated a basic understanding of Western music, it took part in the "world-making" of sounds with its own meaning and coherence.

Familiar with the history of music, I naturally also had some ideas about where music stands in relation to other arts, and in particular in relation to language. Since Goodman put order in my diffused thoughts concerning notation–though he was *unfamiliar* with its historical development–I devoted considerable time to his *Languages of Art* in order to better understand Goodman's unorthodox approach to art and as part of an inquiry into the theory of knowledge. The reading that follows represents my attempt to render Goodman's aesthetics in a "nut-shell," using Goodman's own explications to the major topics which he addresses. I hope, thereby, to introduce the reader to the thinking of a highly venerated philosopher, whose theory of knowledge made no room for a separation between the so called "exact sciences" and the "human sciences," including the arts.

KATZ

KATZ
Goodman's Aesthetics Encapsulated

Goodman's *Ways of World-making* was preceded by his *Languages of Art*, which appeared in 1968 as part of his enquiry into the theory of knowledge. Anchoring the comprehension of the arts in a general theory of symbols, Goodman claims, in *Languages of Art*, that works of art are sets of symbols belonging to *particular* symbolic systems. The manifold means of symbolization, that is, the various ways of world-making, attest to the diversity of human understanding. Since everything that can be referred to by symbols falls within our understanding and since creating and using symbols holds true not only for the arts but for science as well, the difference between art and science, according to Goodman,

> is not that between feeling and fact, intuition and inference, delight and deliberation, synthesis and analysis, sensation and cerebration, concreteness and abstraction, passion and action, mediacy and immediacy, or beauty and truth, but rather a difference in domination of certain specific characteristics of symbols.

By showing how symbols and symbol systems function in the creation and comprehension of our worlds, Goodman removed the barrier between art and science which had prevailed since the seventeenth century, thus breaking with a venerable tradition of philosophical deliberation concerning the arts. His scope is both narrower and wider than that which had prevailed in aesthetic. For example, by concentrating on those aspects which link signs and objects, and accounting for, and only for, objects whose conditions for identification are clear and definite, he excludes intentions, without denying their existence. The aesthetic experience is primarily cognitive as far as Goodman is concerned, whereas factors such as value, intention and the like are culturally determined. Goodman reminds us, however, that attributing inevitable and immutable aspects to cognition is itself a misconception, since in the organization of knowledge it is language which constitutes the prime factor, emphasizing, as it does, cultural rather than universal aspects.

Thus, while arguing, together with Quine, in favor of a holistic view of science, for which deductive inferences are justified by their conformity to valid general rules and, inversely, the rules by their conformity to deductive inferences, Goodman, unlike Quine, anchors both the components as well as the relationship between them in entrenched habits. The rules of deduction, of induction and of logic are neither analytic nor innate; they are, like the experience for which they account, habits of mind susceptible, though stubbornly, to revision and change. The structure of the world of pre-systematic language, says Goodman, is simply "a world-structure under one world description" and not "the structure of the world independent of any description." Among the many true descriptions of the world, accordingly, there are the arts, distinguished by their domination of certain specific characteristics of symbols. Goodman, however, was eager not only to develop a general theory of symbols, but himself made an attempt to describe these certain specific characteristics. It is in connection with his discussion of the specific characteristics of music that Goodman develops his theory of notation.

For a symbolic system to qualify as a Notational System, Goodman tells us, it must answer to five definitional requirements. Two of the requirements are syntactic, and three of them semantic. Briefly, the symbol scheme of every Notational System is notational. It consists of characters ('inscriptions', 'marks', 'utterances') the essential feature of which is an "abstract class of character indifference among inscription," that is, each inscription of character is recognized as a true copy of the character, and no mark may belong to more than one character. The syntactic requirements of a notational system are that the characters be *disjoined* and *finitely differentiated*. Disjointness is assured by a classification that counts every difference as a difference of character. Finite differentiation is assured by a scheme of clearly differentiated inscriptions, so that if two characters have an inscription in common, it must be theoretically possible to determine to which of the two characters the inscription belongs.

Symbol systems consist of symbol schemes correlated with a field of reference. A symbol, however, may or may not denote that which it refers to.

A mark is ambiguous if it has different complaints at different times, even if it is an inscription of a single character. If scores are to be correlated with performances, whatever is denoted by a symbol must comply with it. The three semantic requirements upon notational systems are thus: *un-ambiguity, disjointness* and *finite differentiation*. Un-ambiguity pertains to the invariance in compliance relationship; disjointness stipulates that no two characters have any compliant in common; and finite differentiation assures the theoretical possibility to determine that a given object does not comply with the first or the second of two characters which have different compliance classes if that object does not comply with both.

The above five requirements, Goodman tells us, are not optional, but a must, if a symbol system is to function as a Notational System. Standard musical notation, Goodman suggests, is a prime example of a Notational System. Identity of work and score, he writes,

> is retained in any series of steps, each of them either from compliant performance to score-inscription to true copy. This is ensured by the fact, and only by the fact, that the language in which a score is written must be notational—must satisfy the five stated requirements.

In short, performances of music are not an instance of a musical work, but the end products of the work as defined by its notation. This does not mean that performances do not differ, or may not differ, from each other. In fact, they do because not all the aspects that affect the quality of performances are notational; only those that affect the *identity* of the work are. Developing a notational system like that of music means, says Goodman, having arrived at "a real definition of the notion of a musical work."

Given the immense literature concerning the notion of musical works and the variety of argumentation to which the subject gave rise, Goodman's categorical position about the identity of works may be easily misconstrued. While it is readily understood that a symbol representing an object (1) stands for or denotes that object, and that in order to do so, it must be able (2) to distinguish the object from other objects in its field of reference, it is not readily understood that the discreteness of the objects *themselves* and their field of reference have to be invented, and not only their relationship established. This is certainly so in what Goodman calls a Notational System.

Tracing the development of notation in the West revealed that it persistently eliminated ambiguities and reduced its dependence on any particular style. Once Goodman's five requirements for a notational system were fulfilled *work* preservation, not score preservation, was ensured; the latter is clearly incidental, compared to the paramount significance of the former. Though all symbol systems consist of a symbol scheme correlated with a field of reference, discursive languages–unlike notational systems–meet only the two syntactic requirements, i.e. the disjointness and finite differentiation of characters, but are exempt from the three semantic requirements, that is from un-ambiguity, disjointness, and finite differentiation regarding their field of reference. In discursive languages, accordingly, a definition or set of coextensive definitions is seldom uniquely determined by a member of the class defined, whereas the basic purpose of a notational system may be served only if the compliance relationship is invariant.

A concise summary of Goodman's more comprehensive theory of symbols and the way they function in the arts will contribute a great deal to our understanding of the manner in which they are employed. Given that symbols invariably refer to something, Goodman found it necessary, in his *Languages of Art*, to establish from the outset that resemblance is not necessary for reference and that almost anything may stand for almost anything else. A picture that represents–like a passage that describes–an object refers to and more particularly denotes it. Denotation (what is implied or signified), argues Goodman, is the core of representation and is independent of resemblance. Given that representation is not a matter of imitation, 'reception' and 'interpretation' are interdependent, for in representing an object one does not copy the interpretation, but *achieves* it. Although anything may be denoted, only labels may be exemplified, argues Goodman. Exemplification of an unnamed property usually amounts to exemplification of a nonverbal symbol for which we have no corresponding word or description. The gestures of a conductor, for example, are "labels" applied in analyzing, organizing, and registering what we hear. Though actual labels are often ostensibly applied to fictive things, fictive labels, Goodman reminds us, cannot be applied, for a label that is used exists.

'Exemplification', explains Goodman, is a mode of symbolization related to 'expression'. Though not all exemplification is expression, all expression is exemplification, and what is expressed is *metaphorically* exemplified. Metaphors, however, require attraction as well as resistance, an attraction that overcomes resistance. In metaphor, Goodman tells us, a term with an extension established by habit is applied elsewhere under the influence of that habit; there is both departure from and deference to precedent. When one use of a term precedes and informs another, the second is the metaphorical one. The understanding of metaphor requires recognition that a label functions not in isolation but as belonging to a "family," for we categorize by *sets* of alternatives. The aggregate of the ranges of extension of the labels in a schema Goodman calls 'a realm'. A realm, thus, consist of the objects sorted by the schema, that is, the objects denoted by at least one of the alternative labels. The shift in range that occur in metaphor, Goodman explains, amount to "a migration of concepts, an alienation of categories." It is not, however, the whole 'class' that moves from one realm to realm, nor are attributes somehow extracted from some objects and injected into others. It is, rather, a set of alternative labels that is transported, and the organization they effect in the alien realm is guided by their habitual use in the home realm. Although a schema may be transported almost anywhere, and the choice of territory for invasion is arbitrary, the operation within that territory, Goodman insists, is almost never completely arbitrary. We are free, for example, to apply temperature predicates, say 'warm', to sounds, hues, personalities, and so forth, but which elements in the chosen realm are warm, or warmer than others, is then largely determined. In sum, metaphorical force requires a combination of novelty with fitness, of the odd with the obvious. Metaphor *creates* similarity, and with repetition a transferred application of a schema becomes routine, no longer requiring or making allusion to its base application. Thus "what was novel becomes commonplace, its past is forgotten, and metaphor fades to mere truth."

Given that "what is expressed is metaphorically exemplified," it follows that what expresses sadness, for example, is metaphorically sad, and what is metaphorically sad is *actually* but not literally sad, for it comes under a transferred application of some label coextensive with 'sad'. Thus what is expressed is "possessed", argues Goodman, and what a face or picture expresses need not (but may) be emotions or ideas that the artist wants to convey, or the thoughts or feeling of the viewer or of a person depicted, or the properties of anything else related in some other way to the symbol. The properties a symbol expresses are, however, its own property, but they are acquired property. They are not the features by which the objects that serve as symbols are classified literally, but are metaphorical imports. Furthermore, properties expressed, we learn from Goodman, are not only metaphorically possessed but also "referred to, exhibited, typified, and shown forth." In short, whereas almost anything can denote or even represent almost anything else, a thing can express only what belongs but did not originally belong to it. The difference between expression and literal exemplification, says Goodman, "is a matter of habit, a matter of fact rather than fiat."

Establishment of the referential relationship, as we have seen, is a matter of *singling out* certain properties for attention, of selecting associations with certain objects. Verbal discourse is not least among the many factors that aid in founding and nurturing such associations. Yet musical expressions are no less relative and variable; music may exemplify rhythmic patterns and express peace, pomp, or passion. With respect to verbal symbols, however, Goodman reminds us that ordinary usage is so "undiscriminating" that a word or passage may be said to express not only what the writer thought, felt, intended, or the properties possessed by or ascribed to a subject, but even what is described or stated. Though only the properties it metaphorically exemplifies, *naming* a property and *expressing* it are apparently different matters. Clearly, a tale of fast action may be slow and a description of colorful music drab. To exemplify or express is to *display* rather than describe. From all of these various related modes of symbolization, that is, kinds of reference, the arts may select and organize their "universe" and be themselves in turn informed and transformed.

It is at this point that Goodman introduces his notational theory, but not before having clarified some questions concerning authenticity. His discussion of the subject reveals that in the different arts a work is differently localized. Rembrandt's own brushstrokes must obviously be considered differently than Bach's handwriting, however telling. Goodman distinguishes, accordingly, between 'autographic' and 'allographic' arts, between works that represent individual objects, as in painting, and those that represent a class of performances compliant with the work, as in music. He now proceeds to present his notational theory in order to show that a musical score is in a notation that *defines* a work, and that a picture is not in a notation but is *itself* a work, and that literary script is in a notation and is itself a work. Evidently, in the different arts a work is differently localized.

Though both music and literature are in a notation, taking into account Goodman's five requirements of a notational system, music is both syntactically and semantically articulate, whereas literature is only syntactically articulate but semantically '*dense*', that is, its field of reference is not finitely and un-ambiguously differentiated. In other words, though a literary work is articulate and exemplifies or expresses what is articulated, various reading of the text are always required in order to determine precisely what is exemplified or expressed. While further and projective decisions have to be made with discursive languages, no such questions arise using a notational system as music does. Nothing is, however, intrinsically a representation; status as representation, we learn from Goodman, is relative to symbol system, and a scheme is representational only insofar as it is dense. Hence, despite the definition of works by scores, exemplification of anything beyond the score is reference in a semantically dense system, and a matter of infinitely fine adjustment.

Representation and description are clearly markedly different from exemplification and expression. While representation and description relate a symbol to things it applies to, exemplification relates the symbol to a label that denotes it (and hence indirectly to the things in the range of that label), and expression relates the symbol to a label that metaphorically denotes it (and hence indirectly not only to the given metaphorical but also to the literal range of that label). Thus, to exemplify or express is to display rather than to depict or describe. Goodman's own summary of expression states the following: If 'a' expresses 'b', then (1) 'a' possesses or is denoted by 'b'; (2) this possession or denotation is metaphorical; and (3) 'a' refers to 'b'. Were we to substitute music for 'a' and emotion for 'b', Goodman's summary would state the following: If 'music' expresses 'emotion', then (1) music possesses or is denoted by emotion; (2) this possession or denotation is metaphorical; and (3) it refers to emotion. Let us not forget, however, that expression must be *displayed* and that the utterances of music are *end products* because music is both syntactically and semantically articulate.

Although there is no want of aesthetic theories that deal with music's expressivity or, for that matter, expressivity concerning the other arts and the arts in general, I know of no theory that covers the interrelated functions of symbols pertinent to the arts as rigorously and as succinctly as Goodman's does. Yet there is no denying the importance of Ernest Cassirer's contribution to the philosophy of symbolic logic, with which Goodman was apparently well acquainted. As an arresting representative of Continental philosophy, Cassirer employed his vast learning to unveil the symbolizing activities through which man has expressed himself and given form to his experience. As an analytical philosopher, Goodman's main objective in his *Language of Art* was to unveil the *logic* whereby the denotation of symbols is acquired and circumscribed. Although the symbolizing activities through which man expresses himself are subject to change, affecting the forms to which they give rise, the forms themselves, we learn from Goodman, invariably abide by limiting factors that are necessary for their understanding. Thus how and in what way representation functions in the various arts is independent of their particular choices that are made; works of art must ipso facto take into account the various modes of symbolization, that is, kinds of reference, in order to disclose their preferred objectives.

Patricia Tunstall

Introduction

Tunstall's article "Structuralism and Musicology: An Overview" appeared long before her books on education. Having studied philosophy and musicology, she turned to music education, teaching piano and other musical subjects. Her books clearly focus on the *capacity* of music to transform the lives of children and communities, and on the processes whereby it is achieved. These processes naturally involve socio-psychological factors. In fact, the notion that the arts are able to impact our lives is a premise that accompanied the historical development of Art. History is replete with examples that *display*, and theories that *explain* the "powers" vested in the arts. Goodman, for example, whose theory of knowledge makes no room for a separation between art and science, endeavored to clarify, as we have seen, whereby the "making" of different "worlds" gain the power invested in them. Tunstall's shift from musicology to music education, i.e. from the "humanities" to the "social sciences," more than it exhibits a way whereby knowledge advances it discloses the *temporality* of its internal divisions.

The following section from Tunstall's frequently cited "Structuralism and Musicology" summarizes in a non-technical fashion the fundamental aims, methods and claims of Structuralism and its intellectual history. Structuralism, explains Tunstall, pertains to formal procedures through which the mind structures reality. While the manipulated contents are culture-specific, the procedures themselves are universal in character. Structuralism endeavors, accordingly, to "locate" knowledge and meaning in a "mental system" in search of patterns of structure. These patterns are necessarily of an abstract kind, as distinct from the surface messages presented. Stories, myths, rituals, and other practices are thus assessed through the ways in which their internal components "relate" to each other. Though culture-specific, the ultimate goal of Structuralism consists of "universals" formulated not as ideas but as mental operations that serve humans to organize their world of reality. Structuralism, according to Tunstall, is a latter-day version of Rationalism, although it differs from its 17th-century prototype in that it accommodates cultural and historical diversity and makes use of empirical methods. One may of course argue that these "accommodations" convey a *major* social change, rather than an altered version of rationalism. We ought to remember that it is the "diversities" that triggered the search for a "mental system" that might subsume the differences which they overtly display.

TUNSTALL

from Structuralism and Musicology: An Overview[*]

The past decade has witnessed a growing interest among musicologists in the kind of inquiry known as structuralist. Although structuralism originated as a theory and methodology specific to certain limited disciplines, its relevance to other fields has become increasingly apparent, and its principles and assumptions articulated in increasingly general terms. One of the major trends of twentieth-century thought, it has significant implications for musicology; indeed, some major musicological debates have involved ideas central to structuralist theory, although these ideas are seldom expressed in structuralist terms. It is helpful, therefore, to explore the historical development of that theory at some length - not in order to have new labels to pin on old debates, but to better understand the intellectual history to which those debates are related.

The scope of the subject matter and the limitations of space imposed here will often necessitate somewhat cursory accounts of highly complex fields. The intention of this paper is not, however, an in-depth examination of any single aspect of structuralism, but rather an introductory overview of its basic definitions and procedures.

Structuralism, a theory generated and developed primarily by western European scholars who are the direct inheritors of the Western intellectual tradition, has its philosophical antecedents in the rationalist schools of thought prominent in the seventeenth and eighteenth centuries. Such theorists as Descartes conceived of the thinking human being as inherently rational, and thus as the determining locus of knowledge and truth. Kantian theory was all elucidation of the rational categories that constitute the human mind. French social theorists as diverse as Rousseau and Diderot discussed social functioning from the standpoint of an underlying assumption of the rational nature of man's

[*] From: Patricia Tunstall, "Structuralism and Musicology: An Overview," in *Current Musicology*, 27 (1979, pp.51-64), pp. 51-56.

cognition. The rationalist premises of such figures were reflected not only in the contents but in the formulation of their theories, which involved deductive and speculative rather than inductive processes.

The first challenges to rationalist thought came from within philosophical discourse: empiricists such as Hume and Berkeley argued that the mind has no inherent rational order, but is a repository of the impressions transmitted from the outside world. The nineteenth century, however, brought more formidable challenges. For the first time, the Western tradition of speculation upon the nature of the self was forced into extensive contact with foreign cultures with alien versions of objective reality. Within western European culture itself, radically different worldviews became evident. Never before had such conflicting modes of thought and life demanded recognition: now, however, classes with different social experience were coming into increasing power, and nations with unfamiliar cultures were entering the world economic arena. The evident differences between cultures could not be accounted for by the rationalist assumption of a universal identity of mental categories. The new theories developed to explain these differences were based on a new assumption that of the determining power of environment. In addition, developments in biological science had implications for every field. Emerging theories of evolution provided a new model for understanding human experience in terms of historical progress.

The challenge to rationalism from realms outside of formal philosophical thought thus developed into a powerful and eventually dominant critique. The rationalist assumption that the source of knowledge was the inherent, rational categories of the mind found itself in increasing conflict with theories locating this source elsewhere: in social and cultural experience, in political organization, in historical identity, or in biological nature. Freudian theory, while sharing the rationalist's emphasis on the discovery of universal characteristics of the human subject, implied, however, a refutation of a major rationalist premise: when Freud examined the self, he found not immutable mind but immutable drives–an unconscious which was the very antithesis of reason.

Theorists in all fields, then, rejected the idea of the rational mind and turned to the investigation of other sources of meaning and intelligibility. These theories differed in method as well as object: no longer relying upon deductive elegance, they were couched in the terms of empiricist inquiry and based upon claims of scientific validity. These changes occurred in the emerging discipline of musicology as well as in other fields. Theories that musical processes were determined by universal, invariant mental operations were challenged by explanations of musical activity as conditioned by social, cultural, or historical forces.

It is significant that the discipline of linguistics, in which structuralism first emerged as a systematic theory, has a particularly strong tradition of rationalist ideas. During the late eighteenth century, the French school of "philosophical grammar" had evolved a theory of language based on rationalist premises. Described by one commentator as "the linguistic equivalent of Cartesianism,[1] this school postulated the existence of more and less abstract levels of language, and a transformational process by which less abstract levels were generated out of more abstract ones. Early in the twentieth century, a Swiss linguist named Ferdinand de Saussure revived and developed this line of thinking. Language, he claimed, is a system with logical and autonomous laws. At a level of organization more abstract than what we normally call grammar, a language can be investigated as a set of logical operations. Saussure's seminal distinction was between individual acts of speech ("paroles") and the universe of linguistic conventions upon which individuals draw when they speak ("langue"). Linguistic analysis, therefore, was the investigation of speech in order to discover the organizational properties of language. Saussure stressed that language as a system is not the conscious possession of any individual; rather it is the totality of linguistic rules available in a society, "a sum of impressions deposited in the brain of each member of a community, almost like a dictionary of which identical copies have been distributed to each individual."[2] According to a common formulation, language is a kind of "code"; each instance of individual speech is a "message" constructed with reference to the code. Although the code is not apparent in surface characteristics of speech, and its users are not conscious of it, it can be extrapolated through structural analysis of the relations among elements of a series of messages.

---

[1] Howard Serwer, "New Linguistic Theory and Old Music Theory," in *International Musicological Society: Report of the Eleventh Congress;* Copenhagen, 1972, 2 vols. (Copenhagen: Wilhelm Hansen, 1974), 2:653.

[2] Ferdinand de Saussure, *Course in General Linguistics,* trans. Wade Baskin (New York: McGraw-Hill, 1959), p. 19.

These concepts deviated significantly from many of the social-scientific ideas prevalent at the time. In contrast to the current emphasis upon social context, Saussure's method was to isolate language from its social functions on the assumption that within the elements of language itself could be discovered its essential qualities. Second, Saussure's thesis that these qualities were logically coherent implied the then unpopular premise that the ordering activity of the mind is systematic. Third, in contradistinction to linguistic theories stressing the historical development of languages, Saussure emphasized the importance of non-historical studies, since the system of language accessible to any speaker exists entirely in the present.

The task of the structural analyst, according to Saussure, is to organize a mass of data—a collection of individual utterances—in such a way as to clarify the logical system that comprehends all of them. This involves a process of dismantling and reconstruction, since, in specific utterances, linguistic elements are arranged and distributed so as to obscure the systematic nature of their relations. The linguistic code is thus never deducible from one message. A collection of messages, however, may be broken down into component parts; these parts may then be used to construct a logical model in which their interrelations are explicit. Through the orderly rearrangement of speech elements the fundamental order of a language can be revealed.

Saussure's reconstructive model—adopted by most succeeding structuralists—involves two axes, the syntagmatic and the associative. The horizontal, syntagmatic axis represents "contiguous" relations—that is, how elements are arranged sequentially in speech. The vertical, associative axis represents "thematic" relations, or how elements refer metaphorically or symbolically to other elements. Thus, reading horizontally, the analyst can discover the conventions by which words are combined into a series in speech; vertical configurations will reveal the categories of sound and meaning by which words are classified in memory. Linguistic elements related syntagmatically can occur next to one another; those related associatively can replace one another.

The significance of this model is that it embodies a basic structuralist view of mental ordering activity: the mind can link elements together linearly (and can follow rules for doing so), and it can associate them categorically (again, according to given rules). Crucial to the model is a conception of the mind as active and of mental categories as operations, not ideas. The structure of language explored by Saussure is a complex of operational capacities, not a constellation of images. And it is this feature that makes languages comparable: if the deepest structure of a language is not a set of rules about particular words and grammars, but a set of formal procedures for dealing with all words and all grammars, then this is a level at which all languages may be compared.

Saussure postulated other comparisons as well. Language, he suggested, is only one of several systems of signs operating in society–such systems having fixed correspondences between "signifiers" and "signifieds." In language, the signifiers are sound-images such as words and syllables; its signifieds are the mental concepts indicated by those sound-images. Although language is perhaps the most important system of signs, there are others: "Language is a system of signs that expresses ideas, and is therefore comparable to a system of writing, the alphabet of deaf-mutes, symbolic rites, polite formulas, etc."[3] Any systematic cultural phenomenon is a system of signs, according to Saussure, if it is characterized by a one-to-one relation between each signifier and its signified, and if that relation is not open to individual decision but is fixed by social convention. Linguistics is therefore potentially a field within a general science of signs, which he called "semiology,"

The first to respond to this suggestion was the French anthropologist Claude Levi-Strauss, whose work was decisive for the development of all interdisciplinary structuralist theory and practice. A scholar whose training encompassed both Western philosophical tradition and modern anthropological techniques, Levi-Strauss found in structuralism a way to synthesize his speculative inclinations and his respect for scientific methods. "For the first time," he wrote of structuralism, "social scientists are able to form necessary relations."[4] Working from Saussure's premise that other cultural phenomena were organized like language, he applied the structuralist analytic techniques outlined above to various cultural systems, such as totemistic practices, kinship conventions, and myth repertoires.

In the course of these studies, Levi-Strauss added important dimensions to structuralist theory. First of all, he found that the specific organizational structures discovered in one system of a culture will be similar to those discovered in another. Studies of a Brazilian Indian society provided persuasive evidence

---

[3] Ibid., p, 16.
[4] As quoted in Hayes, ed., Levi-Strauss: *The Anthropologist as Hero* (Boston: MIT Press, 1970).

for this idea. His structuralist investigation of their myths revealed strong systematic relations between the seemingly random elements of the myths: when analytically reorganized, the images, events, and characters of the myths fell into consistent thematic categories (such as honey and tobacco, raw food and cooked food). These categories, in Levi-Strauss's view, were symbolic expressions of a fundamental opposition between nature and culture; and the operations performed upon these symbols in the process of myth generation represented attempts by the culture to render the opposition intelligible. Myths, therefore, were not irrational explanations of natural phenomena; they were logic systems using a vocabulary of natural phenomena to explain the world. Exploring other systems within the same culture, Levi-Strauss discovered that the fundamental categories underlying the elements of myth also underlay other areas of cultural expression. The ways those categories were manipulated within the myths were typical of logical operations governing other kinds of mental activity and understanding. He concluded that the categories and manipulations themselves constituted the structural habits of the culture, the set of cognitive properties underlying all of its various sign systems. The particular value of structuralist anthropology, therefore, was that one could discern the logical structures of a culture in any of its semiological phenomena. The patterns of organization characterizing one system would be the patterns operative in any other, and all systems would be susceptible to the structuralist method of clarifying those patterns.

Levi-Strauss was interested in a still higher level of generalization. He theorized that logic structures were not only consistent among cultural phenomena, they were, at the most abstract level, universal. The ultimate importance of ascertaining such logic structures was that they reflected properties of the human mind itself. The formal procedures through which the mind structured reality were common to all minds; the content manipulated by these procedures was culture-specific, but the procedures themselves were universal in character. All aspects of human experience, then, were governed at the most basic level by a limited number of operational categories inherent in the structure of the mind. In Levi-Strauss's view, these categories were principally binary in nature, such as juxtaposition, inversion, and opposition. It was the task of ethnographers to refine such views: "Ethnographic analysis," he declared, "must try to arrive at invariants beyond the empirical diversity of the human species."[5]

In the work of both Saussure and Levi-Strauss, an analytical process that begins by restricting itself to an isolated object has as its eventual aim the extrapolation of the structures imposed on reality by the mind. The initial exclusiveness of focus is only a preparation for a conclusion at the most general level. This conclusion will not be a hypothesis of universal conceptual, linguistic, or thematic categories; rather it will be a formulation of the organizational properties of the mind that characterize all of its operations.

The connection of this premise to the rationalist philosophical tradition is unmistakable: basic to Cartesian and Kantian theories alike was the notion that all minds operate with the same formal properties, and that these properties are definitively logical. Yet the structuralist theories of Saussure and Levi-Strauss represent a distinctively modern reformulation of this notion.

Seen in the context of Western intellectual history, structuralism is a set of principles neither precisely rationalist nor precisely corresponding to modern ideas of environmental determinism. Like modern social sciences, it proceeds by examining cultural phenomena; like modern natural sciences, it isolates sets of phenomena for purposes of study; but in its ultimate goal–the formulation of cognitive universals–it is close to its heritage of rationalist philosophy. From this heritage it takes the basic assumption of an inherent mental structure that determines experience and knowledge. But it shares with modern social-scientific thought an awareness of the important role of culture in determining specific knowledge and experience, and so postulates universals far more abstract, less bound to specific concepts, than those of philosophical rationalism. Like many modern theories, structuralism postulates decisive limits upon an individual's conscious capacity to choose his forms of thought and action, but it defines those limits as innate to cognition, not as learned. This definition allows it to rely, as did Cartesian thought, upon speculative and deductive analytical techniques; but unlike Cartesian thought, structuralism first depends upon empirical data-gathering and verifying procedures. Structuralism, then, may perhaps be understood as a modern reemergence of rationalist ideas informed and tempered by the insights of modern social, political, and scientific thought.

[5] Ibid., p, 23.

PART III

Conception and Perception Intertwined

III

Conception and Perception Intertwined

Introduction

In this section of the book, I wish to sensitize the reader to the fact that knowledge involves both preconceived notions and inferred understandings. Knowledge and the accumulation thereof rests at all times on insights and discernments, imagination and judgment. Though we as humans create that which guides our understanding, we must be able to differentiate between already formed ideas and new ones, between ideas based on previous observations and distinctions and the ways in which they may be employed in order to further our understanding.

'Conception' is generally viewed as a mental *abstract*, or as a "general idea" inferred or derived from specific instances. John Locke's description of a "general idea" in fact corresponds to a description of the term 'concept'. General ideas, according to Locke, are created by removing the uncommon characteristics from different individuals and retaining only that which they hold in common. Indeed, it is largely accepted that a general conception is formed through abstraction, i.e. by focusing on the common elements among the many images of the members of a class. It has been questioned, however, whether by comparing things with each other and taking note of their agreement, we merely recognize something we already had in mind or discover something that resulted from the comparison. The former position argues that by dropping some of the differences among the real manifestations our intuitive perception strives for an "ideal," representing, as such, some kind of law concerning our intellect. Kant, for example, argued that defining 'concept' as an abstraction of experience is only partly correct since the logical acts of "understanding" rests on our ability to compare *and* reflect, i.e. on the *comparison* among mental images and on the *reflection* whereby they may differ from each other. Kant was clearly more interested in the logical operation by which concepts are generated than in the definition of the term. Nonetheless, according to Kant "to conceive" is essentially to think in abstraction about what is common to a plurality of possible instances.

In cognitive linguistics, abstract concepts are generally viewed as *transformations* of concrete concepts derived from embodied experience. Properties of different domains, accordingly, are selectively mapped onto a "blended space," as it were, similar to the "blends" of metaphors. The transformation of embodied concepts through this kind of mapping clearly deals with concept formation. Plato, as we have seen, advocated a transcendental world of "pure forms," i.e. concepts that lay behind the veil of the physical world of appearance. Plato's ideas are *universal* concepts; they are not derived from abstraction or perception, or as a manner in which we grasp the world.

Abstractions may also be viewed as a process whereby higher concepts are derived from literal ones by retaining only information which is relevant for a particular purpose. As we all know, objects are also often grouped into categories, usually for some specific purpose and are closely related to a process of generating a classification structure. It has been suggested that categorization based on grouping things based on "prototypes" is the basis for human development, and that this process is closely related to our learning about the world via embodiment. In other words, systems of categories are not objectively in the world, but are rooted in people's experience. Conceptual categories, hence, are not necessarily identical for different cultures, or, for that matter, for every individual in the same culture.

Whether mental image, process, or kinds of representation, conceptualization is connected, in one form or another, to comprehension, i.e. to our faculty of understanding that allows us to put knowledge to use. Understanding, thus, represents a more profound level than simply knowing. However, to put knowledge to use invariably depends on strategies which entail an ability to compare groups or categories that contain concept relevant features with groups or categories that do not contain concept relevant features. Concept attainment is in itself a learning process that enables the search for attributes that can be used to distinguish exemplars from non exemplars of various mental categories that help us classify objects, events and ideas.

The following paragraphs aim to serve a double function: (1) to exemplify the process of concept attainment and (2) to provide a short introduction to the subsequent essays.

History is usually told as a succession of periods, each of which is given a name. Elements within a particular period–artistic styles, significant events, socio-political ideas, including popular beliefs–are thought to be related to each other and to characterize the ways whereby periods differ from each other, like for example the Renaissance from the Middle-Ages. Underlying this approach is the notion of *change*. The emphasis on periodicity, however, often obscures *continuity*. The designation of "periods" may be applicable, as well, to a diversity of subject matters and relevant to the changes they underwent. Yet despite their "encompassing" nature, divisions of this kind are likely to overlook the perpetuation of certain habits of thought–predilections and preferences. The "vertical continuities" of *traditions*, for example, clearly deserve no less attention than their "horizontal phases."

Indeed, even if societies undergo periodic change, some underlying themes may endure. Sociological studies have shown that even the attitude to commonplace innovations may reveal long seated norms that promote or retard their acceptance. Moreover, the *reasons,* for example, for rejecting birth-control in India may differ markedly from those provided by orthodox Jews. It has also been observed that the construction of collective memories is a process in which past and present are mutually constitutive. In fact, under the rubric of "Continuity and Change" the social sciences produced many studies that aimed to uncover the *dynamics* of such processes in order to better understand its various manifestations. However, to formalize the *hidden-directives* that affect diverse processes is far from easy since it calls for a "strategy" that would enable their examination beyond the primacy of culture.

Indeed, the above mentioned studies, and many more, led to a search of *programmed instructions* that ostensibly steer the response of social systems to change without forgoing their unique identities. In other words, based on extensive studies and observation, it was assumed that cultures, traditions, political systems and institutions of diverse kinds abide by certain "codes" that impact their behavior. The notion about the persistence of social codes in seemingly changed situations gave rise, in turn, to the examination of the conditions which are more likely to invoke and articulate such codes in practice. In fact, the endorsement of the concept of 'code', and the comprehension of its presumed function, enabled "the putting of acquired knowledge to use."

The following essay "Societal Codes for Responding to Dissent" represents my own attempt "to put knowledge to use." As a musicologist, I was naturally aware of the transformations that took place in the course of music's development in the West. I was likewise aware of the fact that certain local predilections seemed to endure despite the overall characteristics that differentiate one period from another. Certain stylistic features even bare the name of the localities with which they are identified. For example, the 'cantabile'–song-like character–is associated with Italy and the 'agrément'–features of note embellishments–are associated with France. And while the difference between French and Italian opera–including the debates they evoked–is well known, there are endless examples that betray, as it were, "vertical continuities" alongside shared "horizontal changes."

Involved as well in ethno-musicological studies, I was of course also aware of the primacy of culture. But in order to be able to differentiate between the transformational processes of the musical traditions which I investigated, I saw fit to pay closer attention to studies that wrestled with the very *problem* I grappled with, i.e. continuity in the face of change. Consequently, I applied much of what I have learned from these studies to my own field of endeavor. These studies, however, also confirmed what I already knew, namely, that interdisciplinary studies do not require expertise in diverse or related fields, but that they strongly depend on a *thorough understanding* of "what relates to what and whereby." The following investigation of the "workings" of societal codes in fact rested on this very conviction. Musicologists, I believe, have not noticed this study of mine, but my attempt to put my newly acquired knowledge "to use" was well received by the social sciences.

Unlike the unveiling of *hidden directives* with possible structural implications, i.e. processes of "continuity and change" beyond the primacy of culture, the following essay by Rigbi deals with a significant change that took place within Western classical music towards the end of the nineteenth century. In her attempt to delineate the characteristics of the emergent new style, she devised a dichotomous system in which each concept that represents the previous style is opposed by a contrasting concept valid for the new style. While the procedure employs the older style as *reference*, the systematic "negation" of its major characteristics highlights *the extent* of the change that took place. Those familiar with Walter Benjamin's famous essay "The Work of Art in the Age of Mechanical Reproduction" will recall that Benjamin also devised a dichotomous system in which each concept that represents the *traditional* works of art is opposed by a contrasting concept valid for the sphere of *mechanical reproduction*. Accordingly, 'uniqueness', 'distance', 'permanence', 'heterogeneity', and 'cult value' that were the criteria of the sinking "auratic tradition," were superseded by 'reproducibility', 'close range', 'transitoriness', 'homogeneity', and 'exhibition value'. While the prognostic validity of Benjamin's categorical apparatus may raise doubts, it does not affect its analytical value. For example, the observation that 'distance' and 'permanence' belong together, just as, conversely 'close range' and 'transitoriness' do, is independent–as regards truth content–of the continued existence or demise of the "auratic" work of art.

With regard to concepts, Ruth HaCohen's essay reminds us that some of the concepts which we employ in our daily life are "ambiguous" since it is difficult to pinpoint their referents, i.e. to establish what exactly is being indicated. Ambiguity, however, may at times serve a proper function; it may provide a modicum of "flexibility"–a suppleness that leaves room for future clarification, impacted by unforeseen circumstances and novel issues that need addressing. Constitutions, for example, are rarely replaced since some of the concepts which they employ allow for "amendments"–adjustments of sorts. Rather than inviting modifications of kinds, diplomacy, for example, often uses ambiguous concepts in order to *conceal* political intents. Plato, as we have seen, advocated a transcendental world of "pure forms"–concepts that are not derived from the manner in which we grasp the world. History, however, reveals that some of these concepts require clarifications, mindful of the contexts in which they are employed and the purposes they serve. For example, some eighteenth century philosophers attacked Hobbes' social theory–which highlighted the irreconcilable antagonism between *self*-love (egoism) and *social* duty (civic responsibility)–by redefining '*affection*' and its appropriate *space* in order to be able to reconcile man's self-love with social affections. By tracing the transformations which concepts undergo, we stand to gain insight into the procedures whereby humans structure their changing worldviews.

KATZ
Societal Codes for Responding to Dissent*

The fashionable concept of code, as applied to the social sciences, seems most usefully defined in terms of a set of "programmed instructions" directing social systems to respond to a recurrent set of problems in a particular way. The development of the notion of code has been accompanied by an effort at formalization and schematization of these directives using quasi mathematics of information theory, structural linguistics and related fields. If the concept of code is to be of use–that is, if it is to add something that takes us beyond theories of the primacy of culture–it is to this formalization of hidden directives, with their possible structural implications (Levi-Strauss, 1963; Piaget, 1970) and to the adequacy of their description of the processes of continuity and change in familiar social situations that we must look.

Perhaps the most fundamental problem to which to address an inquiry of this kind is the problem of dissent. History, sociology and anthropology are replete with examples of heresy, protest, schism, rebellion and expulsion, as well as alternative examples of merger, accommodation, cooptation and the like. Religion and politics are only the most obvious of the institutional areas in which such problems repeatedly arise. Groups, societies and institutions of all kinds are challenged in the same ways. The patterned set of social relations and rules for the mobilization of these relations to cope with threat, internal or external, are keys to the integrity and continuity of a culture over extended periods of time and wide varieties of ostensibly different situations.[1]

Acculturation studies contain many valuable observations concerning organized efforts to preserve culture–especially those aspects which a group

---

* From: W. Bennis, K. D. Benne & R. Chin, eds., *The Planning of Change,* (New York, 1985), pp. 354-367.

[1] Cf. Eisenstadt (1973) for a discussion of the persistence of such social codes and their reappearance in ostensibly changed situations. Also note the conflictful conditions under which codes are more likely to be invoked and articulated.

values most highly–when the way of life of the group is threatened. For example, it has been emphasized often that the reactions to threat which Linton (1943) called "perpetuative rational nativistic movements" are guided by "boundary maintaining mechanisms."[2] Taking this as his starting point, Freed (1957) made an important contribution to the idea of social codes long before the introduction of the actual word. He suggested "type societies" in acculturation studies. While we shall take issue with him at certain points, we shall make use of Freed's analysis of the two archetypical modes for the successful management of social continuity which he perceives in the *shtetl* culture of the Eastern European Jews, on the one hand, and that of the Pennsylvania Amish, on the other, demonstrating their applicability to a wide variety of groups.

Freed's analysis is limited to structural features, arguing that the social organization of a society and the way it organizes certain of its culture patterns are the critical factors in resisting disintegration. Thus, while all societies have, in one form or another, some boundary-maintaining mechanism, there are but a limited number of distinctive structural forms underlying these mechanisms and capable of contributing to continuity and containing potential deviation. Although we shall deal with it in detail below, it is worth noting here that while Freed's analysis is structural it is also static in the sense that it says nothing about the transformational processes which result from the successive application of such structural responses; in other words, it does not account for problems which have been raised under the heading of "evolutionary invariance" (Baum, 1975) or the "structural implications for derivatives" (Eisenstadt, 1973).

The questions we wish to put are three: (1) whether there are identifiable codes for responding to dissent; (2) whether these codes can be usefully outlined in transformational terms; and (3) whether the preconditions for the development of different kinds of codes can be specified.

Codes for Coping with Dissent

Societies are almost always concerned with their integrity and continuity, although not all to the same degree. As we shall argue below, certain groups

---

[2] For a relevant discussion on "mechanisms of limitation" see Buchler and Nutini (1969).

are more concerned with preserving the integrity of their values, others are more concerned with their continuity as social organizations. Under unusual circumstances, certain groups may care rather little about either.

Societies, groups and organizations which do care about their integrity, continuity or both have to work at ensuring their institutions and have to be prepared continually to cope with the threat of dissent, deviance and innovation. There are two major responses to potential dissent: expulsion and incorporation. Note the similarity to Hirschman's (1970) concepts of "exit" and "voice."[3] Without claiming to exhaust the list of other possible responses, this paper will pay particular attention to a third response which might be called "dispensation," or the licensing of certain individuals or groups to play deviant roles, not so much for their own sake, of course, but to contribute to the stability of the group.

To assume, however, that these responses present themselves as fixed alternatives from which to choose is simply not sound. Indeed, the choice itself is part and parcel of that structure which it serves as a protective mechanism. Moreover, assessments of the consequences of a choice may result in the "decision" to give one of the other alternatives a try. Indeed, oscillating between alternatives may be as much a part of systems which have built-in dilemmas—and there are many of these—as are the clear-cut choices. While characteristic of all groups, the labeling and relabeling of the same phenomena—a particular form of deviance, for example—may thus reflect different degrees of genuine transformation.

It is hardly necessary to provide examples of incorporation and expulsion of potentially deviant groups except for the fact that they may allow us to extrapolate the "schemes" in which motivation, action and consequences are bound. We have at hand, for example, a most telling case of the condemnation and expulsion by the Catholic Church of the Waldensians in 1181–4, and some thirty years later, the recognition and incorporation by the same Church of a

---

[3] Hirschman (1970) came to our attention after this paper was completed. His concern with exiting vs. protesting in response to dissatisfaction is closely related to the argument of this paper. His primary emphasis is on individual rather than group behavior, and in most of his arguments the locus of power resides in the members rather than the organization.

rather similar group, the Franciscans (Leff, 1967). Peter Walde's group, "the poor men of Lyons," was founded about 1170 and preached the emulation of Christ the Man, insisting that the asceticism which that conception implies should be a binding precondition for membership in the Church. They called for Apostolic Christianity, where the Church itself must forgo wealth and privilege. The authority of the Church hierarchy was rejected, and the word of the Scriptures was invoked against the Church itself, which was no longer recognized as the instrument of God's will. Paradoxically, emphasis on Christ, the man, enabled each man to feel more of a God, and implementation of the wishes of the group would have meant, in fact, the dismemberment of the Church.

The Franciscans were inspired by the self-same apostolic ideas. Both groups rejected a mercantile life for one of wandering poverty. But whereas Walde and his group were condemned by the Bishop of Lyons in 1181 and then by Pope Lucius II in 1184, St. Francis' group was recognized by Pope Innocent III in 1210. "Although it is inconceivable," says Leff, "that St. Francis could ever have been a heretic it is more than possible that in different circumstances Walde might have remained within the Church. Conversely, without the insight of Innocent III, St. Francis' and St. Dominic's groups might have been formed into new orders" (p. 419). The Waldensians set up as a splinter group, gaining adherents and surviving the Middle Ages by "bringing practice into conformity with precept"–denouncing the Roman Church and claiming to be the one true apostolic church.

Both Franciscans and Waldensians venerated Christ's poverty. But whereas the Waldensians insisted on the capitulation of the Church, St. Francis viewed the evangelical life as a revelation from God addressed to the individual believer. This distinctive emphasis of the Franciscans, while perhaps even more demanding than that of the Waldensians, made it possible for the Church to incorporate the Franciscans as a pious elite while condemning the Waldensians as heretics.

While the bases of the differential preference of the Church are clear, historically speaking, neither of the responses passed unpaid-for. The ultimate consequence of incorporating groups like the Franciscans and of allowing the growth of more pious enclaves within the Church increased internal differentiation and inevitably fostered the secularization of the Church as a whole. Conversely, by expelling groups like the Waldensians, the Church relinquished its control over the momentous growth of counter-sentiments which accumulated on the outside, unwittingly contributing to the egalitarian ethic and the recognition of common cause among the various dissenting groups.

The "Logic" of Formation and Re-formation

Yet, this inconsistency in the attitude of the Church to deviant and splinter groups may be consistent indeed, and can be described in terms of a code: Let B stand for "Bible," in the broad sense of writings which serve as legitimizing agents; D for "dogma," in the sense of a selected body of articles of faith; and O for "organization." Let the equilibrium between D and O (D⇄O) be our starting point, the point at which orthodoxy became defined and the authority of the Roman Church established.[4] If the structural relation

$$\text{D} \overset{\nearswarrow \text{B} \searrow}{\rightleftarrows} \text{O}$$

stands for the Church (D⇄O) as arbiter of God's will (B) on earth, the following "evolutionary invariants" of "Formation" and "Re-formation" will result from the patterns of incorporation and exclusion respectively; in other words, the successive application of each of the two response patterns will have a distinctive, and cumulative, structural effect over time (see Figure 1).

The cardinal numbers in the schema represent the number of changes undergone in cumulative fashion so that each triangle represents the state of affairs at a given moment in time. The reintroduction of B at each stage represents the renewed appeal to the authority of Scripture to legitimate the change.[5] The right-hand side of the scheme, representing the process which we propose to call Formation, reflects the situation of the Church as

---

[4] We shall not deal with dissent which became such only retrospectively by having failed to be accepted as orthodoxy, but rather with dissent which presented itself as a direct challenge to the Church following its establishment.

[5] It need not be limited to Scripture as we have stated before.

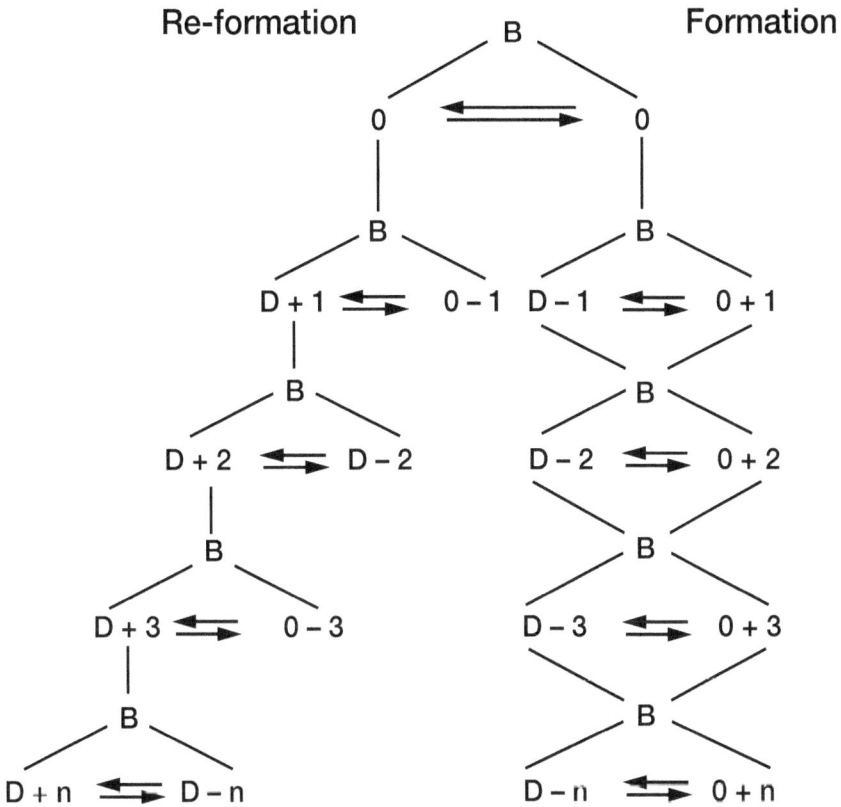

FIGURE 1 Cumulative Structural- Effects of Incorporation and Exclusion

it incorporates the "pious" orders; these developments have their origin in O, the organizational element in the original triangle. The left-hand side of the scheme, under the original D, represents the dispersal of incompatible groups, expulsions or breakaways from the mother Church, which share, however, both the fate and attitudes of heretics. Strictly speaking, both D and O are composites of ends and means, but whereas ends are emphasized over means in the former, means are emphasized over ends in the latter, hence the relationship between the Formation scheme and our original O and the Re-formation scheme and the original D.

The signs minus (–) and plus (+) stand for concession and accretion, or weakening and strengthening, respectively. It will thus be observed that accretion and concession on the left-hand side forces "practice into conformity with precept" in the sense that O is diminished with each increase in D. The right-hand side, however, weakens precept (D) at the expense of practice (O). Ironically, by choosing what seems "best" for the preservation of their institution, we see the "policy-makers"–on the right-hand side–enabling those whom they reject to live up to their professed beliefs. Pragmatism breeds the Gods! Or, less poetically, one may say that institutionalization, centralization, secularization and an orientation to here-and-now go well together, as do ideologization, looser networks of relations and an orientation either to a glorified past or to a utopian future. All of this is implicit in the scheme.

And although we have been referring to religious examples, it should be clear that the same processes apply to other institutions as well, political parties, for example. Troeltsch (1949) and Michels (1949) would be equally applicable here, for the "logic" of Formation and Reformation stands for the dialectics between ideology and power, not only as manifested in universal religions but as it comes to the fore elsewhere as well.

If the analysis presented so far is correct, it suggests a hypothesis concerning the structure of Protestantism: it suggests that the macro-structure which we call Protestantism owes its origin to a "pre-history" of successive failures to become something resembling the mother Church. Rather than modeling itself on the principle of Formation by incorporating successive breakaway groups and incorporating its own dissidents, these sects appear to continue to pursue the exclusionist logic of Re-formation. Should this, in fact, prove to be the case, one may view the Protestant Reformation as an unanticipated consequence of the successive actions of the Catholic Church in breeding egalitarianism and non-conformism which did not organize as a monolithic competitor but, rather, as a loose confederation of groups which came to recognize the common principle underlying their existence. The proposition, in short, concerns the mere dropping of a hyphen.

Exclusion as Social Code

The code implicit in the example of the Catholic Church is one which both excludes and incorporates, according to whether the deviant group gives enough leeway to the establishment to subsume it dogmatically and to relocate it organizationally. Of the two mechanisms, exclusion is the less favored, and indeed can be shown to have costly consequences.

Yet, there appear to be systems which prefer exclusion as a code, and viewed in terms of transformational processes, may even be said to have prospered thereby. Economic systems based on free competition are a case in point.

Our argument may be restated as follows: Just as the Catholic Church excluded certain deviant groups which proved un-subsumable for one or another reason (including lack of imagination) so there may be other groups which exclude themselves. The argument is simple enough, but simply not enough without spelling out its transformational implications. For this kind of schism—whether in religion, politics or economics—leads to a competing church, party or enterprise. That is, the breakaway group establishes the very kind of organization from which it separated and internalizes the same set of "directives" leading to organizational elaboration with its attendant preference for subsuming dissenters, allocating them to a special place, while promoting the growth of oligarchy and centralization.

The case of Protestantism, we suggest, appears to be different. It did not create a competing church but rather a sort of federation of churches. The repeated history of exclusion and rebellion of different groups, equality for the individual and more direct experience through fundamentalism, appears to have been guided by the additional discovery of nonconformity *within themselves*. While exclusion weakens organization by definition, the experience of nonconformity makes room for the idea of the legitimacy of opposition. Taken together it means (1) leave us if you insist on disagreeing, but (2) remember that we, too, were rebels, and (3) our common rebelliousness creates a basis for loosely sticking together. In short, there may arise a pluralistic federation of rebels which together acts like a movement.

The code of exclusion which programs Protestant fundamentalism is illustrated by Freed's (1957) example of the Amish. Freed makes a point of emphasizing the egalitarian character of the group. The maintenance of the group's "nativistic movement" is not in the hands of specialists but is equally the responsibility of all of the adult members of the society. This absence of a group of specialists is correlated in the Amish type of society with strong means of social control (which are readily used) and the frequent expulsion of deviant individuals, and sometimes, of schismatic groups. These splinter groups may form over very minor points.

Clearly, Protestant churches behave in a variety of ways. Some, like the Amish, try to stay out of the world and have trouble relating to others, including–or especially–their own breakaway groups. Others have leaned more toward incorporation, having become–as one might have expected–large and rich and competitive, in many ways, with their Catholic forebears. But in an overall sense, it seems useful to think of Protestantism as "programmed" by exclusion, with the added recognition of commonality. This best of "both-worlds-code," may have contributed to the recognition of the legitimacy of difference, and the rights of minorities, not inside the individual sect (which is exclusionist), but inside the broad domain of Protestantism, and perhaps Western society at large. The separation of church and state and the awareness, often the acceptance, of individual and group difference may prove to be related.

Should this be the case, one may argue that Protestantism was not only expedient to the rise of capitalism, but also to the idea of pluralism in the West. Both relate to the democratization of society before the turn of the curve of diminishing returns.

The evolution of the kibbutz movement provides a parallel example. Its origin is in utopian socialism, emphasizing the desire to live the socialist dogma in person and here-and-now rather than by proxy and "after the revolution." The history of the kibbutz movement includes a series of successive schisms, expressed in the breakaway of groups of kibbutzim from their own kibbutz federations and the breakup of individual kibbutzim due to dogmatic and organizational infighting among their members. Yet, through all of this, the sense of commonality pervades the kibbutzim and the kibbutz federations. Despite all their differences–the differences which forced them apart–they are far the stronger as a result of their awareness of the need to remain together. They require dogmatic homogeneity within the group and recognize the legitimacy of dogmatic pluralism within the movement as a whole. Links of a similar sort sometimes characterize the relationships among splinter groups of other ideological organizations–movements for national liberation, for example–or among terrorist groups espousing a multiplicity of causes with ostensibly little common interest.

Dilemmas and the Dynamics of Codes

Perhaps these "exclusionists" furnish us with another clue to the workings of codes. If codes are directives for action which guide the responses of organizations in situations of choice, it appears that the situations among which they must choose have the character of dilemmas. But dilemmas, by definition, are insoluble; they do not permit a once-and-for-all choice. The dilemma at hand is a good illustration: one cannot continually choose for dogmatic integrity and still hope to remain an organization–any kind of organization. By the same token, one cannot repeatedly choose for organization and hope to remain with a coherent set of beliefs. Organization and dogma are horns of a dilemma, both of which require attention. Thus, by preferring to concern itself with organization, the code of incorporation threatens the *raison d'etre,* while the exclusionist code threatens to empty the pews. Ostensibly, the simple solutions of incorporation and exclusion are both self-destructive.

The more subtle way of examining these codes, therefore, also requires attention to the ways in which each code copes with the "other" horn of the dilemma. The exclusionists do so by making certain–perhaps by having to make certain–that the excluded do not stray too far. Perhaps the idea of federation–among the Protestants or among the kibbutzim–is a typical exclusionist response to the other horn of its dilemma. Similarly, the incorporationists have to see to it that dogma is neither diluted beyond recognition nor so energized that it threatens organizational control. The creation of special orders within the Church for sectarians (so that they are appropriately visible and invisible, accessible at certain times and places, and out-of-reach at others) represents an example of attention to the other horn of the inclusionist dilemma.

Indeed, the challenge that sets the programmed instructions of the code into action is the very dilemma with which the code deals. Dissidence arises when parties seek to modify organization or authority in the name of dogma or dogma in the name of organization. Attending to organization, one invites challenges to authority often couched in the name of dogma. Similarly, attending to dogmatic coherence, one stimulates challenges to dogma often couched in the language of organization.

The Christian church is well experienced in such dilemmas. Its earliest and most continuous problem, perhaps, arises from the competing doctrines of preordination, whereby Man's fate is a function of God's grace–which is un-fathomable–and freedom of will whereby Man's own choice affects his fate.[6] Augustine preached predetermination, but his followers found that the doctrine provided little motivation to strive for the good. Pelagius insisted on the primacy of deliberate acts of will, which, rightly employed, will permit a man to perfect himself and merit the recognition of God. As unanticipated consequence, man dared to equate his own self-determination with God's. Shuttling between the horns of this dilemma is familiar Christian practice.[7] It has led to a multitude of codes, characteristic of the different churches. Calvin's solution–as explicated by Weber–is based on the idea that man's deeds on earth are a kind of quest for grace. In the modern church, says Passmore (1970, p. 100) the dilemma is addressed simultaneously: "the hymns may assume predestination, but the sermons are Pelagian."

Thus, while a code may favor one horn of a dilemma over the other, both horns require attention. And what is true for the dilemma within dogma is no less true for dilemma of dogma and organization. The dilemma generates the need for decision, but the decision can never be final. To the extent that a group favors one type of decision over another–that is, to the extent that the decision isn't simply random oscillation between solutions (between incorporation and exclusion, for example)–we speak of codes. But it is misleading, as we have just seen, to think that leaning toward solutions on one side exempts the group from attention to the other side of its problem. Hence codes must be closely examined for the ways in which they concern themselves–often simultaneously–with both sides of a dilemma.

---

[6] For the thorough discussion on which these paragraphs are based, see John Passmore (1970).

[7] Responding to his critics. Augustine himself, Passmore tells us, formulated the dilemma thus: "If then there is no grace of God, how does He save the world? And if there is no free will, how does He judge the world?" Kulandran (1964, p. 74) sees in this dilemma the struggle between rationalism and mysticism which pervades many religions.

We have had some insight into the ways in which the Catholic code of incorporation and the Protestant code of exclusion–which we have called Formation and Re-formation–look over their shoulders to the co-existence of another side of the dilemma for which they also have developed characteristic responses. We turn now to examine a third code, characteristically Jewish, which also addresses the dilemma of dogma and organization, as it repeatedly demands recognition and, by virtue of its own inherent contradictions, regularly reasserts itself.

Dispensation as Social Code

The sociology of religion–if not of politics–provides us with a third kind of mechanism which deserves attention, in addition to the basic ones of exclusion and incorporation. The key to this code is the idea that deviance may be anticipated and deviants may be "licensed" to carry on with their deviance, for their own good, and even more, for the good of the whole.[8]

This mechanism arises to solve a problem which lies in between the codes of incorporation and exclusion. As we have seen in the case of the Catholic Church, incorporation implies subsuming, and subsuming often requires the allocation of a specific place and role to deviants. The example of the institutionalization of the Franciscan Order makes this clear. Thus, the code of incorporation, as has already been argued, implies differentiation. Exclusion, on the other hand, implies much greater equality both because of its fundamentalist and individualist tendencies and because of its basic suspiciousness of organization and hierarchy. Such sectarian movements are doomed to isolation and perpetual weakness unless they federate, we have argued.

The Jews provide the in-between example. On the whole, their code is inclusionist: every effort is made to keep deviants inside. In traditional orthodoxy, the threat of schism between *hasidim* and *mithnagdim* was overcome by subsuming. In modern Judaism, the schismatic appearances of

---

[8] Hirschman (1970, p. 115) argues that loyalty sometimes induces high officials to remain at their posts even where "exit" would serve the body politic better. Such officials are then allowed to play their dissident roles from within.

Reform and Conservative movements have, on the whole, been retained by incorporation–by invoking, as a last resort, the rule of "a Jew, even though he has sinned, remains a Jew." And like inclusionist churches, parties and the like, we shall expect the Jews to have a differentiated social structure relevant to their perpetuative problems.

On the other hand, the Jews have some of the qualities of sectarianism: they are exclusive, at least insofar as religious contact is concerned. Yet, there is an ever-present concern with the surrounding world, both for reasons of internal security and for reasons of commitment to this-worldly achievement in intellectual and material terms. Their problem is how to preserve a traditional "sectarian" culture and yet partake of the world, how to be exclusive and inclusive at once.

Freed suggests that the Jews of the *shtetl* solved one aspect of this problem by differentiation. The learned–the "specialists" dedicated to the maintenance of the core of the culture–were permitted to continue to learn. This they did in relative isolation, protected by the society from disturbing influences, while the rich supported them materially, gaining prestige thereby. On the whole, the business world was the province of the low and middle-class Jews, and of women, who had low status to begin with. Religious study, in other words, was the aspect of culture selected for perpetuation and special conditions were created to insulate and support its chief practitioners. Changes were accepted in peripheral areas of the culture while keeping the religious sphere uncontaminated. "The class structure," says Freed, "the prestige system, patterns of charity, isolation of religious scholars, and male superiority were integrated, maintaining and preserving the formal aspects of *shtetl* culture" (p. 56).

But Freed does not go far enough. For Jewish tradition makes room for certain kinds of contact with the outside world not only in peripheral areas of the culture, but in its religious sphere as well. In fact, one may argue that had this central focus not been also a pliable focus, the tradition could hardly have survived the challenges of a changing world. To be sure, such pliability must be "programmed" if it is to ensure continuity in the face of change. It must be able to bridge between "particularistic revelation" and universal reason. This, we propose, is achieved through the code of dispensation.

Let HC stand for Holy Community, Ha for *halakha* (the authoritative Jewish *corpus juris*) and T for *Torah* (the Pentateuch: the revealed will of God, esp. the Mosaic laws). The triangle **Ha** $\nearrow$ $\rightleftarrows$ $\nwarrow$**T** represents the core of Jewish tradition. Thus, the Torah (T) was revealed to the holy community (HC), which is governed by the halakha (Ha), which is in accord with the Torah (T). If pliability is to be made room for, obviously it must be located in the jurisdictional corner (Ha) of our triangle, leaving the revelational side untouched. The dispensation code is then structured in the following way:

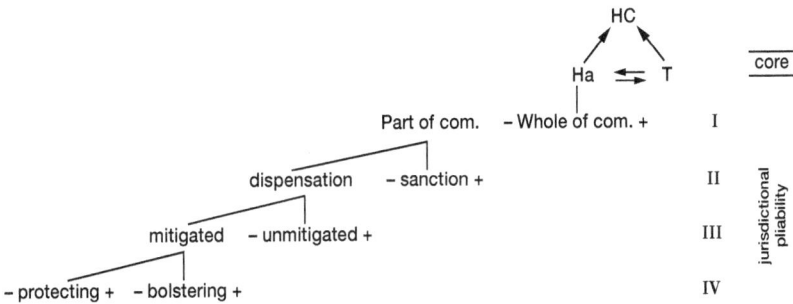

FIGURE 2 The Dispensation Scale

The above scheme is a composite of stages (I-IV). Whenever a challenge presents itself the whole of the scheme is invoked beginning each time at the top. Plus (+) and minus (–) represent "yes" and "no" answers to a series of questions as to who, under what conditions and why a proposed action may be performed when that action is not in obvious accord with the tradition. Not every proposed action requires invoking the entire scheme to its very bottom. How far down to go will depend on the nature of the challenge at hand. The stopping point, however, is invariably dictated by the reaching of a "yes" answer at any level save for the bottom stage (IV), which is decisive as to whether an adjustment could have been made altogether.

It needs to be emphasized, however, that the key point in our proposition is not the number of stages (which for all we know may not be exhaustive) but rather that they work in scale-like fashion, in a two-sided scale in fact, incorporating checks and balances. Thus, purpose or justification is the primary criterion in stage IV, qualification or delimitation in stage III, issue or topic in stage II, and whether it involves the entire community or only part of it in stage I.

Unlike the other two codes, each of which transforms in a unidirectional way with consequences which are irreversible (unless one switches codes), the dispensation code has, so to speak, built-in pliability. It must therefore be invoked as a whole, each time anew. It will be noticed that the orientation of the plus is inward with a double entendre, namely, "reinforcing" of the core values of the group, while the orientation of the minus side is outward, namely "protective" of the group against external threat.

An example will show how the scheme works. As is well known, throughout Jewish history secular studies presented a direct challenge, second to none, to religious studies, either because of their content or as competitors for time, or both. However, not all secular studies have been traditionally perceived as equally threatening to our so-called "specialists." For example, the study of philosophy may have been viewed as a greater threat than the study of biology. The latter, in turn, may have been considered as less "benign" than mathematics and so forth. The above attitudes can easily be projected onto our code. Philosophy, will most likely find itself all the way at the bottom of the scale (if at all), farthest removed from the core because it presents the greatest threat to it. In other words, the license to study philosophy would be granted only after the proposal had been sifted at each successive stage. Thus, in answer to the question at stage I, it would be decided that the study of philosophy was not intended for the community as a whole. If legitimate for only part of the community, the question at stage II is whether it is acceptable for all members of this part or whether it requires a special dispensation. If the latter, stage III asks whether the dispensation is unlimited or whether it is circumscribed or mitigated. If mitigated, stage IV asks what legitimates the mitigated pursuit altogether, and what defines the boundaries which circumscribe it: reinforcement of the inner core of the tradition, or protection against incursions from outside? The answer to all these will determine who may study philosophy and under what conditions.

Assuming that biology is a lesser threat, sifting would probably stop at stage III, while mathematics may well be satisfied by answering the question at stage II.

There have been different schools of thought concerning dispensation for secular studies both over time as well as contemporaneously. The possibility of differences both over time as well as at the "same time" is not so unusual-sounding, save for the fact that in the present case such heterogeneity is legitimized by the dispensation code itself, provided only that each proposal is processed through the scheme as a whole each time it emerges or re-emerges. It is the very strictness of the order, the immutable sequence of the steps which is the source of flexibility and legitimation. If the implications of the dispensation code for continuity and change are apparent, not so the possibilities it harbors for an undulating historical process. The dispensation code is pliable indeed!

Dispensation as a code (employing the very steps outlined above or other steps, but scale-like steps nevertheless) is not only at work in Judaism. The licensing of deviance is a widespread phenomenon, commanding a respectful place in the lives of individuals, in social interactions, social organizations and social systems. Again the kibbutz provides an apt and ready example since it faced and still faces a problem similar to the one discussed here concerning the licensing of higher education: it cannot afford to send everybody off to the university and not every subject is equally legitimate for study.

As we have seen, with respect to another issue, the kibbutz employed the code of exclusion, as we tried to show. Clearly, "when," "how," and "where" need to be specified, since they play a part in the decision to employ one code or another. Is the code then immanent in the issue, or inherent in the culture? This is *the* question.

Conditions for Different Patterns of Response

Three questions were posed at the outset: (1) whether there are identifiable codes for responding to the threat of dissidence, (2) whether these codes can be usefully outlined in transformational terms, and (3) whether the preconditions for the development of different codes can be specified. Two of these questions have already been dealt with. The third received only partial and non-explicit treatment. However, the picture that emerges from our attempted answers to the first two questions is one that challenges the very posing of the third question in terms of "preconditions." For the codes themselves constitute part of those conditions, and there seems nothing that can be viewed apart from, or prior to, the conditions. In this sense they are to be viewed in terms similar to norms; they characterize that by which they are defined.

A comparison of different groups in relation to a specific problem may suggest some key variables relevant to the use of one code in preference to another. Bearing in mind the central concern of this paper with the management of continuity and change, consider the following dimensions in terms of which the several groups may be classified. Thus, with respect to each group, we ask: (1) Is the group stratified relative to the issue of continuity? (2) Does the group want contact with the outside world or is it inward-looking? (3) Does it seek converts or new members? (4) Does the group define itself and its membership as a different kind of people than nonmembers?

Though the variables are tentative in number and perhaps unequal in importance, they are by no means arbitrary. They characterize the groups in brushstroke fashion without attempting a comprehensive definition; indeed, we shall make a case for brushstrokes in the concluding section, below. At any rate, it is evident from Table 1 (below) that the "incorporationist" Catholics and the "exclusionist" Amish are indeed diametrically opposed to each other whereas the Jews occupy an in-between position`- particularistic in parts and universalistic in others. The similarity between the Catholics and the Jews with regard to the first two dimensions should not be allowed to overshadow their differing social functions. Whereas the interest of the Church is centered around the preservation of the institution, that of the Jews focuses on the preservation of the group. The difference between the two with regard to the third and fourth variables highlights this variance in orientation.

TABLE 1			
	Catholic Church	**Jews**	**Amish**
Stratification relative to continuity	Yes	Yes	No
Want contact with outside	Yes	Yes	No
Want converts	Yes	No	No
Define selves as different	No	Yes	Yes

The similarities between the Amish and the Jews should likewise be understood in terms of their somewhat different social functions which, again, are highlighted by the variables on which they differ. Thus, while the Jews and the Amish are primarily interested in the preservation of their respective groups, the Jews, on the whole, stand for difference without separateness from the world, the Amish stand for both separateness and difference.[9]

Other Protestant churches may be classified in terms of these same dimensions. Thus, a chart of this kind may take us some distance toward differentiating among Protestant groups which, as already noted, run the range from "egalitarian" churches like that of the Amish to churches with institutional structures similar to Catholicism. More generally, our comparison suggests that whether or not a group considers itself exclusive and whether or not it desires contact with the outside effects the structure of the group and its patterns of response.

No less interesting is the fact that the different "combinations" reported in Table 1 seem to pertain also to (1) the degree to which the group is alert to the possibility of threat to its continuity, and (2) the perception of the seriousness of such threat. Together, these factors combine to affect (3) the group's perception of its decision time for action. The "type" of response may perhaps be viewed, by extension, as an organic part of a "cyclican" chain reaction, so to speak serving both as consequence and cause. A comparison of the three groups along these lines might look as in Table 2:[10]

---

[9] It should be reiterated that we are discussing the core of Amish culture. In economic affairs, for example, the Amish allow themselves contact through preset intermediaries and are, in fact, very up-to-date farmers. This problem of the differential applicability of codes to central and peripheral aspects of a culture, or indeed the possibility that different codes co-exist with respect to different institutional areas, is an important one, and is related to the recent discussions of theories of institutional "convergence" and "non-convergence." Seeking patterns across institutional areas, Kroeber (1963), for example, stressed convergence. Other scholars argue non-convergence. By the same token, different groups or classes may converge upon each other in certain institutional realms but not in others. A case in point is the convergence of upper and lower classes in the 19th-century waltz craze while maintaining much stricter boundaries in the field of economic behavior. Indeed, the ostensible convergence in the one area may give the false impression of convergence in the other. For data relevant to this historical case, see Katz (1973).

[10] "Awareness," "threat," "decision time for action" are variables often employed in political science in connection with crisis situations. For interrelationship of the three see Charles F. Hermann (1969).

TABLE 2						
	Awareness		Threat		Decision Time for Action	
	Surprise	Anticipated	High	Low	Short	Extended
Jewish		X		X		X
Amish	X		X		X	
Catholic Church	X		X		X	

Should careful historical investigation support the relatedness of code formations to the above, there is much to be learned from this three-dimensional comparison. To begin with, there seems to be direct relationship between awareness of potential threat, perception of threat as serious and decision time for action with respect to heresies. Thus, there are three different bases for response. Secondly, if we attach the codes to these three profiles we find the Catholic Church and not the Jews in the "in-between" position. This suggests that the "dispensation" code is the most inclusionist of the three in that deviation is anticipated and planned for so as to minimize loss to the group.

Conclusion

The purpose of this paper was to suggest an approach to the unveiling of social codes by means of which organizations and communities chart their continuity. While examples have been introduced illustratively, the paper uses these cases as points of departure for the construction of ideal types and bold hypotheses rather than for detailed analysis. To conclude in the same spirit and even to go a step further–always assuming the validity of what has been said so far–we venture to suggest that codes seem to crystallize, morphologically, through a sifting process of actions and reactions, creating content-free dynamic structures.

Such organic growth does not necessarily imply organic use. Thus, one may "borrow" somebody else's code, so to speak, if the issue at hand seems to bear a resemblance to the conditions associated with the alternative code. Just as norms run the entire gamut from very private and personal use to values embracing the entire civilization, so do codes manifest themselves on the micro and macro levels. The larger the group to be embraced, the fewer and more selective the codes become. They gain in *symbolic* importance with each new selection which they survive by virtue of becoming less and less bound to specific situations. Thus a culture as a whole may be identified by an overriding code, with different codes for different subcultures as exemplified by systems and organizations of all kinds. Some of these, in turn, may borrow codes for managing certain issues from others, and so on.

In other words, codes do not vary. Their number seems to be finite and probably relatively small. They appear, however, in a variety of different clusters of different combinations and with different hierarchical orderings. Some aspects of syncretism, levantinism, nouveau-richesse and above all of "cultural earmarks" which come to the fore in processes of modernization, for example, can be explained in terms of borrowing of codes which offset the combinations of the cluster while maintaining the original hierarchical ordering. There is an obvious connection here to studies of diffusion and in particular to questions concerning differential rates of change of parts within a single system (Barnett, 1964).

The higher the code in the hierarchy, we have argued, the less specified the situation in which it is invoked and the more people it encompasses. Hence a code which is to affect everybody in a society, as in the case of innovation, must be accepted by everybody. It follows that (1) the higher the code the less transferable it becomes, and the less readily relinquished (since the more symbolic a code becomes, the more it sheds directives for action); and (2) the heterogeneity of a society facilitates "borrowing" by part but retards the acceptance of that which affects the whole. The relative stability of Western civilization and its unimpaired growth as well as the influence it was able to exert on other civilizations may be attributed certainly in part to its heterogeneity.

The question, then, of whether codes are immanent in the issue or inherent in the culture is a question about relevance, with regard to which issue and culture are interchangeable, depending on ... issue and culture.

Bibliography

Barnett, H. G. "Diffusion Rates," in Robert D. Manners, ed., *Process and Pattern in Culture.* Chicago: Aldine Publishing Company, 1964, pp. 351-362.

Baum, Rainer C. "Authority and Identity: The Case for Evolutionary Invariants." *Sociological Inquiry,* 1975.

Buchler, I. R., and H. G. Mutini. *Game Theory in the Behavioral Sciences.* Pittsburgh: University of Pittsburgh Press, 1969, pp. 1-23.

Eisenstadt, S. N. *Tradition, Change and Modernity.* New York: John Wiley, 1973.

Freed, Stanley A. "Suggested Type Societies in Acculturation Studies." *American Anthropologist,* 1957, 59:55-67.

Geertz, C. *The Interpretation of Cultures.* New York: Basic Books, 1973.

Hermann, Charles F. "International Crisis as a Situational Variable," in James N. Rosenau, ed., *International Politics and Foreign Policy.* Glencoe, Ill.: The Free Press, 1969.

Hirschman, Albert O. *Exit, Voice and Loyalty.* Cambridge, Mass.: Harvard University Press, 1970.

Katz, R. "The Egalitarian Waltz." *Comparative Studies in Society and History,* 1973, 15:368-377.

Kulandran, Sabapathy. *Grace in Christianity and Hinduism.* London: Lutterworth Press, 1964.

Kroeber, A.Z. *Style and Civilizations.* Los Angeles: University of California Press, 1963.

Linton, Ralph. "Nativistic Movements." *American Anthropologist,* 1943, 45:230-40.

Leff, Gordon. *Heresy in the Later Middle -Ages: The Relation of Heterodoxy to Dissent 1250-1450.* New York: Barnes and Noble, 1967.

Lévi-Strauss, C. *Structural Anthropology.* New York: Basic Books, 1963.

Michels, Robert. *Political Parties.* Glencoe, Ill.: The Free Press, 1949. Reprinted in R. K. Merton *et al.,* eds., *Reader in Bureaucracy.* Glencoe, Ill.: The Free Press, 1952.

Passmore, John. *The Perfectability of Man.* New York: Scribner's, 1970.

Piaget, J. *Structuralism.* New York: Basic Books, 1970.

Elisheva Rigbi

Introduction

Elisheva Rigbi is an Israeli musicologist and music critic whose interdisciplinary studies involve Western art music and musical thought of the Fin-de-siècle (roughly 1890-1920). As a result of her thorough investigations of the turn of the 19th century, she proposed a re-configuration of Fin-de-siècle music as a music-historical period in its own right, i.e. as an integral part of the Fin-de-siècle at large, rather than a transitional phase.

As is well known, the year 1900 has served many historians as a demarcation line signifying a major turn in Western thought symptomatically expressed in the attitude toward the past. The Past—unlike *in* the past—was no longer viewed by these historians as a continuous process informing the various intellectual activities of the present. Rather, its relevance to the Present, if any, was regarded as mainly negative. The term 'modern', that had been the hallmark of the time, thus ceased to carry the connotation of mere novelty, whether fad or recent trend. Proclaiming its independence from the past, it came to be used more in the sense of 'modernist', denoting the total break from tradition. Indeed, with the authority of history cast aside, the imagination was set free to produce, in rapid succession, a multitude of new constructs. It is these variegated quasi-concurrent changes that imparted to contemporaries a sense of "history as present."

Fin-de-siècle music has long baffled music historians because of its extreme multifariousness. This music joined together seemingly incommensurable musical elements representing disparate musical styles, thereby precluding any formulation of a period-style according to the customary methods of music historiography. The only way out of this quandary, it seemed, was to regard Fin-de-siècle music as a transition between 19th-century 'Romantic' music and the radical 'New Music' of the 20th century. This was indeed the long-held view. In her *The Modern in Music 1890–1920 against the "Crisis of Historicism" and the Breakdown of the Rational Paradigm: A Critical Analysis of a Style,* (2002) Rigbi offered (1) an overall review of Fin-de-siècle music and musical thought, (2) highlighted the problems attending its aesthetic and historical interpretation, and (3) constructed an ingenious scheme–based on the seminal features that delineate the period as a whole–that substantiated the re-configuration of Fin-de-siècle music as a music-historical period in its own right. Her "Music and Music Historiography in the Fin-de-siècle" (2006) is a critique of contemporary and subsequent historiography of Fin-de-siècle music, while "Musical Prose and Musical Narrativity in the Fin-de-siècle" (2012) compares a major feature of Fin-de-siècle music to the innovations in narrative technique in the modernist novel.

RIGBI
Making Sense of Fin-de-siècle Music

⟨⟨⟩⟩

1

One of the central concerns of the historian is the description and elucidation of change. Since change is a relative concept, this inevitably obliges the historian to operate with constants, i.e. stable entities–real or ideal–in relation to which the change is assessed. Notions of both change and stability interact in the construction of historical periods, each consisting of manifold data that are nevertheless unified by one or more common features posited as constant throughout the extension of the period but not previously or subsequently, so as to distinguish that particular period from its adjacent ones. Without such periodization–as, indeed, without any generalization–the "march of history" would disintegrate into a meaningless multitude of isolated moments.

Periods may be longer or shorter, more or less clearly demarcated, depending on approach and subject matter. In cultural historiography, periods tend to be longer and less clearly demarcated than in political historiography. Obviously, the emergence, or disappearance of an idea are not as easy to pinpoint as, say, coronations or the conquest of royal capitals. They are processes rather than events, less immediately given to experience. Nevertheless, here, too, periodization is based on the interplay of constants and variables. For example: a period-notion such as the "Renaissance" refers to that slice of Western history informed by a common set of ideas and ideals, among them Humanism and the rediscovery and revival of Classical Greek culture. These governing ideals have been manifest in concrete historical reality to varying degrees: the beginning of what we call the Renaissance was probably unnoticed by most contemporaries, since its manifestations were few and far apart. It was only in retrospect, after historians had managed to trace a trajectory of consistent increase in the concrete manifestation of those governing ideals that one could meaningfully speak of the beginnings of the Renaissance in the later 14th century. In other words: in the construction of the period we call 'The Renaissance' it is the governing ideals that function as constants, whereas the data of concrete historical actuality function as variables. It should be stressed that the constants of cultural history are not merely technicalities of historical method, but sources of meaning and very often had real historical impact. The ideals guiding the Renaissance thus not only help the historian make sense of the manifold data, but were an often-declared motivating force in the Renaissance itself.

In music historiography, periodization has relied on a mixed variety of constants. Alongside governing aesthetic ideas we frequently find music-specific features, i.e. elements of the concrete musical material functioning as constants. Thus, for example, the term 'Baroque', which originated outside the musical domain and refers to a general aesthetic of heightened expression, denotes in music historiography a later and longer period than in other domains (ca. 1600 to 1730 or even 1750). This is partly because it is identified with specific musical genres and practices originally associated with the new aesthetic, namely the rise of accompanied monody (e.g. opera) and its eventual derivatives and implications (e.g. the separation of the vocal and instrumental musical paradigms, and the emergence of chordal thinking, ultimately leading to figured bass and the emergence of harmony as an independent musical parameter and a sub-discipline of music theory.) Although 'Baroque' is the most current term in music-historical discourse, it is no incident that the famous German music scholar, Hugo Riemann, one of modern musicology's founding fathers, preferred to call it "the Era of Figured Bass".[1] Indeed, the tendency to rely on musical concretes as constants in the periodization of music history became more pronounced in the 20th century, largely through the influence of the positivistic methods propagated and institutionalized by Guido Adler, another founding father of modern scientific musicology.[2] Such concretely-based approach to music-historical periodization has lead to great achievements, but also has its shortcomings. These are nowhere more evident than when it comes to the music of the Fin-de-siècle

---

[1] See H. Riemann: *Grundriss der Musikwissenschaft*, Leipzig 1908, pp.110, 135-139. Figured bass is a form of musical notation developed in the Baroque that exemplified the new chordal thinking.

[2] On Guido Adler, see below. See also Elisheva Rigbi: "Music & Music Historiography in the Fin-de-siècle ", Richard I. Cohen, ed.: *Image and Sound: Art, Music and History*, Jerusalem, 2007, pp. 301-325.

(roughly 1890-1920), which seems to lack any musical commonality. Indeed, the confusing heterogeneity of fin-de-siècle music was amply remarked upon by contemporaries as its most distinctive feature.[3]

If periodization relies on constants, how should one interpret historically such eclectic material that seems to exhibit no common feature whatsoever? Two options come to mind: (a) search for constants transcending the musical material (e.g. in ideational factors), or (b) disqualify the material as a period in its own right, and regard it rather as a transition between two more unified periods that mixes together remnants of past practices with elements of future styles. It is striking that the historiography of fin-de-siècle music since World War II has overwhelmingly chosen the second option. This indicates not only its increasingly positivistic attitudes but also contrasts sharply with the historiography of other departments of fin-de-siècle culture, where phenomena as diverse as the formulation of relativity theory and symbolist poetry are often subsumed under the common notion of 'change of paradigm', thereby lending the Fin-de-siècle as a whole the unity and meaning of an independent period in cultural history. 'Paradigm' is used here in the sense established by Kuhn to denote the totality of assumptions–implicit and explicit, theoretical and methodological–shared by a cultural community.[4] According to Kuhn, the inherent dynamic of a paradigm inevitably leads from growth to disintegration and, ultimately, to its replacement by a new paradigm. The

---

[3] For example:

Riemann: "A motley such as there has never been, a multitude of crossing and conflicting aspirations, a war between principles that are most decisively contradictory" ("Wohin steuern wir?" [1894] in *Präludien und Studien II,* 1900: 42).

Rudolf Louis: "In, music, too, the present is most monstrously multifarious in its forms and full of contradictions" (*Die deutsche Musik der Gegenwart*, 1909, p.12).

Ernst Kurth: "a fracturing in a thousand different directions ... the most extremely different stylistic moments, working on each other in no order whatsoever" (*Grundlagen des Linearen Kontrapunkts: Bachs melodische Polyphonie,* Bern 1917, p. xi),

Guido Adler: "an architectural style of the Tower of Babel" (on the finale Mahler's Sixth Symphony; Gustav Mahler [1916], in Edward R. Reilly: *Gustav Mahler and Guido Adler: Records of a Friendship,* Cambridge1982, p.56) ,

or: "We are witnessing a confusion and conflict of styles, music is as if gripped in a whirlpool. ..." (*Handbuch der Musikgeschichte II,* 1930: 998).

[4] Thomas Samuel Kuhn: *The Structure of Scientific Revolutions,* Chicago, University of Chicago Press, 2nd enlarged edition, 1970.

paradigm whose collapse has been amply detected throughout fin-de-siècle culture had served the Western community since the Scientific Revolution in the early 17th century, and drew from the belief that it is both possible and desirable to attain objective knowledge by means of Reason. Hence: the "Rational Paradigm".

Irrespectively of this, the music of the Fin-de-siècle, though much studied and recognized for major landmarks, has not been considered as an independent period but rather as a transition from 19th-century "Romanticism" to 20th-century "New Music". This view is based on the emergence in the fin-de-siècle of certain compositional practices that blatantly contradicted musical tradition and that later in the 20th century attained some currency and much prestige. Foremost among these are the "emancipation of dissonance" and the eventual development of the 12-tone system as a replacement for the traditional system of major and minor keys, both participating in what musicians generally call "the breakdown of tonality." Despite increased methodological awareness in recent decades and considerable attention to other seminal musical changes such as the enormous developments in rhythm, timbre and texture, the latter features are usually subordinated to the breakdown of tonality which remains at the core of most accounts of fin-de-siècle music. Accordingly, composers who contributed to the arsenal of technical innovations were foregrounded, while those who continued to use some (or only) tonal materials were marginalized. Although recently, more critical literature has restored many of the latter to scholarly attention and granted the former a more rounded treatment, the *historical* position of fin-de-siècle music as a whole has not been revised.

There are many reasons, both historical and aesthetic, to take issue with this transitional view of Fin-de-siècle music. These have to do, *inter alia*, with the inherent anachronism of the "directional view" of history, especially as regards a time that witnessed its collapse ('Crisis of Historicism').[5] Similar anachronism

---

[5]   On the different senses of 'Historicism' and its "crises," see Georg G. Iggers: "Historicism: The History and Meaning of the Term", *Journal of the History of Ideas* 56/1 (1995): 129-152; idem.: *The German Conception of History: The National Tradition of Historical Thought from Herder to the Present,* revised edition, Middletown, 1983. See also Elisheva Rigbi-Shafrir: *The Modern in Music 1890–1920 against the "Crisis of Historicism" and the Breakdown of the Rational Paradigm: A Critical Analysis of a Style,* PhD dissertation, Jerusalem 2002, ch.3 (in Hebrew); Elisheva Rigbi: "Music and Music Historiography..."

attends the "autonomist" view of music implied by presenting it as an exception to the rest of fin-de-siècle culture.[6] Furthermore, the transitional view of fin-de-siècle music is contradicted by contemporary opinion, which saw the essence of this music in its very eclecticism (not in the breakdown of tonality or any other technical novelty), unanimously regarding it, in itself, as a move away from tradition.[7] Finally, the transitional view cannot provide a key to the aesthetic processing of the music itself, since very often in fin-de-siècle music, the individual piece or movement are no less eclectic than the period as a whole.

All this seems reason enough for trying the other option for periodizing fin-de-siècle music: namely searching for unifying constants that transcend the concrete musical data yet are manifest in them. It also stands to reason that the notion of "change of paradigm," that has successfully subsumed materials as diverse as the rise of structural linguistics and expressionist art, could be used to unify the multifarious abundance of fin-de-siècle music.

2

Implicit in the notion of 'paradigm' as a methodological tool is that all cultural practice–in both sciences and arts (including music)–be regarded as an exemplification of ideational underpinnings, or, in fin-de-siècle parlance, as the objectification of the general *Weltanschauung* ("World-view"). Indeed, this idea has its roots in the Fin-de-siècle, specifically in the thought of Wilhelm Dilthey.[8]

---

[6] The view of music as an autonomous, self-referential "language" is the core of the aesthetic known as 'Absolute Music'. While it is granted that in other departments of art, an autonomy aesthetic was a major feature of fin-de-siècle modernism, there it marked a necessary stage in the abrogation of mimesis and hence represents the breakdown of the Rational Paradigm, whereas in music it was saturated by Rational values and by the fin-de-siècle was very old news. See Carl Dahlhaus: *The Idea of Absolute Music,* Chicago, 1989.

[7] Contemporaries adhered to this view even *after* the emancipation of dissonance and the development of the 12-tone system. See Rigbi-Shafrir: *The Modern in Music..;* Rigbi: "Music and Music Historiography...".

[8] Wilhelm Dilthey (1833-1911), father of the notion of the "Human Sciences" which he based on a philosophically-generalized hermeneutic method, posited the *Weltanschauung* as the largest totality available to humanistic knowledge, from which all particulars draw their meaning but which, reciprocally, can only be known through them.

Each phenomenon may thus be considered in terms of the reciprocal relation between two levels—the one more abstract, consisting of shared assumptions and beliefs, the other more concrete, comprising shared normative practices and the "facts" that they produce. The life of a paradigm, accordingly, may be described in terms of a dialogue between the two levels, conducted through the application of the shared practical norms (and by their means, of the shared general ideas) on a constantly expanding domain. However, this process of expansion and articulation of the paradigm is also the source of its decline, since, inevitably, anomalies are revealed that cannot be accommodated within the ideational framework of the paradigm. When such anomalies accumulate to an extent that can no longer be ignored, they invalidate the ideational tenets, leading to the search for a new paradigm.

The Rational Paradigm, whose demise has been so amply detected throughout fin-de-siècle culture, had been constituted on a dichotomy between subject and object, conceiving of 'truth' as the compliance of the subject with its object of knowledge, the latter construed as *given,* hence as "standing in its own right", i.e. absolute. Fin-de-siècle thought replaced this "copy theory" with a new theory of knowledge, conceived as a free, incessant *creative process* whereby both objects and subjects come into being through their articulation or "objectification" from the indeterminate continuum of "life" or "pure experience" that is the totality prior to all distinction.[9]

In the new man-made, mind-made world of the Fin-de-siècle nothing was given: there were no self-sufficient objects, only objectifications determined and re-determined by their mutual context alone. Although the notion of an inextricable subjective element in all human knowledge has been a recurrent theme of skepticism since antiquity, it had never become mainstream before the Fin-de-siècle—the bulk of the Western tradition had been devoted precisely to combating skepsis and promoting objective certainty. Furthermore, skeptics throughout the ages did not dispute the "copy theory" of knowledge, only its attainability. It was only in the Fin-de-

---

[9] "Life" was the basic category in Dilthey's *Lebensphilosophie.* "Pure experience" was used most famously by William James in his philosophy of Radical Empiricism and Pragmatism.

siècle that thinkers altogether relinquished the "copy" concept, regarding the new creative form of knowledge as a source of stimulation and increased meaning.[10] Finally, this foundational transformation exceeded the realm of philosophical speculation and proliferated throughout cultural practice, giving rise to new forms of knowledge.

A methodological problem arises here: how are we to assess the degree of proliferation? With respect to the subject at hand: how does one translate the epistemological into the acoustic-musical? How are we to map ideas concerning the nature of reality and of knowledge onto the domain of harmonies, rhythms, musical motifs and textures, which seem to say nothing about the world neither about knowledge?[11] The epistemological and the musical must be mediated in terms that are indifferent to content and even to its absence (as is ostensibly the case in instrumental music,) namely formal or structural ones, that are nevertheless demonstrably valid and relevant for both.

In order to arrive at such terms, I extracted from the core ideas of the Rational Paradigm (described above) three formal attributes which, since they inhere at the constituting level, can be expected to be manifest on other levels of paradigmatic articulation (i.e. different departments of culture) as indeed they have been shown to be. They can serve thereby as criteria for assessing the degree to which fin-de-siècle culture–music in particular–exemplifies the general crisis of Reason, their increasing or decreasing expression in the canonic forms of cultural practice indicating (respectively) growth or decline of the paradigm. The distinctive formal features of rational knowledge are as follows:

---

[10] "In our cognitive as well as in our active life," says William James, "we are creative. We add, both to the substance and to the predicate part of reality. The world stands really malleable, waiting to receive its final touches at our hands....Man *engenders* truths upon it...No one can deny that such a role would add both to our dignity and to our responsibility as thinkers." (William James: *Pragmatism* [1907], Cambridge & London 1975, p.123.

[11] As I've shown elsewhere, this non-referential (or self-referential) view of music as "pure" or "absolute" is in itself emblematic of the Rational Paradigm, both substantively and historically. See note 6 above.

1) DISCRETENESS, because of the absolute dichotomy between object and subject; on other levels of cultural articulation it is manifest as elementarism, atomism, associationism ("building-block theories"), reductionism, etc.

2) STABLE IDENTITIES, because of the absolute nature of objectivity; it is manifest, for example, in the epistemological desiderata of unity, universality, consistency, certainty, etc.

3) FIXED ASYMMETRY, or *directionality,* because of the irreversible priority of object to subject, of the world to any knowledge-about-the-world. Directionality may pertain in relation to concrete elements, e.g. in chronological (and musical) order, mechanical interpretations of causality, teleological, genetic and evolutionary explanations, but also less concretely, in any organization based on fixed relations of priority, such as hierarchy or centralization. It pertains also to the very description of the "elements" themselves, as in the traditional dichotomies between essential and accidental, necessary and contingent, part and whole, the abstract and the concrete, the natural and the artificial, etc., all of which were traditionally joined in a fixed asymmetry, even though its precise nature was sometimes a matter of debate.

In contrast to this formal norm of Rationality, I posited a counter-norm of non-Rational knowledge (as described by fin-de-siècle thinkers), marked by the opposite features:

1) CONTEXTUALITY AND INHERENT CONNECTEDNESS instead of discretization, because no objectification is independent of context;

2) DESTABILIZATION OF IDENTITY, because of the unlimited permeability (hence: changeability) of all objectifications, resulting from their unlimited contextuality;

3) PREPONDERANCE OF SYMMETRICAL, HOLISTIC AND CIRCULAR STRUCTURES AND PROCESSES, because of the symmetrization of the dichotomy between subject and object, both regarded as mutually constituent objectifications.

Against these criteria, fin-de-siècle cultural practice as a whole exemplifies a sharp and unmistakable decline in rationality, manifest, for example, in a decrease in directionality. The causal, teleological, genetic, evolutionary and "historical" explanations preferred in the 19th century as *exclusive* hallmarks and guarantors of objectivity (precisely *because* of their directional form) were replaced *en masse* by non-directional, structural, functional, holistic and circular forms of knowledge which now acquired canonic status. Among these, I would mention again the 'Crisis of Historicism' (in its multiple senses) as a crisis of directional notions resulting from their very directionality, and many of its correlates and far-reaching implications in the human sciences. These include, for example, the vindication of the circular method of *Verstehen* (Understanding) in the human sciences (that had previously been regarded as non-scientific) and the emergence to dominance of non-historical human sciences such as structural linguistics or holistic theories in psychology (e.g. Gestalt theory.)[12] In the arts, the proliferation of the crisis is demonstrated through the abrogation of mimesis. In both theory and practice, art no longer aimed to imitate an ostensibly given world, but was free to create its own worlds according to principles which were alike a matter of subjective choice.[13]

Before applying these formal (non)Rational criteria to the music of the fin-de-siècle, one more problem should be addressed: the "transitional view" of fin-de-siècle music is the product of methodologies formulated and institutionalized in those very same years, first and foremost among them Adler's influential method of 'Style Criticism'.[14] If, as I claim, these methods are inappropriate for dealing with fin-de-siècle music, what is one to make of the incongruity arising thereby between the practical and the ideational components of fin-de-siècle musical culture? One could regard it as an indication of crisis within an all-musical paradigm,

---

[12] "For an epistemological analysis of these and other changes in fin-de-siècle human sciences, see Rigbi-Shafrir: *The Modern in Music.*

[13] "Paradigmatic examples in the plastic arts are cubism, expressionism or abstract art, and in literary and art theory "formalism."

[14] See esp. Guido Adler: "Umfang, Methode und Ziel der Musikwissenschaft", *Vierteljahresschrift für Musikwissenschaft I* (1885), pp. 5-20; idem.: *Der Stil in der Musik,* Leipzig 1911; idem.: *Methode der Musikgeschichte,* Leipzig 1919; idem.: "Style Criticism", *Musical Quarterly* XX/2 (1934), pp.172-176.

wherein the concrete components (the musical works) conflict with the ideational (the discourse about them), but in retrospect, the outcome of this conflict would appear to have been the triumph of the ideational over the concrete, since it was the musical works and their composers that have been marginalized whereas the historiographical methods remained normative long into the 20th century. Furthermore, as I've shown elsewhere, these methods conform strongly to the rational desiderata of knowledge.[15] The whole of fin-de-siècle musical culture would then emerge as an anomaly within the greater context of fin-de-siècle culture, bringing us back to the point of departure of this study, having solved nothing.

A more fruitful way of addressing the problem is to regard fin-de-siècle discourse about music not only as the ideational infrastructure of musical practice, but also as its analogue, requiring separate evaluation as to its degree of Rationality, since it, too, is an independent cultural expression of epistemological underpinnings whose upheavals during the Fin-de-siècle were, as described above, at the core of the breakdown of the Rational Paradigm. Here too, such evaluation was accomplished relative to a historically previously-established norm of Rationality, growing conformity to which indicating paradigmatic strength, and increasing deviation—paradigmatic decline. With regard to fin-de-siècle discourse about music, that norm of Rationality included five criteria extracted from an Ideal Type of Rational musical knowledge that I constructed according to the general requirements of Rationality as well as the specific concerns and features of actual 18th–and 19th-century musical discourse (that had exhibited growing conformity with Rational desiderata).[16] The Ideal Type included both speculative and practical components, ordered hierarchically, so that every level in the hierarchy is the justification of the ones "below" and the concretization of the ones "above". At the lowest level, concretizing the whole of musical knowledge was the Ideal Rational musical work.

The five specifically-musical criteria of Rationality are as follows:

---

[15] Rigbi-Shafrir: *The Modern in Music*, pp.159-293; Rigbi: "Music and Music Historiography."
[16] See Rigbi-Shafrir: *The Modern in Music*, ch.4.

a) META-THEORETICAL JUSTIFICATION: Like all Rational-knowledge, the Ideal Rational musical knowledge requires grounding in objectivity, which is inevitably meta-musical, since nothing man-made such as music could ever be considered as a source of objectivity.

b) NORMATIVITY: Like all knowledge aspiring to objectivity, the Ideal Rational musical knowledge inevitably involves evaluating the degree to which the music conforms to objective truth, and is hence more valid.

c) AESTHETIC OBJECTIVISM: Like all knowledge aspiring to objectivity, the ideal Rational musical knowledge refers to the musical "object" in itself, regarding its grounding in objectivity as its "nature" and hence as immanent in it.

d) UNIVERSAL INTEGRATION: In conformity with the specific ideals of Rational knowledge as they developed until the late 19th century, the Ideal Rational musical knowledge strives to integrate all its partial theories and disciplines into a unified whole. Although such integration was never fully achieved, it was unmistakably the increasingly-declared goal of 18th and 19th century musical discourse.

e) AESTHETIC DESIDERATA: As a concretization of the integrated whole of Rational musical knowledge, the Rational musical work should contain its full explanation within itself, follow its own "inner law", so to speak, or in other words, be autonomous and absolute. This is the Rational underpinning of the aesthetic of absolute music and its radicalized form, organicism that viewed each individual musical work as a self-sufficient unity.

When fin-de-siècle musical discourse is reviewed against the criteria developed so far, its large and central portion—that which later became mainstream—emerges as a bastion of Rationality. Included therein, among others, is the work of founding fathers Hugo Riemann and Guido Adler and of music analyst and theorist Heinrich Schenker (1868-1935), whose influence was most pronounced in the USA after World War II, and the theoretical writings of Arnold Schoenberg (1873-1951) - the emblematic modernist composer.[17]

---

[17] For an epistemological analysis of these and other fin-de-siècle musical thinkers, see Rigbi-Shafrir : *The Modern in Music,* pp.159-293; Rigbi: "Music and Music Historiography."

Against this Rational block, one finds figures such as the Czech composer and theorist Leos Janáček (1854-1928), the cosmopolitan composer and virtuoso Ferruccio Busoni (1866-1924), the German critic Paul Bekker (1882-1937), and the musicologist Ernst Kurth (1886-1946), who (with the exception of Janáček) were extremely influential in their day but later marginalized and whose work exhibits markedly non-rational traits. For example, Janáček, Busoni and Kurth all grounded musical knowledge (including music itself) in indeterminate (continuous) entities, producing what were, in effect, their musical versions of fin-de-siècle *Lebensphilosophie* (seen as a non-rational (sub) version of organicism).[18] Both Bekker and Busoni rejected the idea of aesthetic autonomy, Bekker expressly calling for the replacement of the organicist notion of musical form by a notion of "Sociological Form" that considers the artwork as permeated to its core by multiple and ever-changing contexts.[19]

---

[18] Janáček, for example, developed a theory of marked holistic traits, explicitly and exclusively based on emotion and the "conceptualization" of the "stream of consciousness," describing a fundamental theoretical interdependence of musical parameters. In his harmonic thought, he derived all harmony through a *free* and holistic process from what he originally called the "chaotic moment"–an opaque totality which he regarded as the source of beauty and explicitly associated with the "fullness of Life" (*Lebensphilosophie*).

Busoni grounded all music in an incorporeal, infinitely changeable Urmusik ("primordial music") that exists before any tone resounds.

Kurth, notwithstanding the impressive theoretical integration of his oeuvre and the metaphysical status he claimed for the *Urbewegung* (the primordial and chaotic motion) based on the latter both an analytical method and a theory which are markedly holistic (e.g. the energetic/melodic "phase" is theoretically prior to the tones participating in it) and explicitly non-normative. All music is described as a symbol and objectification of the *Urbewegung* rather than its application or derivation. Furthermore, Kurth obliterated the traditional hierarchy of parameters, restoring theoretical dignity not only to melody but also to timbre, traditionally regarded as the least meaningful and essential sound parameter in music but which he regarded as a metaphor for the true nature of music and its culmination before reaching its goal of dissolving back into the primordial stream.

[19] See Bekker: *Das deutsche Musikleben* (1916), introduction. Bekker's socialist political leanings had to do with it, but they, in turn, may have drawn on a climate of *Lebensphilosophie*. Busoni's reasons for rejecting the autonomy aesthetic were more spiritual and idealist. See Ferruccio Busoni: *Sketch of a New Esthetic of Music*, New York 1911 (original published 1907). As a composer, Busoni's consistent practice of intertextuality (through transcription, paraphrase, fragmentation and re-embedding of the works of others and of himself) attests to the abrogation of the organicist ideal of the musical artwork.

Considering that both Rational and non-Rational varieties of musical discourse flourished in the fin-de-siècle, it appears that only later in the 20th century did the Rational–varieties become almost exclusive whereas the non-Rational alternatives were suppressed until the 1980's. The dynamics and details of this reception history are yet to be established. However, it is noteworthy that the non-rational musical theorists were all ardent supporters of the eclectic music of their day, whereas in the Rational block many rejected it. To quote Adler:

> "A time such as our own, when *subjectivism* is almost boundless, cannot produce .... stylized forms. Daring and extravagant experiments are almost always outside the course of *organic* development."
>
> (*Methode der Musikgeschichte* (1919), pp.145-6, italics added).

3

It remains to evaluate the music of the Fin-de-siècle in terms of its degree of Rationality. As noted earlier, there is more-or-less general agreement as to the main features of fin-de-siècle music: the general weakening of traditional tonality (evident in heightened dissonance, increased chromaticism, harmonic colorism, the use of non-Western and novel "artificial" scales, polytonality and atonality), the greatly increased rhythmic complexity, the great developments and foregrounding of timbre (the intricate orchestrations; purely timbral music), melodic phenomena such as "musical prose" and "developing variation", and the general eclecticism and stylistic pluralism. These granted, my disagreement concerns their relative significance as well as their historic and aesthetic interpretation. Whereas the commonly-held view has placed the weakening of tonality at the core of the musical changes of the fin-de-siècle, tending to treat the other features as derivative, I regard all these features– both harmonic (tonal) and otherwise–as the *analogous* and independent expressions of the general breakdown of the Rational Paradigm in fin-de-siècle culture. This is supported by the fact that (a) each of the features occurs in fin-de-siècle music independently of tonal issues, i.e. in both tonal and less-tonal contexts, and (b) each of the features exemplifies the formal features distinctive of non-Rational knowledge surveyed above and thus may be independently interpreted as the expression of the breakdown of the Rational Paradigm.

For example, the stylistic fragmentation and pluralism so emphasized by contemporary writers and for which Mahler, for example, was (in)famous, is clearly a deviation from the Rational ideal of organic, cohesive unity. Likewise Busoni's ideal (and practice) of "Young Classicism", defined as "the mastery, the sifting and the turning to account of all the gains of previous experiments and their inclusion in strong and beautiful forms" to create an art both "old and new at the same time."[20] This is particularly striking against the exactly contemporaneous institutionalization of Adler's concept of style as an organic unity and the "highest ideal unification" at the core of the young discipline of musicology.[21]

In the domain of melody and rhythm, the multi-faceted phenomenon of musical prose, associated primarily with composers Max Reger and Schoenberg but practiced by many other contemporaries as well, has been shown to be not only a case of melodic or rhythmic pluralism but also the antithesis of organicism. In view of the centuries-long connotation of 'prose' with chaos, it is telling that the usage 'musical prose', originally negative, was first sanctioned only in the fin-de-siècle.[22]

That the weakening of traditional Western major-minor tonality has been fore-grounded by the customary transitional view of fin-de-siècle music is in itself an indication of the Rational underpinnings of "establishment" music historiography during much of the 20th century, reflecting the primacy of harmony in the Rational hierarchy of musical knowledge described above. However, once we leave Rational ground, the weakening of tonality can be easily

[20] Busoni: "Young Classicism" (1920), *The Essence and Oneness of Music, and Other Papers,* Westport, Connecticut, 1979, p. 20.

[21] On Adler's attitude to stylistic hybridity in general and in Mahler in particular, see Rigbi-Shafrir: *The Modern in Music,* pp.200-215; Rigbi: "Music and Music Historiography", p.318, n35, 322-324.

[22] On the changing meanings of 'musical prose', see Rigbi (2012). See also Hermann Danuser: *Musikalische Prosa.* Regensburg 1975, and Carl Dahlhaus: "Musical Prose" *Schoenberg and the New Music,* Cambridge, 1988, pp. 105–127.

accommodated in the context of the demise of the Rational Paradigm. If Western tonality is based on a hierarchical system of tones subordinated to a single tonal center (the tonic), then its weakening means a decrease in the Rational-features of unity and directionality. This holds true for all its diverse manifestations. For example: the heightened dissonance and chromaticism of fin-de-siècle music obscure the hierarchic differentiation between the tones and chords of the system, thereby weakening the sense of tonal orientation. Harmonic colorism leads to similar results. Polytonality, i.e. the simultaneous use of multiple keys, subverts the tonal mechanism of unity by using it to undermine unity itself. In the "exotic" and "artificial" scales employed in fin-de-siècle music, the hierarchy of tones is looser, usually leading to a weaker, more local (or absent) sense of tonic center (e.g. Debussy's whole-tone scale, inspired by Balinese music), this besides clashing directly with the tonal system's traditional Rational claim to objectivity. From this perspective, the 12-tone system developed by Schoenberg towards the end of World War I and hailed in many transitional accounts of fin-de-siècle music as the "goal" and culmination of the transition, represents a step "backwards" toward Rationality: although explicitly designed as non-hierarchic (non-directional), it was nevertheless intended as an instrument of unity.

Finally, the great development and foregrounding of timbral aspects, as in the orchestrations of Mahler, Strauss, Debussy and Schreker, or in Schoenberg's and Webern's experiments in *Klangfarbenmelodie* ("Tone-color melody"), is a direct challenge to Rational values, especially in view of the traditionally marginal status of timbre as a parameter of musical sound in both theory and practice. This marginality stemmed precisely from the fact that as a sound-Gestalt–a homogeneous global quality of sound that overrides the plurality of its simple acoustic determinants–timbre cannot be quantified or systematically organized.[23] In other words: timbre eludes rationalization. As I've shown elsewhere, in its broadest sense, timbre as manifest in fin-de-

---

[23] In contrast, pitch and pitch relations (that define intervals, scales, keys, chords) are fully determined by exact fundamental frequencies and relations thereof. Similarly, temporal (rhythmic) aspects in Western music are fully accounted for in terms of exact numerical proportion of durations. This is reflected, inter alia, in Western musical notation, that fully determines pitch and duration of tones while leaving relatively imprecise indications concerning their timbre and intensity, or none at all.

siècle music may be regarded as the irrational twin of Adler's notion of 'style', institutionalized into musicological method at the very same time, and relates to it as *Lebensphilosophie* relates to organicism. Both 'style' and timbre are holistic, global qualities, but whereas Adlerian 'style' was explicitly an organic unity, an ordered complex of clear and distinct elements, timbre is an obscure, fused totality that musically obliterates its own constituent elements.[24] The musical consequences were, as expected, a sharp decline in all three formal attributes of Rationality: the greater the timbral-richness and salience in fin-de-siècle music, the greater the salience of the sensuous and momentary and the weaker the sense of structure and direction. When one is submerged in ineffably iridescent sound, one does not and indeed cannot remember how one got there neither can one form musical expectations. The full sensuous presence of sound is a totality that leaves little room for a sense of (musical) past or future, let alone of a linear progression from the one to the other. Small wonder that most of the Rational critics of the fin-de-siècle rejected the timbral-riches of its music, often regarding them as morally reprehensible.[25]

[24] Adler explicitly identified style as a Gestalt quality. See e.g. Adler: *Methode der Musikgeschichte*, pp. 111-113; idem.: "Style Criticism". Also see E.M. von Hornbostel, 'Gestaltpsychologisches zur Stilkritik', *Studien zur Musikgeschichte: Festschrift für Guido Adler zum 75. Geburtstag*, Wien 1930, pp. 12-16; M. Weber, "Empiricism, Gestalt Qualities, and determination of Style: Some Remarks Concerning the Relationship of Guido Adler to Richard Wallaschek, Alexius Meinong, Christian von Ehrenfels, and Robert Lach", M. Leman (ed.), *Music, Gestalt and Computing: Studies in Cognitive and Systematic Musicology* (Lecture Notes in Artificial Intelligence 1317), Berlin 1997, pp. 42-56.

[25] For example: music theorist and critic August Halm, the son of a Lutheran minister who had studied for the ministry himself, explicitly rejected the rich orchestrations of fin-de-siècle music as "Luxury music" and largely disregarded orchestration in his study of Bruckner's symphonies (1913). Adler devoted to instrumentation a mere one and a half pages out of 89 devoted to "Sound as a stylistic factor" in *Der Stil in der Musik* (1911), calling it "coloristic dress", implying thereby that it is but a superficial coating on the more essential attributes of music.

It is noteworthy that Schoenberg, after having experimented with independent timbral music both as a composer (1909, op.16 no.3 "Klangfarbenmelodie") and as a theorist (1911; pp. 421-422), retreated to a more traditional view of timbre (orchestration) as subservient to the traditional structural determinants of music, namely harmony and motivic and thematic factors. See Schoenberg: "The Future of Orchestral Instruments" (1924), *Style and Idea* edited by Leonard Stein, London 1975, pp. 322-330.

4

In conclusion, the absence of commonalties within fin-de-siècle music does not preclude its interpretation as a meaningful period in music history. Such periodization has been achieved by reference to the Rational ideal and image of knowledge interpreted in musically applicable terms. This "commonality" has been employed here as a *negative model* and the musical data evaluated according to their deviation from it. Therefore it may be said to have resided outside the historical material. Nevertheless, this model is fully validated culture-historically, since it served as a significant reference for contemporaries, as well. Indeed, the demise of the Rational Paradigm was most conspicuously on their minds, and the "loss of objectivity" at the heart of fin-de-siècle sensibility.

Works Cited

Adler, Guido: "Umfang, Methode und Ziel der Musikwissenschaft", *Vierteljahresschrift für Musikwissenschaft I* (1885): 5-20.

—— *Der Stil in der Musik,* Leipzig, Breitkopf & Härtel, 1911.

—— *Gustav Mahler* (²1916), in Edward R. Reilly: *Gustav Mahler and Guido Adler: Records of a Friendship,* Cambridge, Cambridge University Press, 1982, pp.13-73.

—— *Methode der Musikgeschichte,* Leipzig, Breitkopf & Härtel, 1919/ ᴿ1971, Gregg International Publishers, Westmead UK.

—— (ed.) *Handbuch der Musikgeschichte,* Berlin-Wilmersdorf, Heinrich Keller, ²1930.

—— "Style Criticism", *Musical Quarterly XX/2* (1934), pp.172-176.

Bekker, Paul: *Das deutsche Musikleben,* Berlin, Schuster & Loeffler, 1916.

Busoni, Ferruccio: *Sketch of a New Esthetic of Music,* translated by Th. Baker, New York, Dover, ᴿ1962 (original published 1907).

—— *The Essence and Oneness of Music, and Other Papers,* translated by Rosamond Ley, Westport, Connecticut, Hyperion Press, ᴿ1979.

Dahlhaus, Carl: *Schoenberg and the New Music,* translated by Derrick Puffett & Alfred Clayton, Cambridge, Cambridge University Press,1988.

—— *The Idea of Absolute Music,* translated by R. Lustig, Chicago, University of Chicago Press, 1989.

Danuser, Hermann: *Musikalische Prosa,* Regensburg, Gustav Bosse Verlag, 1975.

Hornbostel, E.M. von: 'Gestaltpsychologisches zur Stilkritik', *Studien zur Musikgeschichte: Festschrift für Guido Adler zum 75. Geburtstag,* Wien 1930, pp. 12-16.

Iggers, Georg G.: The German Conception of History: The National Tradition of historical Thought from Herder to the Present, revised edition, Wesleyan University Press, Middletown, 1983.

—— "Historicism: The History and Meaning of the Term", *Journal of the History of Ideas 56/1* (1995), pp. 129-152.

James, William: *Pragmatism: A New Name for Some Old Ways of Thinking,* Harvard, Harvard University Press, 1975 (first published: 1907).

Kuhn, Thomas Samuel: *The Structure of Scientific Revolutions,* Chicago, University of Chicago Press, 2nd enlarged edition, 1970.

Kurth, Ernst: Grundlagen des Linearen Kontrapunkts: Bachs melodische Polyphonie, Bern, Max Drechsel, 1917.

Louis, Rudolf: *Die deutsche Musik der Gegenwart,* München & Leipzig, Georg Müller, 1909.

Riemann, Hugo: *Präludien und Studien II,* Leipzig, Hermann Seemann Nachfolger, 1900.

—— *Grundriss der Musikwissenschaft,* Leipzig, Quelle & Meyer, 1908.

Rigbi, Elisheva: "Music and Music Historiography in the Fin-de-siècle", *Image and Sound: Art, Music, History,* ed. by Richard I.. Cohen, Jerusalem, Shazar Center (Israel Historical Society), 2007, pp.301-325 (in Hebrew).

—— "Musical Prose and Musical Narrativity in the *Fin-de-siècle*", in Michael Klein & Nicholas Reyland, eds.: *Music and Narrative after 1900,* Bloomington, IN., Indiana University Press, 2012.

Rigbi-Shafrir, Elisheva: The Modern in Music 1890–1920 against the "Crisis of Historicism" and the Breakdown of the Rational Paradigm: A Critical Analysis of a Style, PhD dissertation, Hebrew University of Jerusalem, 2002 (in Hebrew, English summary & TOC).

Schoenberg, Arnold: "The Future of Orchestral Instruments" (1924), *Style and Idea,* edited by Leonard Stein, London, Faber and Faber, 1975, pp. 322-330.

— *Theory of Harmony*, translated by Roy Carter from the 3rd edition (1922), Berkeley & Los Angeles, University of California Press, 1978 (first published: 1911).

Weber, M.: "Empiricism, Gestalt Qualities, and determination of Style: Some Remarks Concerning the Relationship of Guido Adler to Richard Wallaschek, Alexius Meinong, Christian von Ehrenfels, and Robert Lach", M. Leman (ed.), *Music, Gestalt and Computing: Studies in Cognitive and Systematic Musicology* (Lecture Notes in Artificial Intelligence 1317), Berlin 1997, pp. 42-56.

Ruth HaCohen

Introduction

Professor Ruth HaCohen is a member of the department of musicology at the Hebrew University of Jerusalem. Her studies seek to explicate the role played by Western music and related art forms in shaping and reflecting wide cultural processes from the 17th to the 20th century. She focuses on formations and transformations of sonic forms that penetrate and interact with political, cultural and religious universes.

Together with Ruth Katz, HaCohen explored the concerted efforts of musicians and theoreticians since the seventeenth century to fathom new modes of emotional expression and signification, beyond mimetic renditions. She examined as well the "strategies of signification" in musical works by Bach, Wagner and Schoenberg. Her integrated theoretical perspective encompassed conceptual transformations, such as the role of music in shaping religious experience in both Jewish and Christian contexts.

Her book *The Music Libel Against the Jews* won the Kinkeldey Award (for the most distinguished book in musicology published during 2011) and the Polonsky Prize (for originality and creativity in Humanistic Studies). The book traces the trajectory traversed from the medieval "noise accusation" against the Jews through the partial embracement of Jews within the European sonic sphere. The book is sensitive both to the sociological context, which grapples with exclusivist communitarian or nationalist motivations, and the aesthetic context which addresses the application of criteria to rationalize the difference between noise and music.

Together with Yaron Ezrahi she completed a study on the *Coproduction of Music and Politics*, tracing three major modes of interrelations between music and politics in the West. 'Analogy', accordingly, refers to situations which enlist the harmonizing powers of music so as to confer its values on a political (or religious) regime. 'Instantiation' refers to the use of "sonic means" that animate regimes, minorities and individuals, facilitating their socio-political embodiment. 'Transformation' is viewed as a mode through which music partakes in affecting new moral attitudes or in subverting existing ones.

All of HaCohen's studies, not only the ones I mentioned, attest to the flourishing of interdisciplinary activities nowadays and the creativity which it engenders.

HaCOHEN

Between Compassion and Sympathy: The Search for a Proper Space for an Ambiguous Concept

We all employ concepts in our daily lives, rarely stopping to examine what they actually refer to and the possible meanings which they may entail. It can also be shown that well-established concepts do not stand still, but undergo changes regarding their assumed referents and what is understood thereby. The concept 'childhood,' for example, while invariably pointing to the initial phase of human lives, underwent considerable change in the course of history, highlighting different aspects deserving attention. It is well known that even converting texts from one language to another often defies literal translation, since concepts may carry different nuances in different languages. Moreover, that which holds true for different languages also holds true for different cultures.

While examining the transformations that took place in the "language" of music between the 17th and the 19th centuries, I became keenly aware of the ways in which music "gave voice" to seminal changes that took place in the social sphere concerning human interactions, involving concepts like 'compassion' and 'sympathy' and the efforts vested in their clarification and relationship. Indeed, my musical expedition revealed that the peculiarities of music provided an arena well suited to exemplify "fellow-feelings" and "collective responsibility." In what follows I shall try to show–albeit in brush-stroke fashion–how different endeavors impacted each other, conveying shared concerns.

From 'Compassion' to 'Sympathy': Defining the Boundaries of Inquiry

'Compassion' and 'Sympathy', derived respectively from Latin and Greek, are, etymologically speaking, identical. In the course of their long use in the English language, they have come to share certain semantic markers, while diverging in others. 'Compassion' is found already in Middle English, denoting both suffering *together with* another, as well as being *moved by* the suffering or distress of another.[1] 'Sympathy' entered English usage only towards the end of the sixteenth century, in both senses, but was primarily used for denoting an affinity (real or supposed) between certain things, by virtue of which "they are similarly or correspondingly affected by the same influence," or "attracted towards each other."[2] Affinity was understood, in turn, in physiological, psychological or moral terms, calling for investigation into possible shared properties between sympathetically attracted entities and/or the nature of the common influence they entertain.

Sympathy in Renaissance thought functioned, according to Foucault, "as a principle of mobility," rather than mere inference, activating "an instance of the *Same* so strong and so insistent that it will not rest content to be merely one of the forms of likeness" (Foucault 1973:23-4). With the advance of the New Science, the Renaissance principle of sameness was constrained by new conceptions of mathematical and philosophical commensurability, transforming 'sympathy' into an analytical category for exploring *causal* relations irrespective of distance. Likewise, Pythagoras' exemplary reduction of qualities to quantities (sound to proportions) underwent considerable change concerning both the symbolic function of numbers and of that which they symbolize. In fact, the sympathy between reverberating strings became the paradigm for the mode of thought that increasingly undermined magical and astrological teachings. While preserving the element of sameness, it penetrated, as such, aesthetic and moral discourses, impacting both the understanding of compassion and the ways in which it functions.

The introduction of 'sympathy' into art theory stemmed as well–as I have argued elsewhere (HaCohen 2001)–from a crisis *within* the mimetic tradition that itself was affected by the rise of new scientific methods. In the figurative terms of the period, it can be found embodied in the persona of Echo, the compassionate nymph, who gradually eclipsed Narcissus, the self-centered

---

[1] For lack of space I am limiting the discussion to the English language, though interactions with and comparisons to other European languages in this regard is highly instructive.

[2] See *Oxford English Dictionary,* <Sympathy>; accessed 3 July 2013.

deity (Ovid's *Metamorphoses*, Book III). The idea of "fellow-feeling" emerged from a convergence of several trajectories, conflating insights gathered from three separate theoretical fields that mushroomed at the time: the physiological and behavioral study of the passions, moral philosophy and art theory. Together they stimulated the inquiry of "fellow-feelings" in terms of emotion, attitude and artistic strategy–bequeathing this complexity to subsequent generations.

Drawing on the thought of a few exemplary thinkers, let me illustrate the search for a theoretical space able to reconcile the ambiguous concept that emerged from the convergence among these different terms (to which one should add pity as well). My search, historically grounded, included an investigation into the concept's ontology and epistemology, which came to denote sympathy not only with suffering personae but also with people in other emotional states. The ontological aspect concerned the reality or validity of fellow-feelings, the epistemological aspect concerned the mental operations entailed in their activation, those pertaining to the faculty of imagination-reflection, comparison and action planning. Whether or not this endeavor yielded unequivocal resolutions, they certainly divulged the inherent complexity compassion/sympathy entails.

The ontological element was crucial and affected the epistemological. The fact that in philosophical discourse compassion, since Plato and Aristotle, had been confined mainly to theatrical experience meant that it was destined to be considered secondary if not a "fictional" mental state, and thus of inferior moral consequences. Stressing the central role music played in this development, I claim that the phenomenology of the auditory in general, and of the prevalent musical language in particular, lent themselves to manifestations of sympathy that transcended fictional forms, and enabled a clearer tracing of the mechanism which this mental state involved, betraying a new awareness of the role of fellow-feelings in the universes of the modern individual and society.

The Transformation of 'Compassion' in light of Diverse Understandings of its Referent (Feeling, Attitude or Moral Duty)

The attempt to define "fellow-feelings" clearly required answers to preliminary questions, such as: to what extent is suffering *with* different from being moved *by*? Is the first only a contagious state of mind, stemming from a certain "existential togetherness" and the other a more voluntary emotion, attesting to the overcoming of an existential distance between the compassionate person and the sufferer? Indeed, from Antiquity up to our own times, there has not been an agreement on the extent to which compassion is a feeling, an attitude, or a moral duty. When considered as a feeling or an emotion–clearly one of a secondary order–it became clear that while no external signs necessarily define its expression (unlike other affective states), the primary affections on which it draws are not definite either. As an attitude, it has not been clarified whether compassion is related to an inborn disposition or is an acquired trait and to what extent it may be inculcated. In both cases it appeared to implicate the imagination, but in so doing threatened its own validity as a reliable state of mind. As a moral duty, it has raised the question how far compassion (or later sympathy) should extend, whom it should include and how to choose among types of sufferers (Scheler 1954; Schopenhauer 1995; Eliot 1995; Hartman 1997, Boltansky 1999). In different times, some questions were picked up; others were neglected. All, however, were implied in almost every discussion of compassion/sympathy's "surprising effects" (Marshall 1988). In early modern times, theorists and moralists could freshly engage compassion predicaments by redefining the boundaries between reality, art, and imagination.

As in other cases of the history of ideas, the legacy of classical thinkers was rather determinant. Plato and Aristotle both conceived of pity (ἔλεος) as a bridge between illusion and reality, protagonists and antagonists, speaker and audience. Both agreed that it touches upon fear (φόβος) and involves a notion of propriety, since not everybody deserves to be pitied. But whereas Plato banished pity from his state, together with theater, poetry and painting (Plato 1963: 605), Aristotle welcomed it into the realms of art and life. The reason for their opposing views lies in their different ontologies and divergent political worldviews. Plato, the idealist, denies illusionary representations in his utopian state, considering them as a third-rate reality, insisting on valor as a supreme personal quality rather than mercy. Aristotle, the empiricist, embraced the psychological and political effects of well-made illusions (i.e.

tragedies), and was tolerant towards the variety of human dispositions. Yet he distinguished between real pity and theatrical pity, viewing the former as encouraging *moral action,* while the latter as demanding *emotional participation* (Aristotle 1968; 1961; 1934). Bifurcated between life and art, morality and passion, the Aristotelian ἔλεος became a challenge that later generations tried to overcome without relegating pity to an imaginary, lower moral sphere or, alternately, draining it of emotional involvement.

Fellow-feelings: Between a Theatre of Emotions and a Moral Order

The transformation of 'compassion' into 'sympathy' between the early 17th century and the late 19th century may be exemplified by reference to a few landmark thinkers from Descartes through Rousseau, to Adam Smith and George Eliot. All of them were engaged in moral and aesthetic issues central to 'sympathy', though they were differently preoccupied. For Descartes, pity is confined to "reality," to the realm where the "passions of the soul" can be viewed in action and thus channeled and controlled (Descartes 1985). Still, he could not exclude the "theatrical" from penetrating the psycho-physiological mechanism he attributed to pity. For Rousseau, on the other hand, pity is a primary passion, a literary theme, a moral principle, and a cohesive political power. His ideas supplied basic coordinates for developments in the arts, those which brought about new sensibilities concerning sympathy. Adam Smith insisted on the mutuality of sympathy in a decent society, constructing a comprehensive moral theory on its elusive base. And while George Eliot borrowed many of his ideas, she sought to reconnect the moral advantages Smith identified with sympathy to the artistic sphere, particularly to music, which she viewed as a most pertinent arena for enhancing their effect. Smith's and Eliot's ideas, however, would be better assessed after having considered certain developments in the art of music.

As with Plato and Aristotle, so with Descartes: the moral entitlement of the object of pity to a better fate is a crucial condition for feelings of pity. Fear, though unnamed, likewise inhabits the psychological arena of the Cartesian feeler of pity: Descartes argues that there are "those who think of the evil afflicting others as capable of befalling themselves" (Descartes 1985:

395). Like Plato, Descartes' account of pity is imbued with normative moral notions. His compassionate personae are derogated for being moved to pity "more by the love they bear towards themselves than by the love they have for others."

Yet Descartes also recognized a more virtuous compassion, one experienced "like that [pity] caused by the tragic actions we see *represented on the stage*; it is more external, affecting the senses more than the interior of the soul, which still has the satisfaction of thinking that it is *doing its duty* in feeling compassion for those afflicted" (ibid. my italics). No real emotions accompany this sort of compassion, for Descartes, and no real affinity with the afflicted person. Actually the compassion felt in this case is for the weakness of those who cannot endure their suffering with forbearance. Descartes' virtuous pity has, thus, almost nothing in common with everyday pity. It is devoid of emotions (fear, sadness or love) and of moral urgency, reduced, instead, to a pure, calculated attitude, betraying self-satisfaction, with a grain of arrogance.[3]

Rousseau turns this picture upside down. Identifying what he terms as natural pity, he views it as "the source of all morality," preceding the use of all reflection. Combined with love of self (*l'amour de soi*), which it moderates, and further moderated by it, pity introduces us to the loving and gentle passions, far removed from vanity, indifference and nontransparent social intercourse (Rousseau 1964: 130; Starobinsky 1988: 210). Derrida and others will argue that pity's innateness according to Rousseau does not sever it from the reflective faculties (Derrida 1998: 173). Thus for Rousseau, reflectivity is built on feelings of affinity and perception of unbearable difference between the compassionate persona and the sufferer (Rousseau 1966: 32). Only thus could pity serve Rousseau as a regulating power for the formation of the moral society. Rousseau's 'pity' is thus an interactive human disposition, inseparable from cognitive and moral growth, and indispensable to social order: a mode of feeling, cogitation and behavior, guaranteeing a sympathetic society.

---

[3] This is reminiscent of how Richard Wagner eventually "viewed" the matter, in his important letter to Mathilde Wesendonk. See Wagner 1853-1871: 84.

The Emergence of Sympathetic Sonorities where Mimetic Illusion Failed

Rousseau positioned music close to pity in his appraisal of the arts and language: a natural mode of expression unmarred by artificial and corrupt manifestations of human civilization. Moreover, he viewed the art of sound–in contradistinction to that of color and design–even in its later developments, as endowed with powers to bring society back to a state of solidarity and transparency it had long lost. No wonder he considered the connection between music and sympathy as abiding. Together with later advocates of music's sympathetic powers, Rousseau highlights music's enveloping and enwrapping capacity, stemming from the phenomena of sound and singing. Artistic developments in the century that transpired between Descartes and Rousseau added additional components to these basic qualities: While painting and literature were estranging themselves from the direct expression of emotions, sensitizing audiences to the deceptive potential of artistic devices and to the intricacies of illusion and hazards of reflections, major trends in the art of music sought to merge illusion and reality, deception and truth. Music was said to dwell on sympathy as a major mode of configuring sound that affects both insiders of fictive worlds as well those who watch them, not to speak of sound played in the real world, unconditioned by dramatic illusion.

The place of music in regard to sympathy may be seen in three main areas, which were given special attention by composers and theorists in the course of the 17th and 18th century: *time*, *texture* and *expression*. Music, accordingly, has its own experiential duration, concomitantly conveying a symbolic temporal dimension. Music can bring disparate levels of reality to the same time frame, convening personae of all kinds and ranks, close and distant in time and spirit, embracing them in sympathetic action that transcends "reality." This general propensity was heightened, in the 17th century, through tonal configurations that rendered continuous movement from one tonal area to another through diatonic modulations. Concomitantly, the increasing use of chromatic and enharmonic modulations enabled the dissection, and immediate projection, of musical utterances from a remote tonal area to a central one.[4] Unexpected sympathetic mobilizations, annihilating symbolic distances, could be thus effected.

Regarding *texture*, music was increasingly configured through echoing textures of various kinds, and other repetitive devices that enhanced the notion of sameness, affinity and reverberations. These new textural configurations were devised in the search for ways to communicate sympathetic reciprocation, conveyed by the poetic texts chosen by composers. Once these textural arrangements prevailed, whether vocal or instrumental, music appropriated sympathy as its major affective principle.

This basic sympathetic condition was further enhanced by means of the ever-expanding scope of its *expressive* vocabulary, regarding various emotional states. This vocabulary was defined mainly in terms of melody, harmony, and rhythm, and was encoded mainly through textual labels. Despite the fact that this vocabulary was a recent innovation, the musical gestures it gave rise to were readily perceived by listeners to be immediate and natural, especially when compared to verbal utterances (Katz and HaCohen 2003). Sympathy, metaphorically connoted in music, was enriched by this development. The kinds of emotion to which it could join   sadness, joy, anxiety, longing etc.— became more distinct and assumed a vitality and directness that allowed it to overcome fictional, historical and other barriers that separated sympathizers from sympathized. Music was thus able to accentuate an important component in the arousal of sympathy that was less prominent in drama and life: sympathy produced via *expression,* by "look and gestures," as Adam Smith

---

[4] Tonal harmony crystallized during the 17th century and became the most pervasive and enduring perceptual and conceptual frame of reference for organizing large and small stretches of music, through its highly cohesive, generative, and hierarchical tonal relations. It rendered each musical composition into a sophisticated recursive "text", the units of which could be defined in terms of higher and lower syntactical units. It also defined, through the same musical materials (tones and chords), the rules of transition from each unit (called key or tonal area)—main or subsidiary—to the next. The transition from one key to the next was termed modulation, of which the chromatic and the enharmonic were more abrupt and poignant.

suggested (Smith 1976: 11) rather than by *incidents*, as Aristotle claimed. Moreover, this expression was soon to be perceived as a "universal language" due to the non-lexical nature of musical communication, which rendered it more immediate and direct.

From Adam Smith to George Eliot: Moving beyond Immediate Affinities

Though not explicitly referenced in his treatise on the sentiments, Adam Smith, the Scottish philosopher, must have understood the capacity of music to express and emote (Katz and HaCohen 2003a: 405-411). An empiricist, he also acknowledged the limited emotional and imaginary resources of normal people to reach out beyond the near and familiar, and did not denigrate the idea that basic fear may motivate fellow feelings (HaCohen 2011: 77-79). Concomitantly, he insisted on the reciprocal nature of sympathy, akin to the musical texture that became the norm of the day. He even argued that mutuality takes the edge of the pain of the suffering persona, enabling the sympathetic dyad to further overcome distance. Still he had to admit, which he did, that effective compassion for far away victims of catastrophe or misfortune is rare. Transparency (of expression), closeness, mutuality and cultural affinity are, according to Smith, the space – social and ideational - in which one should seek for sympathy, and for 'sympathy'.

George Eliot, a thinker and a novelist, demanded more from her fellow-citizens as well as from her protagonists, but acknowledged human limitations, following Smith and his like. Where and how can one go beyond the four components of transparency, closeness, mutuality and cultural affinity? While transparent expression is a condition of sympathy, one can move, through the power of imagination, to conceive not only of the suffering persona inner state but of the circumstances–social political and biographical–that brought him/her to that condition, reducing judgmental attitude. And though one more naturally sympathizes with one's neighbor more than with a distant victim, there are still many sufferers whom we exclude through various "othering" strategies. Indeed, mutual response creates a better ground for the sympathetic act, but it does not have to be immediate, facing the miserable situation of the sufferer. Cultural shareability is a condition for basic understanding, but as Eliot shows, it can exceed expectations, teaching the sympathetic dyad to transcend difference, while learning the new and the different in the world of the remote other. Again, echoing music for Eliot is a great inspiration for her major essay on sympathy–the novel *Daniel Deronda* (published 1776), but her musical examples also point to less familiar and immediate sonic possibilities that can equally encourage sympathetic feelings (HaCohen 2011). The proper space for sympathy is thus broader than imagined by Smith, without being tainted by normative and arrogant approaches. While acknowledging that sameness is the basic condition of the sympathetic act, imagination and reflection are also required to reach out to people who seek our sharing sentiments and sometimes also our ameliorating actions.

Bibliography

Aristotle (1968) *Poetics; A Translation and Commentary for Students of Literature*, translated by Leon Golden, commentated by O.B. Hardison (Englewood Cliffs, N.J.: Prentice Hall).

Aristotle (1961 [1948]). *The Politics of Aristotle*, translated with an introduction by Ernest Barker (Oxford: Oxford University Press).

Aristotle (1934). *Aristotle's Rhetoric* in *Poetics Aristotle, On Style, Demetrius*, edited by Rev. T.A. Moxon (London: Dent).

Boltanski, Luc (1999). *Distant Suffering: Morality, Media and Politics*, trans. Graham

Burchell (Cambridge: Cambridge University Press).

Derrida, Jacques (1998 [1967]). *Of Grammatology*, corrected ed., translated by Gayatri Chakravorty Spivak (Baltimore: The Johns Hopkins University Press).

Descartes, René (1961 [1618]). *Compendium of Music*, translated by W. Robert (New York: The American Institute of Musicology).

Descartes, René (1985 [1649]). *The Passions of the Soul*, in *The Philosophical Writings of Descartes*, vol.1, translated by J. Cottingham, R. Stoothoff, and D. Murdoch (Cambridge: Cambridge University Press).

Foucault, Michel (1972). *The Order of Things: An Archaeology of the Human Sciences* (New York: Vintage Books).

HaCohen, Ruth (2001). "The Music of Sympathy in the Arts of the Baroque; or, the Use of Difference to Overcome Indifference," *Poetics Today* 22:3: 607-650.

HaCohen, Ruth (2011). *The Music Libel Against the Jews* (New Haven: Yale University Press).

Hartman, Geoffrey H. (1997). *The Fatal Question of Culture* (New York: Columbia University Press).

Katz, Ruth and HaCohen, Ruth (2003). *Tuning the Mind: The Prefiguration of the Cognitive Turn by the Arts* 2 vols. (New Brunswick: Transaction).

Katz, Ruth and HaCohen, Ruth (2003a). *The Arts in Mind: Pioneering Texts of a Coterie of British Men of Letters*, edited and annotated (New Brunswick: NJ: Transaction).

Marshall, David (1988). *The Surprising Effects of Sympathy* (Chicago: University of Chicago Press).

Plato (1963). *The Collected Dialogues*, edited by Edith Hamilton and Hunington Cairns (New York: Bollingen Foundation, Pantheon Books).

Rousseau, Jean-Jacques (1964). *The First and Second Discourses*, ed. Roger D. Masters (New York: St. Martin's Press).

Rousseau, Jean-Jacques (1966). *Essay on the Origin of Languages,* in *On the Origin of Language,* trans. by John H. Moran and Alexander Gode (Chicago: Chicago University Press).

Scheler, Max (1954 [1931]). *The Nature of Sympathy,* translated by Peter Heath (London: Routledge and Kegan Paul).

Schopenhauer, Arthur (1995). *On the Basis of Morality,* translated by E.F.J Payne (Oxford: Berghahn Books).

Smith, Adam (1976 [1759]). *The Theory of Moral Sentiments,* edited By D. D. Raphael and A.L. Macfie, (Oxford: Clarendon Press).

Starobinsky, Jean (1988 [1971]). *Jean-Jacques Rousseau, Transparency and Obstruction,* translated by A. Goldhammer (Chicago: The University of Chicago Press).

Wagner, Richard (1853-1871). *Tagebuchblätter und Briefe an Mathilde Wesendonk,* eingeleitet und erläutert von R. Sternfeld (Berlin: Deutsche Buch-Gemeinschaft).

PART IV

Mind and Brain Relationship

IV

Mind and Brain Relationship

Introduction

In my introduction to section III, I stated that it is largely accepted that a general conception is formed through abstraction, i.e. by focusing on the common element among the many images of members of a class. Yet taking note of the *agreement* among things raised some unresolved questions: Do we by comparing things to each other recognize something we already had in mind, or something that resulted from the comparison? Does our intuitive perception strive for some kind of "ideal" by dropping the differences that may obscure coherence? Where and how do perceptions turn into conceptions that facilitate communication? Although we regularly use concepts inadvertently, and some of us may even be aware of their linguistic significance, we may be oblivious, nonetheless, to major queries which the subject entails.

The history of art, as we have seen, takes ample note of the social transformations and the collective attitudes that impact stylistic change and aesthetic desiderata. Discussing Gombrich (in section II), I emphasized that though he was fully aware of the collective attitudes that impact art, he was primarily interested in what can be learned from the historical development of art that tells us something about our *mental* makeup that enables visual representations and the comprehension of their displayed images. Assuming that the production of art must involve some kind of *interrelationship* between visual perception and visual representation led Gombrich to investigate the ways in which artists grappled with this fundamental problem. Gombrich, accordingly, examined the "practical" problems that artists faced and the means they adopted to solve them. The artist, Gombrich believed, needs a medium and a schema–a "vocabulary," as it were–that can be modified, since artists do not simply examine the nature of the physical world, but the nature of our reactions to it. Thus artists, throughout history, have learned more from the "inventions" of other artists, than through direct observations of nature. They have learned from each other to depict the visual world with increased attention to visual perception, though unaware that they were addressing a seminal issue that will require further study and investigation. At any rate, in *Art and Illusion* Gombrich revealed that there is no rigid distinction between perception and illusion. He contributed, thereby, a way of looking into the invisible realm of the mind.

Ever since the scientific revolution of the late sixteenth and early seventeenth century, the advancement of knowledge no longer rested on the belief that the laws of nature may be extrapolated from the visible world. The revolution challenged the very premise that the regulations of the "Divinely-Ordered" universe may be revealed through their worldly manifestations. The revolution, in fact, sought to extrapolate from the perceptible world the *invisible* laws of nature, laws that may better explain their multiple actualizations. However, the unveiling of *secret* "designs" and "intent" invariably involves procedures that enable their discovery. Yet the procedures themselves must be construed so as to fit the undertaken tasks. Though often subjected to processes of "trial and error," procedures of this kind may also stumble inadvertently on "intervening" factors that require attention of their own. Indeed, the unveiling of the *secret laws of nature* is an ongoing-process that steadily alerts us to problems we have not been aware of, while addressing those of which we have been aware.

Given the ongoing process delineated above, it is no wonder that the history of science–and, for that matter, the advancement of knowledge by and large–should be replete with conceptual transformations of various kinds, involving diverse fields of endeavor. Yet despite the steady mushrooming of knowledge and the many trajectories which it encompasses, the advancement of knowledge increasingly clarifies "what relates to what and whereby." Moreover, conceptions, methodologies, and the application of various technologies, are continuously transferred from one field to another in order to better understand the interrelationships among diverse fields of investigation. Indeed, via processes of this kind it became increasingly evident how we, as humans, create our world of knowledge. All of this raises however a fundamental question about us as *humans*: What enabled us to undertake so grand an enterprise?

Philosophy was never oblivious to this primary question, although it addressed the issue indirectly, as it were. Aristotle, for example, raised interesting questions concerning the "truly real" in nature: Is the truly real known by inference or directly, objectively or subjectively, as part of the world of phenomena or of *human understanding*? All of these questions, and more, were also asked subsequently, subjected to refined scrutiny, yielding interesting insights and enlightening arguments. Plato, as we have seen, gave ideas a primary ontological validity. That which is apprehended by the *intellect*, he claimed, is more real than all else, hence the timelessness and immutability of ideas. In fact, all of the theories that dealt with the *grounds* of knowledge seem to have grappled in one way or another with the nature of Man no less than they grappled with the laws of Nature. The distinction, for example, between 'body' and 'soul', which preoccupied philosophers for centuries, reveals–via the interesting debates which it enlisted–man's concerted effort to understand his uniqueness, though indecisive about *wherein* or *where* it was "located." And long before philosophical deliberations gave rise to psychological investigations, which eventually gave rise to cognitive studies, Descartes distinguished between the 'mind' and the material body, claiming that the former is indivisible whereas the latter is. Indeed, wherever one turns in the various branches of philosophy Man occupies either center stage or a major role behind the scenes. Evidently, investigations of fundamental queries do not emerge *ad nihilo* in the orbit of knowledge.

Philosophy has of course been preoccupied with questions concerning the "innate" versus the "learned" for a long time. Yet the advancement of several offshoots of scientific investigations brought questions pertaining to "nature versus nurture" to the forefront. From biology to psychology, from the behavioral sciences to education, and more, the dividing lines between the "bequeathed" and the "acquired" have become central issues in dire need of clarifications and guidance. In fact, the cognitive turn in epistemology in the second half of the eighteenth century constituted a crucial turning point that markedly precipitated the investigation of the brain. It commenced with 'perception' as a subject worthy of study and continued with 'cognition' and with attempts to better grasp the impact of the former on the latter. How the mind *processes* information remained, nevertheless, unclear. Moreover, the antecedent position of perception became increasingly challenged. Experiments of diverse kinds have shown that the distinctions among elements–those that we have learned to recognize *as such*–largely determine what we perceive. In short, what we are "looking for" may impact what we see. It is of course far more complicated than it seems, since it suggests that the study of the brain must, willy-nilly, also address the mind/brain conundrum, which must evidently engage a goodly number of *interdisciplinary* studies. Interestingly, it is our mind that asks the questions which the brain enabled us to ponder, and the unveiling of the *secrets* of the brain is expected to disclose the "means" and "in what way" we comprehend and proceed to fashion our world.

The history of science has witnessed many conceptual transformations, not least owing to technological advances that facilitated diverse research projects. Yet the study of the brain underwent a fundamental transformation due to the advances in imaging technology that made it possible to *actually see* the brain for the first time. The functional magnetic resonance imaging (fMRI), for example, allows neuroscientists to trace the brain activity while in action. It has also allowed for the tracing of different areas of the brain, revealing that each of the cerebral structures is specialized for one or more specific tasks. However, despite this development and other techniques, neuroscientists are still far from unveiling the multiple "secrets" that philosophers and scientists have been debating for millennia, i.e. the mysteries of the *human mind*. How the brain forms abstractions is, of course, a central problem in cognitive neurology, but there is still a large gap between the processing of the brain and the processes of the mind, which the former helps to produce. Recent research, accordingly, does not only focus on how the brain works, but also on the ways in which it impacts our mind, i.e. those features that are primarily attributed to mankind. These include aspects such as thought, feelings, creativity, memory, sentiments and more, without denying several of these attributes to other living creatures.

As stated above, the mind/brain conundrum engages many interdisciplinary studies. A fairly number of these studies focus on the mental processes that accompany the production and the perception of the various arts. In fact, the brain is nowadays viewed as a kind of '*Gesamtkunstwerk*'–a magisterial "artwork," a design that determines and controls all of our activities and abilities, from the simple raising of a hand to the most complicated of intellectual activities. Already in the nineteenth century, the eminent physiologist Herman Helmholz (1821–1894) suggested that we unconsciously infer from fragmentary clues–gathered by our senses from the environment–a *holistic representation* of visual reality. The world we see, he suggested, is neither "objective" nor "direct," but a subjective and indirect representation constructed *internally* by the nervous system. In other words, in contrast to the view that the development and operation of perception is entirely dependent on direct engagement with the external world, he suggested that what appears in our conscious mind is to some degree independent from what exists in the world. A century later, Giacomo Rizzolatti announced the discovery of mirror neurons (1992), a special class of neurons that do not only galvanize, while carrying out a certain action, but also when that action is merely witnessed. It has been argued that these neurons may be important for understanding the actions of other people and for learning new skills by imitation. Some researchers, however, believe that these neurons may be related to language abilities, while others believe that they may constitute the basis for the human capacity for emotion, such as empathy. Given these and many other findings, may cast light not only on the "processing activity" of the brain, but also on the processes that attended its development.

As of now, more can still be said about the developments produced by the human mind than can be said about the complex activities of the brain. Already in the early part of the eighteenth century, Vico suggested in his *Scienza Nuova* that there can be a "science of mind" that is the history of its development, a science that can be traceable through the "evolution of symbols" and their altering patterns, functions, structures, and uses. It may be recalled that the systematic reflection and analysis of human consciousness, provided Cassirer with a firm basis for all of human knowledge, including scientific knowledge (see Cassirer, section I). In fact, Cassirer's symbolic forms contain, unto themselves, the significations of human experience in its variety; they do not create a distinction between the symbolizing activity of consciousness and its schematizing function. They represent a fusion, as it were, between the activity and its function, embodying jointly the ways in which human beings construct their reality in the world which they created. Cassirer's approach to symbolic forms in fact rests on the notion that humans create their own universe of *symbolic meaning* that structures and shapes their perception of reality and that only thus can they conceive of progress in the form of human culture. The world, in other words, is not directly perceived via sensory perception, but via the means humans create whereby it is perceived.

The examples I cited above hardly represent the many interesting theories that sprouted in the course of history concerning the mind. The examples only intended to illustrate some of the arguments that theories of this kind enlisted. Although this is not the place to linger on theories concerning the mind, I wish to emphasize that however interesting these theories turned out to be, they fell short of revealing the actual "mechanisms" that enabled their development, i.e. the "processing" of the brain. Nonetheless, it must be remembered that it is theories of this kind and more that gradually led to the investigation of the brain. Nor should one forget the technological developments that enabled the study of the brain. Indeed, nothing starts from scratch in the vast orbit of knowledge!

The study of the brain, nowadays, clearly occupies a central position among scientific inquiries. The object, however, is not only theoretical, i.e. to better understand our mental functioning, but in order to be able to address neurological disease therapeutically. The essays included in this section of the book only exemplify the sort of "reasoning" that accompanies some seminal studies of the brain. * From Zeki's essay we learn that the primordial function of the visual brain is the acquisition of knowledge by registering the *constant* and *essential* characteristics of objects. Since these characteristics are also the primordial function of art, neurobiologists are encouraged to take advantage of art as a field that may contribute to the investigation and understanding of the workings of the brain. * From Harth's essay we learn how difficult it is to track down the "seat" of *consciousness*. His account, which begins with neuro-chemicals and ends with qualities, connects the emergence of the *self* to "physical forces." Unlike Zeki, Harth holds to the opinion that the "particulars" of brain function are so complex that it will never be possible to test the hypothesis that behavior can be explained in terms of brain structure and function that can have predictive value.

Semir Zeki

Introduction

Semir Zeki is a neuroscientist whose work involves a multi-disciplinary approach that brings together neuroscientists, cognitive scientists and those in the humanities, to address questions that are of deep concern to science and society. With a background in anthropology and medicine, his main interest focuses on the organization of the primate visual brain. He has published many articles and several books based on his discoveries concerning visual areas of the brain and their functional specialization for different visual attributes such as color and motion. He was likewise able to show that the processing sites in the visual brain are also perceptual sites.

In 1994, Zeki began to study the neural basis of creativity and the aesthetic appreciation of art, resulting in a book entitled *Inner Vision: an Exploration of Art and the Brain*. By 2001 he had founded the Institute of Neuroaesthetics, which is mainly based in Berkeley, California. As the initiator of neuroaesthetics, he has lectured in diverse institutions around the world including museums, art galleries, academies of art and diverse scientific societies. He holds many positions related to neuroscience, and serves on the editorial boards of many journals specializing in neurobiology.

Neuroaesthetics is a relatively recent discipline that approaches aesthetic perception scientifically, benefiting from the advances that have taken place in the technological sphere. As a neuroscientist at the University College London, Zeki runs the university's nstitute of neuroaesthetics. His interest in the study of the visual brain through art, and the emotions through literature and music, rests on a genuine familiarity with writers and philosophers of past centuries who tried to grasp the essence of aesthetic experiences and to define the concept of 'beauty'. However, aware of the fact that these thinkers never had the opportunity *to see* what takes place in the brain when confronted with works of art, he saw fit to apply the techniques of neuroscience to aesthetics so as to better understand the acts of creativity, the reactions to them, and their interdependence. In fact, his studies led him to suggest that artists may be viewed as "instinctive neurologists," i.e. as creators equipped with an *innate understanding*, as it were, concerning the way the brain "looks" at the world. Convinced that the primordial function of seeing is not a passive process, he –like Gombrich (see section II)–believes that artists were continuously trying to find a "visual language" in order to convey the partaking of the brain in what we see and experience.

According to Zeki, the development and operation of perception–at least in the case of visual cognition–is dependent on direct engagement with the external world. Without appropriate sensory stimulation the visual components of the brain fail to develop the capacity for instantaneous object recognition that sighted people take for granted. Aware of both Locke and Kant, the physiologist Helmholtz (see the introduction to this section) had already suggested, based on his investigations, that we unconsciously infer a *holistic* representation of visual reality through fragmentary clues gathered from the external environment by our senses. The world we see, he suggested, is a subjective and indirect representation constructed internally by our nervous system. According to Zeki, the primordial function of the visual brain is the acquisition of knowledge by registering the *constant* and *essential* characteristics of objects, which are as well the primordial function of art. Since all artistic works clearly involve in their conceptions and techniques certain neurobiological aspects, neurobiologists are encouraged to take advantage of art as a field that may contribute to the investigation and understanding of the working of the brain.

In the introduction to section III, I stated that conceptions are generally viewed as *mental abstracts*, or as "general ideas" inferred or derived from specific instances. Abstraction has also been viewed as a process whereby higher concepts are derived from literal ones by retaining only information which is relevant for a particular task. Even before it was possible to actually see the brain, it was accepted that processes of this kind involve mental capacities that enable their activation. Indeed, how the brain forms abstractions is a central problem in cognitive neurobiology. Abstraction, according to Zeki, is a process in which "the particular is subordinated to the general, so that what is represented is applicable to many particulars." Abstraction, he suggests, is not only an efficient step in the acquisition of knowledge, but relieves the brain from an overload of particulars. This may be imposed by the limitations of our memory system which overrides the need to recall every detail. Given that art also involves abstraction, it likewise externalizes the inner workings of the brain. In fact, neuroaesthetics studies the neural basis of artistic creativity convinced that there cannot be a satisfactory theory of aesthetics that is not neurobiologically based.

The history of science has seen many conceptual transformations in diverse fields, yet none were as promising as those that sprouted in the wake of the cybernetic revolution. Brain studies, nowadays, seem to tackle all of our basic faculties–memory, perception, sentiments, consciousness, and more–in the hope to acquaint us with ourselves. Although we are becoming more and more acquainted with ourselves, there is still a huge gap between the mind and what we presently know about the brain, i.e. why we think, feel, and behave as we do, namely, the attributes that make us human.

ZEKI
Art and the Brain[*]

ᶜᴳ᷎

Les causeries sur l 'art sont presque inutiles.
–*Paul Cézanne* (Gerstle Mack, *La Vie de Paul Cézanne,* quoted in
Gray, 1953).

*More often than not, [people] expect a painting to speak to them
in terms other than visual, preferably in words, whereas when a
painting or a sculpture needs to be supplemented and explained by
words it means either that it has not fulfilled its function or that the
public is deprived of vision.* –*Naum Gabo* (Gabo, 1962)

I

Much has been written about art, but not in relation to the visual brain–through
which all art, whether in conception or in execution or in appreciation, is
expressed. A great deal, though perhaps not as much, has been written about the
visual brain, but little in relation to one of its major products, art. It is therefore
hardly surprising that the connection between the functions of art and the
functions of the visual brain has not been made. The reason for this omission
lies in a conception of vision and the visual process that was largely dictated by
simple but powerful facts, derived from anatomy and pathology. These facts
spoke in favor of one conclusion to which neurologists were ineluctably driven,
and that conclusion inhibited them, as well as art historians and critics, from
asking the single most important question about vision that one can ask: Why
do we see at all? It is the answer to that question that immediately reveals a
parallel between the functions of art and the functions of the brain, and indeed

[*] From: *Journal of Consciousness Studies,* 6, No. 6-7, 1999, pp. 76-96.

ineluctably drives us to another conclusion–that the overall function of art is an extension of the function of the brain. In that definition are the germs of a theory of art that has solid biological foundations and that unites the views of modem neurobiologists with those of Plato, Michelangelo, Mondrian, Cezanne, Matisse, and many other artists.

The concept of the functions of the visual brain inherited by modem neurobiologists was based on facts derived between 1860 and 1970. Chief among these was the demonstration by the Swedish neuropathologist Salomon Henschen and his successors in Japan and England that the retina of the eye is not diffusely connected to the whole brain, or even to half the brain, but only to a well-defined and circumscribed part of the cerebral cortex. First called the visuo-sensory cortex and later the primary visual cortex (area V1), it therefore constituted 'the only entering place of the visual radiation into the organ of psyche' (Flechsig, 1901). This capital discovery led to a prolonged battle between its proponents and its opponents, who thought of it as 'une localisation à outrance' (Vialet, 1894); they had conceived of the visual input to the brain as being much more extensive and as including large parts of the cerebral cortex that were known to have other functions, a notion more in keeping with the doctrine of the French physiologist Pierre Flourens. The predecessor of the American psychologist Karl Lashley, Flourens had imagined that each and every part of the cortex is involved in every one of its activities. It was not until early this century that the issue of a single visual area located in an anatomically and histologically defined part of the cortex was settled in favor of the localizationists (Monbrun, 1939). There was much else to promote the idea of V1 as the 'sole' visual centre. It had a mature appearance at birth, as if ready to 'receive' the visual 'impressions formed on the retina',[1] whereas the cortex surrounding it matured at different stages after birth, as if the maturation depended upon the acquisition of experience; this made of the latter higher cognitive centers, the *Cogitatzionszentren,* whose function was to interpret the visual image received by V1, or so neurologists imagined.

---

[1] These are the terms of neurologists, not mine; they were current until the last two decades.

As well, lesions in V1 lead to blindness, the position and extent of which is in direct proportion to the position and size of the lesion; by contrast, lesions in the surrounding cortex resulted in vague visual syndromes, referred to first as mind blindness *(Seelenblindheit)* and then as agnosia, following the term introduced by Freud. Together, these facts conferred the sovereign capacity of 'seeing' on V1, leading neurologists to conceive of it as the 'cortical retina', the cerebral organ that receives the visual images 'impressed' upon the retina, as on a photographic plate—an analogy commonly made. Seeing was therefore a passive process, while understanding what was seen was an active one; this notion divided seeing from understanding and assigned a separate cortical seat to each.

This concept left little room for the fundamental question of why we see. Instead, seeing was accepted as a given. Asked the question today, few would suppose that it is so we can appreciate works of art; most would give answers that are specific, though related in general to the survival of the species. The most general of these answers would include all the specific ones and define the function of seeing as *the acquisition of knowledge about the world* (Zeki, 1993). There are, of course, other ways of obtaining that knowledge—through the sense of touch or smell or audition, for example—but vision happens to be the most efficient way of obtaining it, and there are some kinds of knowledge, such as the color of a surface or the expression on a face, that can only be obtained through vision.

It takes but a moment's thought to realize that obtaining that knowledge is no easy matter. The brain is only interested in obtaining knowledge about those permanent, essential, or characteristic properties of objects and surfaces that allow it to categorize them. But the information reaching the brain from these surfaces and objects is in continual flux. A face may be categorized as a sad one, thus giving the brain knowledge about a person in spite of the continual changes in individual features, viewing angle, or even the identity of the face viewed; or the destination of an object may have to be decided by its direction of motion, regardless of its speed or distance. An object may have to be categorized according to color, as when judging the state of ripeness of an edible fruit. But the wavelength composition of the light reflected from an object is never constant; it changes continually, depending upon the time of day, without entailing a substantial shift in its color. The ability of the brain to assign a constant color to a surface or a constant form to an object is generally referred to as color or object constancy. But perceptual constancy is a much wider phenomenon. It also applies, for example, to faces that are recognizable when viewed from different angles and regardless of the expression worn. There is also what I shall call situational constancy, when the brain is able to categorize an event or a situation as festive or sad and so on, regardless of the particular event. There is even a narrative constancy when, for example, the brain is able to identify a scene as the 'Descent from the Cross', regardless of variations in the detail or the style of the painting. The brain, in each case, extracts from the continually changing information that reaches it only what is necessary for it to identify the characteristic properties of what it views; it has to extract constant features in order to be able to obtain knowledge about them and to categorize them. Vision, in brief, is an active process that depends as much upon the operations of the brain as upon the external, physical environment; the brain must discount much of the information reaching it, select only what is necessary in order to obtain knowledge about the visual world, and compare the selected information with its stored record of all that it has seen. A modern neurobiologist should approve heartily of Matisse's statement that 'Voire, c'est déjà une operation créatrice, qui exige un effort' (Matisse, 1972, p. 365).

How the brain achieves this remarkable feat remains a puzzle; indeed, the question has only been seriously addressed in the last thirty years, which have witnessed a prolific output of work on the visual brain. Among the chief discoveries is that it is composed of many different visual areas that surround V1 (Zeki, 1978). Each group of areas is specialized to process a particular attribute of the visual environment by virtue of the specialized signals that each receives from V1 (*ibid.*). Cells specialized for a given attribute such as motion or color are grouped together in anatomically identifiable compartments within V1, and different compartments connect with different visual areas outside V1, thus conferring their specializations on the relevant areas (Livingstone & Hubel, 1984; 1987; Shipp & Zeki, 1985). V1 acts much like a post office, distributing different signals to different destinations; it is but the first, though essential, stage in an elaborate machinery designed to extract the essential information from the visual world. What we now call the visual brain is therefore V1 plus the specialized visual areas with which it connects, directly and indirectly. We therefore speak of parallel systems devoted to processing simultaneously different attributes of the visual world, a system comprising the specialized cells in V1 plus the specialized areas to which these cells project. Vision, in brief, is modular. The reasons for evolving a strategy to process in parallel the different attributes of the visual world have been debated, but it seems plausible to suppose that they are rooted in the need to discount different kinds of information when acquiring knowledge about different attributes (Zeki, 1993). With color, it is the precise wavelength composition of the light reflected from a surface that has to be discounted, whereas with size it is the precise viewing distance, and with form, the viewing angle.

Recent evidence has shown that the processing systems are also perceptual systems in that activity in each can result in a percept without reference to the other systems (Zeki, 1998); each processing-perceptual system terminates its perceptual task and reaches its perceptual endpoint at a slightly different time than the others, thus leading to a perceptual asynchrony in vision—color is seen before form, which is seen before motion, with the advantage of color over motion being of the order of 60-100 ms (Moutoussis & Zeki, 1997). Thus visual perception is also modular. In summary, the visual brain is characterized by a set of parallel processing-perceptual systems and a temporal hierarchy in visual perception (Zeki, 1998).

These findings lead me to propose that there is also a modularity, a functional specialization, in visual aesthetics. When area V4, the color centre, is damaged, the consequence is an inability to see the world in color (Zeki, 1990). But other attributes of the visual scene are perceived normally. When area V5, the motion centre, is damaged, the consequence is an inability to see objects when in motion, although other attributes are seen normally. Damage to a region close to V4 leads to a syndrome characterized by an inability to see familiar faces. There are other specific syndromes—for example, the inability to recognize certain categories of objects—and neurology is continually uncovering new syndromes of selective visual loss. I do not mean, of course, to imply that the aesthetics of color are due solely to the activity in V4 or the aesthetics of kinetic art are due solely to the activity in V5; I am suggesting only that the perception of color and of motion is not possible without the presence and healthy functioning of these areas. It does little good to ask a patient with a V4 lesion to appreciate the complexities of fauvist art or a patient with a V5 lesion to view the works of Tinguely. These are aesthetic experiences of which such patients are not capable.

II

The definition that I have given above of the function of the visual brain–a search for constancies with the aim of obtaining knowledge about the world–is applicable with equal vigor to the function of art. I shall thus define the general function of art as a search for the constant, lasting, essential, and enduring features of objects, surfaces, faces, situations, and so on, which allows us not only to acquire knowledge about the particular object, or face, or condition represented on the canvas but to generalize, based on that, about many other objects and thus acquire knowledge about a wide category of objects or faces. In this process, the artist must also be selective and invest his work with attributes that are essential, discarding much that is superfluous. It follows that one of the functions of art is an extension of the major function of the visual brain. Indeed, philosophers and artists often spoke about art in terms that are extremely similar to the language that a modem neurobiologist of vision would use, except that he would substitute the word 'brain' for the word 'artist.' It is striking, for example, to compare Herman von Helmholtz's statement about 'discounting the illuminant', in which a colored surface is viewed (in order to assign a constant color to it), with the statement of Albert Gleizes and Jean Metzinger in their book *Cubism*. Discussing Gustave Courbet, they wrote, 'Unaware of the fact that in order to display a true relation we must be ready to sacrifice a thousand apparent truths, he accepted, without the slightest intellectual control, all that his retina presented to him. He did not suspect that the visible world can become the real world only by the operation of the intellect' (Gleizes & Metzinger, 1913). I interpret 'intellect' to mean the brain or, better still, the cerebral cortex. In order to represent the real world, the brain (or the artist) must discount ('sacrifice') a great deal of the information reaching it (or him), information that is not essential to its (or his) aim of representing the true character of objects.

It is for this reason that I hold the somewhat unusual view that artists are neurologists, studying the brain with techniques that are unique to them and reaching interesting but unspecified conclusions about the organization of the brain. Or, rather, that they are exploiting the characteristics of the parallel processing-perceptual systems of the brain to create their works, sometimes even restricting themselves largely or wholly to one system, as in kinetic art. These conclusions are on canvas and are communicated and understood through the visual medium, without the necessity of using words. This may surprise them since most of them, naturally enough, know nothing about the brain, and a good many still hold the common but erroneous belief that one sees with the eye rather than with the cerebral cortex. Their language, as well as the language of those who write about art, betrays this view. But however erroneous their views about the seeing organ or the role of the visual brain may be, it is sufficient to glance at their writings to realize the extent to which they have defined the function of art in a way that a modern neurobiologist would not only understand but feel very sympathetic to. Thus Henri Matisse once said, 'Underlying this succession of moments which constitutes the superficial existence of things and beings, and which is continually modifying and transforming them, one can search for a truer, more essential character, which the artist will seize so that he may give to reality a more lasting interpretation' (Matisse, 1978). Essentially, this is what the brain does continually–seizing from the constantly changing information reaching it the more essential one, distilling from the successive views the essential character of objects and situations. Similar statements abound, and it is sufficient to give just one more example. Jacques Rivière, the art critic, wrote: 'The true purpose of painting is to represent objects as they really are, that is to say, differently from the way we see them. It tends always to give us their sensible essence, their presence, this is why the image it forms does not resemble their appearance ... ' because the appearance changes from moment to moment (Rivière, 1912). A neurologist could hardly have improved on that statement in describing the functions of the visual brain. He might say that the function of the brain is to represent objects as they really are, that is to say, differently from the way we see them from moment to moment if we were to take into account solely the effect that they produce on the retina.

To summarize, therefore, both the brain and one of its products, art, have the task of, in the words of artists themselves, depicting objects as they are. And both face the problem of how to distill from the ever-changing information in the visual world only that which is important in order to represent the permanent, essential characteristics of objects. Indeed, this was almost the basis of Kant's philosophy of aesthetics, to represent perfection; but perfection implies immutability, and hence arises the problem of depicting perfection in an ever-changing world. I shall therefore define the function of art as being a search for constancies, which is also one of the most fundamental functions of the brain. The function of art is therefore an extension of the function of the brain–the seeking of knowledge in an ever-changing world.

III

Plato was among the most prominent of those who lamented the poverty of art. Without saying so, and indeed without ever referring to the brain, he implicitly compared the limitations of art to the infinite capacities of the brain. His most explicit statement in this regard occurs in Book X of *The Republic,* where he dismisses painting as a mimetic art, one that could represent only one aspect of a particular example of a more general category of an object. To him there was the general ideal of a given form, which was the embodiment of all the examples of that form; then there was a particular form that was but one example of the more general, 'universal' form; and finally, there was painting, which captured but one facet, one image, of one particular form. 'The Greeks,' Sir Herbert Read tells us (Read, 1964), 'with more reason, regarded the ideal as the real, and representational art as merely an imitation of an imitation of the real.[2]

---

[2] This does not represent the view of all ancient Greeks; Aristotle, Plato's student, turned away from it.

Plato's contempt for painting was really linked to his theory of forms and ideals. The example he gives in Book X is that of a couch. To him, there is only one real couch, the one created by God; this is the idea of a couch, and it has a universal existence. One can therefore obtain real knowledge only about this one ideal couch. Of particular couches–as made by a craftsman (δημιουργος), or represented in a single view in a painting, or reflected in a mirror–there can only be an opinion, and an unverifiable one at that.[3] Put in mathematical terms, we can only obtain real and reliable knowledge about ideal circles, triangles, and straight lines. Viewing painted circles and straight lines without reference to the Ideal leads only to a superficial impression and an opinion, which may turn out to be true or false. Plato implied that, at least to get nearer to the Ideal, painting should change direction in order to represent as many facets of an object or situation as possible, since this would give more knowledge about the object. What Plato only implied, Schopenhauer made explicit many centuries later when he wrote that painting should strive 'to obtain knowledge of an object, not as a particular thing but as Platonic Ideal, that is, the enduring form of this whole species of things', a statement that a modem neurobiologist could easily accommodate in describing the functions of the visual brain (Schopenhauer, 1964). Indeed, to a neurobiologist, a brain that is not able to do this is a sick, pathological brain. Painting, in other words, should be the representation of the constant elements, the essentials that would give knowledge of all couches; it should represent constancies. As John Constable put it in his *Discourses:* 'The whole beauty and grandeur of Art consists... in being able to get above all singular forms, local customs, particularities of every kind. ... [The painter] makes out an abstract idea of their forms more perfect than anyone original' (Constable, 1836), the 'abstract idea' presumably being Constable's term for the Platonic Ideal.

---

[3] The example that Plato gives, that of a couch, is derived from the kind of furnishing used in the symposia frequented by Plato and his elite circles. The Idea is created by God, the craftsman (δημιουργος) makes a first example of it, and artists subsequently represent different single views of the craftsman's creation.

There is something unsatisfactory about the Platonic Ideal from a neurobiological point of view, because the Ideal has an existence that is external to the brain and without reference to it; we can only have an opinion of that which we perceive, 'whereas knowledge is of a super-sensible eternal world' (Russell, 1946). Implicitly more dependent upon brain function, and thus more acceptable neurobiologically, are the views of Kant and Hegel. Their views exalt art, which is seen as being able to represent reality better than the 'ephemera of sense data,' since the latter changes from moment to moment. Hegel deals with the Idea that is derived from the Concept. In a painting, the brain, having 'accumulated a treasure, can now freely disgorge [it] in a simple manner without the far-flung conditions and arrangements of the real world.' By this process of 'disgorging,' and thus of externalizing and concretizing, the Concept becomes the Idea. The Idea, then, is merely the external representation of the Concept that is in the brain, the Concept that it has derived from ephemeral sense data. It is, in fact, the product of the artist. Art, including painting, therefore, 'furnishes us with the things themselves, but out of the inner life of the mind'; through art, 'instead of all the dimensions requisite for appearance in nature, we have just a surface, and yet we get the same impression that reality affords' (Hegel, 1975). It is through this translation of the Concept into the Idea that Dutch painting, for example, 'has recreated ... the existent *and fleeting appearance of nature* as something generated afresh by man' *(ibid.,* emphasis added).

Although the views of Plato and Hegel may appear antipodean, the difference between the two is in fact neurobiologically irrelevant if we try to give a neurobiological definition of the Platonic Ideal and the Hegelian Concept. The first step in such a definition, relevant to Plato's views but less so to Hegel's, is a neurobiological doctrine: forms do not have an existence without a brain. This may seem an audacious statement to make, but it is supported by numerous clinical and physiological studies that have shown that individuals who are born blind and to whom vision is later restored find it very difficult, if not impossible, to learn to see even a few forms, and these they soon forget. The question that the learned Mr. Molyneux asked in John Locke's *Essay Concerning Human Understanding* - whether a man born blind and who had learned to distinguish between forms by touch alone would be able to distinguish them by sight alone when vision is restored to him—has been answered negatively many times by clinical studies (see e.g., von Senden, 1932). Physiological studies, particularly those of David Hubel and Torsten Wiesel, have shown that even when the genetically determined visual apparatus is intact at birth, the organism must be exposed to visual stimuli after birth, after which visual education becomes much less important (Hubel & Wiesel, 1977). There is, in other words, a critical period for vision, just as there appears to be for emotional development (Harlow, 1972). Artists have often wished that they could see and paint the world as a child does—for the first time, innocently, without what they suppose to be the prejudice of the developed and possibly even corrupted influence of a brain that has knowledge of the world. Picasso admired the art of children and Matisse wanted to paint like them, as does Balthus (Zeki & Balthus, 1995); Monet wished that he could have been born blind, with vision restored to him later in life so that he could see pure form 'without knowing what the objects were that he saw before him' (Perry, 1927). They are all yearning for something that is physiologically almost impossible. The visual apprenticeship of children occurs at a very early age, before two, and begins immediately after birth, long before the motor apparatus has developed sufficiently to be able to execute a painting. In its conceptual immaturity and technical simplicity, the art of a four-year-old child may be touching and even exciting, but it is the art of a visual brain that is already highly developed and that has acquired much knowledge about the world. The innocence that artists yearn for is, in terms of the brain, a myth.

If neurologically no forms, ideal or otherwise, exist without a brain that is properly nourished, how can we define the Platonic Ideal and the Hegelian Concept in neurological terms? I would propose that both can be equated with the brain's stored memory record of all the views of all the objects that it has seen, from which it has formed a Concept or an Ideal of these objects such that a single view of an object makes it possible for the brain to categorize that object. Indeed, in Plato's system, we can only recognize and categorize objects of which our immortal souls have seen examples constructed by δημιουργος; (see, for example, Plato's *Meno).* In this sense, therefore, the Platonic system acknowledges the importance of a stored record, though without making reference to the brain. The recognition that we can only categorize objects that we have already seen (and therefore have a general representation of) nevertheless constitutes a far-reaching insight and brings Plato's position close to a modem neurobiological one. Neurobiology would have to depart from the Platonic system in saying not only that this general representation is built by the brain but also that there can be no Ideals without the brain.

We know a little, but not much, about the brain's stored visual memory system for objects. We know that it must involve a region of the brain known as the inferior convolution of the temporal lobes, because damage here causes severe problems in object recognition. Although very much in their infancy, recent physiological studies have started to give us some insights into the more detailed physiological mechanisms involved (Logothetis *et al.,* 1995). When a monkey, an animal that is close to man, is exposed to different views of objects that it has never encountered before (objects generated on a television screen), recordings from single cells in its inferior temporal cortex can show how they respond when these same objects are subsequently shown on the screen again. Most cells respond to one view only, and their response declines as the object is rotated in such a way as to present increasingly less-familiar views. A minority of cells respond to only two views, but only a very small proportion, amounting to less than one per cent, respond in a view-invariant manner. Whether they respond to one or more views, the actual size of the stimuli or the precise position in the field of view in which they appear make little difference to the responses of the cells. On the other hand, no cells have ever been found that are responsive to views with which the animal has not been familiarized; hence, exposure to the stimulus is necessary, from which it follows that the cells may be plastic enough to be 'tuned' to one or more views of an object. In summary, many cells, each one responsive to one view only, may be involved during recognition of an object, with the whole group acting as an ensemble. But the presence of that small one per cent of cells that respond in a view-invariant manner suggests also that form constancy may be the function of a specialized group of cells, since one percent represents an enormous number in absolute terms.

When undertaking their work, artists generally are concerned not with philosophical views but rather with achieving desired effects on canvas–by experimenting, by 'sacrificing a thousand apparent truths' and distilling the essence of their visual experience. We are told, for example, that Cézanne's work is 'a painted epistemology' *(Erkenntnis Kritik),* since Cézanne supposedly shared Kant's ideology (Novotny, 1932). But Cézanne, in particular, put paid to all these empty speculations even before they were made when he said that 'les causeries sur l'art sont presque inutiles' (Mack, 1935). I agree with Kahnweiler when he states, 'J'insiste, en passant, sur le fait qu'aucun de ces peintres ... n'avait de culture philosophique, et que les rapprochements possibles–avec Locke et Kant surtout–d 'une telle attitude leur étaient inconnus, *leur classement étant, d'ailleurs, instinctif plus que raisonné.'* (Kahnweiler, 1946, p. 326; emphasis added).[§] The preoccupation of artists has instead been less exalted and more similar to the physiological experiments described earlier: exposing themselves to as many views of their subject as possible and thus obtaining a brain record from which they can distill on canvas the best combination. If, in executing his work, the artist is indifferent to these polar views–Plato on the one hand, and Hegel and Kant on the other–so should the neurobiologist be, if he accepts my equation of the Platonic Ideal and the Hegelian Concept with the brain's stored record of what it has seen. Whether art succeeds in presenting the real truth, the essentials, or whether it is the only means of getting to that truth in the face of constantly changing and ephemeral sense data, the opposing views are at least united in suggesting that there is (Hegel) or that there should be (Plato and Schopenhauer) a strong relationship between painting and the search for essentials. And my equation of both the Hegelian Concept and the Platonic Ideal with the brain's stored record means that the difference between the two, from a neurological point of view, is

---

[§] Kahnweiler: "I insist, in passing, that none of these painters...had a philosophical background, and that the possible connections of such an attitude to Locke and Kant, in particular, were unknown to them, *their classification being, rather, more instinctive than reasoned."* (Editor's translation).

insignificant. There have been artists who have, again without reference to the brain or its stored record, tried deliberately and with much success to contradict the stored memory record of the brain. Many of the works of René Magritte go against everything that the brain has seen, learned, and stored in its memory. There is no Platonic Ideal or Hegelian Concept here because the brain has no representation of such bizarre scenes. It is an act of the imagination that fascinates the brain, which tries to make sense of a scene that goes against all its experience and for which it can find no solution.

IV

To a neurobiologist viewing the art scene without being involved in it, it seems to be Cubism that most explicitly, without acknowledging it or perhaps even being aware of it, set out to answer that deep paradox between reality and appearance alluded to by Plato–although this is my interpretation, not that of Cubists. Cubism, the most radical departure in Western art since Paolo Uccello and Piero della Francesca introduced perspective into painting, 'was a sort of analysis', a static representation of the result of 'moving around an object to seize several successive appearances, which, fused in a single image, reconstitute it in time' (Kahnweiler, 1946). The aims of Cubist painting, which was an attempt 'to discover less unstable elements in the objects to be represented', were well stated by the French critic Jacques Rivière, and they read as if they were an account of the aims of the brain *(ibid.)*. Rivière wrote that, 'The Cubists are destined ... to give back to painting its true aims, which is to reproduce ... objects as they are.' But to achieve this, 'lighting must be eliminated' because 'it is the sign of a particular instant.... If, therefore, the plastic image is to reveal the essence and permanence of things, it must be free of lighting effect.... It can therefore be said that lighting prevents things from *appearing as they are....* Sight is a successive sense; we have to combine many of its perceptions before we can know a single object well. But the painted image is fixed ... ' Perspective must also be eliminated because it 'is as accidental a thing as lighting. It is the sign ... of a particular position in space. It indicates not the situation of objects but the situation of a spectator.... Perspective is also the sign of an instant, of the instant when a certain man is at a certain point' (Rivière, 1912; original emphasis). That statement is one that a modern neurobiologist would applaud, for the brain likewise never sees the objects and surfaces that make up the visual world around us from a single point or in a standard lighting condition. Instead, objects are viewed at different distances, from different angles and in different lighting conditions, yet they maintain their identity.

The solution that Cubism brought to this problem was to try to mimic the functions of the brain, though with far less success. The precursor of Cubist painting is generally agreed to be Picasso's *Les Demoiselles d'Avignon,* a forceful painting about which a great deal has been written, much of it neurologically and visually uninformative. What is especially interesting visually is the ambiguity in the figures, especially the one seated to the bottom right; she could be facing us or facing sideways. This ambiguity was much exploited by both Picasso and the cofounder of Cubism, Georges Braque. The elimination of the point of view became a prominent feature of many of Picasso's portraits, so that the subject could seemingly be facing one direction or another. In later representative paintings such as *The Violin Player,* Picasso introduced so many different points of view that the painting ceased to be recognizable to the human brain, the final result being only recognizable as a violin player through its title. A brain ignorant of that title can hardly construe this as a violin player. The brain regularly views objects and people from different angles and is able to integrate these different views in an orderly way, allowing it to recognize and obtain knowledge about what it is viewing. The attempt by Cubism to mimic what the brain does, to create a perceptual constancy for objects regardless of viewing angle, was, in the neurobiological sense, a failure–a heroic failure perhaps, but a failure nevertheless. My neurobiological interpretation is that it is indeed because of this failure that Cubism changed course and entered its later, synthetic phase; it is certain that Mondrian saw it that way, for he abandoned Cubism and accused it of 'not accept[ing] the logical consequences of its own discoveries [and] developing abstraction towards its ultimate goal, the expression of pure reality' (Mondrian, 1986, pp. 338-41). In the synthetic phase, Kasimir Malevich tells us, 'objective nature is merely *the starting point– the motivation–for the creation of new forms,* so that the objects themselves can scarcely, if at all, be recognized in the pictures' (Malevich, 1959, p. 102; original emphasis). But the new forms that Synthetic Cubism created were ultimately derived from the forms in nature that the artist was exposed to, and perhaps the best proof of this is found in the objective titles given to the paintings. It is difficult for the brain of a spectator to decipher what many of the creations of Synthetic Cubism represent. It was probably also difficult for Picasso himself, which is presumably one reason why he used objective and recognizable titles to describe his paintings. Nilsen Lauvrik, who was hostile to Cubism, described *Woman with a Mustard Pot* as 'one of the most engaging puzzles of a very puzzling art. This is sharply emphasized by the delight and pride of every spectator who is successful in solving the puzzle by finding in these enigmatic charts some sort of a tangible, pictorial justification of the title appended thereto.... The discovery of the 'mustard pot' would scarcely have been possible without the happy cooperation of the title with the spectator's previous knowledge of the actual appearance of a mustard pot' (Laurvik, 1913).

V

From the neurobiological point of view, representational art was a good deal more successful in meeting the brain's incessant demands for constancy. Here I will consider neurologically the work of two different artists, Vermeer and Michelangelo, both of whom–unknowingly and in different ways–satisfied this demand far better than the product of the heroic but neurobiologically flawed experiments of the Cubists.

A great deal has been written about Vermeer, 'un artiste à jamais inconnu', as Proust astutely called him (Proust, 1952, p. 128). His technical brilliance, his use of perspective and rich chromatism are all common knowledge. But in viewing a painting such as *Man and Woman at the Virginal* (displayed at Buckingham Palace), it is not these features that attract and move the ordinary viewer. Paul Claudel, among others, has commented on the banality of Vermeer's subjects: an interior, a maid pouring milk, a girl weighing gold, another reading a letter, a music lesson–all daily events seemingly without special significance (Claudel, 1946, p. 240). But there is, in Claudel's words, something 'eerie, uncanny' about them.[4] In a good many of his paintings, the viewer is invited to look inside, as if through a keyhole, but not to enter.[5] He is a voyeur, peering into the private moments of private, unknown, individuals; what they are doing, or saying, or thinking is a mystery. It is this aspect of Vermeer, I believe, that has the immediate power to attract and provoke, and his technical virtuosity is used in the service of that psychological power, not as an end in itself, unsurpassed though it may be.

Where does this psychological power come from and what, in any case, do we mean by psychological power? A painting like *Man and Woman at the Virginal* derives its grandeur, I believe, from the way in which its technical virtuosity is used to generate ambiguity. I use the term ambiguity here to mean its ability to represent simultaneously, on the same canvas, not one but several truths, each as valid as the others. These several truths revolve around the relationship between the man and the woman. There is no denying that there is some relationship between them. But is he her husband, her lover, a suitor, or a friend? Did he actually enjoy the playing or does he think that she can do better? Is the harpsichord really being used or is she merely playing a few notes while concentrating on something else, perhaps something he told her, announcing a separation or a reconciliation, or maybe something a good deal more banal? All these scenarios have equal validity in the painting, which can thus satisfy several 'ideals' simultaneously. Through its stored memory of similar past events, the brain can recognize in this work the ideal representation of many situations and can categorize the scene represented as happy or sad. This gives ambiguity, a characteristic of all great art, a different, and neurological, definition: not the vagueness or uncertainty found in dictionaries, but, on the contrary, certainty— the certainty of many different and essential conditions, each equal to the others, all expressed in a single painting, profound in its faithful representation of so much.

---

[4] Claudel used the English terms since there is no good French equivalent.
[5] Here I disagree with Claudel, who says that the spectator is immediately invited in. This is true of some but not most of Vermeer's work; a notable exception is *Girl with a Pearl Earring* (Marithuis, The Hague).

The Vermeer painting satisfies Schopenhauer's wish that a painting should 'obtain knowledge of an object, not as particular thing but as Platonic Ideal, that is to say, the enduring form of this whole species of thing' (Schopenhauer, 1964). In any of a number of situations, the scene depicted is what one might actually expect. There is a constancy about it, which makes it independent of the precise situation and applicable to many. The painting is indeed 'a vision of two distant people 'alone together' in a space moved by forces beyond the ken of either' (Snow, 1979, p. 214), a scenario effectively exploited by Michelangelo Antonioni in some of his films, and most notably in *L'Avventura* and *l'Eclisse,* where once again the viewer becomes imaginatively involved in trying to guess the thoughts of the protagonists. Though it may come as a surprise, there is in this respect and in terms of the brain a certain neurobiological similarity between the paintings of Vermeer and those of the Cubists, especially the later variety that cultivated an ambiguity, in the sense that I have used the term. Writing of Cubism, Gleizes and Metzinger tell us that 'certain forms should remain implicit, so that the mind of the spectator is the chosen place of their concrete birth' (Gleizes and Metzinger, 1913). There could be no more admirable description of the work of Vermeer, where very nearly all is implicit. As with forms and objects in Cubist art, the brain of the spectator is the chosen birthplace of many situations in Vermeer's paintings, each one of equal validity as the others. The true solution remains 'à jamais inconnu', because there is no true solution, there is no correct answer. It is therefore a painting for many conditions.

Situational constancy is a subject that neurology has not yet studied; indeed, the problem itself has not been addressed. We have hardly begun to understand the simpler kinds of constancy, such as form or color, and it is not surprising that neurologists should not have even thought of studying so complex a subject. I would guess from the kind of physiological experiment described above that, in broad outline, exposure of an individual to a few situations would be sufficient to extract the elements that would be common to all similar occasions. But what brain mechanisms are involved remains a mystery today.

It was perhaps the masters of Cycladic art in the sixth century BC who understood earlier than most that the brain must be the place of birth of implicit forms. They created works that emphasized a few organs - the lips or the nose, for example–and left it to the imagination of the beholder to complete the form. Michelangelo achieved much the same effect by leaving many of his sculptures unfinished. Why he did so remains a question of debate; my interpretation is that this was one solution to the problem of representing the many facets of spiritual beauty and divine love–it was too great a task even for the mighty Michelangelo. We know that he usually refused to execute portraits, believing that he could not represent all the beauty that his brain had formed a Concept of. Two exceptions are his portraits of Andrea Quaratesi and of Tommaso de' Cavalieri, the young nobleman who had overwhelmed him with his beauty and had come to dominate his emotional life in his later years, unleashing a furious creative energy of great brilliance. But the difficulty of portraying physical beauty was nothing compared to that of depicting spiritual beauty and divine love. As a devout Catholic, Michelangelo found that love in the life of Jesus, and particularly in the last moments on the Cross and after the Descent from it, the subject of several of his sculptures. By leaving many of his sculptures unfinished– for example, the *Rondanini Pietá* and the *San Matteo*–Michelangelo invites the spectator to be imaginatively involved, and the spectator's view will fit many of the Concepts, the stored representations, in his brain. The forms that the unfinished work merely suggests become concretely realized only in the spectator's brain. There is an ambiguity here too, and therefore a constancy about these unfinished works, but the ambiguity is reached by a different route. Perhaps the most definitive hint at what Michelangelo intended is found in his *Rime* or *Sonnets,* where, next to his works, he best expounds his views on art and beauty. In one, dedicated to Vittoria Colonna, Marchesa di Pescara, he wrote:

> The greatest artists have no thought to show that
> Which the marble in its superfluous shell does not contain
> To break the marble spell is all that the hand
> That serves the brain can do.[6]

---

[6] I have used the translation by Symonds; other translations do not use the word brain. The actual word used for brain in the original is *intelleto*. In Latin, *intellectus* means perception or 'a perceiving'–see Clements (1961), p. 15–and Symonds has astutely, in my view, rendered it into 'brain'.

VI

The Alexandrian Neo-Platonist Plotinus, with whose writings Michelangelo was surely acquainted, remarked, 'The form is in the sculptor long before it ever enters the stone' (Plotinus, 1964), a biological truth that enables the sculptor to fashion his work and the spectator to appreciate it. But if the form is in the artist (and the spectator), maybe neither need the forms in the outside world at all. That was the real starting point for the work of the Russian Suprematist Kasimir Malevich, a neurobiologically interesting artist, who wrote that 'art wants nothing further to do with the objective world as such.' The use of the word 'further' here gives biological credibility to Malevich's doctrine because, as discussed above, the brain needs to be visually nourished at critical periods after birth so as not to remain almost indefinitely blind. So the nonobjective sensation and art of which Malevich speaks is really the introspective art of a brain that is well acquainted with the objective world; it has already selected all the information necessary to be able to identify and categorize objects. And true to its aims of being a search for essentials and constants, we find that, as art developed more and more in the modern era, much of it became better and better tailored to the physiology of the parallel processing-perceptual systems and the visual areas that we have only recently discovered, and specifically to the physiology of single cells in them. The physiology of these areas is itself tailored to extract the essential information in the visual environment—there exists an *Einfühlung,* that untranslatable term signifying a link between the 'preexistent' forms within the individual and the forms in the outside world that are reflected back, the 'art de peindre des ensembles nouveaux empruntés non à la réalité visuelle, mais à celle que suggèrent à l'artiste l' instinct et l'intuition', as Guillaume Apollinaire said of Cubism (Apollinaire, 1986).[★7]

★ Apollinaire: "[the] art of painting new combinations, borrowed not from visual reality but from that suggested to the artist by instinct and intuition." (Editor's translation).

7 Apollinaire does not use the term *Einfühlung.* The notion of *Einfühlung* in art was first elaborated by the German philosopher Robert Vischer in a work entitled *Über das optische Formgefühl.* Wilhelm Worringer developed the notion further and applied it to abstract art in his doctoral thesis at Berne University, published in 1908, entitled *Abstraktion und Einfühlung,* but Worringer sought other, non-neurobiological, explanations for the then developing abstract art. See Vallier (1980).

Physiologically, the *Einfühlung* is expressed in what I have called the art of the receptive field and I shall give but two brief examples of it here.[8] The receptive field is one of the most important concepts to emerge from sensory physiology in the past fifty years. It refers to the part of the body (in the case of the visual system, the part of the retina or its projection into the visual field) that, when stimulated, results in a reaction from the cell, specifically, an increase or decrease in its resting electrical discharge rate. To be able to activate a cell in the visual brain, one must not only stimulate in the correct place (i.e., stimulate the receptive field) but also stimulate the receptive field with the correct visual stimulus, because cells in the visual brain are remarkably fussy about the kind of visual stimulus to which they will respond. The art of the receptive field may thus be defined as that art whose characteristic components resemble the characteristics of the receptive fields of cells in the visual brain and which can therefore be used to activate such cells.

One group of cells, discovered by David Hubel and Torsten Wiesel in 1959, will only respond to lines of particular orientation, since the orientational preferences of different cells are different and each responds increasingly more grudgingly as one departs from the preferred orientation until the response disappears at the orthogonal orientation. Such cells are a prominent feature of area V1 and some other areas surrounding it, notably V3, but they are also found in other areas. They are usually considered to be the physiological 'building blocks' of form perception, though how one moves from such cells to the creation of forms remains unknown. It is interesting that the line is among the most prominent features of the 'nonobjective' art of Malevich and his successors. Lines are the predominant and sometimes only feature in the paintings of artists as diverse as Olga Rozanova, Barnett Newman, Robert Motherwell, Ellsworth Kelly, Gene Davis, Robert Mangold and Ad Reinhardt, to mention but a few. Together with the rectangle and the circle, they were considered by Malevich to be the most elemental aspect of the nonobjective world. Mondrian, too, came to emphasize lines but reached

---

[8] See also Zeki (1997). A more detailed account is given in my forthcoming book, *Inner Vision*.

that conclusion from an intellectually (though perhaps not physiologically) different route. Art, he believed, 'shows us that *there are also constant truths* concerning forms,' and it was the aim of objective art, as he saw it, to reduce all complex forms to one or a few universal forms, the constant elements that would be the constituent of all forms. Thus, as he said, to 'discover consciously or unconsciously the fundamental laws hidden in reality' and 'to create pure reality plastically it is necessary to reduce natural forms to the *constant elements*' (Mondrian, 1986, pp. 338-41; original emphasis). He sought, in other words, the Platonic Ideal for form (though he did not describe it in these terms). This search led to the vertical and horizontal lines, or so he believed. These 'exist everywhere and dominate everything.' Moreover, the straight line 'is a stronger and more profound expression than the curve' because 'all curvature resolves into the straight, no place remains for the curved' (Mondrian, 1986, pp. 75-81). He wrote, 'Among the different forms, we may consider those as being neutral which have neither the complexity nor the particularities possessed by natural forms or abstract forms in general' *(ibid.).*

This emphasis on line in many of the more modern and abstract works of art, in all probability, is derived not from a profound knowledge of geometry but simply from the experimentation of artists to reduce the complexity of forms into their essentials or, to put it in neurological terms, to try and find out what the essence of form as represented in the brain may be. This is my interpretation, not that of artists, but I cannot see that it is any less valid than other interpretations. Kahnweiler, the art dealer, tells us, 'C'est uniquement l'apparition, chez les Cubistes, de lignes droites ... qui a fait croire à une geometrie dont il n'y a, en réalité, nulle trace. Ces droites ... reflets de la base même, de l'a priori, de toute perception visuelle humaine, se retrouvent, en fait, dans toute oeuvre d'art plastique des que le souci d'imitation a disparu' (Kahnweiler, 1946).* This is as explicit a statement as any - coming from

---

* Kahnweiler: "It is only the appearance, with the Cubists, of straight lines...that made one believe in a geometry of which there is no trace in reality. These straight...reflections of the very base, of the *a priori* of human visual perception are, in fact, found in all works of plastic art from which the concern for imitation has disappeared." (Editor's translation).

one who, if not an artist himself, was at least well acquainted with artists and their work–that the artist is trying to represent the essentials of form as constituted in his visual perception, which I take to mean the brain. Gleizes and Metzinger, both artists, emphasized the straight lines and the relationship that they have to each other, as did Mondrian. They wrote, 'The diversity of the relations of line to line must be indefinite; on this condition it incorporates quality, the incommensurable sum of the affinities perceived between that which we discern and that which pre-exists within us' (Gleizes and Metzinger, 1913). Once again, I interpret 'that which pre-exists within us' to mean that which is in our brains. Although Gleizes and Metzinger are discussing here the relations between lines, it is nevertheless lines that they have chosen to emphasize. Equally interesting are the speculations of Mécislas Golberg, a man said to have had a powerful influence on Matisse. In his book *La Morale des lignes* he emphasized lines, especially the vertical and the horizontal, and dreamed of a return to geometry, 'mais une géométrie mitigée, soumise elle-même à des lois de simplification et d 'unification,' which he thought was important for 'le dépouillement de la réalité dans sa forme la plus abstraite', which in turn was essential for 'la simplification et la modernisation du dessin' (Golberg, 1976, p. 413).[†] And although he attached subjective sentiments to the vertical and the horizontal, it is nevertheless these that he thought of as important in modernizing art. 'And is this not already a very appreciable contribution to artistic evolution and, above all, to the intelligence of contemporary art where the line, presented sometimes without the support of a traditional 'subject', has to be interpreted and understood by itself and for itself?' (Aubery, 1965).

I do not mean to imply that it is uniquely the stimulation of the orientation–selective cells in the brain that results in the aesthetic experience produced by a Malevich or a Barnett Newman, but only that the constituent elements of

---

† Golberg: "... but a qualified geometry, subordinated to the laws of simplification and unification" (which he thought was important for) "the analysis of Reality into its most abstract form" (which in turn was essential for) "the simplification and modernization of Art."(Editor's translation).

these works are a powerful stimulus for these cells and, moreover, that a brain deprived of such cells–either because of blindness during the critical period after birth or through pathological reasons–will not be able to appreciate these paintings at all. Given the importance that lines have assumed in much of modern and abstract painting, and given that lines constitute probably the most basic visual stimulus with which to excite a very important category of cell in the cortex, it is interesting to ask whether the relationship between the two is entirely fortuitous.

It is in kinetic art that we find one of the best examples of the art of the receptive field, and its evolution powerfully shows how an art form became better tailored to the physiology of a specific visual area in the brain–area V5, in which visual motion is emphasized.[9] Kinetic art was born out of a dissatisfaction, ostensibly due to social and political reasons, with an art form that seemed to exclude movement or the fourth dimension, as Naum Gabo called it. The demand for its inclusion was strongly featured in the *Futurist Manifesto* of Naum Gabo and Antoine Pevsner and in Marinetti's *Manifesto of Futurism*. For all the shrill demands, especially from the Italian artists, movement was usually represented statically, as in Giacomo Balla's paintings or those of Umberto Buccioni. There are a few early exceptions, such as Gabo's *Kinetic Sculpture,* but they are rare. Marcel Duchamp, influenced by the chronophotography of Jules Etienne Marais in France, began to produce paintings that suggested movement statically; of these the most famous is perhaps *Nude Descending the Staircase II.* From about 1910 onwards, motion was very much on Duchamp's mind although he did not exploit it explicitly, perhaps because he did not know how to do so or had not yet settled on the best way of doing so. Perhaps Rickey is right in asserting that 'Duchamp showed, by deferring his work with movement for years and confining it to optical phenomena, that his concern therein was dadaist and superficial' (Rickey, 1963). At any rate, by 1913 he had produced his famous *Bicycle Wheel,* the 'Ready-Made,' which he called a *Mobile.* Although usually immobile when exhibited in an art gallery, it is commonly thought of

[9] For a more detailed treatment of this subject, see Zeki and Lamb (1994).

as a precursor to kinetic art, even though Duchamp himself did not consider this or machines in general to be artistic objects, referring to them as 'non-art' (Lebovici, 1991). Indeed, the *Bicycle Wheel* was to him only one ready-made among many, which included such interesting objects as urinals—'art without an artist', he called it, a concept that later was to be exploited so well commercially by Andy Warhol, who, it is said, showed the world that anything could be made famous for fifteen minutes. The real incorporation of motion in Duchamp's hands came much later, when he produced his *Rotoreliefs* in the 1920s.

Duchamp was not alone in trying to emphasize motion, but the gulf between the idea and its implementation in works of art was not much easier for other artists; it required some degree of technical mastery, of getting at least parts of the work of art into motion, which is perhaps one reason why its actual incorporation into works of art was to take a relatively long time. The surrealists, too, who desired a retreat from all that was rational and predictable, found in motion the unpredictability for which they had yearned. Picabia designed imaginary machines, such as his *Machine tournez vite* and his *Parade amoureuse*, the latter somewhat reminiscent of Duchamp's *La mariée* and, like it, lacking the real motion that it exalted. Until Calder invented his mobiles, the generation of motion depended upon machines, and machines did not seem beautiful or desirable works of art to everyone, not even to the cynical Duchamp.

It was in fact Alexander Calder who best developed the art of the mobile, popularized it, and planted it in the popular mind. In many ways, the mobile was an ingenious invention. It was not dependent upon any profound knowledge of motors and engineering, although Calder's first mobiles were power driven. Mobiles, in other words, were relatively easy to execute. Motion was the dominant element, and to aid the dominance Calder decided to limit himself largely to the use of black and white, the two most contrasting colors, as he called them. Red was to him the color best opposed to these two, but all the secondary colors 'confused' the clarity of the mobiles (Calder, 1952).

One of the specializations in the human visual brain is that for visual motion. This specialization is centered on area V5, where all cells are selectively responsive to motion and the great majority are also selective for the direction of motion, responding vigorously when the stimulus moves in one direction but remaining silent or even being inhibited when it moves in the opposite or 'null' direction. These cells are indifferent to the color of the stimulus and usually indifferent to the form as well; indeed, most of them respond best when the stimulus is a spot that is a fraction of the receptive field size. It is interesting to consider here how the mobiles of Calder stimulate the cells of area V5. Viewed from a distance, each element of the mobile is a sort of spot, small or large, depending upon its size. Once it moves in the appropriate direction within the receptive field of a cell in V5, it will lead to a vigorous response from it. In a mobile, of course, the different elements will move in different directions, and each element will stimulate not one but many cells, each cell (or group of cells) being specifically tuned to respond to motion in the respective direction in which the element of the mobile is moving. There are many other interesting features about our perception of mobiles that I have discussed elsewhere (Zeki & Lamb, 1994), but the important point to emphasize here is that in its development, kinetic art, especially in the hands of Calder, resulted in works that act as perfect stimuli for the cells of V5. Another important feature that perhaps reinforces the view that I present here–that artists try to learn something about the organization of the visual brain, though with techniques unique to them–is found in the general emphasis on movement and in a lack of emphasis on color and form, mirroring so well the physiology of V5.

In giving the above two examples, it is worth emphasizing that there is much about the perception of lines and of motion that we still do not understand physiologically, and it is therefore impossible to relate directly the experience of even one line to what really happens in the brain. If viewed at a sufficiently close distance, even a single vertical line, for example, may fall on the receptive fields of many cells that are specific for the vertical orientation; how the brain combines the responses of these cells to indicate a continuous vertical line is a mystery that neurology has not yet solved, nor has it solved the question of how it may differentiate one vertical line from other vertical lines that are distinct from it and indeed differentiate the entire tableau from what surrounds it. No less puzzling is the coherence in a work of kinetic art, where the brain can interpret different elements that fall on different receptive fields as forming part of the same work. However, these unsolved neurological problems should not inhibit us from noting that what the physiologists call the building blocks of form–the oriented lines–are the same ones that artists, keen on representing the constant elements of form, have used and that what physiologists consider to be the building blocks in the perception of motion–the cells that respond to motion in a given direction–are the very ones used by an artist such as Calder in his mobiles.

VII

Jean-Paul Sartre was quite ecstatic about the work of Calder. He wrote, 'La sculpture suggère le mouvement, la peinture suggère la profondeur ou la lumière. Calder ne suggère rien: il attrape de vrais mouvements vivants et les façonne. Ses mobiles ne signifient rien, ne renvoient à rien qu'à eux mêmes: ils sont, voilà tout; ce sont des absolus' (Sartre, 1964).[‡] This is not an uninteresting observation, and one can draw at least a superficial parallel between his absolutes and the absolutes of form that were such an obsession of Mondrian and others. The search for these absolutes leads to abstraction. Abstraction has been used to describe many different schools and movements; I use it here in its broadest sense, to signify works in which neither the work itself nor its constituent parts represent any recognizable objects in the visual world (non-iconic abstraction). It is obvious that in this context, abstract art differs radically from representational art. The question is whether there is a significant difference in the pattern of brain activity when subjects look at abstract as opposed to representational art?

A hint that there may be substantial differences can be found in recent imaging experiments from our laboratory, which have been inspired in part by the fauvist dream of liberating colors to give them more expressive power. But from what can color be 'liberated'? It is not easy to liberate it from form for good physiological reasons. The fauvists therefore settled on a different solution, which

---

‡ Sartre: "Sculpture suggests movement, painting suggests depth or light. Calder does not suggest anything: he captures real live movements and shapes them. His mobiles do not signify anything, nor do they refer to anything but themselves: they are, therefore, everything; these are absolutes." (Editor's translation)

was to invest objects with colors that are not usually associated with them, as André Derain's *View of Charing Cross Bridge* and other fauvist paintings testify. Unknown to them, and only uncovered in our imaging experiments, they were exploiting different neurological pathways in the visual brain than the ones used in representational art in which objects are vested in the 'correct' colors.

Color is a biological signalling mechanism that exemplifies very well the brain's quest for knowledge under continually changing conditions. It is common knowledge that the basis of color vision is found in light–which itself has no color, being electromagnetic radiation–having many different wavelengths, stretching from red (long wave) at one end to blue (short wave) at the other, and the fact that different surfaces have different efficiencies for reflecting light of different wavelengths. What the brain seemingly does is to compare the efficiency of different surfaces for reflecting light of the same wavebands and thus make itself independent of the actual amount of light of any given waveband reflected from a single surface, since the latter changes continually depending upon the illuminant in which the surface is viewed. If the brain assigned a color to a surface as a function of the wavelength composition of the light reflected from it–characterizing it as green when it reflects more green (middle-wave) light and blue when it reflects more blue (shortwave) light, with the dominant wavelength constituting a sort of code that the brain has to decipher–then the brain would be at the mercy of any and every change in wavelength composition reflected from the surface. Instead the brain has evolved an ingenious mechanism, whose neural implementation remains obscure, to take the ratio of light of a given wavelength reflected from a surface and its surrounds. While the precise amount of light of a given wavelength reflected from a surface changes, the ratio of light of that same waveband reflected from the surface and from surrounding surfaces always remains the same. Color is therefore a construction of the brain, an interpretation that it gives to the reflective efficiency of different surfaces for the different wavelengths of light, which is why James Clerk Maxwell referred to color as 'a mental science.' But to be able to take ratios, there must be a boundary between one surface and the surrounding surface, and that boundary has a shape–hence the impossibility (except in very rare pathological conditions) of divorcing color, and thus liberating it, from shape. Color therefore follows the logic of the brain's operations. André Malraux was right when he drew attention in *Les Voix du silence* to Cézanne's remark that 'Il y a une logique colorée; le peintre ne doit obéissance qu'à elle, jamais à la logique du cerveau', describing it as 'cette phrase maladroite [qui] nous révèle pourquoi, sur l'essentiel de son art, tout peintre de génie est un muet' (Malraux, 1951, p. 344), although I would have preferred it if Malraux had said 'devrait être muet' instead.◊

It is obvious that at the ratio-taking, computational stage there are no 'wrong' colors. Making a square red is as good as making it blue. Edwin Land's paradigm in studying color vision consisted of an abstract multicolored scene with no recognizable objects, rather like the paintings of Mondrian. When humans view such a scene the increase in regional activity in their brain occurs in area V4, the color centre. But colors are not normally viewed in this way; they are instead properties of surfaces and objects. What happens in the brain when humans view colored objects and scenes depends upon whether the objects are dressed in the right or the wrong colors, but in either case it is different from the activity produced by colors in the abstract, as in a Mondrian. If the objects are dressed in normal colors a more extensive part of the brain, including the frontal lobes, becomes active in addition to V4. But if they are dressed in abnormal colors, as in fauvist paintings, a different set of areas (in addition to V4) becomes active (Zeki and Marini, 1998).

These results are replete with neurological interest, but in the present context they allow us to draw two interesting conclusions. The first is that abstract paintings in color do not need to recruit those additional brain areas that are mobilized when we view representational art in color. The second is that the fauvists had unwittingly uncovered certain truths about the organization of the visual brain about which they were and remain ignorant—namely, that their art used pathways that are quite distinct from the ones used by representational art that portrays objects in normal colors.

◊ Cézanne: "There is a logic of color; a painter owes his obedience to it alone, never to the logic of the brain." Malreaux: "that awkward phrase [that] reveals to us why, on the essence of his art, every painter of genius is a mute." The author here corrects to "should be mute". (Editor's translation).

VIII

I have tried, using only a few examples, to explain that we have learned enough about the visual brain in the past quarter of a century to begin to study the biological foundations of aesthetics. Aesthetics, like all other human activities, must obey the rules of the brain of whose activity it is a product, and it is my conviction that no theory of aesthetics is likely to be complete, let alone profound, unless it is based on an understanding of the workings of the brain. There is, of course, much that has been left unsaid in this brief essay–about topics such as portrait painting, impressionist art, or op art–but these different tendencies can also be discussed within the overall context of a search for knowledge. There are other questions that are difficult to write about at present: why some artists are drawn to paint in a particular genre, why some of us prefer certain schools to others, the role of the imagination in producing works of art, the relationship between artistic creativity and sexual impulses (since they are both reproductive processes), the emotive power of works of art, the role of culture and historical knowledge in appreciating and interpreting works of art. But I have been exploring a topic here that is new and have concerned myself exclusively with the perceptive aspects. There is much that has yet to be discovered and described.

The approach that I have adopted may seem distasteful to some. Art, they might say, is an aesthetic experience whose basis is opaque and indeed should remain so. It has derived much of its value from the different way in which it arouses, satisfies, and disturbs different individuals, and to profane physiologically the secrets of fantasy in this way implies that what happens in one brain is very similar to what happens in other brains when we view works of art. There is substance to that argument. But we should consider that what happens in different brains when we view works of art *is* very similar, at least at an elementary level, which is one reason why we can communicate about art and through art without the need for the written or spoken word. And no profound understanding of the workings of the brain is likely to compromise our appreciation of art any more than our understanding of how the visual brain functions is likely to compromise the sense of vision. On the contrary, an approach to the biological foundations of aesthetics is likely to enhance the sense of beauty–the biological beauty of the brain.

Acknowledgments

I gratefully acknowledge the help I received from the staff of the J. Paul Getty Museum in California while I was a visiting museum scholar there at the kind invitation of Mr. John Walsh, Director of the Museum. I am also much indebted to Professor K. Bartels and to Andreas Bartels for their insightful comments, especially concerning the Platonic doctrines. 'Art and the Brain' is reprinted by permission of *Daedalus,* Journal of the American Academy of Arts and Sciences, from the issue entitled, 'The Brain', Spring 1998, **127** (2), pp. 71-103.

References

Apollinnaire, Guillaume (1986), *Les Peintres cubistes: Méditations esthétiques* (Paris: Berg International).

Aubery, Pierre (1965), 'Mécislas Golberg et l'art moderne', *Gazette des Beaux Arts,* **66,** pp. 339-44.

Calder, Alexander (1952), Extract from *Témoignages pour l'art abstrait,* ed. Julien Alvard and Roger van Gindertael (Paris: Editions Art d'aujourd'hui).

Claudel, Paul (1946), *L'oeil écoute* (Paris: Gallimard).

Clements, *R.I.* (1961), *Michelangelo's Theory of Art* (New York: New York University Press, 1961).

Constable, John (1836), *Syllabus of a Course of Lectures on the History of Landscape Painting* (London: Royal Institution of Great Britain).

Flechsig, Paul (1901), 'Gehirnphysiologie und Willenstheorien', Fifth International Psychology Congress, pp. 73-89; trans. Gerhardt von Bonin in *Some Papers on the Cerebral Cortex* (Springfield, IL: Thomas, 1960).

Gabo, Naum (1962), *Of Divers Arts* (New York: Pantheon Books).

Gleizes, Albert and Metzinger, Jean (1913), *Cubism* (London: Fisher Unwin).

Golberg, Mécislas (1976), *La Morale des lignes,* quoted in Ellen C. Oppler, *Fauvism Reexamined* (New York: Garland Publishing).

Gray, Christopher (1953), *Cubist Aesthetic Theories* (Baltimore, MD: The Johns Hopkins Press).

Harlow, H. (1972), 'Love created - love destroyed - love regained', in *Modèles animaux du comportement humain,* no. 198 (Paris: Editions du Centre National de la Recherche Scientifique).

Hegel, G.W.F. (1975), *Aesthetics,* vol. I, trans. T.M. Knox (Oxford: Clarendon Press).

Hofstader, Albert and Kuhns, Richard (ed. 1964), *Philosophies of Art and Beauty* (Chicago, IL: University of Chicago Press).

Hubel, David H. and Wiesel, Torsten N. (1977), 'The Ferrier Lecture - Functional architecture of macaque monkey visual cortex', *Proceedings of the Royal Society of London,* Series B, **198**, pp. 1-59.

Kahnweiler, Daniel Henry (1946), *Juan Gris: Sa vie, son oeuvre, ses écrits* (Paris: Gallimard).

Laurvik, Nilsen (1913), *Is It Art? Post-Impressionism, Futurism, Cubism* (New York: The International Press).

Lebovici, E. (1991), 'Bouge, moeurs et réssuscite', *Art studio,* **22**, pp. 6-21.

Livingstone, Margaret S. and Hubel, David H. (1984), 'Anatomy and physiology of a color system in the primate visual cortex.' *Journal of Neuroscience.* **4**. DD. 309-56.

Livingstone, Margaret S. and Hubel, David H. (1987), 'Connections between layer 4B of Area 17 and the thick cytochrome oxidase stripes of Area 18 in the squirrel monkey', *Journal of Neuroscience,* **7**, pp. 3371-7.

Logothetis, N.K. *et al.* (1995), 'Shape representation in the inferior temporal cortex of monkeys', *Current Biology,* **5**, pp. 552-63.

Mack (1935), *La Vie de Paul Cézanne,* quoted in Gray, *Cubist Aesthetic Theories.*

Malevich, Kasimir (1959), *The Non-Objective World,* trans. Howard Dearstyne (Chicago, IL: P. Theobald).

Malraux, André (1951), *Les Voix du silence* (Paris: La Pléiade).

Matisse, Henri (1972), *Ecrits et propos sur l 'art* (Paris: Hermann).

Matisse, Henri (1978), 'Notes d'un peintre', in *Matisse on Art,* ed. Jack D. Flam (Oxford: Phaidon). Originally published in *La Grande Revue,* LII (24), pp. 731-45.

Monbrun, A. (1939), 'Les Affections des voies optiques rétrochiasmatiques et de l'écorce visuelle', in *Traité d'Ophtalmologie,* vol. 6, ed. Baillart *et al.* (Paris: Masson).

Mondrian, Piet (1986), *The New Art - The New Life: The Collected Writings of Piet Mondrian* (Boston, MA: G.K. Hall).

Moutoussis, Konstantinos and Zeki, Semir (1997), 'A direct demonstration of perceptual asynchrony in vision', *Proceedings of the Royal Society of London,* Series B, **264**, pp. 393-9.

Novotny, Fritz (1932), 'Das Problem des Menschen Cézannes im Verhaeltnis zu Seiner Kunst,' *Zeitschrift für Aesthetik und Allegemeine Kunstwissenschaft,* **26**, p. 278.

Perry, L. C. (1927), 'Reminiscences of Claude Monet from 1889-1909,' *American Magazine of Art,* **XVIIII,** quoted by John Gage, *Colour and Culture* (London: Thames and Hudson, 1993).

Plotinus (1964), *Ennead V, Eighth Tractate: On the Intellectual Beauty,* republished in Hofstadter and Kuhns (1964).

Proust, Marcel (1952), *Vermeer de Delft* (Paris: La Pléiade).

Read, Herbert (1964), *The Philosophy of Art* (London: Faber and Faber).

Rickey, George W. Rickey (1963), 'The morphology of movement: A study of kinetic art', *Art Journal,* **22,** pp. 220-31.

Rivière, Jacques (1912), 'Present tendencies in painting', *Revue d 'Europe et d 'Amérique,* **March,** pp. 384-406. Reprinted in *Art in Theory,* ed. Charles Harrison and Paul Wood (Oxford: Blackwell, 1992).

Russell, B. (1946), *History of Western Philosophy* (London: Allen and Unwin).

Sartre, Jean-Paul (1964), 'Situations III', trans. Wade Baskin, in *Essays in Aesthetics* (London: Peter Owen Ltd.).

Schopenhauer, Arthur (1964), *The World as Will and Idea,* 3rd book, from Hofstader and Kuhns (1964).

Shipp, S. and Zeki, S. (1985), 'Segregation of pathways leading from Area V2 to Areas V4 and V5 of macaque monkey visual cortex', *Nature,* **315,** pp. 320-325.

Snow, Edward (1979), *A Study of Vermeer* (Berkeley, CA: University of California Press).

Vallier, D. (1980), *l'Art Abstrait* (Paris: Librarie Générale Française).

Vialet, M. (1894), 'Considerations sur le centre visuel cortical à propos de deux nouveaux cas d'hémianopsie suivis d'autopsie', *Archives d'Ophtalmologie,* **14,** pp. 422-6.

von Senden, Marius (1932), *Space and Sight* (London: Methuen and Co.).

Zeki, S.M. (1978), 'Functional specialization in the visual cortex of the rhesus monkey', *Nature,* **274,** pp. 423-8.

Zeki, S. (1990), 'A century of cerebral achromatopsia', *Brain,* **113**, pp. 1721-77.

Zeki, S. (1993), *A Vision of the Brain* (Oxford: Blackwell).

Zeki, S. (1997), 'The Woodhull Lecture: Visual art and the visual brain', *Proceedings of the Royal Institute of Great Britain,* **68,** pp. 2-63.

Zeki, S. (1998), 'Parallel processing, asynchronous perception and a distributed system of consciousness in vision', *The Neuroscientist,* **4**, pp. 365-72.

Zeki, S. and Lamb, M. (1994), 'The neurology of kinetic art', *Brain,* **117**, pp. 607-36.

Zeki, S. and Balthus (1995), *La Quête de l 'essentiel* (Paris: Les Belles Lettres).

Zeki & Balthus (1993), 'Semir Zeki, in conversation with Balthus', *Connaisance des Arts.*

Zeki, S. and Marini, M. (1998), 'Three cortical stages of colour processing in the human brain', *Brain,* **121,** pp. 1669-85.

Erich Harth

Introduction

Knowledge, as we have seen, begets knowledge. As an ongoing process, it advances by sensitizing us to problems we have either overlooked or were unable to tackle at an earlier time. The acquisition of knowledge–like all grand enterprises–produced a "division of labor," a division that underwent considerable fluctuations in the course of history. "What belongs where" and "what relates to what" was steadily impacted by discoveries obtained in diverse fields of investigation that evoked new queries or suggested unforeseen relationships, and, occasionally, the interdependence between them.

This by no means implies that the fundamental division of Knowledge or some sub-divisions thereof were necessarily annulled thereby. It highlighted, instead, the nature of the process–the routes and means that mankind developed in order to comprehend the universe he is part of and the place he occupies in the world he inhabits. Since we, as humans, create that which guides our understanding (including that of Nature), cross relationships and contingencies of sorts are, in effect, to be expected, even if their exact indicators and conditions cannot be predicted. The process also reveals that seeming independent areas of investigation may be subsumed at times by others, while sections of established fields of endeavor may occasionally carve zones of their own. Nonetheless, the enormity of the enterprise requires at all times some kind of division of labor. Established disciplines, though impacted by the developments that are taking place elsewhere, also have "histories" of their own, i.e. sequences of "trails and error" that characterize their developments. Even in the case of a widely shared problem, these histories influence the way in which a problem may be conceptualized and operationalized.

The study of the brain clearly involves many disciplines, and the mind/brain conundrum has given rise to many interdisciplinary studies. Brain research, as we have seen, underwent a fundamental transformation due to the advance in imaging technology that made it possible not only to *see* the brain for the first time, but also to trace its activity while in action. The brain, moreover, is nowadays viewed as a kind of magisterial "design" that determines and controls all of our activities, from the raising of a hand to the most complicated of intellectual activities. No wonder that the study of the brain should have given rise, among else, to various theories concerning its own "history," i.e. the course of its development. Yet "how" and "where" to begin remains an open question.

As professor of physics at Syracuse (now retired), Erich Harth is the author of several books concerning the nature of human consciousness. In his various works, Harth attempted to account for a "continuum" that commences with cells and neuro-chemicals and ends with qualities, such as 'imagination', 'creativity' and–above all–with the being we identify as "self." His theory tries to explain how the brain creates the conscious self by addressing many questions that involve the relationship between the nature of human beings and the physical world. In his thought provoking book *The Creative Loop: How the Brain Makes a Mind*, Harth attempted to answer and clarify problems all of which are related, in one way or another, to the key question: "where does our consciousness come from?" The book suggests a central thesis concerning how the mind works, a thesis that is based on an elaborate theory about "feedback loops" whereby neurons are capable of forming the things produced by the brain. Like many others, Harth is after the "seat" of consciousness. His account, which begins with neurochemicals and ends with qualities, connects the emergence of the "self" to the physical world.

Harth's creative loop theory is based on connections between "higher" cortical brain regions and "lower" cortical regions. Higher and lower refer to the relative position in a neural network. That which is closer to a sensory input organ is lower and that which is further removed from a sensory input–through connections between cells of the brain–is higher. According to Harth, the use of the loop, from higher to lower brain regions and back from lower to higher brain regions, is what allows us to "think" of the world. Although it renders an intelligent description of the physical working of our brain, the creative loop theory, according to neuroscientists, fails to answer many questions related to our mental experiences.

Harth has been criticized by neuroscientists for suggesting an "easy" solution to the most complicated scientific puzzles that humans have ever faced, namely, the *mind/brain* conundrum. Whilst the scientific study of the mind tried hard to rid itself of introspection, Harth is accused for bringing it back through his particular theory of consciousness. Although Harth hardly addresses the subjects that concern neuroscientists, he apparently rejects their basic tenet, i.e. that mind can be explained as the function of brain. Neuroscientists, on their part, claim that Harth's creative loop theory *does not* explain "how a brain makes a mind." For example, it does not deal with how memories are stored in the brain tissue and then recalled at later times. Harth, however, holds to the opinion that the "particulars" of brain function are so complex that it will never be possible to test the hypothesis that behavior can be explained in terms of brain structure and function that can have predictive value. In short, Harth rejects the idea that "stored information," which creates a wealth of associations and emotions–complexities imposed by culture– may eventually achieve a detailed analysis in terms of a "seamless chain" of microscopic neural events.

The following essay rests on the theory according to which our brains are characterized by sensory pathways that "allow higher cortical centers to control neural activity patterns at peripheral sensory areas." The latter are supposed to involve "recursive interactions between central symbols and peripheral images." This process, according to Harth, is the "fundamental mechanism underlying most cognitive functions." Harth attributes the beginnings of 'art' and 'language' to this pre-existing internal process, made possible by the enlarged human prefrontal cortex. Consciousness, accordingly, emerges from the brain because it has been "put there" by a lifetime of experience. We would not understand 'consciousness', concludes Harth, even if we could follow in detail "the dynamics of a hundred billion neurons" without knowing much about "the society and culture in which we are immersed."

Since no physical theory exists that is congruent with sensory experience, the object of the scientific study of consciousness is to discover how we "convert" data from the world into our experience. Philosophy was clearly aware of the phenomena of consciousness. In fact, philosophical discussions of consciousness provided some insights into the nature of consciousness and supplied interesting arguments that unveiled the complexity involved. Indeed, though difficult to define, philosophers tried–in one way or another, and under different names–to define this *manifest* marvel. However, due to the discoveries of neuroscience we know that the brain performs countless functions that are *not* part of our conscious experience. And though most of the processes of the brain are non-conscious, the output contributes no doubt to our experience. Since the "integrated" output of brain processes deal with all kinds of sensations, it gave rise, naturally, to attempts to unveil the "signals" (via electric, magnetic, and other means) that register consciousness. However, "how" and "where" experiences take place still remains *the* question. In the absence of an agreed theory of consciousness, scientists continue to search for the neural "correlates" of consciousness. The correlates consist of events in the brain that accompany events in conscious experience.

HARTH
*The Emergence of Art and Language in the Human Brain**

*Our brains are characterized by sensory pathways that are highly **reflexive,** allowing higher cortical centers to control neural activity patterns at peripheral sensory areas. This feature is characterized as an **internal sketchpad** and involves recursive interactions between central symbols and peripheral images. The process is assumed to be the fundamental mechanism underlying most cognitive functions. The paper attempts to portray the beginnings of art and language as natural extensions of these preexisting internal processes, made possible by the greatly enlarged human prefrontal cortex. It views these highly social activities as originating in subjective, private discourse between the emerging self and its externalized expressions.*

Artistic expression and language proficiency are among the least understood functions of the human brain. They are also exclusive to our species. While many attempts have been made to understand language functions in terms of cerebral processes, little has been said about the brain's involvement in the production and appreciation of works of art. We find it puzzling that prehistoric humans, at the height of the last Ice Age, when life must have been extremely harsh, found the leisure and the passion to decorate vast caves with magnificent paintings and sculptures.

How is art related to brain functions? Twenty four hundred years ago Plato, in his *Republic,* considered *painting* and *thinking* to be antonyms. To think is to transcend the obvious, to go beyond appearances to the true *'essence'* of a thing, whereas painting to him was copying an appearance, thus twice removed from reality. But to the late French philosopher Maurice Merleau-Ponty, the thinker and the painter pursue similar goals, namely to conjure up images in order to

* From: *Journal of Consciousness Studies,* 6, No. 6-7,1999, pp. 97-115

gain new insights. Jacques Derrida (1987) sees art as a self-referent production in which the mind 'returns to itself, comes back to consciousness and cognizance ... returning to it in a circle'.

Until recently it has seemed reasonable to compare human language with forms of animal communication, and to attempt to see language as arising from the primitive signals animals send to one another as warnings or mating calls. It has become more and more apparent, however, that it is difficult to bridge the enormous gap between human and animal communication. Linguists generally point out that no animal signals qualify as language, not even the signs chimpanzees and gorillas have acquired after intensive training. Terrence Deacon (1997) makes the strong point that no *simple languages* exist anywhere in the animal kingdom.

The Danish linguist Ib Ulbaek (1992) suggested a radical departure from the attempts to trace language origins to animal communication. Instead, he perceives continuity between the higher forms of animal *cognition* and human language. In this view, which has since been reiterated by others (e.g. Wilkins & Wakefield, 1995), language arises from already existing cognitive structures and thinking processes.

In this paper I will investigate the role particular cognitive features and their neuroanatomical foundations may play in the origin of both artistic and language skills. The stress here is on *origin*. Clearly, both art and language have undergone profound evolutions of their own whose cultural dimensions are beyond the range of the present discussion.

In the *sketchpad model*, Harth *et al.* (1987) and Harth (1995), have presented a neural mechanism by which images and symbols interact in the human brain during conscious cognition. I want to suggest now that in art and language these processes are extended beyond the confines of the individual by *externalizing* images and symbols.

Images and Symbols

In the first step of sensory perception the brain forms images of the objects that are to be perceived. I use the visual system as an example, but much of the discussion is applicable to other sense modalities.

Images

The neural activity patterns in the first few stages of post-retinal visual processing are *images* in the sense that they are facsimiles of the raw visual stimulus patterns generated by the eyes. If an outside observer could view them, he or she would recognize them as representing the imaged real objects (Tootell *et al.,* 1982). As a requirement of this *retinotopic* organization, neighboring cells in the retina connect to neighboring cells in the next few stages of processing, the lateral geniculate nuclei (LGN) in the thalamus, and cortical projection area V1. *Receptive fields* of neurons in these areas–defined as regions in the visual field to which these neurons are sensitive are generally small, but increase in size as we ascend the sensory pathway. Already in V1, one finds single cells that respond to oriented lines and edges, thus combining the responses of a number of neurons of the preceding stage (Hubel & Wiesel, 1959). At even higher levels of cortical processing single neurons are found to be sensitive to color, or motion, or a variety of complex patterns. The imagistic character of neural activity thus gradually disappears and gives way to *symbolic* representation.[1]

We may ask, naively, why all this processing is necessary in the first place. Isn't all relevant information contained in the primary sensory image? There are three simple reasons why these images by themselves cannot convey anything:

1. The neural patterns in the early stages of processing lack *coherence;* they are collections of millions of unconnected *local* events, like dabs of color in a pointillist painting. Each point is part of the picture, but no point can tell us whether we are looking at a face or a tree.

2. The information lacks *embeddedness.* It is devoid of memory, and without associations to previous events.

3. The images are transient, leaving no record to be connected with subsequent patterns.

---

[1] The term symbolic is used here merely to distinguish this neural activity from one that preserves some of the topographic character of the stimulus object. This differs from Jung's definition of symbols, but conforms to that of Deacon (1997).

It is important to remind ourselves, also, that a significant gap exists between an object and its images, however *realistic*. Animals will generally not recognize the object of a painting, or even of a color photograph, while humans excel in the recognition of incomplete or noisy images, but readily distinguish them from the real objects they resemble. Even the wonders of virtual reality will not fool us, unless we are intent on being fooled.

Clearly, delicate cognitive steps are involved in the perceptive process, i.e. in going from receiving the image to perception. The network of associations we use in daily living require the extraction and independent representation of *features*. Thus, to be able to say that the color of a certain flower reminds us of the color of a sunset, we must first have extracted the color feature from both objects.

Accordingly, in the visual system, series of feature extractors, or analyzers, are found along several parallel pathways, beginning at VI. Receptive fields of neurons increase in size as we ascend the sensory pathways. The neural responses now no longer display the input patterns; instead, individual cells or cell groups represent, or *symbolize,* features by virtue of their afferent connectivity.

Symbols

We have seen why the neural images formed at primary sensory areas cannot by themselves account for the cognitive reception of sensory messages. Nor can central symbolic representations alone accomplish the task. No conscious perception exists without cortical activation by brainstem structures (Moruzzi & Magoun, 1949), or an intact thalamus. Although symbols constitute a certain amount of integration, as reflected by their large receptive fields, they are themselves scattered over large cortical areas. The color of the bird I am looking at is represented in one cortical area, its shape in another, motion in a third. Nowhere are all the cognitive elements reunited. This is the *binding problem.* Then there is the question of how the symbols are related back to the feature they are expressing. Hamad called this the *symbol grounding problem* (Harnad, 1990).

Locality

We have come to what is perhaps the most difficult question: Is there *any way* by which all this information could be brought together short of having it viewed by an intelligent observer? This is the *homunculus* problem. As long as the information remains distributed among any number of neurons we face the same problem of *locality* that we encountered with the original image.

To break through this limitation of *locality* would require a quantum phenomenon physicists call *entanglement,* which can exist between certain pairs of elementary particles under very special conditions. No one has shown convincingly that scattered neurons could be so *entangled.*

The idea has become popular (e.g. Eckhorn *et al.,* 1988; Crick & Koch, 1990) that binding could be achieved through temporal coherence of neurons firing in repetitive and synchronized manner. Undoubtedly, such correlations between the activities of scattered neurons serve important functions, but it is not clear how they can solve the binding problem. Simultaneity is easily defined by the physiologist who is able to monitor different neurons at one time and compare the traces of their activities on an oscilloscope screen. But the meaning of time *within* the neural mass is made obscure by the multiplicity of pathways between neurons and the different propagation velocities of the signals. For simultaneity to have binding functions there would have to be a *simultaneity detector* of sorts.

But suppose there were true convergence in the brain, with all the feature-analyzers reporting their findings to a single neuron. This might solve the binding problem, but it would require this neuron to be a *'gnostic unit,'* to perceive, to feel, to comprehend. It is difficult to ascribe such faculties to a single cell that, embedded in the matrix of neural tissue, *knows* only the amounts of transmitter molecules that have reached its receptor sites.

Perception

What happens in the brain–other than the formation of neural images and symbols–when we view an object, pay attention to it, think about it? The processes are immensely complex. Only certain elements are halfway understood. Beside the evident problems of binding and symbol grounding, there is the problem of *selection.* Not everything that appears in the image is contemplated. Some features are enhanced, others suppressed. From functional magnetic resonance imaging (fMRI) studies Kastner *et al.* (1998) have shown that responses to simultaneously presented visual stimuli tend to suppress one another, but that *directed attention* can unblock that effect. Crick (1984) speaks of a *searchlight* that plays over the scene and is controlled by a structure in the thalamus called the *nucleus reticularis*. Associations are made, and past memories brought to the fore. Baddeley (1986) introduced the useful concept of a *working memory,* a region or process in which stored memories are reactivated. Goldman-Rakic (1987) and others believe that working memory is located in the prefrontal lobe of the neocortex. Activities there are diffuse, showing no clear topographic relation to either sensory or motor space (Perecman, 1987; Stuss & Benson, 1986). We call these representations *symbolic.*

Finally, there is the very fundamental problem of *control*: what is it that *selects* the features to be emphasized and the trajectory the mind will follow? The stream of consciousness is not always, and not exclusively, driven by the senses. We form *mental images* that may be a modification of the sensory input, or completely independent of the visual scene before us. In general, they may reflect a competition between sensory reality and cortical fancy.

What is the nature of *mental* images? Are they truly topographically arranged, quasi-sensory neural activities, or are we really talking about symbolic representations interacting with one another? This has been a controversy among psychologists for some time, with the *symbolic* interpretation championed for example by Z.W. Pylyshyn (1975). Recent investigations (Kosslyn, 1994; Shepard & Cooper, 1982; Finke, 1996) strongly suggest the *imagistic* interpretation. There is in our cognitive handling of these images something that requires picture-like properties. A simple thought experiment mentioned by Steven Pinker (1997, p. 291) adds weight to that interpretation: If you are asked to form a mental image of a banana lying *next to* a lemon, your image will have the banana either to the left or the right of the lemon. There is no in-between, but the verbal symbol '*next to*' does not distinguish between the alternatives. Thus, if the mental 'image' were entirely symbolic the left-right decision would remain unresolved. Finally–and this will be an important point–I will make the reasonable assumption that topographic *mental* images appear at places in the brain where similar sensory images are found, i.e. at cortical projection areas or perhaps as peripheral as thalamic relay nuclei.

Deacon (1997) has pointed out that the dominant control wielded by a greatly enlarged prefrontal cortex over the rest of the brain is a uniquely human development. He calls it the *'front-heavy brain.'* It is the prefrontal cortex that is supposed to exert *executive control,* deciding somehow what sensory features to select for special attention (Wickelgren, 1997).

In behavioral studies with primates, Hasegawa *et al.* (1998) have shown that 'top-down processes originating from the prefrontal cortex can regulate retrieval from the modality-specific posterior association cortex, even in the absence of direct sensory input'.

The complexity of the interaction between images and symbols is pointed up in the following story about a man who approached Picasso complaining about his painting *Demoiselles d'Avignon.* 'Why don't you paint women the way they really look?' he wanted to know. 'And how do they *really* look?' Picasso asked. At that, the man pulled a photograph of his wife from his wallet. 'Like *this,*' he answered. Picasso studied the picture for a while and then handed it back to the man. 'She's small, isn't she,' he said, 'and flat.'

The story points up the arbitrariness in any pictorial representation, and its subtle link to the symbolic structures in our heads. We often take these links for granted but are reminded of their fundamentally subjective character when we find animals unable to recognize members of their own species in paintings or color photographs. We will come back to this point later when talking about the cerebral basis of art.

The Sketchpad Model

In 1976 I proposed a model of visual perception in which images formed at peripheral sensory areas were further manipulated by top-down control depending on the symbolic responses at higher levels. I proposed an optimization–or hill-climbing[2] process that favored expression of those images that elicited particularly strong central responses (Harth, 1976).

The model in its more recent version (Harth *et al.,* 1987; Harth, 1995; 1997) is based on reciprocal pathways between thalamic relay nuclei and corresponding cortical projection areas, and on the effect of brainstem centers and prefrontal cortex on the reticular nucleus of the thalamus (NRT). The latter occupies a strategic location between the thalamic relay nuclei and their cortical projection areas. I have assumed that diffuse feedback from brainstem to NRT guides the hill-climbing process that acts on the sensory images. By its simultaneous action on all thalamic relay nuclei it is thus able to produce a unitary, poly-modal experience.

In a series of computer simulations, and with the circuitry based in part on the work of Yingling & Skinner (1977) and Steriade *et al.* (1986), we were able to show that extremely noisy input patterns could be improved by feedback from central feature detectors (Harth *et al.,* 1987). In the corresponding neural system this would imply the ability not just to modify afferent patterns, but to weave patterns entirely under central control.

Consciousness

The model stresses what I consider an important feature of perception and conscious processes in general: neural representations (other than motor commands) do not function at any level as *outputs* or *final states,* to be displayed on, what Daniel Dennett (1991) has derisively called, a *'Cartesian theater'.* Just as it is the only known function of single neurons to send messages to other cells, so the cell groups that constitute imagistic or symbolic representations serve only to interact with other representations at higher or lower levels. Thus, instead of a process of sequential mappings with a questionable ultimate destination of the information, perception appears as a continuous recursive *bootstrap* process.

The *stream of consciousness* is seen as a succession of single items selected by association and happenstance out of a multitude of partially activated traces existing side-by-side in working memory. Consciousness is a process of serialization (through selection) of massive parallel information received

---

[2] A process in which parameters are adjusted so-as-to maximize a function.

through the senses. The bottleneck which accounts for the narrowness of the conscious channel is more likely to arise in the selection process itself than from insufficiency of representational neural space.

Top-down control of images introduces what has been called the *inverse problem* (v. Baeyer, 1985): How can the extensive neural processing that leads from images to symbols be inverted so that symbols can both modify and recreate images? The task can be achieved by hill-climbing processes as previously shown (Harth, 1976; 1995; 1997; Harth *et al.,* 1987). I have also discussed the inherent slowness of the process and mentioned alternate inversion mechanisms (Harth, 1996).

The model can account also for the two most puzzling aspects of conscious cognition, the problems of *binding* and of *symbol grounding.* *Binding* of separate features of sensory reality is achieved here not through spatial convergence of responses or through their temporal alignment, but through the reinforcement, under symbolic control, of all pertinent imagistic features. No homunculus is required here. By the same mechanisms, the symbolic representations are *grounded* through their synergistic interaction with the appropriate images. I envision a continuous loop of symbolization of existing images and the de-symbolization, or re-imaging of central symbolic activity. There are, of course, as Pinker (1997, pp. 284) has pointed out, different levels of mental imagery, from the strictly topographic to the partially symbolic.

Consciousness is often described as an *emergent* phenomenon, based in and emerging out of the complexity of the neural machinery. This is a form of reductionism in which consciousness remains utterly incomprehensible. If consciousness emerges from the brain it is only because it has been *put* there by a lifetime of experience. This was not just a matter of *downloading* a stream of sensory information, but the chewing, digesting, and regurgitating of the ingested stream. We would not understand consciousness even if we could follow in detail the dynamics of a hundred billion neurons without knowing much about the society and culture in which we are immersed. This 'social construction of consciousness' was recently discussed by Burns and Engdahl (1998).

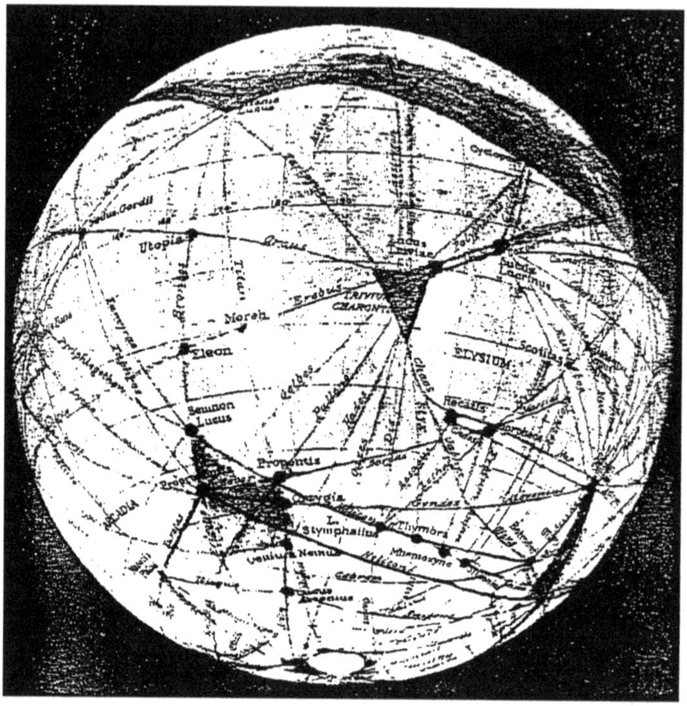

Figure 1
Canals on Mars as reported by the American astronomer Percival Lowell
(1906).

Top-down control

The visual images displayed at topographically organized areas such as the lateral geniculate nucleus (LGN) in the thalamus, or visual projection area VI in the cortex, reflect not just the messages conveyed by the retina but the attentional and selective influence of higher cortical levels. In extreme cases the images may be almost completely dominated by cortical fancy.

A striking example of this was presented by the American astronomer Percival Lowell who firmly believed that *canals* existed on Mars, and who convinced himself of seeing them through his telescope (Fig. 1). Lowell's own remarks are revealing: 'To observe Mars', he writes, 'is to embark upon the enterprise not in body but in mind'. He describes this vision of the appearance and waning of the canals in this striking way (Lowell, 1906):

> Gone as quickly as it came, he (the observer) will instinctively doubt his own eyesight. ... By persistent watch, however, ... *backed by the knowledge of what he is to see,* he will find its coming more frequent, more certain, and more detailed. (Italics mine.)

By his own admission, it is the mind telling the eyes what to see. It is as though a dialogue were being carried on between symbolic centers in prefrontal cortex and peripheral visual projection areas where the telescope's image of Mars is represented.

> *'There is nothing there'*, report the senses.
> *'There must be. I know there are canals'*, answers the working memory.
> *'Ah, I see them now'*, say the senses.

Neural dialogue

The idea of the brain conversing with itself is not new. The number of neural fibers descending from the cortex to the thalamus far exceeds the number of the afferent sensory fibers. Reciprocity of connections is found at nearly every stage of processing. My model more specifically asserts that by top-down control the brain uses the more peripheral topographic areas of the sensory brain as an *internal sketchpad* in a cyclic process of controlling and observing.

The superposition of mental imagery and visual reality in Lowell's description of Mars argues for a common neural space in which they both are displayed. The simplest interpretation would have the canals appear, at least in rudimentary form, in peripheral visual areas such as the LGN or V1.

The term *reflection* is therefore an appropriate description of most thinking processes. (Exceptions are the symbol-symbol associations that occur, for example, in mathematical reasoning.) Unlike the case of the physical reflection of light or sound, each reverberation here generally contributes more information.

The outcome of the process is virtually unpredictable since we are dipping into a reservoir of enormous complexity containing traces of everything we have ever seen, heard, or thought. We observe and we confabulate. Like Rodin's *Thinker*, we are often oblivious to what goes on around us. This *bootstrap process*—I have called it the *creative loop* (Harth, 1993)—is the source of all human creativity and inventiveness, though it can often (as in Lowell's case) lead us astray.

Every act of invention or creation involves trial patterns in the head that are being judged for their adequacy and modified until they appear satisfactory. I came across this passage out of Karl Marx's *Das Kapital* quoted by the Vietnamese linguist Tran Duc Thao (1984).

> What distinguishes the worst architect from the best of bees is this, that the architect raises his structure in the imagination before he erects it in reality.

The evolution of the neural circuitry that gives us the power to insert into sensory reality the products of our symbolic transactions has been of enormous adaptive value. By using and testing mental imagery, it has enabled humans to invent the first primitive stone tools, and, over a period of some two and a half million years, develop tool-making into a sophisticated technology. The resulting adaptive advantage may easily account for the spectacular growth of the prefrontal cortex over the same stretch of time. Deacon (1997) has called this a mind-body *co-evolution*. It is this cognitive evolution that we can readily trace back to lower mammals and that Ulbaek (1992) believes responsible for the eventual invention of language.

Creativity and Invention

Most forms of creativity and invention result from the spontaneous interplay between images and symbols. The underlying neurodynamics, while largely deterministic, has probabilistic and chaotic ingredients (Freeman, 1994; Harth, 1983) that make prediction of its future course impossible, even in principle. I have pointed out (Harth, 1983) that one of the characteristics of living systems in general, and of the nervous system in particular, is the tight coupling between microscopic and macroscopic features of the system. In phenomena similar to Hermann Haken's *synergetics,* this allows minute fluctuations to percolate upward through hierarchies of structures and give rise to significant macroscopic phenomena (Haken, 1983).

We must presuppose the existence of a delicate balance between randomness and guidance to avoid meaningless chaos on the one hand and stagnation on the other. The situation here is comparable to the balance between the rate of random mutations and the strength and speed of natural selection in evolution. A high rate of random mutations–brought about for instance by a significant rise in background radiation–will have lethal consequences. The other extreme of total genetic stability will make every species a dead end. (Of course, there would not be any species in a no-mutation world.)

Woolf (1997) pointed out that the continuity of thought in the absence of sensory stimulation may be due to continuous excitation fed into the cortical network by a system of spontaneously active cholinergic neurons that are located in the basal forebrain and in a region between pons and mesencephalon.

Given these dynamic principles, we can now understand the generation of spontaneous trains of images in a recursive or *bootstrap* fashion. The psychologist Merlin Donald (1991) speaks of '*autocuing*' as the spontaneous recall of memories without environmental cues. He believes that this is involved in the transition from the 'episodic memory' of apes to the brain of *Homo sapiens*.

The features of selectivity and exclusivity that I discussed before allow us to direct our attention to specific items. They also limit the range of cognitive tasks we are able to perform. We have difficulty thinking simultaneously of more than one thing. Thus, while the *sketchpad-in-the-head* enabled our distant ancestors to manufacture primitive tools, the design of more complex machinery would have been impossible without *external* sketching and storing. We don't know what ancient Leonardo first advanced technology by making sketches. But for a long time *Homo sapiens* just drew, sculpted and painted, apparently with no practical end in mind. We find this profoundly puzzling.

Representational Art: External Images Discovered

Drawing, painting and sculpting are late arrivals in human affairs. Of course, we cannot exclude the possibility that much earlier efforts have been lost, but few historians would put the beginnings of representational art much before about 60,000 years ago. This was long after the last increase in human brain-size or any other discernible biological changes (Mithen, 1996). Unlike tool-making, the earliest artistic efforts were almost certainly the exclusive work of our own species, *Homo sapiens*. The artistic *explosion* that began some 40,000 years ago, roughly the time of the demise of the Neanderthals, culminated in the magnificent paintings and sculptures we find in the caves of Southern France and Spain. We asked this question at the outset: What made humans devote so much time, passion, and labor to this endeavor?

We are now in a position to offer an educated guess. We stand at the end of what Deacon called the *co-evolution* between mind and brain, which saw the growth of the human brain, especially the prefrontal cortex, driven by the adaptive advantages of superior cognitive functions. (I leave open for the moment the question whether language was the dominant driver as Deacon suggests.) I interpret the cognitive portion of the process in terms of the sketchpad model as involving ever more intensive use of mental imagery in the performance of ever more sophisticated tasks.

These images are mostly ephemeral and lack both realism and specificity. We generally can tell between an object imagined and the real thing, but can still recognize the image and utilize it in sketchpad fashion. This ability to connect imperfect images with the appropriate symbols appears to be a central feature of human intelligence.

It seems a small step from this to the recognition of *external* images. A cloud, fortuitously shaped like a rabbit, projected onto the retina of some distant hominid, may have been the first external *image* recognized. At another time, he or she may have been startled by what seemed like the image of a horse's head on a rock wall. These images were truly in the heads of the beholders. No animal could have seen anything in them. Their resemblance is much too remote. Finding such external images must rank among man's great *discoveries*.

I am reminded here of two contemporary paintings. One, by the American Mark Tansey, is entitled *The Innocent Eye Test* (Plate 1).[3] In it a group, evidently scientists, observe a 'real' cow as they unveil a life-sized painting of cows. One man, notepad in hand, stands ready to record the cow's reaction. There isn't any. Why doesn't she recognize her likenesses?

What we almost fail to see is that there are no cows there. The one being 'observed by the scientists' is as much a facsimile as the ones in the fake canvas. And that made me think of Magritte's famous painting of a pipe with the inscription' *Ceci n'est pas une pipe*.' What do you mean, 'This is not a pipe?' we want to say. 'Of course it's a pipe!' But a cow would know better. It is a colored piece of canvas.

Now, back to our ancient ancestor, who saw a rabbit in a cloud and a horse's head on a rock wall. The faint resemblance suggests improvement. There is not much you can do with a cloud, but the rock could be made to look more horsy. The world's first sculptor then reached for a primitive rock chisel and the random *simulacrum* was changed into a *facsimile*, a thing *made* to resemble.

I chose a horse's head in this hypothetical scenario because, much later, at the peak of the artistic explosion in the Upper Paleolithic, the delicate features of a horse's head were carved into the rock wall at Commarque, Southern France. Not all of it was done by the artist, however. There was a crack in the wall that made a perfect nostril and a natural bulge that became the horse's cheekbone. Plato was wrong when he characterized the artist as simply copying nature. In seeing a flaring nostril in that crack in the wall the artist perceived the *essence* of the horse.

There is a surprising consensus about the intrinsic uselessness of art. Pinker, who in his *How the Mind Works* makes a strong argument for the shaping of most aspects of the human mind through evolutionary mechanisms, makes an exception for art–along with literature, music, wit, religion, and philosophy–as 'biologically frivolous and vain' (1997, p. 521). Denis Donaghue speaks of 'the uselessness of art', which he considers 'its finest tribute' (1983, p. 67).

But, is art really useless?

Placing images into the outside world was a step that was to have enormous consequences. I described its beginning as an adventitious, almost playful, act, and perhaps play it remained for some time. The sheer joy of discovering

---

[3] Plate 1 is displayed at the end of this essay.

novel channels between external images and symbols residing deep in the brain probably preceded any ritualistic or religious significance. But play is far from a useless activity. A child learns by playing. It is the art of make-believe and presupposition. *Homo sapiens* have rightly been called *Homo ludens*; perhaps another appropriate name would be *Homo pingens*, the image maker.

Note that the process of sculpting or painting conforms with what I believe has been the basic mechanism of thinking for hominids since they began to manufacture stone tools. Higher mammals must also avail themselves of this skill. 'Chimpanzees are curious manipulators of objects', Pinker (1997, p.356) points out. It is reported that a chimpanzee will move a box to reach a banana that is attached to the roof of his cage. It must have had something like a mental image of the solution. On the other hand, a dog with its leash wound tightly around a tree is unable to free itself by simply *un*winding it.

Drawing, painting, and sculpting have provided humans with a greatly enlarged and more permanent *sketchpad*. Along the way, art has become a social activity, with creators, spectators, critics, and styles. But its original form, *sketching*, whether in two or three dimensions, was, and still is, a solitary activity. The creative act has always been a private dialogue between the artist and his or her medium. It is as though another layer had been added to the hierarchy of cerebral stages that reflect ideas, changing them from images to symbols and back again to images. In that sense art is an enhanced way of *thinking*.

Sketching eventually took off in a different direction and became the mainstay of all science and technology, from the sand sketches of Archimedes to Leonardo's *notebooks*, the anatomical studies of Vesalius, and contemporary engineering drawings.

Language: External Symbols Invented

I described the origin of art as an almost inevitable event for a brain that had become as highly reflective and self-referent as that of *Homo sapiens*. It is not quite so easy to explain the emergence of language. The subject is fraught with so much uncertainty that for a long time speculations were frowned upon as being beyond scientific dominion. This is in part due to the fact that, unlike artistic expression, the spoken word is the most fleeting of human activities.

The time of origin of speaking is uncertain by more than two million years. This period is bracketed at one end by the speculation that language co-evolved with our increasing brain size (Deacon, 1997), beginning perhaps with primitive expressions uttered by *Homo habilis*. At the other end, it is frequently claimed that the artistic explosion of the Upper Paleolithic was part of a more general *cultural* explosion that included also the beginnings of language. Deacon, who favors the view that language powered the evolutionary engine, and hence must have begun long before the Upper Paleolithic, plays down the significance and grandeur of that epoch, speaking of an 'overzealous extrapolation from human artifacts to human mind' (Deacon, 1997, p. 370).

I do not want to enter the controversy about the timing of language origin, except to point out that the biological evolution of the brain from *Homo erectus* to *Homo sapiens* could have been driven solely by the adaptive advantages gained from the enhanced cognitive functions, of which tool-making is just one of the manifestations, and may not have required the invention of language. Language could have emerged much later and without further genetic intervention, taking advantage of what Wilkins and Wakefield (1995) called the *re-appropriation* of previous evolutionary changes. The geneticist Christopher Wills (1993) called attention to the remarkable ability of our brains 'to encompass a totally new skill without any genetic change whatsoever'.

It is not just the time that is uncertain about the origin of language. The gap between speaking *Homo sapiens* and non-speaking creatures is so profound, we don't know how it could have been bridged. Spoken language presupposes some salient biological changes not seen in lower animals. These involve a greatly enlarged brain with dedicated speech centers and the evolution of the organs of speech production, such as a properly positioned larynx and other modifications to the vocal tract. Equally important, brain and speech apparatus had to be reciprocally matched to bring about the brain's delicate control over the appropriate muscles, and the ready interpretation of speech sounds.

These puzzles have been approached along two principal avenues. The *adaptionist* stance envisions a gradual Darwinian evolution toward speaking, driven by the adaptive advantages gained at each step. This view is most eloquently represented by Deacon (1997) who sees language *co-evolving* along with its biological prerequisites.

By contrast, the *nativist* position, represented chiefly by Noam Chomsky (1972), Jerry Fodor (1975), and, more recently, Derek Bickerton (1995), envisions the acquisition of a *language module* that is unique to *Homo sapiens* and contains not only the wherewithal of speech production and perception but also a set of rules of syntax and grammar, that they believe to be innate and universal. This theory bridges the gap by fiat and tells us little about how it all came about.

The first of these approaches, evolution of language through adaptive advantages, is often questioned on the basis of the following argument. For speaking to have an adaptive advantage, it must be produced by a speaker *and* understood by a listener. It seems unlikely that the two hurdles could have been overcome simultaneously by a single selective process. It is as though writing were useless before the invention of printing. The chances are neither of the two would have come about. This point is expressed for example by the American anthropologist Sonia Ragir (1992):

> Selection for genetically determined language capacity is problematic from any perspective. Where is the advantage of speech if only one person has the capacity to talk – or ten, or one hundred scattered through a population ranging across a continent?

Ragir suggests that language is a cultural achievement, comparable to technological advances, rather than resulting from adaptive biological changes.

Private speech

I want to suggest that language, as communication, is such a cultural development, but perhaps *subsequent* to speech, that was originally– *monologue*. Unlike Ragir, I believe that speech is of value to the speaker even when it is not understood by others, and unlike Blachowicz (1997), I regard *talking to oneself* to be truly *monologue,* rather than a dialogue between 'cognitively different partners'.

The importance of private speech (and its mute cousin inner speech) in our cognitive development has been recognized by Piaget (1955), Vygotsky (1962), and more recently Berk (1992; 1994). Vygotsky, unlike Piaget, argues that private speech is secondary to social communication. This is perhaps true in the development of speech in children who are immersed in ready-made language from the day they are born. It may not be the way language originated. The erroneous analogy between language and animal calls led us to overemphasize the interpersonal use of speech. At the dawn of language, the invention of any new linguistic symbol must always have been an individual act. The word must first mean something to the speaker who can then convey its meaning to another person. But, before doing so, she is likely to acquire familiarity with the symbol through use in quiet or articulated soliloquy.

I also want to make this point: semantics must precede syntax. Vocabularies come before grammar. A word symbol for *love* must have existed long before linguists could wonder why 'John loves Mary' is different from 'Mary loves John'. Thus, when I speak of the beginnings of language, I am referring to initially haphazardly juxtaposed symbols, or what Bickerton (1995, p. 51) calls a *lexicon without syntax* or a *protolanguage*. Syntax must have evolved gradually to avoid misunderstandings rather than emerging full-blown as a result of some happy genetic accident.

The attempt to connect human speech with animal calls has been the standard approach to the question of language origin. It has met with little success. One difficulty has to do with the fact that we find little advance in animal communication as we ascend the evolutionary ladder. The dance of bees probably conveys more information than the varied calls of apes. There are no *'simple languages'* (in the sense Deacon, 1997, defines the term) anywhere in the animal kingdom, although studies on non-human primates have demonstrated a capacity for symbol use.

Another difficulty has to do with neuroanatomy. Deacon (1992) points out that the neural centers responsible for the production of calls in monkeys are in the midbrain, the diencephalon, and limbic cortex. If human speech originated from animal calls, we would expect these areas to evolve further and become our speech centers. Instead, human speech is almost entirely controlled by the neo-cortex, involving, among others, the well-known language areas of Broca and Wernicke.

Ulbaek's suggestion that the roots of language should be sought not in animal communication but in animal cognition opens a promising new approach. 'Language exists', says Ulbaek (1992), 'because it is founded on an already existing structure, viz. cognition or thinking'.

Man had become adept at juggling images and symbols between layers of his brain. This was the intellectual heritage he may have picked up from the distant common ancestor he shared with the apes. Language was *made possible*, in the opinion of Wilkins and Wakefield (1995) by new neural structures joining the parietal, occipital and temporal lobes of the brain, and forming an 'association area of association areas'. This resulted in the ability to form associations that are *'modality-neutral'* and hence conducive to forming higher order symbols. This happened at the time *Homo habilis* appeared in the fossil record, some two million years ago. With the concurrent expansion of the prefrontal cortex the *'front-heavy'* brain eventually found its mental images too crowded and too short-lived, and man began to place images in the outside world. Sometime, before or after that event, he did the same with symbols and found that it helped him to think.

The use of language as an instrument of thought is questioned by Pinker (1997, p. 70) on the basis of its 'clutter' of articles, prepositions, and the like, and its frequent ambiguity. He states that, 'If one string of words in English can correspond to two meanings in the mind, meanings in the mind cannot be strings of words in English.' His example was the ambiguous news headline *Bundy Beats Date with Chair* that announced Bundy's stay of execution. Pinker believes that an abbreviated form of coding, he calls *mentalese,* is the language of thought.

But we *also* frequently use everyday language with all its syntactic flourishes and prepositional *clutter* in our thinking, and talk to ourselves as though talking to another person. What is the function of these monologues? Are we merely telling ourselves something we already know?

I see mentalese and formal language as complementary. Where one skips lightly among topics without benefit of grammar or syntax, the other, formal and precise, is useful in establishing cognitive beachheads and to leave memory traces of what has been accomplished. Pilots verbally go through their pre-takeoff and landing checklists, and any writer can attest to the fact that the even more formalized use of language in writing is often the source of novel ideas.

Bickerton (1995, p. 40) makes the point that the human species 'instead of becoming clever enough to invent language', was 'blundering into language and, as a direct result of that, becoming clever'. I would amend that the *blundering* could only occur at the end of a long evolution of his cognitive faculties.

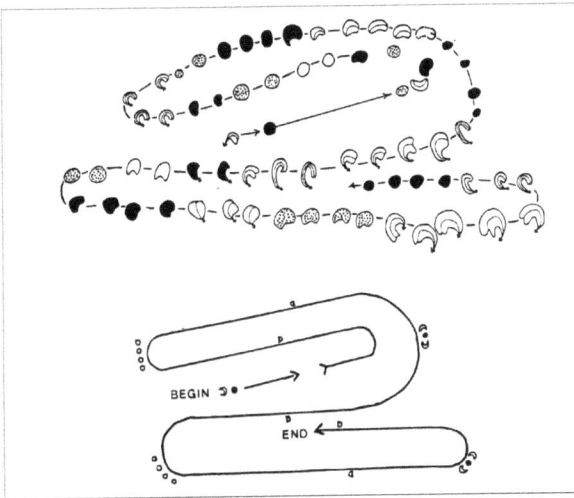

Figure 2 Bone plaque with token representation of a lunar calendar, c. 28,000 years ago (after Marshack, 1992).

The first external symbols may have been *tokens*. Without being able to count, we would have difficulty telling numbers greater than five or seven. If somebody had ten reindeer and one was lost, he would not know the difference. Before humans invented numbers or tokens they could not count the days between full moons or the number of moons in a season. When this became sufficiently troublesome, they invented *tokens*: perhaps small notches cut into bark for each day and a big cut for each moon. Some of the tokens cut into bone or stone survived, like the bone plaque found in Blanchard, France (Fig. 2). It shows 69 marks of different round or crescent shapes that snake back and forth across the small plaque. The Harvard archaeologist Alexander Marshack (1992) speculates that they represent phases of the moon.

Arranging the notches in groups may have been a further advance, the way we still arrange lines in groups of fives when checking off events. Eventually, symbols were invented to stand not for events but for numbers, thus creating perhaps the first abstractions. The transition may have been virtually unnoticed; the first three Roman numerals are still indistinguishable from the tokens. The first four Arabic numerals also appear to betray their token origin (Fig. 3).

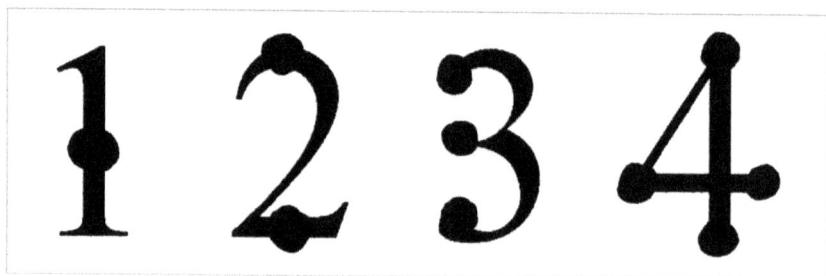

Figure 3 Token origin of Arabic numerals?

The change was profound, however. The tokens represented specific events, whether days, or moons, or reindeer. The numeral had shed all specific reference and could be applied to all countable things. It is quite possible that, in the case of numbers, the written symbol preceded the spoken one.

If numerals were the first written symbols, they were not always a matter of communication. More likely they served as a kind of *memo-pad,* telling the writer something for safekeeping and future reference. In ancient Peru, Inca and pre-Inca civilizations had no written language, but numerical records were kept on knotted ropes, called *quipus,* by a class of accountants (Bushnell, 1969). To this day, counting (overt or silent) is still a most essential non-communicative form of private speech.

From Babble to Babel

Workers in the field of comparative linguistics attempt to trace back the genealogy of languages in order to find common roots. These studies have identified a number of language families like the Indo-European group, the Uralic languages, and others; each member of a family is presumed to be derived from a common ancestor.

This practice, called *lumping,* is pushed to the limit by some who see a single common ancestor to the different known language families. They call it *Nostratic.* It is attributed to a group of hunter-gatherers who lived in Europe, Northern Africa, and parts of Asia some 15,000 years ago. Some linguists went so far as to suggest that all languages that were ever spoken descended from a single original invention, a *proto-protolanguage* whose remnants may still be discerned today by sophisticated linguistic studies.

These *radical lumpers* are criticized by the *splitters* who regard many similarities between languages as arising more through cultural exchanges than common origins. They believe in a multiple origin of languages. Comparative linguistics thus brings us face-to-face with the most elusive of questions: How did language originate?

We may pick up some hints by looking at language acquisition by children without trying to revive that old myth about ontogeny recapitulating phylogeny. Here we find that a critical period exists in early childhood for the acquisition of a *first language.* This talent disappears if, for one reason or another, the child has not been exposed to language during the first few years of his life. In 1797 a *feral* child of age twelve, the *Wild Boy of Aveyron,* was found in southern France. Despite intensive efforts by a tutor, he never learned to speak. Another famous case, Genie, born in 1957 in Los Angeles, was raised under the most brutal conditions and without access to any spoken words. After being rescued at age 13, Genie was able to acquire a limited vocabulary, but never achieved normal speech. IQ tests showed her to be above normal on all but linguistic tasks.

Does this rule of a critical period also apply to language invention? This would imply that the first human speakers must have been children.

Before speaking, children, beginning at age 5 or 6 months, are engaged in a period of forming a great variety of vocal sounds, we call *babbling.* This activity is at first non-imitative, having little to do with the particular phonemes he or she is surrounded with. Even deaf children babble. Pinker (1994) describes this stage: 'The infant is like a person who has been given a complicated piece of audio equipment, bristling with unlabeled knobs and switches, but missing the instruction manual'.

Put differently, to produce even the most primitive vocalization *at will*, the infant must eventually *connect* the auditory signature of a given phoneme with the set of motor commands necessary to produce it. The German neuroanatomists Valentino Braitenberg and A. Schlitz (1992) pointed out that this would require an inordinate amount of specific neural wiring at correspondingly great genetic cost. Braitenberg suggests that something like a *'random noise generator'* induces the human infant to babble. The randomly produced phonemes are perceived by the auditory system, and the repeated associations between 'a phoneme heard and one produced', trains the brain and the speech apparatus to produce phonemes *at will*. Houde and Jordan (1998) have recently shown that the motor programs controlling speech can be redesigned if the aural feedback to the speaker is altered.

In view of this, it is unlikely that our distant ancestors were genetically *wired* in a way that we are not. They too had to babble before they could speak.

If we had to think of a single evolutionary step that lifted humanity out of muteness, it was perhaps nothing more than the infant's urge to babble, or Braitenberg's 'random noise generator'.

The ancient infant was, of course, not immersed in language like his modern counterpart. The path from babble to speaking could still have been long and complicated, but not fundamentally mysterious.

The spontaneous creation of a language has often been questioned. There is the story of the Danish twins who, about the turn of the century, were abandoned at age two. When observed years later they are said to have developed a language of their own. It resembled Danish but was unintelligible to outsiders. The story may be apocryphal. We have no well-documented proof that a language can still arise without speaking examples.

The American psychologist E.L. Thorndike once suggested that a fortuitous attachment of meaning to one of the infant's random utterances, changing a phoneme or string of phonemes into a symbol, may have been the beginning of language. He called the process *babbleluck*. The babbleluck symbol, of course, had meaning initially only to the babbler.

Children, in fact, spend much time talking to themselves. This was first observed by the French psychologist Jean Piaget (1955). Later, Merleau-Ponty

(1973), who wrote extensively on language and perception, stated that what looks like conversation among children is often a 'collective monologue,' as 'two or more children, while appearing to be answering one another, are in reality only pursuing their own monologues, without taking into account the reaction of others'. Early speech is, as Piaget calls it, *egocentric*. Dialogue appears to be a secondary use of language. We may picture ancient hominids muttering to themselves while going about their hunting and gathering.

The recognition that monologue is an important phase of language (rather than an aberration) removes the bottleneck of requiring the simultaneous development of speech and communication. Bickerton (1995) recognizes the usefulness of monologues in freeing us from being concerned exclusively with present sensory reality. He calls this *'off-line thinking,'* and states that it has 'liberated us from "on-line" mentality to which other species are confined'.

The above discussion has some further implications regarding the origin of language, arguing against the existence of a single ancestral language from which all others descended. Instead, I view vocal symbols as the invention of individuals, followed by a gradual spreading of their meanings first among small groups of people, families and tribes who lived together in intimate contact. If the same phenomenon occurred among many isolated communities, languages evolved from many roots by aggregation as the size of communicating groups increased.

Summary

I have proposed that artistic expression and language arise in a natural way from cognitive processes that are traceable to early primate evolution. A common characteristic of these is the formation of quasi-sensory images, so-called *mental images*, under control by prefrontal cortical structures referred to as *working memory*. Such images are of necessity fleeting and incomplete. This led to a greatly enhanced ability to 'see patterns' in random configurations we encounter in the world around us. The manipulation of such *external* images came to supplement the narrow channel and ephemeral character of the *sketchpad-in-the-head* and became the beginning of the artistic enterprise.

The origin of language, the second of the exclusively human mental attributes, poses more severe problems since no early forms are extant. Instead, we are facing a profound discontinuity between animal calls and human oral communication. Ulbaek's suggestion that language is a continuation of animal *cognition,* rather than of animal communication, opens up a novel and promising approach.

The particular cognitive development I have suggested here as the basis for both art and language involves the reciprocal interaction between peripheral sensory imagery and corresponding central symbolic neural representations. Language involves the externalization of symbols and their re-introduction into the nervous system through sensory perception. It has often been assumed that speaking conveys no adaptive advantage without it being comprehended by listeners. But the simultaneous emergence of speakers and listeners represents a major hurdle to the emergence of language as communication.

I have assumed that language may have begun as *monologue,* just as children, in the early stages of speaking, talk mostly to themselves. The value of monologue, even for the adult human, lies in its facilitation of thought processes that exhibit the basic pattern of recursive manipulation of symbols and images. Both artistic expression and language are *thinking tools,* their mode of operation patterned after preexisting internal cognitive processes.

References

Baddeley, A.D. (1986), *Working Memory* (Oxford: Oxford University Press).

von Baeyer, H.C. (1985), 'The inverse problem', *The Sciences,* Nov/Dec.

Berk, L.E. (1992), 'Children's private speech: An overview of theory and the status of research', in *Private Speech,* ed. Diaz and Berk (Hillsdale, NJ: Lawrence Erlbaum).

Berk, L.E. (1994), 'Why children talk to themselves', *Scientific American,* November, pp. 78-83.

Bickerton, D. (1995), *Language and Human Behavior* (Seattle: University. of Washington).

Blachowicz, J. (1997), 'The dialogue of the soul with itself', *Journal of Consciousness Studies,* **4** (5-6), pp. 485-508.

Braitenberg, V & Schutz, A. (1992), In Wind *et al.* (1992), pp. 89-102.

Burns, TR. & Engdahl, E. (1998), 'The social construction of consciousness', *Journal of Consciousness Studies,* **5** (1), pp. 67-85.

Bushnell, G.H.S. (1969), *Peru* (New York: Praeger).

Chomsky, N. (1972), *Language and Mind* (New York: Harcourt Brace Jovanovich)

Crick, F. (1984), 'Function of the thalamic reticular complex. The searchlight hypothesis', *PNAS,* **81**, pp. 4586-90.

Crick, F. & Koch, C. (1990), 'Towards a neurobiological theory of consciousness', *Seminars in Neuroscience,* **2**, pp. 263-75.

Deacon, T.W. (1992), In Wind *et al.* (1992), pp. 121-62.

Deacon, T.W. (1997), *The Symbolic Species* (New York: W.W. Norton).

Dennett, D. (1991), *Consciousness Explained* (Boston, MA: Little Brown).

Derrida, J. (1987), *The Truth in Painting* (Chicago: University of Chicago Press).

Diaz, R.M. & Berk, L.E. (ed. 1992), *Private Speech* (Hillsdale, NJ: Erlbaum).

Donaghue, D. (1983), *The Arts Without Mystery* (Boston, MA: Little Brown).

Donald, M. (1991), *Origins of the Modern Mind* (Cambridge, MA: Harvard).

Eckhorn, R. *et al.* (1988), 'Coherent oscillations; a mechanism of feature linking in the visual cortex?', *Biological Cybernetics,* **60**, pp. 121-30.

Finke, A. (1996), 'Imagery, creativity, and emergent structure', *Consciousness & Cognition,* **5,** pp. 381-93.

Fodor, J.A. (1975), *The Language of Thought* (Cambridge, MA: Harvard).

Freeman, W.J. (1994), 'Neural networks and chaos', *J. Theoret. Biol.,* **171**, pp. 13-18.

Goldman-Rakic, P.S. (1987), In *Handbook of Physiology,* ed. F. Plum & V.B. Mountcastle (Bethesda, MD: American Physiol. Soc.) pp. 375-417.

Haken, H. (1983), *Synergetics: An Introduction* (Berlin: Springer Verlag).

Harnad, S. (1990), 'The symbol grounding problem', *Physica D,* **42**, pp. 335-46.

Harth, E. (1976), 'Visual perception: a dynamic theory', *Biological Cybernetics,* **22**, pp. 169-80.

Harth, E. (1983), 'Order and chaos in neural systems: an approach to the dynamics of higher brain functions', *Trans. IEEE SSMC,* **13**, pp. 782-9.

Harth, E. (1993), *The Creative Loop. How the Brain Makes a Mind* (Reading, MA: Addison- Wesley).

Harth, E. (1995), 'The sketchpad model. A theory of consciousness, perception and imagery', *Consciousness & Cognition,* **4**, pp. 346-68.

Harth, E. (1996), 'Self-referent mechanisms as the neural basis of consciousness', in *Toward a Science of Consciousness,* ed. S.R. Hameroff *et al.* (Cambridge, MA: MIT Press).

Harth, E. (1997), 'From brains to neural nets to brains', *Neural Networks,* **10**, pp. 1241-55.

Harth, E., Unnikrishnan, K.P. & Pandya, A.S. (1987), 'The inversion of sensory processing by feedback pathways: a model of visual cognitive functions', *Science,* **237**, pp. 184-7.

Hasegawa, I., Fukushima, T., Ihara, T. & Miyashita, Y. (1998), 'Callosal window between prefrontal cortices: cognitive interaction to retrieve long-term memory', *Science,* **281**, pp. 814-18.

Houde, J.F. & Jordan, M.I. (1998), 'Sensorimotor adaptation in speech production', *Science,* **279,** pp.1213-16.

Hubel, D.H. & Wiesel, T.N. (1959), 'Receptive fields of single neurons in the cat's striate cortex', *J. Physiol.,* **148,** pp. 574-91.

Kastner, S., De Weerd, P., Desimone, R. & Ungerleider, L.G. (1998), 'Mechanisms of directed attention in the human extrastriate cortex as revealed by functional MRI', *Science,* **282,** pp. 108-11.

Kosslyn, S.M. (1994), *Image and Brain* (Cambridge, MA: MIT Press).

Lowell, P. (1906), *Mars and its Canals* (London: Macmillan).

Marshack, A. (1992), In Wind *et al.* (1992), pp. 421-48.

Merleau-Ponty, M. (1973), *Consciousness and the Acquisition of Language,* trans. H.J. Silverman (Evanston: Northwestern University Press).

Mithen, S. (1996), *The Prehistory of the Mind* (London: Thames & Hudson).

Moruzzi, G. & Magoun, H.W. (1949), 'Brain stem reticular formation and activation of the EEG', *Electroencephalogr. & Clin. Neurophysiol.,* **1,** pp. 455-73.

Perecman, E. (1987), *The Frontal Lobes Revisited* (New York: IRBN Press).

Piaget, J. (1955), *The Language and Thought of the Child,* trans. M. Gabin (Cleveland, OH: Meridian).

Pinker, S. (1994), *The Language Instinct: How the Mind Creates Language* (New York: Morrow).

Pinker, S. (1997), *How the Mind Works* (New York: W.W. Norton).

Pylyshyn, Z.W. (1975), 'Do we need images and analogues?', *Proc. Conf. on Theoretical Issues in Natural Language Processing, MIT (1975).*

Ragir, S. (1992), In *Language Origin: A Multidisciplinary Approach,* ed. J. Wind *et al.,* (Dordrecht: Kluwer), pp. 39-48.

Shepard, R.N. & Cooper, L.A. (1982), *Mental Images and their Transformations* (Cambridge, MA: MIT Press).

Steriade, M., Domich, L. & Oakson, G. (1986), 'Reticularis thalami neurons revisited: activity changes during shifts in states of vigilance', *J. Neurosc.,* **6,** pp. 68-81.

Stuss, D. & Benson, D. (1986), *The Frontal Lobes* (New York: Raven Press).

Tootell, R.B.H., Silverman, M.S., Switges, E. & De Valois, R.L. (1982), 'Deoxyglucose analysis of retinotopic organization in primate striate cortex', *Science,* **218,** pp. 902-4.

Trân Duc Thao (1984), *Investigations into the Origin of Language and Consciousness* (Dordrecht: Reidel).

Ulbaek,l. (1992), In Wind *et al.* (1992), pp. 265-78.

Vygotsky, L. (1962), *Thought and Language* (Cambridge: Cambridge University Press).

Wickelgren, I. (1997), 'Getting a grasp on working memory', *Science,* **275**, pp. 1580-2.

Wills, C. (1993), *The Runaway Brain. The Evolution of Human Uniqueness* (London: Harper-Collins).

Wilkins, W.K. & Wakefield, J. (1995), 'Brain evolution and neurolinguistic preconditions', *Behavioral and Brain Sciences,* **18,** pp. 161-226.

Wind, J. *et al.* (ed. 1992), *Language Origin: A Multidisciplinary Approach* (Dordrecht: Kluwer).

Woolf, N.J. (1997), 'A possible role for cholinergic neurons of the basal forebrain and pontomesencephalon in consciousness', *Consciousness & Cognition,* **6,** pp. 574-96.

Yingling, C.D. & Skinner, J.E. (1977), In *Progress in Clinical Neurophysiology,* Vol. 1, ed. J.E. Desmedt (Basel: Karger), pp. 70-6.

Plate 1: Mark Tansey: *The Innocent Eye Test,* 1981, oil on canvas.
Curt Marcus Gallery, 578 Broadway, New York, NY 10012.

Concluding Remarks

The reader will have realized, no doubt, that the writings in this volume rest on two basic presuppositions, namely, that the acquisition of knowledge is a *man-made* process and that knowledge *begets* knowledge. It will have been noticed, as well, that I saw fit to assert, time and again, that humans use ideas to *think with* about ideas in their ongoing efforts to ascertain *what relates to what and whereby*. The acquisition of knowledge–the enormity of the enterprise and the pace of its development–necessitated at all times a division of labor, a division that was continuously impacted by novel insights due to seminal new "findings." Indeed, sifting processes of all kinds accompanied the quest for knowledge, increasingly sensitive to what belongs where and is relevant to what and in what way.

As stated in the preface, this volume neither represents the history of ideas, nor does it deal with 'reference' in pure philosophical terms. Aware of the concerted efforts that attended and still attend many of the concepts employed in this volume, I allowed myself, nonetheless, to call attention to some of the concepts that scholars employ, as "tools," in order to arrive at a better understanding of the issues their investigations involve. Language, as we all know, is one of those collective enterprises that are invariably anchored in *shared* understandings of sorts. I chose, hence, to focus on concepts we use in our daily lives, unaware, however, of the *multiple* functions they may serve in establishing what *refers* to what and *whereby*. Language, in fact, occupies a central position in the many-fold inferences that fuel the advance of knowledge, provided one fully understands how it is used and for what purpose. Though important at all times, a thorough understanding of the different functions that familiar terms may serve in diverse contexts carries special weight concerning interdisciplinary studies. It must be remembered nonetheless that the quest for knowledge–as a *collective* enterprise–invariably employed the capacity of humans to create language, since it is in language that Culture *and* cultures are formed.

'Knowledge' often implies a familiarity with facts–information or skills acquired through experience or education. But it also refers, as we have seen, to the theoretical understanding of a subject. Theories concerning the method or grounds of knowledge have occupied philosophers from time immemorial. According to Aristotle, for example, 'understanding' is akin to knowing why things are a certain way. While there is no shortage of theories that explain 'knowledge', there is still no single agreed upon definition of the concept. The acquisition of knowledge evidently involves complex cognitive processes, such as perception, memory, association and reasoning, all of which are subject to change. Despite the impressive epistemological inquiries over the centuries, given the enormity and complexity of the world of knowledge that humans have managed to bring about, it is impossible to exhaust all that might be relevant to the understanding of a given problem, not to speak of an entire domain. Even the remarkable development of science and technology–considering their significant contributions to how knowledge is acquired and advanced–engendered *as such* concerted inquiries. Yet nothing has changed the simple fact that knowledge is primarily transferred through language, symbolic representations and replication based on observation.

Although it is generally assumed that the past cannot foretell what the future has in store, much can be learned from the historical unfolding of the acquisition of knowledge that occupied mankind. For example, despite the changes that knowledge underwent, people tended to believe, at any given moment, that things behave in a *regular* manner; that patterns in the behavior of objects will *persist* into the future and throughout the *unobserved* present. Given this tendency, how should one understand the development of knowledge and its *forward* thrust? Questions of this kind were in fact asked, engendering interesting answers. Philosophy was never oblivious to the various "collectives" which humans create and to their efforts to improve the conditions of their members. Nor did philosophy overlook the "strength of mind" that characterizes mankind. However named or defined, whether innate or acquired, this "obscure," but taken for granted "potency" accompanied the acquisition of knowledge through its historical development. Interestingly, via steadily redefining its functions and shifting its "location," our *developed* Mind gradually drew attention to our *unknown* Brain, and our metaphysical soul to our experience of consciousness.

Philosophy, we learn, gave rise to the *behavioral* sciences. The latter emerged in all likelihood due to the growth of knowledge which made it increasingly difficult to establish unwavering "truth claims." The behavioral sciences in fact examined the circumstances and conditions that *alter* thoughts, perspectives and ways of life. The focus on external factors that influence the behavior of people created a renewed interest in the *human* attributes that allow people to behave the way they do. Aside of their material bodies and vital senses, people also display emotions and a power of "will" that evidently take part in their thought and action. While the social sciences increasingly contributed to our understanding of our *social* behavior, psychology tried to uncover the "spirit" that enables humans to perform the tasks they see fit to undertake, or fail to accomplish. It is psychology, in particular, that gave rise to cognitive studies, which nowadays engulf our biological "make-up" in order to better understand why and wherefore we feel, act and behave as we do.

The advance of knowledge is, of course, a far more complex and convoluted development than the "brush-stroke" delineation that I presented above. Independent fields of investigation were at times subsumed, as we have seen, by others, while sections of established fields at times carved their own "areas" of investigation. The advance of knowledge–which necessitates at all times a division of labor–gave rise to both diachronic as well as synchronic developments. And despite the impact that diverse fields may have exerted on each other at different times, it is nonetheless possible to trace the histories of diverse fields of knowledge–philosophy, mathematics, physics, chemistry, technology, medicine, etc. All I wished to convey via my "short-handed" delineation is how difficult it is to establish *enduring* inductive inferences.

Philosophy, naturally, addressed this ostensible difficulty. Without entering into the philosophical debates that dealt with the subject, allow me just to state that it is largely owing to the empirical observations of Hume and the thinking of those whom he influenced (including Kant) that the problem of induction surfaced as it did, casting doubts about the human powers of reason. Hume contributed vastly to the notion that our knowledge is restricted to what can be experienced, rather than to our ability to conceive. Due to the operation of our faculties, observed Hume, we are able to form beliefs that go beyond our experiences, but knowledge, he insisted, cannot be claimed on that basis. In opposition to the rationalists (primarily Descartes), Hume suggested that we reason inductively by regularly associating conjoined events, and that it is the *mental act of association* that is the basis of our concept of causation. According to Hume, the underlying foundation of the sciences–regardless of kind–is "Human Nature" which can only know things it directly experiences. Mental behavior is thus governed by *acquired* ability, and our use of induction is justified solely by our idea of the constant conjunction of causes and effects. The science of human nature must hence be based on experience and observation. Moreover, we must study the essence of our mind like any other external body, i.e. through experiments and observation of particular effects. Hume clearly advocated empirical inquiry, instead of philosophical speculations. It is the latter, however, that enabled Hume to gain the insights which led to his remarkable conclusions.

Given the abundance of important figures in the history of Western philosophy, the astute reader must have guessed why I chose, in particular, to "resurrect" Hume. You may recall that I opened my concluding remarks by reminding the reader that the writings in this volume rest on two basic presuppositions, namely that the acquisition of knowledge is a *man-maid* process and that knowledge *begets* knowledge. But I also saw fit to remind the reader of my oft used maxim, i.e. that humans use ideas to *think with* about ideas in their efforts to ascertain "what relates to what and whereby." The sifting processes that accompanied the quest for knowledge reveal that knowledge is primarily acquired through "constant conjunction" of "causes and effects." Indeed, the writings included in this volume exemplify how complex ideas are formed from *associative* chains of ideas that rest on our experience. The observation that humans *reason inductively* by constantly *associating* conjoined events, caused Hume to declare that "causal relations" are *semantically* equivalent to propositions about our experiences and that it is a *mental act of association* that apparently constitutes the basis for our knowledge. He concluded, moreover, that the principles required for connecting our ideas are neither theoretical nor rational, but *natural operations* of our mind. Having recognized our cognitive limitations, he identified three principles of connection that advance human inquiries: resemblance, contiguity, and "cause and effect." Even the few oversimplified sentences that I accorded to Hume suffice to explain why he is viewed by many as one of the founding fathers of cognitive science.

Aware of the history of ideas and the inherent complexity of the advancement of knowledge, the present volume only intended to upgrade the awareness of its readers to some familiar "tools" that scholars employ in their investigations. These "readily accessible" tools also serve many interdisciplinary studies. Indeed, interdisciplinary studies–which raised considerable doubts in the past–have become central to the acquisition of knowledge nowadays. However, since knowledge is primarily transferred through language, the transfer of "ideas" from one field to another requires full understanding of the way in which they are used and understood where they come from. By focusing on language as a "practical apparatus" that humans devised in order to understand each other and the world they inhabit, I wished to highlight five basic tenets: 1) Knowledge, like language, is a collective enterprise. 2) Humans use ideas to *think with* about ideas. 3) Ideas interrelate via referential sequences. 4) Knowledge advances in humanly intelligible ways. 5) As a collective enterprise, knowledge advances, as it were, in "connected vessels." These tenets, if correct, go a long way to dispel the accepted divisions among the sciences and to offset the grudging attitude to the humanities. Despite their different aims and different trajectories, the arts and the sciences are all guided and governed by the referential "devices" that mankind has created and by the limits and the potentials of our natural makeup.

www.ingramcontent.com/pod-product-compliance
Lightning Source LLC
Chambersburg PA
CBHW062358090426
42740CB00010B/1326